Lecture Notes in Computer Science 3424

Commenced Publication in 1973
Founding and Former Series Editors:
Gerhard Goos, Juris Hartmanis, and Jan van Leeuwen

David Martin   Andrei Serjantov (Eds.)

Privacy Enhancing Technologies

4th International Workshop, PET 2004
Toronto, Canada, May 26-28, 2004
Revised Selected Papers

 Springer

Volume Editors

David Martin
University of Massachusetts Lowell, Department of Computer Science
One University Ave., Lowell, Massachusetts 01854, USA
E-mail: dm@cs.uml.edu

Andrei Serjantov
University of Cambridge, Computer Laboratory
William Gates Building, 15 JJ Thomson Avenue, Cambridge CB3 0FD, UK
E-mail: aas@arachsys.com

Library of Congress Control Number: 2005926701

CR Subject Classification (1998): E.3, C.2, D.4.6, K.6.5, K.4, H.3, H.4, I.7

ISSN   0302-9743
ISBN-10   3-540-26203-2 Springer Berlin Heidelberg New York
ISBN-13   978-3-540-26203-9 Springer Berlin Heidelberg New York

Springer is a part of Springer Science+Business Media

springeronline.com

Printed in Germany

Typesetting: Camera-ready by author, data conversion by Scientific Publishing Services, Chennai, India
Printed on acid-free paper   SPIN: 11423409   06/3142   5 4 3 2 1 0

Preface

The first workshop in this series was held at the International Computer Science Institute in Berkeley and was published as LNCS 2009 under the name "Workshop on Design Issues in Anonymity and Unobservability." Subsequent Privacy Enhancing Technologies (PET) workshops met in San Francisco in 2002 (LNCS 2482) and Dresden in 2003 (LNCS 2760). This volume, LNCS 3424, holds the proceedings from PET 2004 in Toronto. Our 2005 meeting is scheduled for Dubrovnik, and we hope to keep finding new and interesting places to visit on both sides of the Atlantic – or beyond.

An event like PET 2004 would be impossible without the work and dedication of many people. First and foremost we thank the authors, who wrote and submitted 68 full papers or panel proposals, 21 of which appear herein.

The Program Committee produced 163 reviews in total. Along the way, they were assisted in reviewing by Steven Bishop, Rainer Bohme, Sebastian Clauß, Claudia Díaz, Richard E. Newman, Ulrich Flegel, Elke Franz, Stefan Kopsell, Thomas Kriegelstein, Markus Kuhn, Stephen Lewis, Luc Longpre, Steven Murdoch, Shishir Nagaraja, Thomas Nowey, Peter Palfrader, Lexi Pimenidis, Klaus Ploessl, Sivaramakrishnan Rajagopalan, Marc Rennhard, Leo Reyzin, Pankaj Rohatgi, Naouel Ben Salem, Sandra Steinbrecher, Mike Szydlo, Shabsi Walfish, Jie Wang, Brandon Wiley, and Shouhuai Xu.

We invited two prominent speakers to speak at the workshop: Ross Anderson explained the "Economics of Security and Privacy", and Andreas Pfitzmann covered "Research on Anonymous Communication in German(y) 1983–1990." In addition, we held two panel discussions, two lively rump sessions, and we enjoyed a number of memorable social activities. Slides from many of the presentations are available at http://petworkshop.org/

A successful workshop depends not only on an interesting program, but also on a hospitable venue and attention to detail. Alison Bambury did a fantastic job coordinating the local arrangements. Roger Dingledine managed the stipend pool, funded by Microsoft Corporation, the Information and Privacy Commissioner's Office (Ontario), the Centre for Innovation Law and Policy at the University of Toronto, and Bell University Labs. The stipend fund helped more than 20 people attend the workshop. Paul Syverson led the committee to determine the recipients of the PET Award for Outstanding Research, also funded by Microsoft Corporation. Finally, Richard Owens, PET 2004's General Chair, oversaw the whole event and ensured that everything happened as planned and within budget. We offer our thanks to all of you, and to everyone who contributed their time, interest, and resources to the 2004 PET Workshop.

January 2005

David Martin
Andrei Serjantov
Program Committee Co-chairs

Privacy Enhancing Technologies 2004
Toronto, Canada
May 26–28, 2004
http://petworkshop.org/

Program Committee

Alessandro Acquisti, Heinz School, Carnegie Mellon University, USA
Caspar Bowden, Microsoft EMEA, UK
Jean Camp, Kennedy School, Harvard University, USA
Richard Clayton, University of Cambridge, UK
Lorrie Cranor, School of Computer Science, Carnegie Mellon University, USA
George Danezis, University of Cambridge, UK
Roger Dingledine, The Free Haven Project, USA
Hannes Federrath, Universität Regensburg, Germany
Ian Goldberg, Zero Knowledge Systems, Canada
Philippe Golle, Palo Alto Research Center, USA
Marit Hansen, Independent Centre for Privacy Protection Schleswig-Holstein,
    Germany
Markus Jakobsson, RSA Laboratories, USA
Dogan Kesdogan, Rheinisch-Westfälische Technische Hochschule Aachen,
    Germany
Brian Levine, University of Massachusetts, Amherst, USA
David Martin, University of Massachusetts, Lowell, USA
Andreas Pfitzmann, Dresden University of Technology, Germany
Matthias Schunter, IBM Zurich Research Lab, Switzerland
Andrei Serjantov, University of Cambridge, UK
Adam Shostack, Informed Security Inc., Canada
Paul Syverson, Naval Research Lab, USA

General Chair

Richard Owens, University of Toronto, Canada

Sponsoring Institutions

Microsoft Corporation
Information and Privacy Commissioner's Office (Ontario)
Centre for Innovation Law and Policy at the University of Toronto
Bell University Labs

Table of Contents

Anonymity and Covert Channels in Simple Timed Mix-Firewalls[*]

Richard E. Newman[1], Vipan R. Nalla[1], and Ira S. Moskowitz[2]

[1] CISE Department,
University of Florida,
Gainesville, FL 32611-6120
{nemo, vreddy}@cise.ufl.edu
[2] Center for High Assurance Computer Systems, Code 5540,
Naval Research Laboratory,
Washington, DC 20375
moskowitz@itd.nrl.navy.mil

Abstract. Traditional methods for evaluating the amount of anonymity afforded by various Mix configurations have depended on either measuring the size of the set of possible senders of a particular message (the anonymity set size), or by measuring the entropy associated with the probability distribution of the messages possible senders. This paper explores further an alternative way of assessing the anonymity of a Mix system by considering the capacity of a covert channel from a sender behind the Mix to an observer of the Mix's output.

Initial work considered a simple model [4], with an observer (Eve) restricted to counting the number of messages leaving a Mix configured as a firewall guarding an enclave with one malicious sender (Alice) and some other naive senders (Clueless$_i$'s). Here, we consider the case where Eve can distinguish between multiple destinations, and the senders can select to which destination their message (if any) is sent each clock tick.

1 Introduction

In [4] the idea of measuring the lack of perfect anonymity (quasi-anonymity) via a covert channel was initiated. This idea was formalized in [5]. Our concern in this paper is to identify, and to calculate the capacity of, the covert channels that arise from the use of a Mix [8, 6] as an exit firewall from a private enclave (as briefly addressed in [4–Sec. 4].) In general, we refer to a covert channel that arises, due to a state of quasi-anonymity, as a quasi-anonymous channel [5]. The quasi-anonymous channel also serves the dual role of being a measure of the lack of perfect anonymity. [1] uses a similar model for statistical attacks in which Eve correlates senders' actions with observed output.

---

[*] Research supported by the Office of Naval Research.

D. Martin and A. Serjantov (Eds.): PET 2004, LNCS 3424, pp. 1–16, 2005.

2   Exit Mix-Firewall Model

There are $N + 1$ senders in a private enclave. Messages pass one way from the private enclave to a set of M receivers. The private enclave is behind a firewall which also functions as a timed Mix [6] that fires every tick, t, hence we call it a simple timed Mix-firewall. For the sake of simplicity we will refer to a simple timed Mix-firewall as a Mix-firewall in this paper. One of the $N + 1$ senders, called Alice, is malicious. The other N clueless senders, $\text{Clueless}_i, i = 1, \ldots , N$, are benign. Each sender may send at most one message per unit time t to the set of receivers. All messages from the private enclave to the set of receivers pass through public lines that are subject to eavesdropping by an eavesdropper called Eve. The only action that Eve can take is to count the number of messages per t going from the Mix-firewall to each receiver, since the messages are otherwise indistinguishable. Eve knows that there are $N + 1$ possible senders. The N clueless senders act in an independent and identical manner (i.i.d.) according to a fixed distribution $C_i, i = 1, \ldots , N$. Alice, by sending or not sending a message each t to at most one receiver, affects Eve's message counts. This is how Alice covertly communicates with Eve via a quasi-anonymous channel [5].

Alice acts independently (through ignorance of the clueless senders) when deciding to send a message; we call this the *ignorance assumption*. Alice has the same distribution each t. Between Alice and the N clueless senders, there are $N + 1$ possible senders per t, and there are $M + 1$ possible actions per sender (each sender may or may not transmit, and if it does transmit, it transmits to exactly one of M receivers).

We consider Alice to be the input to the quasi-anonymous channel, which is a proper communications channel [9]. Alice can send to one of the M receivers or not send a message. Thus, we represent the inputs to the quasi-anonymous channel by the $M + 1$ input symbols $0, 1, \ldots , M$, where $i = 0$ represents Alice not sending a message, and $i \in \{1, \ldots , M\}$ represents Alice sending a message to the ith receiver R_i. The "receiver" in the quasi-anonymous channel is Eve.

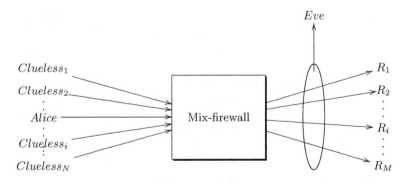

Fig. 1. Exit Mix-firewall model with N clueless senders and M distinguishable receivers

Eve receives the output symbols $e_j, j = 1, \ldots, K$. Eve receives e_1 if no sender sends a message. The other output symbols correspond to all the different ways the $N + 1$ senders can send or not send, at most one message each, out of the private enclave, provided at least one sender does send a message.

For the sake of simplicity we introduce a dummy receiver R_0 (not shown above). If a sender does not send a message we consider that to be a "message" to R_0. For $N + 1$ senders and M receivers, the output symbol e_j observed by Eve is an $M + 1$ vector $\langle a_0^j, a_1^j, \ldots, a_M^j \rangle$, where a_i^j is how many messages the Mix-firewall sends to R_i. Of course it follows that $\sum_{i=0}^{M} a_i^j = N + 1$.

The quasi-anonymous channel that we have been describing is a discrete memoryless channel (DMC). We define the channel matrix M as an $(M+1) \times K$ matrix, where $M[i,j]$ represents the conditional probability that Eve observes the output symbol e_j given that Alice input i. We model the clueless senders according to the i.i.d. C_i for each period of possible action t:

$$P(Clueless_i \ doesn't \ send \ a \ message) = p$$

$$P(Clueless_i \ sends \ a \ message \ to \ any \ receiver) = \frac{q}{M} = \frac{1-p}{M}$$

where in keeping with previous papers, $q = 1 - p$ is the probability that $Clueless_i$ sends a message to any one of the M receivers. When $Clueless_i$ *does* send a message, the destination is uniformly distributed over the receivers $R_1, \ldots, R_M$. We call this the **semi-uniformity assumption**. Again, keep in mind that each clueless sender has the same distribution each t, but they all act independently of each other.

We model Alice according to the following distribution each t:

$$P(Alice \ sends \ a \ message \ to \ R_i) = x_i$$

Of course, this tells us that

$$x_0 = P(Alice \ doesn't \ send \ a \ message) = 1 - \sum_{i=1}^{M} x_i \ .$$

We let A represent the distribution for Alice's input behavior, and we denote by E the distribution of the output that Eve receives. Thus, the channel matrix M along with the distribution A totally determine the quasi-anonymous channel. This is because the elements of M take the distributions C_i into account, and M and A let one determine the distribution describing the outputs that Eve receives, $P(\text{Eve receives } e_j)$.

Now that we have our set-up behind our exit Mix-firewall model, we may now go on to analyze various cases in detail. Additional cases and more detail are available in [7].

3   Capacity Analyses of the Exit Mix-Firewall Model

The mathematics of the problem gets quite complex. Therefore, we start with some simple special cases before attempting to analyze the problem in general.

The mutual information between A and E is given by

$$I(A, E) = H(A) - H(A|E) = H(E) - H(E|A) = I(E, A).$$

The capacity of the quasi-anonymous channel is given by [9]

$$C = \max_A I(A, E) \, ,$$

where the maximization is over the different possible values that the x_i may take (of course, the x_i are still constrained to represent a probability distribution). Recall $M[i, j] = P(E = e_j | A = i)$, where $M[i, j]$ is the entry in the ith row and j^{th} column of the channel matrix, M. To distinguish the various channel matrices, we will adopt the notation that $M_{N.M}$ is the channel matrix for N clueless senders and M receivers.

3.1   One Receiver ($M = 1$)

Case 1 — No clueless senders and one receiver ($N = 0, \ M = 1$)
Alice is the only sender, and there is only one receiver R_1. Alice sends either 0 (by not sending a message) or 1 (by sending a message). Eve receives either $e_1 = \langle 1, 0 \rangle$ (Alice did nothing) or $e_2 = \langle 0, 1 \rangle$ (Alice sent a message to the receiver). Since there is no noise (there are no clueless senders) the channel matrix M is the 2×2 identity matrix and it trivially follows that $P(E = e_1) = x_0$, and that $P(E = e_2) = x_1$.

$$M_{0.1} = \begin{array}{c} \\ 0 \\ 1 \end{array} \overset{\begin{array}{cc} e_1 & e_2 \end{array}}{\begin{pmatrix} 1 & 0 \\ 0 & 1 \end{pmatrix}}$$

Since $x_0 = 1 - x_1$, we see that[1] $H(E) = -x_0 \log x_0 - (1 - x_0) \log(1 - x_0)$. The channel matrix is an identity matrix, so the conditional probability distribution $P(E|A)$ is made up of zeroes and ones, therefore $H(E|A)$ is identically zero. Hence, the capacity is the maximum over x_0 of $H(E)$, which is easily seen to be unity[2] (and occurs when $x_0 = 1/2$). Of course, we could have obtained this capacity[3] without appealing to mutual information since we can noiselessly send one bit per tick, but we wish to study the non-trivial cases and use this as a starting point.

Case 2 — N clueless senders and one receiver ($M = 1$)
This case reduces to the *indistinguishable receivers* case with N senders. This is the situation analyzed in [4] with both an exit Mix-firewall that we have

---

[1]   All logarithms are base 2.
[2]   The units of capacity are bits per tick t, but we will take the units as being understood for the rest of the paper. Note that all symbols take one t to pass through the channel.
[3]   This uses Shannon's [9] asymptotic definition of capacity, which is equivalent for noiseless channels (in units of bits per symbol).

been discussing and an entry Mix-firewall, with the receivers behind the latter. Alice can either send or not send a message, so the input alphabet again has two symbols. Eve observes $N + 2$ possible output symbols. That is, Eve sees $e_1 = \langle N+1, 0 \rangle$, $e_2 = \langle N, 1 \rangle$, $e_3 = \langle N-1, 2 \rangle$, $\cdots$, $e_{N+2} = \langle 0, N+1 \rangle$. A detailed discussion of this case can be found in [4].

3.2   Some Special Cases for Two Receivers ($M = 2$)

There are two possible receivers. Eve has knowledge of the network traffic, so Alice can signal Eve with an alphabet of three symbols: 1 or 2, if Alice transmits to R_1 or R_2, respectively, or the symbol 0 for not sending a message. Let us analyze the channel matrices and the entropies for different cases of senders.

The symbol e_j that Eve receives is an 3-tuple of the form $\langle a_0^j, a_1^j, a_2^j \rangle$, where a_i^j is the number of messages received by i^{th} receiver.[4] The index $i = 0$ stands for Alice not sending any message. The elements of the 3-tuple must sum to the total number of senders, $N + 1$,

$$\sum_{i=0}^{2} a_i = N + 1 \ .$$

Case 3 — No clueless senders and two receivers ($N = 0$, $M = 2$)
Alice is the only sender and can send messages to two possible receivers. The channel matrix is trivial and there is no anonymity in the channel.

$$
\mathrm{M}_{0.2} = \begin{array}{c} 0 \\ 1 \\ 2 \end{array}
\begin{pmatrix}
1 & 0 & 0 \\
0 & 1 & 0 \\
0 & 0 & 1
\end{pmatrix}
$$

with column headers $\langle 1,0,0 \rangle$, $\langle 0,1,0 \rangle$, $\langle 0,0,1 \rangle$.

The subscript 0.2 represents one sender (Alice alone) and two receivers. The 3×3 channel matrix $\mathrm{M}_{0.2}[i, j]$ represents the conditional probability of Eve receiving the symbol e_j, when Alice sends to the Receiver i. '0' stands for not sending a message.

The mutual information I is given by the entropy $H(E)$ describing Eve

$$I(E, A) = H(E) = -x_1 \log x_1 - x_2 \log x_2 - (1 - x_1 - x_2) \log(1 - x_1 - x_2).$$

The capacity of this noiseless covert channel is $\log 3 \approx 1.58$ (at $x_i = 1/3$, $i = 0, 1, 2$). This is the maximum capacity, which we note corresponds to zero anonymity.

---

[4] Recall that the a_i^j's of the output symbol are not directly related to A, which denotes the distribution of Alice.

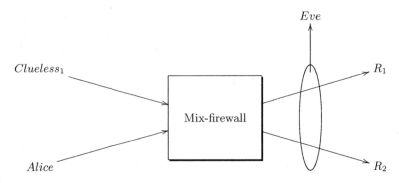

Fig. 2. Case 4: system with $N = 1$ clueless sender and $M = 2$ receivers

Case 4 — $N = 1$ clueless sender and $M = 2$ receivers
There are only six symbols that Eve may receive since there are six ways to put two indistinguishable balls into three distinct urns.

Let us consider the channel matrix.

$$
M_{1.2} = \begin{array}{c} \\ 0 \\ 1 \\ 2 \end{array}
\begin{array}{cccccc}
\langle 2,0,0 \rangle & \langle 1,1,0 \rangle & \langle 1,0,1 \rangle & \langle 0,2,0 \rangle & \langle 0,1,1 \rangle & \langle 0,0,2 \rangle \\
\left(\begin{array}{cccccc}
p & q/2 & q/2 & 0 & 0 & 0 \\
0 & p & 0 & q/2 & q/2 & 0 \\
0 & 0 & p & 0 & q/2 & q/2
\end{array} \right)
\end{array}
$$

The 3×6 channel matrix $M_{1.2}[i, j]$ represents the conditional probability of Eve receiving the symbol e_j when Alice sends to R_i. As noted, the dummy receiver R_0 corresponds to Alice not sending to any receiver (however this is still a transmission to Eve via the quasi-anonymous channel).

Given the above channel matrix we have:

$$
\begin{aligned}
H(E) = -\{ & px_0 \log[px_0] \\
& + [qx_0/2 + px_1] \log[qx_0/2 + px_1] \\
& + [qx_0/2 + px_2] \log[qx_0/2 + px_2] \\
& + [qx_1/2] \log[qx_1/2] + [qx_1/2 + qx_2/2] \log[qx_1/2 + qx_2/2] \\
& + [qx_2/2] \log[qx_2/2] \}.
\end{aligned}
$$

The conditional entropy is given by

$$
H(E|A) = -\sum_{i=0}^{2} \left[p(x_i) \sum_{j=1}^{6} p(e_j|x_i) \log p(e_j|x_i) \right] = h_2(p) ,
$$

where $h_2(p)$ denotes the function

$$
\begin{aligned}
h_2(p) &= -(1-p)/2 \log((1-p)/2) - (1-p)/2 \log((1-p)/2) - p \log p \\
&= -(1-p) \log((1-p)/2) - p \log p .
\end{aligned}
$$

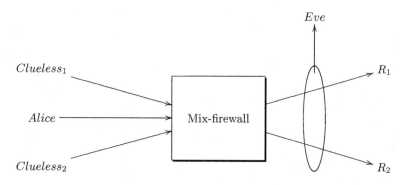

Fig. 3. Case 5: system with $N = 2$ clueless senders and $M = 2$ receivers

The mutual information between Alice and Eve is given by:

$$I(A, E) = H(E) - H(E|A) \ .$$

and the channel capacity is given by:
$$C = \max_A I(A, E)$$
$$= \max_{x_1, x_2} \ -\{px_0 \log[px_0]$$
$$+[qx_0/2 + px_1] \log[qx_0/2 + px_1]$$
$$+[qx_0/2 + px_2] \log[qx_0/2 + px_2]$$
$$+[qx_1/2] \log[qx_1/2] + [qx_1/2 + qx_2/2] \log[qx_1/2 + qx_2/2]$$
$$+[qx_2/2] \log[qx_2/2]\} - h_2(p).$$

Note that the maximization is over x_1 and x_2, since x_0 is determined by these two probabilities (holds for any N). This equation is very difficult to solve analytically and requires numerical techniques. Figure 4 shows the capacity for this case with the curve labeled $N = 1$. From the plot the minimum capacity is approximately 0.92, when $p = 1/3$.

Case 5 — $N = 2$ clueless senders and $M = 2$ receivers
With two clueless senders and two receivers, Eve may receive ten symbols since there are ten different ways to put three indistinguishable balls into three distinct urns.

$$M_{2.2} = \begin{array}{c} 0 \\ 1 \\ 2 \end{array} \begin{pmatrix} \langle 3,0,0\rangle & \langle 2,1,0\rangle & \langle 2,0,1\rangle & \langle 1,2,0\rangle & \langle 1,1,1\rangle & \langle 1,0,2\rangle & \langle 0,1,2\rangle & \langle 0,3,0\rangle & \langle 0,2,1\rangle & \langle 0,0,3\rangle \\ p^2 & pq & pq & q^2/4 & q^2/2 & q^2/4 & 0 & 0 & 0 & 0 \\ 0 & p^2 & 0 & pq & pq & 0 & q^2/4 & q^2/4 & q^2/2 & 0 \\ 0 & 0 & p^2 & 0 & pq & pq & q^2/2 & 0 & q^2/4 & q^2/4 \end{pmatrix}$$

The 3×10 channel matrix $M_{2.2}[i, j]$ represents the conditional probability of Eve receiving e_j when Alice sends a message to receiver R_i.

Figure 4 shows the capacity for this case in the curve labeled $N = 2$. Again, the minimum capacity is found at $p = 1/3 = 1/(M + 1)$. From the plot the minimum capacity is approximately 0.62, when $p = 1/3$.

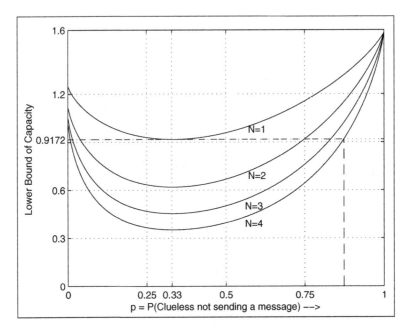

Fig. 4. Capacity for $M = 2$ receivers and $N = 1$ to 4 clueless senders

Case 6 — General Case: N clueless senders and M receivers

We now generalize the problem to N clueless senders and M receivers (refer again to Figure 1). There are $N + 1$ indistinguishable transmissions (including null transmissions) and they are sent into $M + 1$ distinct receivers (urns) (this also includes the null transmission, which by convention goes to R_0, not shown in the figure). Combinatorics tells us then that there are $K = \binom{N+M+1}{N+1}$ possible symbols e_j.

The rows of our channel matrix correspond to the actions of Alice. The ith row of $M_{N.M}$ describes the conditional probabilities $p(e_j|x_i)$. By convention e_1 always corresponds to every sender not sending a message (which is equivalent to all senders sending to R_0). Therefore e_1 is the $M+1$ tuple $\langle N+1, 0, \ldots, 0 \rangle$. Given our simplifying semi-uniformity assumption for the clueless senders' distribution, this term must be handled differently.

The first row of the channel matrix is made up of the terms $M_{N.M}[0,j]$. (We will not always explicitly note that $j = 1, \ldots, \binom{N+M+1}{N+1}$.) Here, Alice is not sending any message (i.e., she is "sending" to R_0), so Alice contributes one to the term a_0^j in the $M + 1$ tuple $\langle a_0^j, a_1^j, a_2^j, \ldots, a_M^j \rangle$ associated with e_j. In fact, this tuple is the "long hand" representation of e_j. Therefore the contributions to the $M + 1$ tuple $\langle a_0^j - 1, a_1^j, a_2^j, \ldots, a_M^j \rangle$ describe what the N clueless senders are doing. That is, $a_0^j - 1$ clueless senders are not sending a message, a_1^j clueless senders are sending to R_1, etc. Hence, the multinomial coefficient $\binom{N}{a_0^j-1, a_1^j, \ldots, a_M^j}$

tells us how many ways this may occur.[5] For each such occurrence we see that the transmissions to R_0 affect the probability by $p^{a_0^j - 1}$, and the transmissions to $R_i, i > 0$, due to the semi-uniformity assumption, contribute $(q/M)^{a_i^j}$. Since the actions are independent, the probabilities multiply, and since $a_0^j - 1 + a_1^j + \cdots + a_M^j = N$, we have a probability term of $p^{a_0^j - 1}(q/M)^{N+1-a_0^j}$. Multiplying that term by the total number of ways of arriving at that arrangement we have that:

$$M_{N.M}[0, j] = \binom{N}{a_0^j - 1, a_1^j, \ldots, a_M^j} p^{a_0^j - 1}(q/M)^{N+1-a_0^j} .$$

The other rows of the channel matrix are $M_{N.M}[i, j]$, $i > 0$. For row $i > 0$, we have a combinatorial term $\binom{N}{a_0^j, a_1^j, \ldots, a_{i-1}^j, a_i^j - 1, a_{i+1}^j, \ldots, a_M^j}$ for the N clueless senders, a_0^j of which are sending to R_0 and $N - a_0^j$ of which are sending to the $R_i, i > 0$. Therefore, we see that under the uniformity assumption,

$$M_{N.M}[i, j] = \binom{N}{a_0^j, a_1^j, \ldots, a_{i-1}^j, a_i^j - 1, a_{i+1}^j, \ldots, a_M^j} p^{a_0^j}(q/M)^{N-a_0^j}, i > 0 .$$

We show the plots of the mutual information when the clueless senders act (assumed throughout the paper) in a semi-uniform manner *and* when Alice also sends in a semi-uniform manner (i.e., $x_i = (1 - x_0)/M$, $i = 1, 2, \ldots, M$). We **conjecture** based upon our intuition, but do not prove, that Alice having a semi-uniform distribution of destinations $R_1, \ldots, R_M$ when the clueless senders act in a semi-uniform manner maximizes mutual information (achieves capacity). This has been supported by all of our numeric computations for capacity. With this conjecture, we can reduce the degrees of freedom for Alice from M to 1 (her distribution A is described entirely by x_0), which allows greater experimental and analytical exploration.

The channel matrix greatly simplifies when both the clueless senders and Alice act in a *totally uniform manner*. That is, when $x_0 = 1/(M + 1)$, then $x_i = (1 - x_0)/M = 1/(M + 1)$ for all x_i, and $p = 1/(M + 1)$. We have $M_{N.M}[0, j] = \binom{N}{a_0^j - 1, a_1^j, \ldots, a_M^j} p^{a_0^j - 1}(q/M)^{N+1-a_0^j}$, which simplifies to

$$M_{N.M}[0, j] = \binom{N}{a_0^j - 1, a_1^j, \ldots, a_M^j}(\tfrac{1}{M+1})^N . \text{ We also have}$$

$$M_{N.M}[i, j] = \binom{N}{a_0^j, a_1^j, \ldots, a_{i-1}^j, a_i^j - 1, a_{i+1}^j, \ldots, a_M^j} p^{a_0^j}(q/M)^{N-a_0^j}, i > 0,$$

which simplifies to $M_{N.M}[i, j] = \binom{N}{a_0^j, a_1^j, \ldots, a_{i-1}^j, a_i^j - 1, a_{i+1}^j, \ldots, a_M^j}(\tfrac{1}{M+1})^N, i > 0$. Note that this form holds for $i = 0$ also, due to the total uniformity of the C_i.

To determine the distribution E describing Eve we need to sum over the columns of the channel matrix and use the total uniformity of A. $P(E = e_j) = \sum_i P(E = e_j | A = i) P(A = i)$ $i = 0, \ldots, M$. This gives us

$$P(E = e_j) = (\tfrac{1}{M+1})^N \sum_{i=0}^M \binom{N}{a_0^j, \ldots, a_{i-1}^j, a_i^j - 1, a_{i+1}^j, \ldots, a_M^j} = (\tfrac{1}{M+1})^N \binom{N+1}{a_0^j, \ldots, a_M^j}.$$

From this we can compute the entropy $H(E)$ without too much trouble

$$H(E) = (\tfrac{1}{M+1})^N \sum_j \binom{N+1}{a_0^j, \ldots, a_M^j} \left(N \log(M+1) - \log \binom{N+1}{a_0^j, \ldots, a_M^j} \right). \text{ However, the}$$

conditional entropy is more complicated, but is expressible. Therefore, we wrote

---

[5] The multinomial coefficient is taken to be zero, if any of the "bottom" entries are negative.

Matlab code to calculate the mutual information, which is conjectured to be the capacity, when both the clueless senders and Alice act in a semi-uniform manner. Local exploration of nearby points all yield lower mutual information values.

4   Discussion of Results

Figure 4 shows the capacity as a function of p with $M = 2$ receivers, for $N = 1, 2, 3, 4$ clueless senders. In all cases, the minimum capacity is realized at $p = 1/3$, and the capacity at $p = 1$ is identical to $\log 3$. As N increases, the capacity decreases, with the most marked effects at $p = 1/3$.

In Figure 4, the capacity (of course under the semi-uniformity assumption for C_i)) was determined numerically for any choice of A. However, for the remaining plots, we applied the semi-uniformity conjecture (that Alice is better off behaving semi-uniformly if that is what the clueless senders do). Thus, x_0 is the only free variable for Alice's distribution in what follows.

The mutual information as a function of x_0 is shown in Figure 5 for $M = 2$ receivers and $N = 1$ clueless sender for $p = 0.25, 0.33, 0.5, 0.67$. Here, note that the curve with $p = 0.33$ has the smallest maximum value (capacity), and that the value of x_0 at which that maximum occurs is $x_0 = 0.33$. The x_0 value that maximizes the mutual information (i.e., for which capacity is reached) for the other curves is not 0.33, but the mutual information at $x_0 = 0.33$ is not much less than the capacity for any of the curves.

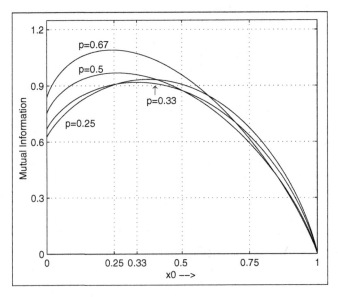

Fig. 5. Mutual information vs. x_0 for $M = 2$ receivers and $N = 1$ clueless sender, for $p = 0.25, 0.33, 0.5, 0.67$

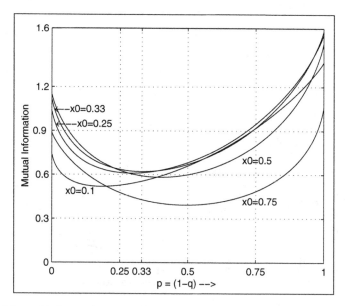

Fig. 6. Mutual information vs. p for $N = 2$ clueless senders and $M = 2$ receivers

Figure 6 shows the mutual information curves for various values of x_0 as a function of p, with $N = 2$ clueless senders and $M = 2$ receivers. Note that the curve for $x_0 = 1/(M+1) = 1/3$ has the largest minimum mutual information, and also has the greatest mutual information at the point where $p = 1$, i.e., when there is no noise since Clueless_1 is not sending any messages. The capacity for various values of p is, in essence, the curve that is the maximum at each p over all of the x_0 curves, and the lower bound on capacity occurs at $p = 1/3 = 1/(M+1)$.

Also observe that the $x_0 = 0.33$ curve has the highest value for $p = .33$, but for other values of p, other values of x_0 have higher mutual information (i.e., Alice has a strategy better than using $x_0 = 0.33$). However, the mutual information when $x_0 = 0.33$ is never much less than the capacity at any value of p, so in the absence of information about the behavior of the clueless senders, a good strategy for Alice is to just use $x_0 = 1/(M + 1)$. These observations are illustrated and expanded in the next two figures. Note the differences in concavity between Figure 5 and Figure 6. We will discuss concavity again later in the paper.

Figure 7 shows the optimal value for x_0, i.e., the one that maximizes mutual information and hence, achieves channel capacity, for $N = 1, 2, 3, 4$ clueless senders and $M = 3$ receivers as a function of p. A similar graph in [4] for $M = 1$ receiver is symmetric about $x_0 = 0.5$, but for $M > 1$ the symmetry is multidimensional, and the graph projected to the (p, x_0)-plane where the destinations are uniformly distributed is not symmetric. However, note that the optimum choice of x_0 is $1/(M + 1)$ both at $p = 1/(M + 1)$ and at $p = 1$, that is, when the clueless senders either create maximum noise or when they do not transmit at all (no noise). As N increases, the optimum x_0 for other values of

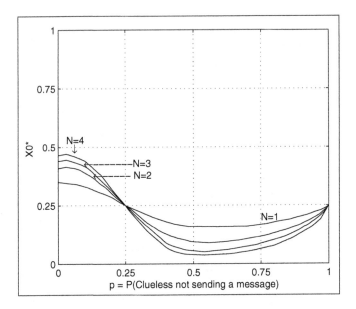

Fig. 7. Value of x_0 that maximizes mutual information for $N = 1, 2, 3, 4$ clueless senders and $M = 3$ receivers as a function of p

p is further from $1/(M + 1)$. Also observe that Alice's best strategy is to do the opposite of what the clueless senders do, up to a point. If they are less likely to send messages ($p > 1/(M + 1)$), then Alice should be more likely to send messages ($x_0 < 1/(M + 1)$), whereas if Clueless$_i$ is more likely to send messages ($(p < 1/(M + 1)$), then Alice should be less likely to send messages ($x_0 > 1/(M + 1)$).

Figure 8 shows the degree to which the choice of $x_0 = 1/(M + 1)$ can be suboptimal, for $N = 1, 2, 3, 4$ clueless senders and $M = 3$ receivers. The plot shows the mutual information for the given p and $x_0 = 1/(M + 1)$, normalized by dividing by the capacity (maximum mutual information) at that same p. Hence, it shows the degree to which a choice of $x_0 = 1/(M + 1)$ fails to achieve the maximum mutual information. For $N = 2$, it is never worse than 0.94 (numerically), but for $N = 4$, its minimum is 0.88. The relationship of suboptimality for other choices of M and N, or for other distributions is not known.

In Figure 9, we show the lower bound on capacity of the channel as a function of p for $N = 1$ clueless sender and various values of M receivers. Numerical results show that this lower bound increases for all p as M increases, and the lower bound on the capacity for a given M occurs at $p = 1/(M + 1)$, which is indicated by the dotted lines in the figure.

For Figure 10, we take the capacity at $p = 1/(M + 1)$, which we found numerically to minimize the capacity of the covert channel, and plot this lower bound for capacity for many values of N and M. We retain the assumption that $x_i = (1 - x_0)/(M + 1)$ for $i = 1, 2, ..., M$, that is, given the semi-uniform

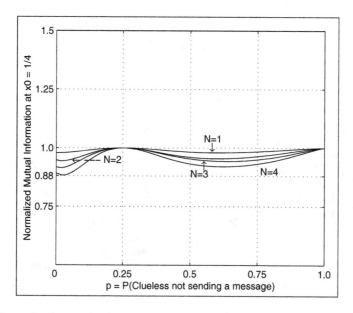

Fig. 8. Normalized mutual information when $x_0 = 1/4$ for $N = 1, 2, 3, 4$ clueless senders and $M = 3$ receivers

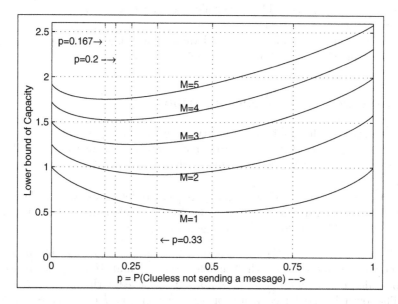

Fig. 9. Lower bound on capacity for $N = 1$ clueless sender and $M = 1$ to 5 receivers

distribution of transmissions to the receivers by the clueless senders, it is best for Alice to do likewise. Along the surface where $N = 0$, we have the noiseless channel, and the capacity is $\log(M + 1)$, which is also the upper bound for

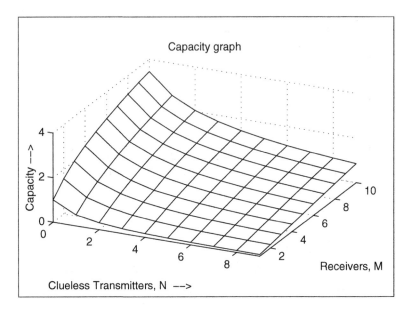

Fig. 10. Capacity lower bound for $N = 0$ to 9 clueless senders and $M = 1$ to 10.

capacity for all N and M. The values along the surface when $M = 1$ give us the same values we derived in [4].

Equations and curves for additional values and ranges of N and M may be found in a forthcoming technical report [7].

5   Comments and Generalizations

We first note that the maximum capacity of this (covert) quasi-anonymous channel is $\log(M + 1)$ for M distinguishable receivers, and is achievable only if there are no other senders ($N = 0$) or if none of them ever send ($p = 1$), i.e., when the channel is noiseless.

Here are some of the observations from the different cases considered, under the semi-uniform assumption for the clueless senders and the semi-uniform conjecture for Alice, followed by some generalizations.

1. The capacity $C(p, N, M)$, as a function of the probability p that a clueless sender remains silent, with N clueless senders and M receivers, is strictly bounded below by $C(\frac{1}{M+1}, N, M)$, and is achieved with $x_0 = 1/(M + 1)$.
2. The lower bound for capacity for a given number M of receivers decreases as the number N of clueless senders increases,
   $C(\frac{1}{M+1}, N, M) > C(\frac{1}{M+1}, N + 1, M)$.
3. The lower bound for capacity for a given number N of clueless senders increases as the number M of distinguishable receivers increases,
   $C(\frac{1}{M+2}, N, M + 1) > C(\frac{1}{M+1}, N, M)$.

These observations are intuitive, but we have not shown them to be true numerically in the general case (we did for the case that $M = 1$ in [4]). It is interesting to note that increasing the number of distinguishable receivers increases the covert channel capacity, which in some sense *decreases* the (sender) anonymity in the system (Alice has more room in which to express herself). This is a bit contrary to the conventional view of anonymity in Mix networks, where more receivers tends to provide "greater anonymity." In this light, we note that Danezis and Serjantov investigated the effects of multiple receivers in statistical attacks on anonymity networks [2]. They found that Alice having multiple receivers greatly lowered a statistical attacker's certainty of Alice's receiver set.

While the graphs and numerical tests support that the "worst" thing the clueless senders can do is to send (or not) with uniform probability distribution over the R_i, $i = 0, 1, 2, ..., M$, we have not proven this mathematically. Nor have we proven that, under these conditions, the best Alice can do is to send (or not) to each receiver R_i with uniform probability, $x_i = 1/(M + 1)$ for $i = 0, 1, 2, ..., M$, although the numerical computations support this. The proof in [4] of these conjectures for the case where $M = 1$ relied, in part, on the symmetry about $x_0 = 0.5$, which is not the case when $M > 1$, so another approach must be used. However, we should still be able to use the concavity/convexity results from [4]. Note that our conjecture that the best that Alice can do is to send in a semi-uniform manner, and the results illustrated in Figure 8, seem to be an extension of the interesting results of [3].

6   Conclusions and Future Work

This paper has taken a step towards tying the notion of capacity of a quasi-anonymous channel associated with an anonymity network to the amount of anonymity that the network provides. It explores the particular situation of a simple type of timed Mix (it fires every tick) that also acts as an exit firewall. Cases for varying numbers of distinguishable receivers and varying numbers of senders were considered, resulting in the observations that more senders (not surprisingly) decreases the covert channel capacity, while more receivers increases it. The latter observation is intuitive to communication engineers, but may not have occurred to many in the anonymity community, since the focus there is often on sender anonymity.

As the entropy H of the probability distribution associated with a message output from a Mix gives the effective size, 2^H, of the anonymity set, we wonder if the capacity of the residual quasi-anonymous channel in an anonymity system provides some measure of the effective size of the anonymity set for the system as a whole. That is, using the covert channel capacity as a standard yardstick, can we take the capacity of the covert channel for the observed transmission characteristics of clueless senders, equate it with the capacity for a (possibly smaller) set of clueless senders with maximum entropy (i.e., who introduce the maximum amount of noise into the channel for Alice), and use the size of this latter set as the effective number of clueless senders in the system. This is illustrated in Figure 4, with the vertical dashed line showing that $N = 4$ clueless senders that remain silent with probability $p = 0.87$ are in some sense equivalent to one clueless sender that sends with $p = 0.33$.

The case in which the Mix itself injects dummy messages into the stream randomly is not distinguishable from having an additional clueless sender. However, if the Mix predicates its injection of dummy messages upon the activity of the senders, then it can affect the channel matrix greatly, to the point of eliminating the covert channel entirely. We are also interested in the degree to which the Mix can reduce the covert channel capacity (increase anonymity) with a limited ability to inject dummy messages.

In future work we will analyze the situation where we have different (and more realistic) distributions for the clueless senders. We are also interested in different kinds of exit point Mix-firewalls, such as threshold Mixes, timed Mixes (where the time quantum is long enough to allow more than one message per sender to be sent before the Mix fires), timed-pool Mixes, and systems of Mixes.

Acknowledgements

We thank the reviewers and Andrei Serjantov for their helpful comments.

References

1. George Danezis and Andrei Serjantov. Statistical disclosure or intersection attacks on anonymity systems. In *Information Hiding, Sixth International Workshop.* Springer-Verlag, LNCS, 2004.
2. George Danezis and Andrei Serjantov. Statistical disclosure or intersection attacks on anonymity systems. In *IH 2004, Springer LNCS TBD,* page TBD, Toronto, Canada, May 2004.
3. E.E. Majani and H. Rumsey. Two results on binary input discrete memoryless channels. In *IEEE International Symposium on Information Theory*, page 104, June 1991.
4. Ira S. Moskowitz and Richard E. Newman and Daniel P. Crepeau and Allen R. Miller. Covert channels and anonymizing networks. In *ACM WPES,* pages 79-88, Washington, October 2003.
5. Ira S. Moskowitz and Richard E. Newman and Paul F. Syverson. Quasi-anonymous channels. In *IASTED CNIS,* pages 126-131, New York, December 2003.
6. Andrei Serjantov and Roger Dingledine and Paul Syverson. From a trickle to a flood: Active attacks on several mix types. In F.A.P. Petitcolas, editor, *IH 2002, Springer LNCS 2578,* pages 3652, Noordwijkerhout, the Netherlands, October 2002.
7. Richard E. Newman and Vipan R. Nalla and Ira S. Moskowitz. Covert channels and simple timed mix-firewalls. NRL Memorandum Report to appear, NRL, 2004.
8. David Chaum. Untraceable electronic mail, return addresses, and digital pseudonyms. *Communications of the ACM,* 24(2):84-88, 1981.
9. Claude E. Shannon. The mathematical theory of communication. *Bell Systems Technical Journal,* 30:50-64, 1948.

Practical Traffic Analysis: Extending and Resisting Statistical Disclosure

Nick Mathewson and Roger Dingledine

The Free Haven Project
{nickm, arma}@freehaven.net

Abstract. We extend earlier research on mounting and resisting passive long-term end-to-end traffic analysis attacks against anonymous message systems, by describing how an eavesdropper can learn sender-receiver connections even when the substrate is a network of pool mixes, the attacker is non-global, and senders have complex behavior or generate padding messages. Additionally, we describe how an attacker can use information about message distinguishability to speed the attack. We simulate our attacks for a variety of scenarios, focusing on the amount of information needed to link senders to their recipients. In each scenario, we show that the intersection attack is slowed but still succeeds against a steady-state mix network. We find that the attack takes an impractical amount of time when message delivery times are highly variable; when the attacker can observe very little of the network; and when users pad consistently and the adversary does not know how the network behaves in their absence.

1   Introduction

Mix networks aim to allow senders to anonymously deliver messages to recipients. One of the strongest attacks against current deployable designs is the *long-term intersection attack*. In this attack, a passive eavesdropper observes a large volume of network traffic and notices that certain recipients are more likely to receive messages after particular senders have transmitted messages. That is, if a sender (call her Alice) maintains a fairly consistent pattern of recipients over time, the attacker can deduce Alice's recipients.

Researchers have theorized that these attacks should be extremely effective in many real-world contexts, but so far it has been difficult to reason about when these attacks would be successful and how long they would take.

Here we extend a version of the long-term intersection attack called the statistical disclosure attack [13] to work in real-world circumstances. Specifically, whereas the original model for this attack makes strong assumptions about sender behavior and only works against a single batch mix, we show how an attacker can learn Alice's regular recipients even when:

D. Martin and A. Serjantov (Eds.): PET 2004, LNCS 3424, pp. 17–34, 2005.

- Alice chooses non-uniformly among her communication partners, and can send multiple messages in a single batch.
- The attacker lacks *a priori* knowledge of the network's average behavior when Alice is not sending messages.
- Mixes use a different batching algorithm, such as Mixmaster's dynamic-pool algorithm [25, 30] or its generalization [17].
- Alice uses a mix network (of any topology, with synchronous or asynchronous batching) to relay her messages through a succession of mixes, instead of using just a single mix.
- Alice disguises when she is sending real messages by sending padding traffic to be dropped by mix nodes in the network.
- The attacker can only view a subset of the messages entering and leaving the network (so long as this subset includes some messages from Alice and some messages to Alice's recipients).
- The cover traffic generated by other senders changes slowly over time. (We do not address this case completely.)

Each deviation from the original model reduces the rate at which the attacker learns Alice's recipients, and increases the amount of traffic he must observe.

Additionally, we show how an attacker can exploit additional knowledge, such as distinguishability between messages, to speed these attacks. For example, an attacker who sees message contents can take into account whether messages are written in the same language or signed by the same pseudonym, and thereby partition messages into different classes and analyze the classes independently.

The attacks in this paper fail to work when:

- Alice's behavior is not consistent over time. If Alice does not produce enough traffic with the same recipients, the attacker cannot learn her behavior.
- The attacker cannot observe how the network behaves in Alice's absence. If Alice always sends the same number of messages, in every round, forever, a passive attacker cannot learn who receives messages in Alice's absence.
- The attacker cannot tell when Alice is originating messages.

We begin in Section 2 by presenting a brief background overview on mix networks, traffic analysis, the disclosure attack, and the statistical disclosure attack. In Section 3 we present our enhancements to the statistical disclosure attack. We present simulated experimental results in Section 4, and close in Section 5 with recommendations for resisting this class of attacks, implications for mix network design, and a set of open questions for future work.

2   Previous Work

Chaum [10] proposed hiding the correspondence between sender and recipient by wrapping messages in layers of public-key cryptography, and relaying them through a path composed of *mixes*. Each mix in turn decrypts, delays, and re-orders messages, before relaying them toward their destinations. Because some mixes might be controlled by an adversary, Alice can direct her messages through a sequence or 'chain' of mixes in a network, so that no single mix can link her to her recipient.

Many subsequent designs have been proposed, including Babel [21], Mixmaster [25], and Mixminion [14]. We will not address the differences between these systems in any detail: from the point of view of a long-term intersection attack, the internals of the network are irrelevant so long as the attacker can observe messages entering and leaving the network, and can guess when a message entering the network is likely to leave.

Another class of anonymity designs aims to provide low-latency connections for web browsing and other interactive services [6, 9, 18, 28]. We do not address these systems here because short-term timing and packet counting attacks seem sufficient against them [31].

Attacks against mix networks aim to reduce the anonymity of users by linking anonymous senders with the messages they send, by linking anonymous recipients with the messages they receive, or by linking anonymous messages with one another. For detailed lists of attacks, consult [2, 27]. Attackers can trace messages through the network by observing network traffic, compromising mixes, compromising keys, delaying messages so they stand out from other traffic, or altering messages in transit. They can learn a given message's destination by flooding the network with messages, replaying multiple copies of a message, or shaping traffic to isolate a target message from other unknown traffic [30]. Attackers can discourage users from using honest mixes by making them unreliable [2, 19]. They can analyze intercepted message text to look for commonalities between otherwise unlinked senders [26].

2.1   The Long-Term Intersection Attack

Even if we foil all the above attacks, an adversary can mount a *long-term intersection attack* by correlating times when senders and receivers are active [8].

A variety of countermeasures make intersection attacks harder. Kesdogan's stop-and-go mixes [23] provide probabilistic anonymity by letting users specify message latencies, thereby broadening the range of time when messages might leave the mix network. Similarly, batching strategies [30] as in Mixmaster and Mixminion use message pools to spread out the possible exit times for messages.

Rather than expanding the set of messages that might have been sent by a suspect sender, other designs expand the set of senders that might have sent a target message. A sender who also runs a node in the mix network can conceal whether a given message originated at her node or was relayed from another node [5, 20, 29]. But even with this approach, the adversary can observe whether certain traffic patterns are present when a user is online (possibly sending) and absent when a user is offline (certainly not sending) [33, 34].

A sender can also conceal whether she is currently active by consistently sending decoy (dummy) traffic. Pipenet [11] conceals traffic patterns by constant padding on every link. Unfortunately, a single user can shut down this network simply by not sending. Berthold and Langos aim to increase the difficulty of intersection attacks with a scheme for preparing plausible dummy traffic and having other nodes send it on Alice's behalf when she is offline [7], but their design has many practical problems.

Finally, note that while the adversary can perform this long-term intersection attack entirely passively, active attacks (such as blending attacks [30] against a suspected sender) can help him reduce the set of suspects at each round.

2.2   The Disclosure Attack

In 2002, Kesdogan, Agrawal, and Penz presented the disclosure attack [22], an intersection attack against a single sender on a single batch mix.

The disclosure attack assumes a global passive eavesdropper interested in learning the recipients of a single sender Alice. It assumes that Alice sends messages to m recipients; that Alice sends a single message (recipient chosen at random from m) in each batch of b messages; and that the recipients of the other $b-1$ messages are chosen at random from the set of N possible recipients.

The attacker observes the messages leaving the mix and constructs sets R_i of recipients receiving messages in batch i. The attacker then performs an NP-complete computation to identify m mutually disjoint recipient sets R_i, so that each of Alice's recipients is necessarily contained in exactly one of the sets. Intersecting these sets with subsequent recipient sets reveals Alice's recipients.

2.3   The Statistical Disclosure Attack

In 2003, Danezis presented the statistical disclosure attack [13], which makes the same operational assumptions as the original disclosure attack but is far easier to implement in terms of storage, speed, and algorithmic complexity. Unlike its predecessor, statistical disclosure only reveals *likely* recipients; it does not identify Alice's recipients with certainty.

In the statistical disclosure attack, we model Alice's behavior as an unknown vector $\vec{v}$ whose elements correspond to the probability of Alice sending a message to each of the N recipients in the system. The elements of $\vec{v}$ corresponding to Alice's m recipients will be $1/m$; the other $N-m$ elements of $\vec{v}$ will be 0. We model the behavior of the covering "background" traffic sent by other users as a known vector $\vec{u}$ each of whose N elements is $1/N$.

The attacker derives from each output round i an observation vector $\vec{o_i}$, each of whose elements corresponds to the probability of Alice's having sent a message to each particular recipient in that round. That is, in a round i where Alice has sent a message, each element of $\vec{o_i}$ is $1/b$ if it corresponds to a recipient who has received a message, and 0 if it does not. Taking the arithmetic mean $\overline{O}$ of a large set of these observation vectors gives (by the law of large numbers):

$$\overline{O} = \frac{1}{t} \sum_{i=i}^{t} \vec{o_i} \approx \frac{\vec{v} + (b-1)\,\vec{u}}{b}$$

From this, the attacker estimates Alice's behavior:

$$\overrightarrow{v} \approx b \frac{\sum_{i=1}^{t} \overrightarrow{O_i}}{t} - (b - i)\overrightarrow{u}$$

Danezis also derives a precondition that the attack will only succeed when $m < \frac{N}{b-1}$, and calculates the expected number of rounds to succeed (with 95% confidence for security parameter $l = 2$ and 99% confidence for $l = 3$) [12]:

$$t > \left[m \cdot l \left(\sqrt{\frac{N-1}{N}(b-1)} + \sqrt{\frac{N-1}{N^2}(b-1) + \frac{m-1}{m}} \right) \right]^2$$

3   Extending the Statistical Disclosure Attack

3.1   Broadening the Attack

Here we examine ways to extend Danezis's statistical disclosure attack to systems more closely resembling real-world mix networks. We will simulate the time and information requirements for several of these attacks in Section 4 below.

Complex Senders, Unknown Background Traffic: First, we relax the requirements related to sender behavior. We allow Alice to choose among her recipients with non-uniform probability, and to send multiple messages in a single batch. We also remove the assumption that the attacker has full knowledge of the distribution $\overrightarrow{u}$ of cover traffic sent by users other than Alice.

To model Alice's varying number of messages, we use a probability function P_m such that in every round Alice sends n messages with probability $P_m(n)$. We still use a behavior vector $\overrightarrow{v}$ to represent the probability of Alice sending to each recipient, but we no longer require Alice's recipients to have a uniform $1/m$ probability. Alice's expected contribution to each round is thus $\overrightarrow{v} \sum_{n=0}^{\infty} n P_m(n)$.

To mount the attack, the attacker first obtains an estimate of the background distribution $\overrightarrow{u}$ by observing a large number t' of batches to which Alice has *not* contributed any messages.[1] For each such batch i, the attacker constructs a vector $\overrightarrow{u_i}$, whose elements are $1/b$ for recipients that have received a message in that batch, and 0 for recipients that have not. The attacker then estimates the background distribution $\overrightarrow{u}$ as:

$$\overrightarrow{u} \approx \overline{U} = \frac{1}{t'} \sum_{i=1}^{t'} \overrightarrow{u_i}$$

---

[1] The attack can still proceed if few such Alice-free batches exist, so long as Alice contributes more to some batches than to others. Specifically, the approach described below (against pool mixes and mix networks) can exploit differences between low-Alice and high-Alice batches to infer background behavior.

The attacker then observes, for each round i in which Alice *does* send a message, the number of messages m_i sent by Alice, and computes observations $\overrightarrow{o_i}$ as before. Taking the arithmetic mean of these $\overrightarrow{o_i}$ gives us

$$\overline{O} = \frac{1}{t}\sum_{i=1}^{t}\overrightarrow{o_i} \approx \frac{\overline{m}\cdot\overrightarrow{v} + (b-\overline{m})\overline{U}}{b} \quad \text{where } \overline{m} = \frac{1}{t}\sum m_i$$

From this, the attacker estimates Alice's behavior as

$$\overrightarrow{v} \approx \frac{1}{\overline{m}}\left[b\cdot\overline{O} - (b-\overline{m})\overline{U}\right]$$

Attacking Pool Mixes and Mix Networks: Most designs have already abandoned fixed-batch mixes in favor of other algorithms that better hide the relation between senders and recipients. Such algorithms include timed dynamic-pool mixes, generalized mixes, and randomized versions of each [17, 30]. Rather than reordering and relaying all messages whenever a fixed number b arrive, these algorithms store received messages in a *pool*, and at fixed intervals relay a *fraction* of the pooled messages based on the pool's current size.

When attacking such a mix, the attacker no longer knows for certain which batches contain messages from Alice. Instead, the attacker can only estimate, for each batch of output messages, the probability that the batch includes one or more of Alice's messages.

Following Díaz and Serjantov's approach in [17], we treat these mixing algorithms as follows: a mix relays a number of messages at the end of each round, depending on how many messages it is currently storing. All messages in the mix's pool at the end of a round have an equal probability of being included in that round's batch. Thus, we can characterize the mix's pooling algorithm as a probability function $P_{\text{MIX}}(b|s)$—the probability that the mix relays b messages when it has s messages in the pool.

We denote by $P_R^i(r)$ the probability that a message arriving in round i leaves the mix r rounds later. We assume that the attacker has a fair estimate of P_R.[2] Now, when Alice sends a message in round i, the attacker observes round i through some later round $i + k$, choosing k so that $\sum_{j=k+1}^{\infty} P_R^i(j)$ is negligible. The attacker then uses P_R to compute $\overline{O_w}$, the mean of the observations from these rounds, weighted by the expected number of messages from Alice exiting in each round:

$$\overline{O_w} = \sum_{i}\sum_{r=0}^{k} P_R^i(r)\cdot m_i\cdot\overrightarrow{o_{i+r}} \approx \frac{\overline{m}\cdot\overrightarrow{v} + (\overline{n}-\overline{m})\overrightarrow{u}}{\overline{n}}$$

To solve for Alice's behavior $\overrightarrow{v}$, the attacker now needs an estimate for the background $\overrightarrow{u}$. The attacker gets this by averaging observations $\overrightarrow{u_i}$ from

---

[2] The attacker can estimate P_R by sending test messages through the mix, or by counting the messages entering and leaving the mix and deducing the pool size.

batches with a negligible probability of including messages from Alice. Such batches, however, are not essential: If the attacker chooses a set of $\overrightarrow{u_i}$ such that each round contains (on average) a small number $\delta_a > 0$ of messages from Alice, averaging them gives:

$$\overline{U'} \approx \frac{\delta_a}{n} \overrightarrow{v} + \frac{1 - \delta_a}{n} \overrightarrow{u}$$

and the attacker can solve again for $\overrightarrow{v}$ in the earlier equation for $\overline{O_w}$, now using

$$\overrightarrow{u} \approx \frac{1}{1 - \delta_a} \left[\overline{n} \cdot \overline{U'} - \delta_a \cdot \overrightarrow{v} \right]$$

Senders can also direct their messages through multi-hop paths in a network of mixes. While using a mix network increases the effort needed to observe all messages leaving the system, it has no additional effect on intersection attacks beyond changing the system's delaying characteristics. Assume (for simplicity) that all mixes have the same delay distribution P_R, and that Alice chooses paths of length ℓ_0. The chance of a message being delayed by a further d rounds is now

$$P'_R(\ell_0 + d) = \binom{\ell_0 + d - 1}{d} (1 - P_D)^{\ell_0} P_D^d$$

Danezis has independently extended statistical disclosure to pool mixes [12]; Danezis and Serjantov have analyzed it in detail [15].

Dummy Traffic: Alice can also reduce the impact of traffic analysis by periodically sending messages that are dropped inside[3] the network.

Although this padding can slow or stop the attacker (as discussed below in Section 4), the change in the attack is trivial: Alice's behavior vector $\overrightarrow{v}$ no longer adds to 1, since there is now a chance that a message from Alice will not reach any recipient. Aside from this, the attack can proceed as before, so long as Alice sends more messages (including dummies) in some rounds than in others.

Partial Observation: Until now, we have required that the attacker, as a global passive adversary, observe all the messages entering and leaving the system (at least, all the messages sent by Alice, and all the messages reaching Alice's recipients). This is not so difficult as it might seem: to be a "global" adversary against Alice, an attacker need only eavesdrop upon Alice, and upon the mixes that deliver messages to recipients. (Typically, not all mixes do so. For example, only about one third of current Mixminion servers support delivery.)

---

[3] Alice might also send dummy traffic to ordinary recipients. This approach has its problems: how should Alice generate cover texts, or get the list of all possible recipients? In any case, it is unclear whether Alice can obscure her true recipients without sending equal volumes of mail to all of her non-recipients as well, which is impractical.

A non-global attacker's characteristics depend on which parts of the network he can observe. If the attacker eavesdrops on a fraction of the *mixes*, he receives a sample[4] of the messages entering or leaving the system. If such an attacker can see some messages from Alice and some messages to her recipients, he can guess Alice's recipients, but will require more rounds of observation.

Alternatively, an attacker who eavesdrops on a fraction of the *users* receives *all* messages sent to or from those users but no messages sent to or from other users. So long as one of these users is Alice, the network (to such an attacker) is as if the messages sent by Alice to unobserved recipients were dummy messages. Now the attack converges only against observed recipients: the attacker learns which of observed recipients get messages from Alice, and which do not.

Time-variant Background Traffic: If Alice's behavior changes completely and radically over time, long-term intersection attacks cannot proceed: the attacker cannot make enough observations of any version or subset of Alice's behavior to converge on a $\overline{v}$ for any of them.

On the other hand, if Alice's behavior $\overrightarrow{v}$ remains consistent while the behavior of the background traffic $\overrightarrow{u}$ changes slowly, the attacker still has some hope. Rather than estimating a single $\overline{U}$ from rounds to which Alice does not contribute, the attacker estimates a series of successive $\overline{U_i}$ values based on the average behavior of the network during comparatively shorter durations of time. The attacker observes $\overrightarrow{o_i}$ and computes the average of $\overrightarrow{o_i} - \overline{U_i}$, as before. Now,

$$\overrightarrow{v} \propto \frac{1}{t} \sum_{i=1}^{t} \overrightarrow{o_i} - \overline{U_i}$$

So if an attacker can get good local estimates to $\overrightarrow{u}$, the intersection attack proceeds as before.

Attacking Recipients: Finally, we note that an attacker can find recipients as well as senders by using slightly more storage and the same computational cost.

Suppose the attacker wants to know who is sending anonymous messages to a given recipient Bob. The analysis remains the same: the attacker compares sender behavior in rounds from which Bob probably receives messages with behavior in rounds from which Bob probably doesn't receive messages. The only complication is that the attacker cannot tell in advance when Bob will receive a message. Therefore, the attacker must remember a window of recent observations at all times, such that if Bob later receives a message, the chance is negligible that the message was sent before the first round in the window.

3.2   Strengthening the Attack

Section 3.1 extended the original statistical disclosure attack to link senders and recipients in a broader range of circumstances. In this section, we discuss ways to reduce the required amount of traffic by incorporating additional information.

---

[4] But possibly a biased sample, depending on Alice's path selection algorithm.

Partitioning Messages: The attack is simplified if some output messages are *linkable*—that is, if they are likelier to originate from the same sender than are two randomly chosen messages. We consider a special case of linkability, in which we can *partition* messages into separate classes such that messages in the same class are likelier to have the same sender than messages chosen at random.

For example, in a typical pseudonym service, each sender has one or more pseudonyms and each delivered messages is associated with a pseudonym. To link senders and recipients, an attacker only needs to link senders to their pseudonyms. He can do so by treating pseudonyms as virtual message destinations: instead of collecting observations $\vec{o_i}$ of recipients who receive messages in round i, the attacker now collects observations $\vec{o_i}$ of linkable classes (e.g. pseudonyms) that receive in round i. Since two distinct senders don't produce messages in the same linkability class, the elements of Alice's $\vec{v}$ and the background $\vec{u}$ are now disjoint, and thus easier for the attacker to separate.

It's also possible that the partitioning may not be complete: sometimes many senders will send messages in the same class. For example, two binary documents written with the same version of MS Word are more likely to be written by the same sender than two messages selected at random.[5]

To exploit these scenarios, the attacker chooses a set of c partitioning classes (such as languages or patterns of use), and assigns each observed output message a probability of belonging to each class. Instead of collecting observation vectors with elements corresponding to recipients, the attacker now collects observation vectors whose elements correspond to number of messages received by each ⟨recipient, class⟩ tuple. (If a message might belong to multiple classes, the attacker sets the corresponding element of each possible class to the probability of the message's being in that class.) The attack proceeds as before, but messages that fall in different classes no longer provide cover for one another.

Exploiting *a priori* Suspicion: Finally, the attacker may have reason to believe that some messages are more likely to have been sent by the target user than others. For example, if we believe that Alice studies psychology but not astrophysics, then we will naturally suspect that a message about psychology is more likely to come from Alice than is a message about astrophysics. Similarly, if users have different views of the network, then an attacker will suspect messages exiting from mixes Alice probably doesn't know about less than other messages.

To exploit this knowledge, an attacker can (as suggested in the original statistical disclosure paper) modify the estimated probabilities in $\vec{o_i}$ of Alice having sent each delivered message.

---

[5] Encrypting all messages end-to-end would address most of these attacks, but is difficult in practice. Most recipients do not run anonymity software, and many don't support encrypted email. Thus, many messages still leave today's mix networks in plaintext. Furthermore, today's most popular encryption standards (such as PGP and SMIME) have enough variation for an attacker to tell which implementations could have generated a given message.

4   Simulation Results

In Section 3.1, we repeatedly claim that each complication of the sender or the network forces the attacker to gather more information. But how much?

To find out, we ran a series of simulations of our attacks, first against the model of the original statistical disclosure attack, then against more sophisticated models. We describe our simulations and present results below.

The Original Statistical Disclosure Attack: Our simulation varied the parameters N (the number of recipients), m (the number of Alice's recipients), and b (the batch size). The simulated "Alice" sends a single message every round to one of her recipients, chosen uniformly at random. The simulated background sends to $b - 1$ additional recipients per round, also chosen uniformly at random. We ran 100 trial attacks for each chosen $\langle N, m, b \rangle$ tuple. Each attack was set to halt when the attacker had correctly identified Alice's recipients, or when 1,000,000 rounds had passed. (We imposed this cap to keep our simulator from getting stuck on hopeless cases.)

Figure 1 presents the results of our simulation (the low-m curves are at the bottom). As expected, the attack becomes more effective when Alice sends messages to only a few recipients (small m); when there are more recipients to whom Alice does not send (large N); or when batch sizes are small (small b).

Complex Sender Behavior and Unknown Background Traffic: The next simulation examines the consequences of a more complex model for background traffic, and of several related models for Alice's behavior.

We model the background as a graph of N communicating parties, each of whom communicates with some of the others. We build this graph according to the "scale-free" model [3, 4]. Scale-free networks share the "six degrees of separation property" (for arbitrary values of six) of small-world networks [32], but also mimic the clustering and 'organic' growth of real social networks, including citations in journals, co-stars in IMDB, and links in the WWW. For these trial attacks, the background messages were generated by choosing nodes from

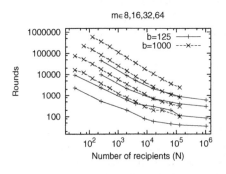

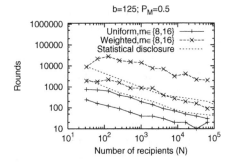

Fig. 1. Statistical disclosure model: median rounds to guess all recipients

Fig. 2. Unknown background: median rounds to guess all recipients

the graph with probability proportional to their connectedness. This simulates a case where users send messages with equal frequency and choose recipients uniformly from among the people they know.

We simulated trial attacks for different values of N (number of recipients) and m (number of Alice's recipients). Instead of sending one message per batch, however, Alice now sends messages according to a geometric distribution with parameter P_M (such that Alice sends n messages with probability $P_m(n) = (1 - P_M)P_M^n$). We tried two methods for assigning Alice's recipients: In the 'uniform' model, Alice's recipients are chosen according to their connectedness (so that Alice, like everyone else, is likelier to know well-known people) but Alice still sends to her recipients with equal probability. In the 'weighted' model, not only are Alice's recipients chosen according to their connectedness, but Alice also sends to them proportionally to their connectedness. We selected these models to examine the attack's effectiveness against users who behave with the same model as other users', and against users who mimic the background distribution.

The results are in Figure 2, along with the results for the original statistical disclosure attack as reference. As expected, the attack succeeds easily, and finishes faster against uniform senders than weighted senders for equivalent values of $\langle N, m, b \rangle$. Interestingly, the attack against uniform senders is *faster* than the original statistical disclosure attack—because the background traffic is now clustered about popular recipients, Alice's recipients stand out more.

Attacking Pool Mixes and Mix Network: Pooling slows an attacker by increasing the number of output messages that could correspond to each input message. To simulate an attack against pool mixes and mix networks, we abstract away the actual pooling rule used by the network, and instead assume that the network has reached a steady state, so that each mix retains the messages in its pool with the same probability (P_{delay}) every round. We also assume that all senders choose paths of exactly the same length.

Unlike before, 'rounds' are now determined not by a batch mix receiving a fixed number b of messages, but by the passage of a fixed interval of time. Thus, the number of messages sent by the background is no longer a fixed $b - n_a$ (where n_a is the number of messages Alice sends), but now follows a normal distribution with mean $BG = 125$ and standard deviation set arbitrarily to $BG/10$.[6]

To examine the effect of pool parameters, we fixed m at 32 and N at 2^{16}, and had Alice use the 'uniform' model discussed above. The results of these simulations are presented in Figure 3. Lines running off the top of the graph represent cases in which fewer than half of the attacks converged upon Alice's recipients within 1,000,000 rounds, and so no median could be found.

---

[6] It's hard to determine standard deviations for actual message volumes on the deployed remailer network: automatic reliability checkers that send messages to themselves ("pingers") contribute to a false sense of uniformity, while some users generate volume spikes by sending enormous fragmented files, or maliciously flooding discussion groups and remailer nodes. Neither group blends well with the other senders.

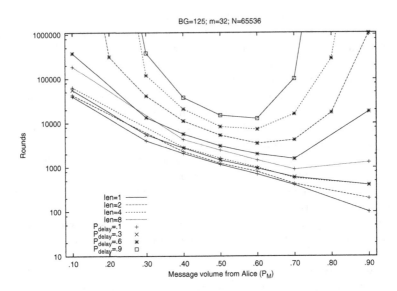

Fig. 3. Pool mixes and mix networks: median rounds to guess all recipients

From these results, we see that increased variability in message delay slows the attack by increasing the number of output messages that may correspond to any input message from Alice, effectively 'spreading' each message across several output rounds. More interestingly, pooling is most effective at especially high or especially low volumes of traffic from Alice: the 'spreading' effect here makes it especially hard for the attacker to discern rounds that contain messages from Alice when she sends few messages, or to discern rounds that don't contain Alice's messages when she sends many messages.

The Impact of Dummy Traffic: Several proposals exist for using dummy messages to frustrate traffic analysis. Although several of them have been examined in the context of low-latency systems [24], little work has been done to examine their effectiveness against long-term intersection attacks.

First, we choose to restrict our examination (due to time constraints) to the effects of dummy messages in several cases of the pool-mix/mix network simulation above. Because we are interested in learning how well dummies thwart analysis, we choose cases where, in the absence of dummies, the attacker had little trouble in learning Alice's recipients.

Our first padding strategy ("independent geometric padding") is based on the algorithm used in current versions of Mixmaster: Alice generates a random number of dummy messages in each round according to a geometric distribution with parameter P_{junk}, independent of her number of real messages.

This strategy slows the attack, but does not *necessarily* stop it. As shown in Figure 4, independent geometric padding is most helpful when the mix network

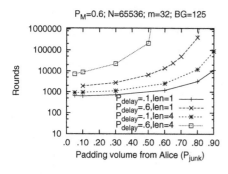

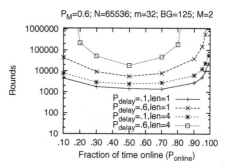

Fig. 4. Independent geometric padding: median rounds to guess all recipients

Fig. 5. Imperfect threshold padding: median rounds to guess all recipients

has a higher variability in message delay to 'spread' the padding between rounds. Otherwise, Alice must send far more padding messages to confuse the attacker.

Our second padding strategy ("imperfect threshold padding") assumes that Alice attempts to implement the otherwise unbreakable threshold padding strategy (always send M messages total in every round, adding dummies up to M and delaying messages after M as necessary), but that she is only sometimes online (with probability P_{online}), and cannot send real messages or padding when she is offline. (This will be typical for most real-world users attempting to implement threshold padding in a world of unreliable hardware and network connections.)

Figure 5 shows the result of imperfect threshold padding. As before, Alice benefits most from padding in networks with more variable delays. Interestingly, in the low delay-variability cases (short paths, low P_{delay}), padding does not thwart the attack even when Alice is online 99% of the time.

For our final dummy traffic simulation, we assume that Alice performs threshold padding consistently, but that the attacker has had a chance to acquire a view of the network's background behavior before Alice first came online.[7] Here, our goal was to confirm our earlier suspicion that padding helps not by disguising how many messages Alice sends, but by preventing the attacker from learning how the network acts in Alice's absence.

Figure 6 compares results when Alice uses consistent threshold padding and the attacker knows the background to results when Alice does not pad and the background $\vec{u}$ is unknown. Not only can an attacker who knows the background distribution identify Alice's recipients with ease, regardless of whether she uses padding, but such an attacker is *not* delayed by increased variability in message delays.

---

[7] As usual, we assume that the background traffic patterns are unchanging. If background traffic changes significantly over time, Alice can defeat this attack by joining the network, sending nothing but padding until the network's background characteristics have changed on their own, and only then beginning to send her messages.

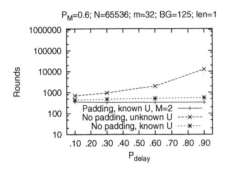
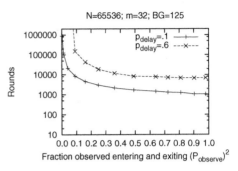

Fig. 6. Full padding, background known: median rounds to guess all recipients

Fig. 7. Partial observation: median rounds to guess all recipients

The Impact of Partial Observation: Finally, we examine the degree to which a non-global adversary can mount a statistical disclosure attack.

Clearly, if Alice chooses only from a fixed set of entry and exit mixes as suggested by [34], and the attacker is watching none of her chosen mixes, the attack will fail—and conversely, if the attacker is watching all of her chosen mixes, the attack proceeds as before. For our simulation, therefore, we assume that all senders (including Alice) choose all mixes as entry and exit points with equal probability for each message, and that the attacker is watching some fraction f of the mixes. We simulate this by revealing each message entering or leaving the network to the attacker with probability $P_{observe} = f$. The attacker sees a message when it enters *and* when it exits with probability $(P_{observe})^2$.

The results in Figure 7 show that the attacker can still implement a long-term intersection attack even when he is only observing part of the network. When most of the network is observed ($P_{observe} > 70\%$ in our results), the attack is hardly impaired at all. As more of the network is concealed ($.4 < P_{observe} < .7$) the attack becomes progressively harder. Finally, as $P_{observe}$ approaches 0, the required number of rounds approaches infinity.

5   Conclusions

Our results demonstrate that long-term end-to-end intersection attacks can succeed even in the presence of complicating factors. Here we suggest several open questions for future work, and offer recommendations for mix network designs.

A More Realistic Model: Our model differs from reality in five major ways. First, although real social networks behave more like scale-free networks than like the original disclosure attack's model, our **models for user behavior** still have room for improvement. Real users do not send messages with a time-invariant geometric distribution: most people's email habits are based on a 24-hour day, and a 7-day week. Early research on traffic patterns in actual mix networks [16] suggests that this variation is probably significant.

Second, **real user behavior changes over time**. Section 3.2 discusses how an attacker might handle a scenario where the background traffic changes slowly over time, and perhaps a similar approach would also help against a sender whose recipients were not constant. In the absence of a model for time-variant user behavior, however, we have not simulated attacks for these cases.

Third, it seems clear that systems with **message linkability**, such as pseudonymous services, will fall to intersection attacks far faster than anonymizing services without linkability. How linkable are messages "in the wild," how much does this linkability help an attacker, and how can it be mitigated?

Fourth, real attackers are not limited to passive observation. We should generalize our attacks to incorporate information gained by an **active attacker**. Past work on avoiding blending attacks [30] has concentrated on preventing an attacker from being certain of Alice's recipients—but in fact, an active attack that only reveals slight probabilities could speed up the attacks in this paper.

Fifth, Alice has incentive to **operate a mix**, so an attacker cannot be sure if she is originating messages or just relaying them [1]. Can we treat this relayed traffic (which goes to actual recipients) as equivalent to padding (which goes to no recipients)? Can Alice employ this relayed traffic for a cheaper padding regime, without opening herself up to influence from active attacks?

Other Questions for Future Research: Our analysis has focused on the impact of Alice's actions on Alice alone. How do Alice's actions (for example, choice of padding method) affect other users in the system? Are there incentive-compatible strategies that provide good security for all users?

It would be beneficial to find closed-form equations for expected number of rounds required to mount these attacks, as Danezis does for statistical disclosure.

Many of our simulations found "sweet spots" for settings such as mix pool delay, message volume, padding volume, and so on. Identifying those points of optimality in the wild would be of great practical help for users. Systems could perhaps then be designed to adaptively configure their pooling strategies to optimize their users' anonymity.

Implications for Mix Network Design: First, **high variability** in message delays is essential. By 'spreading' the effects of each incoming message over several output rounds, variability in delay increases each message's anonymity set, and amplifies the effect of padding.

Padding seems to slow traffic analysis, especially when the padding is consistent enough to prevent the attacker from gaining a picture of the network in Alice's absence. On the other hand, significant padding volumes may be too cumbersome for most users, and perfect consistency (sending padding from the moment a network goes online until it shuts down) is likely impractical.

Users should be educated about the effects of **message volume**: sending infrequently is relatively safe, especially if the user doesn't repeat the same traffic pattern for long.

Mix networks should take steps to **minimize the proportion of observed messages** that a limited attacker can see entering and exiting the network. Possible approaches include encouraging users to run their own mixes; choosing messages' entry and exit points to cross geographical and organization boundaries; and (of course) increasing the number of mixes in the network.

Much threat analysis for high-latency mix networks has aimed to provide perfect protection against an eavesdropper watching the entire network. But unless we adopt an unacceptable level of resource demands, it seems that some highly distinguishable senders will fall quickly, and many ordinary senders will fall more slowly, to long-term intersection attacks. We must stop asking whether our anonymity designs can forever defend every conceivable sender. Instead, we should attempt to quantify the risk: *how long* our designs can defend *which senders* against an adversary who sees *how much*.

Acknowledgments

Thanks go to Gerald Britton, Geoffrey Goodell, Novalis, Pete St. Onge, Peter Palfrader, Alistair Riddoch, and Mike Taylor for letting us run our simulations on their computers; to Peter Palfrader for helping us with information on the properties of the Mixmaster network; and to George Danezis for his comments on drafts of this paper.

References

1. Alessandro Acquisti, Roger Dingledine, and Paul Syverson. On the economics of anonymity. In Rebecca N. Wright, editor, *Financial Cryptography*. Springer-Verlag, LNCS 2742, 2003.
2. Adam Back, Ulf Möller, and Anton Stiglic. Traffic analysis attacks and trade-offs in anonymity providing systems. In Ira S. Moskowitz, editor, *Proceedings of Information Hiding Workshop (IH 2001)*, pages 245–257. Springer-Verlag, LNCS 2137, 2001.
3. Albert-Lázló Barabási and Réka Albert. Emergence of scaling in random networks. *Science*, 286:509–512, October 1999.
4. Albert-Lázló Barabási, Réka Albert, and Hawoong Jeong. Mean-field theory for scale-free random networks. *Physica A*, 272:173–187, 2000.
5. Krista Bennett and Christian Grothoff. GAP – practical anonymous networking. In Roger Dingledine, editor, *Proceedings of Privacy Enhancing Technologies workshop (PET 2003)*. Springer-Verlag, LNCS 2760, March 2003.
6. Oliver Berthold, Hannes Federrath, and Stefan Köpsell. Web MIXes: A system for anonymous and unobservable Internet access. In H. Federrath, editor, *Proceedings of Designing Privacy Enhancing Technologies: Workshop on Design Issues in Anonymity and Unobservability*, pages 115–129. Springer-Verlag, LNCS 2009, July 2000.
7. Oliver Berthold and Heinrich Langos. Dummy traffic against long term intersection attacks. In Roger Dingledine and Paul Syverson, editors, *Proceedings of Privacy Enhancing Technologies workshop (PET 2002)*. Springer-Verlag, LNCS 2482, April 2002.

8. Oliver Berthold, Andreas Pfitzmann, and Ronny Standtke. The disadvantages of free MIX routes and how to overcome them. In H. Federrath, editor, *Proceedings of Designing Privacy Enhancing Technologies: Workshop on Design Issues in Anonymity and Unobservability*, pages 30–45. Springer-Verlag, LNCS 2009, July 2000.
9. Philippe Boucher, Adam Shostack, and Ian Goldberg. Freedom systems 2.0 architecture. White paper, Zero Knowledge Systems, Inc., December 2000.
10. David Chaum. Untraceable electronic mail, return addresses, and digital pseudonyms. *Communications of the ACM*, 4(2), February 1982.
11. Wei Dai. Pipenet 1.1. Usenet post, August 1996. `<http://www.eskimo.com/~weidai/pipenet.txt>` First mentioned to the cypherpunks list, Feb. 1995.
12. George Danezis. *Better Anonymous Communications*. PhD thesis, University of Cambridge, December 2003.
13. George Danezis. Statistical disclosure attacks: Traffic confirmation in open environments. In Gritzalis, Vimercati, Samarati, and Katsikas, editors, *Proceedings of Security and Privacy in the Age of Uncertainty, (SEC2003)*, pages 421–426, Athens, May 2003. IFIP TC11, Kluwer.
14. George Danezis, Roger Dingledine, and Nick Mathewson. Mixminion: Design of a type III anonymous remailer protocol. In *2003 IEEE Symposium on Security and Privacy*, pages 2–15. IEEE CS, May 2003.
15. George Danezis and Andrei Serjantov. Statistical disclosure or intersection attacks on anonymity systems. In *Proceedings of Information Hiding Workshop (IH 2004)*. Springer-Verlag, 2004 (forthcoming).
16. Claudia Díaz, Len Sassaman, and Evelyne Deweiite. Comparison between two practical mix designs. Forthcoming, 2004.
17. Claudia Díaz and Andrei Serjantov. Generalising mixes. In Roger Dingledine, editor, *Proceedings of the Privacy Enhancing Technologies workshop (PET 2003)*. Springer-Verlag, LNCS 2760, March 2003.
18. Roger Dingledine, Nick Mathewson, and Paul Syverson. Tor: The Second-Generation Onion Router. In *Proceedings of the 13th USENIX Security Symposium*, August 2004.
19. Roger Dingledine and Paul Syverson. Reliable MIX Cascade Networks through Reputation. In Matt Blaze, editor, *Financial Cryptography*. Springer-Verlag, LNCS 2357, 2002.
20. Michael J. Freedman and Robert Morris. Tarzan: A peer-to-peer anonymizing network layer. In *Proceedings of the 9th ACM Conference on Computer and Communications Security (CCS 2002)*, Washington, DC, November 2002.
21. Ceki Gülcü and Gene Tsudik. Mixing E-mail with Babel. In *Network and Distributed Security Symposium (NDSS 96)*, pages 2–16. IEEE, February 1996.
22. Dogan Kesdogan, Dakshi Agrawal, and Stefan Penz. Limits of anonymity in open environments. In Fabien Petitcolas, editor, *Proceedings of Information Hiding Workshop (IH 2002)*. Springer-Verlag, LNCS 2578, October 2002.
23. Dogan Kesdogan, Jan Egner, and Roland Büschkes. Stop-and-go MIXes: Providing probabilistic anonymity in an open system. In *Proceedings of Information Hiding Workshop (IH 1998)*. Springer-Verlag, LNCS 1525, 1998.
24. Brian N. Levine, Michael K. Reiter, Chenxi Wang, and Matthew Wright. Timing attacks in low-latency mix-based systems. In Ari Juels, editor, *Financial Cryptography*. Springer-Verlag, LNCS (forthcoming), 2004.
25. Ulf Möller, Lance Cottrell, Peter Palfrader, and Len Sassaman. Mixmaster Protocol — Version 2. Draft, July 2003.

26. Josyula R. Rao and Pankaj Rohatgi. Can pseudonymity really guarantee privacy? In *Proceedings of the 9th USENIX Security Symposium*, pages 85–96. USENIX, August 2000.
27. J. F. Raymond. Traffic Analysis: Protocols, Attacks, Design Issues, and Open Problems. In H. Federrath, editor, *Designing Privacy Enhancing Technologies: Workshop on Design Issue in Anonymity and Unobservability*, pages 10–29. Springer-Verlag, LNCS 2009, July 2000.
28. Michael G. Reed, Paul F. Syverson, and David M. Goldschlag. Anonymous connections and onion routing. *IEEE Journal on Selected Areas in Communications*, 16(4):482–494, May 1998.
29. Michael Reiter and Aviel Rubin. Crowds: Anonymity for web transactions. *ACM Transactions on Information and System Security*, 1(1), June 1998.
30. Andrei Serjantov, Roger Dingledine, and Paul Syverson. From a trickle to a flood: Active attacks on several mix types. In Fabien Petitcolas, editor, *Proceedings of Information Hiding Workshop (IH 2002)*. Springer-Verlag, LNCS 2578, October 2002.
31. Andrei Serjantov and Peter Sewell. Passive attack analysis for connection-based anonymity systems. In *Computer Security – ESORICS 2003*. Springer-Verlag, LNCS (forthcoming), October 2003.
32. Duncan J. Watts and Steven H. Strogatz. Collective dynamics of 'small-world' networks. *Nature*, 393:440–442, June 1998.
33. Matthew Wright, Micah Adler, Brian Neil Levine, and Clay Shields. An analysis of the degradation of anonymous protocols. In *Network and Distributed Security Symposium (NDSS 02)*. IEEE, February 2002.
34. Matthew Wright, Micah Adler, Brian Neil Levine, and Clay Shields. Defending anonymous communication against passive logging attacks. In *IEEE Symposium on Security and Privacy*, pages 28–41. IEEE CS, May 2003.

The Traffic Analysis of Continuous-Time Mixes

George Danezis

University of Cambridge, Computer Laboratory,
15 JJ Thomson Avenue, Cambridge CB3 0FD, United Kingdom
George.Danezis@cl.cam.ac.uk

Abstract. We apply the information-theoretic anonymity metrics to continuous-time mixes, that individually delay messages instead of batching them. The anonymity of such mixes is measured based on their delay characteristics, and as an example the exponential mix (sg-mix) is analysed, simulated and shown to use the optimal strategy. We also describe a practical and powerful traffic analysis attack against connection based continuous-time mix networks, despite the presence of some cover traffic. Assuming a passive observer, the conditions are calculated that make tracing messages through the network possible.

1   Introduction

Building blocks for anonymous communication operating by batching input messages in rounds, such as threshold or pool mixes, have recently been the subject of extensive study [15, 16, 6, 17]. The same is not true for mixes that operate in continuous-time, by individually delaying messages. An example of these is the *sg-mix* construction presented by Kesdogan *et al* [10]. Its inventors present an analysis of its anonymity, but this cannot easily be generalised to other mix strategies.

We will present a new framework for analysing the anonymity provided by mix strategies that individually delay messages. In order to make the analysis easier, we assume that the rate of arrival of messages to the mixes is Poisson distributed. Using the work presented here, different mix strategies can be analysed but we choose to illustrate our method with an analysis of the exponential mix (sg-mix), both because it is relatively simple and because it has been extensively mentioned in the literature. Furthermore, a section is devoted to showing that given some latency constraints the exponential mix is the mixing strategy providing maximal anonymity.

We then present a powerful attack that given enough packets, can break the anonymity provided by connection-based mix networks functioning in continuous-time. The attack relies on detecting an input traffic pattern, at the outputs of the mixes or network, using signal detection techniques. A detailed description is given on how to perform this attack, and confidence intervals are provided to assess the reliability of the results. The attack can be used effectively against many proposed anonymous communications systems such as Onion Routing [13], Freedom [4], TARZAN [7] or MorphMix [14].

D. Martin and A. Serjantov (Eds.): PET 2004, LNCS 3424, pp. 35–50, 2005.
© Springer-Verlag Berlin Heidelberg 2005

2   Delay Characteristic and Anonymity

The main aim of a mix, as introduced by Chaum [5], is to hide the correspondence between the input and output messages it relays. First it makes its inputs and outputs bitwise unlinkable, which means that a third party cannot link them by observing their bit patterns without knowledge of the cryptographic keys used to perform the transform. Secondly it blurs the timing correlations between inputs and outputs by batching, introducing appropriate random delays and reordering messages. Continuous-time mixes achieve this by delaying each message individually and independently of the others.

We can say that a particular mix strategy is described by its *delay characteristic*. This is a function $f(\beta|\alpha)$ that represents the probability a message injected in the mix at time α leaves the mix at time β, where $\alpha \leq \beta$. Since $f(\beta|\alpha)$ is a conditional probability distribution, it is normalised.

$$\forall \alpha. \int_{\alpha}^{+\infty} f(\beta|\alpha)\, d\beta = 1. \tag{1}$$

The *inverse delay characteristic*, $f'(\alpha|\beta)$, of the same mix strategy is a probability distribution that describes the likelihood a message being ejected at time β was injected at time α. Again because it is a conditional probability distribution it is normalised.

$$\forall \beta. \int_{-\infty}^{\beta} f'(\alpha|\beta)\, d\alpha = 1. \tag{2}$$

The two characteristics are related, since the second f' can be calculated using Bayes theorem from f. Some knowledge of the probability of arrivals at particular times is necessary to perform this conversion. To simplify things, we will consider that arrivals are Poisson distributed with a rate λ_α. In a Poisson process, the probability of an arrival is independent from other arrivals or the time α.

$$f'(\alpha|\beta) = \frac{f(\beta|\alpha)\Pr[\text{Arrival at } \alpha]}{\int_{-\infty}^{\beta} f(\beta|\alpha)\Pr[\text{Arrival at } \alpha]\, d\alpha} \tag{3}$$

$$= \frac{f(\beta|\alpha)}{\int_{-\infty}^{\beta} f(\beta|\alpha)\, d\alpha} \tag{4}$$

Therefore, given the delay characteristics and some assumptions about the traffic in the network we can calculate the inverse delay characteristic. These will allow us to measure the effective sender and receiver anonymity for this mix strategy.

We will use the metric introduced in [15] to calculate the sender anonymity provided by a mixing strategy. This metric is based on defining a random variable that describes the possible senders of a message and calculating the entropy of its underlying probability distribution. The entropy is then a measure of the anonymity provided, and can be interpreted as the amount of information an attacker is missing to deterministically link the messages to a sender.

We assume that in a time interval $(\beta - T, \beta)$, K messages arrive at the mix, where K is distributed according to a Poisson distribution with parameter λ_α. These messages arrive at times $X_{1...K}$ each distributed according to a uniform distribution $U(t)$ over the time interval of length T (as required by the Poisson distribution).

Given the inverse delay characteristic of the mix $f'(\alpha|\beta)$, the sender anonymity $\mathcal{A}$ provided by the mix can be calculated. It represents the entropy of the probability distribution describing how likely each of the inputs X_i is to be output at a particular time β.

$$\mathcal{A} = \sum_{i=1}^{K} \frac{f'(X_i|\beta)}{\sum_{j=1}^{K} f'(X_j|\beta)} \log \frac{f'(X_i|\beta)}{\sum_{j=1}^{K} f'(X_j|\beta)} = \tag{5}$$

$$= \frac{1}{\sum_{j=1}^{K} f'(X_j|\beta)} \left(\sum_{i=1}^{K} f'(X_i|\beta) \log f'(X_i|\beta) \right) - \log \sum_{j=1}^{K} f'(X_j|\beta) \tag{6}$$

From the Law of Large Numbers[1] we know that the sums converge to:

$$\sum_{j=1}^{K} f'(X_j|\beta) \rightarrow \frac{K}{T} \rightarrow \lambda_\alpha \tag{7}$$

$$\sum_{i=1}^{K} f'(X_i|\beta) \log f'(X_i|\beta) \rightarrow \frac{K}{T} \int_{\beta-T}^{\beta} f'(t|\beta) \log f'(t|\beta) dt \rightarrow \lambda_\alpha \mathcal{E}[f'(\alpha|\beta)] \tag{8}$$

Thus the fraction K/T converges to λ_α, which is the rate of arrival of messages to the mix and the integral (8) reduces to the entropy of the inverse delay characteristic function $\mathcal{E}[f'(\alpha|\beta)]$. Therefore the sender anonymity of a continuous mix with delay characteristic f' and a rate of arrival λ_α can be expressed.

$$\mathcal{A} \rightarrow \mathcal{E}[f'(\alpha|\beta)] - \log \lambda_\alpha \tag{9}$$

Putting this into words, the effective sender anonymity set size of the mixing strategy will converge towards the relative entropy of the inverse delay characteristic, as defined by Shannon [19], minus the logarithm of the rate at which messages are received. Similarly the recipient anonymity set size can be calculated using the same techniques and the delay characteristic of the mix strategy.

2.1 The Exponential Mix

In order to illustrate the calculations above we analyse the exponential mix. The exponential mix has been presented as a mixing strategy by Kesdogan *et*

---

[1] For large K and T, $\lim_{K \to \infty} \sum_{j=1}^{K} f'(X_j|\beta) = K \int_{\beta-T}^{\beta} U(t) f'(t|\beta) dt \rightarrow \frac{K}{T}$. Note that for the approximation we do not assume the rate to be large, but simply the observation period T to be large enough to observe some traffic.

al [10]. In their design additional features are implemented to avoid $(n-1)$ attacks [8, 16], that we are not concerned with in this work.

The exponential mix can be abstracted as an $M/M/\infty$ queue. We assume, as required from the calculations above, the arrival rates of messages to be Poisson distributed with rate λ_α. Each of the messages that arrives at the mix is delayed according to a random variable that follows the exponential distribution with parameter μ. Therefore the delay characteristic of the exponential mix is:

$$f(\beta|\alpha) = \mu e^{-\mu(\beta-\alpha)}. \tag{10}$$

From equation (4) we can calculate the inverse delay characteristic f'. Due to the nature of the exponential distribution, it is equal to the delay characteristic f.

$$f'(\alpha|\beta) = \frac{f(\beta|\alpha)}{\int_{-\infty}^{\beta} f(\beta|\alpha)\,d\alpha} = f(\beta|\alpha) = \mu e^{-\mu(\beta-\alpha)} \tag{11}$$

Using the inverse delay characteristic, and (9) we can now calculate the expected sender anonymity ($\mathcal{E}[\cdot]$ is the entropy function).

$$\mathcal{A} = \mathcal{E}[\Pr[\alpha]] \to \mathcal{E}[f'(\alpha|\beta)] - \log \lambda_\alpha = \tag{12}$$

$$= \int_{-\infty}^{\beta} \mu e^{-\mu(\beta-\alpha)} \log \mu e^{-\mu(\beta-\alpha)}\,d\alpha - \log \lambda_\alpha = -\log \frac{\lambda_\alpha e}{\mu} \tag{13}$$

To check the above result (since it relies on the approximations (7) and (8)) a simulation was run for some values of λ_α and μ, and the results were compared with the metric predictions in equation (13). The inverse delay characteristic was used to calculate the probability assigned to a number of messages arriving at a mix. The number of messages was Poisson distributed according to λ_α, and their time of arrival was chosen uniformly. Their delay was a random variable distributed according to the exponential distribution with rate μ. The absolute difference between the predictions (figure 1(a)) and the simulation (figure 1(b)) is shown in figure 1(c).

The main divergence of the simulated results from the predicted results, is in the region where the metric predicts positive values for the entropy. This is intuitively impossible and indeed is the largest error from the actual simulation results. The conditions for which the model, that the equation (13) describes, should not be considered accurate is described by:

$$-\log \frac{\lambda_\alpha e}{\mu} > 0 \Rightarrow \mu > \lambda_\alpha e \tag{14}$$

It is clear that an $M/M/\infty$ queue with a departure rate μ larger than the arrival rate λ_α would not provide much anonymity most of the time. The average time a message would spend in the mix is $\frac{1}{\mu}$ while the average time between message arrivals is $\frac{1}{\lambda_\alpha}$, which is larger. Therefore the mix would behave on average as a first-in first-out queue.

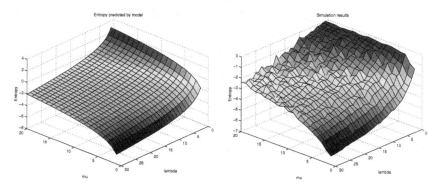

(a) Predictions for exponential mix   (b) Simulation of exponential mix

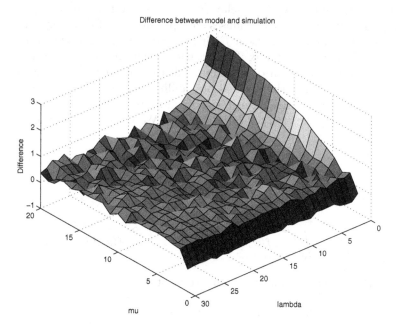

(c) Absolute difference between prediction and simulation

Fig. 1. Simulation of exponential mix for different μ and λ

2.2   The Latency of a Mix Strategy

The delay characteristic of a mix can also be used to calculate the latency introduced by a mix strategy and its variance. This can be done trivially since the latency of the mix strategy is the expectation $E[\cdot]$ of the delay characteristic function $f(\beta|\alpha)$.

$$E[f(\beta|\alpha)] = \int_{\alpha}^{+\infty} (\beta - \alpha) f(\beta|\alpha) \, d\beta \tag{15}$$

Similarly the variance $V[\cdot]$ of the delay can be calculated using the expectation:

$$V[f(\beta|\alpha)] = \int_{\alpha}^{+\infty} (E[f(\beta|\alpha)] - (\beta - \alpha))^2 f(\beta|\alpha) \, d\beta \tag{16}$$

For the exponential mix the mean delay is $\frac{1}{\mu}$ and its variance is $\frac{1}{\mu^2}$.

2.3   Optimal Mixing Strategies

So far, we have described how to measure the anonymity and latency of a continuous-time mix, given its delay strategy. Naturally, the next problem is finding a mix strategy that maximises entropy, and therefore anonymity.

We need to find a distribution f with a particular mean a, which represents the average latency of the mix. Since a packet can only leave the mix after it arrived, the function f can only occupy half the timeline, namely the interval $[0, +\infty)$. We prove that the optimal probability distribution f is the exponential probability distribution. This result was first proved by Shannon [19] using techniques from the calculus of variations [22]. We want to minimise:

$$E[f(x)] = -\int_{0}^{-\infty} f(x) \log f(x) dx \tag{17}$$

Subject to the constraints:

$$a = \int_{0}^{-\infty} x f(x) dx \qquad \text{and} \qquad \int_{0}^{-\infty} f(x) dx = 1 \tag{18}$$

Then by the calculus of variations [22] we must solve:

$$\frac{\partial(-f(x) \log f(x) + \lambda x f(x) + \mu f(x))}{\partial f} = 0 \tag{19}$$

$$\Rightarrow -1 - \log f(x) + \lambda x + \mu = 0 \tag{20}$$

$$\Rightarrow f(x) = e^{\lambda x + \mu - 1} \tag{21}$$

After incorporating the constraints, the resulting function is:

$$f(x) = \frac{1}{a} e^{-\frac{1}{a} x} \tag{22}$$

This is exactly the exponential mix as analysed in section 2.1, which is therefore optimal.

3   Traffic Analysis of Continuous Mixes

In the previous sections we have considered the anonymity of single packets mixed using a continuous-time mixing strategy. Continuous-time mixes can approximate circuit-based systems that implement minimal mixing, in order to provide real-time communications. In such systems a number of packets, all belonging to the same stream, are quickly routed through the same path in the network.

The Onion Routing project [20] first drew the community's attention to the need for traffic padding to protect against fine-grained traffic analysis. Since then some publications have discussed traffic analysis and possible defences against it [1, 12]. Others refer to the same problem in the context of intersection attacks [3, 2, 9] and present padding as a potential protection.

Some previous work has drawn attention to the vulnerabilities of anonymous systems to "timing" attacks [14], while Kesdogan et al [9] present a concrete attack. Serjantov et al [18] present a traffic analysis attack based on counting packets on the links, while Levine et al [11] uses more fine grained traffic patterns to trace them. We will now present a very general way of performing traffic analysis on streams of packets travelling through the same route in a continuous-time mix network. We show that after a certain number of messages, that can be calculated, the communication can be traced with high confidence.

3.1   Concrete Traffic Analysis Techniques

We denote as $f(t)$ the function that describes the traffic, to be traced, feeding into a continuous mix with delay characteristic $d(x)$. We assume that all messages described by $f(t)$ belong to the same stream, and will therefore be ejected on the same output link. We will assume that there are two output links. The attacker's aim is to determine on which output link the stream is redirected.

On the first link we observe messages coming out at times $X_{1 \cdots n}$ and on the second link messages come out at times $Y_{1 \cdots m}$ in the time interval $[0, T]$. H_0 represents the hypothesis the input stream $f(t)$ is interleaved in the first channel described by the observations X_i, and H_1 that is in the second corresponding with Y_i.

In order to detect the streams we will make some approximations. We will create two model probability distributions C_X and C_Y and will assume that all messages in the output channels are independent samples out of one of these distributions. The difference between C_X and C_Y is due to our attempt to model the noise in the two output channels. We will also consider that all the other messages are uniformly distributed in the interval $t \in [0, T]$ according to the distribution $U(t) = u$.

When H_0 is true the stream under observation is interleaved in the observations X_i. We will model each of them as following the probability distribution:

$$C_X(t) = \frac{\lambda_f(d * f)(t) + (\lambda_X - \lambda_f)U(t)}{\lambda_X} \tag{23}$$

The probability distribution $(d * f)(t)$ is the convolution of the input signal with the delay characteristic of the mix. The probability a message delayed by $d(x)$ is output at time t given an input stream of messages described by $f(t)$ is described by this convolution.

$$(d * f)(t) = \int d(x) f(t - x) dx \tag{24}$$

Furthermore λ_f is the rate of messages in the input signal, while λ_X is the rate of the output channel. Finally $U(t) = u$ is the uniform distribution in the interval $[0, T]$.

Similarly if hypothesis H_1 is true, the signal is interleaved in the observations Y_i that follow the distribution:

$$C_Y(t) = \frac{\lambda_f (d * f)(t) + (\lambda_Y - \lambda_f) U(t)}{\lambda_Y} \tag{25}$$

In order to decide which of the two hypothesis is valid, H_0 or H_1, we can calculate the likelihood ratio of the two alternative hypothesis.

$$\frac{\mathcal{L}(H_0 | X_i, Y_j)}{\mathcal{L}(H_1 | X_i, Y_j)} = \frac{\prod_{i=1}^n C_X(X_i) \prod_{j=1}^m u}{\prod_{i=1}^n u \prod_{j=1}^m C_Y(Y_j)} > 1 \tag{26}$$

We choose to accept hypothesis H_0 if condition (26) is true, and hypothesis H_1 otherwise. Section 3.3 will show how we calculate our degree of confidence when making this choice.

3.2 A Simple Example

Figure 2 shows six diagrams illustrating the traffic analysis attack. The first column represents, from top to bottom, the signal that we inject in a mix and the two output channels, one of which contains the delayed signal. The right hand side column represents the delay characteristic of the network, an exponential distribution in this case (sg-mix), the "model" that is created by convolving the input signal with the delay characteristic and, at the bottom, the log-likelihood ratio.

The cover traffic or "noise" in the above experiments is assumed to be a Poisson process. Noise is added both to the channel that contains the stream under surveillance (in this case link 1, X_i) and the other link (Y_i). The rate of the signal $f(t)$ in the traffic analysis graphs shown above is 50 messages, while the noise added in X_i has a rate of 150 messages. The second link contains random padding with a rate of 200 messages (Y_i). The delay characteristic $d(x)$ chosen to illustrate the traffic analysis technique is exponential with a departure rate of 30. The graphs therefore illustrate the traffic analysis of a sg-mix node. The decision graph presents the logarithm of the likelihood, ratio $\log \frac{\mathcal{L}(H_0 | X_i, Y_j)}{\mathcal{L}(H_1 | X_i, Y_j)}$, as an attacker would compute it at each point in the simulation time. After 700 simulation ticks the log-likelihood ratio is clearly positive indicating that H_0 should be accepted.

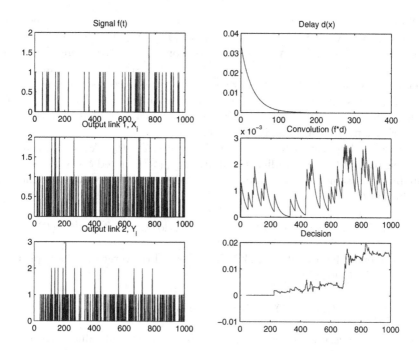

Fig. 2. Final and intermediate results of traffic analysis

3.3   Performance of the Traffic Analysis Attack

There are two question that need to be answered concerning the traffic analysis attack presented. First the conditions under which it is at all possible must be established. Second the number of observations necessary to get reliable results has to be calculated.

By simple mathematical manipulations with logarithms, we can derive that the likelihood ratio test, applied to select the most appropriate hypothesis can be expressed using sums of random variables:

$$\mathcal{L}_{H_0/H_1} = \frac{\mathcal{L}(H_0|X_i, Y_j)}{\mathcal{L}(H_1|X_i, Y_j)} = \frac{\prod_{i=1}^n C_X(X_i) \prod_{j=1}^m u}{\prod_{i=1}^n u \prod_{j=1}^m C_Y(Y_j)} > 1 \qquad (27)$$

$$\Rightarrow \log \mathcal{L}_{H_0/H_1} = \sum_{i=1}^n \log C_X(X_i) - \sum_{j=1}^m \log C_Y(Y_j) + (m-n) \log u > 0 \qquad (28)$$

The expression above is equivalent to (26) the rule by which we choose the hypothesis to accept. The condition for which the attack is possible is that the decision rule (28) must not equal zero. This could be the case if both C_X and C_Y were uniform distributions. Even through the inequality might hold it does not give us any measure of confidence in the result. We will therefore attempt to find bounds within which we are confident that the decision is correct.

Note that the two sums will converge to the expectations $nE\left[\log C_X(X)\,|\,X_i \sim X\right]$ and $mE\left[\log C_Y(Y)\,|\,Y_j \sim Y\right]$. The notation $X_i \sim X$ means that the samples X_i are sampled from the distribution X, and the samples Y_j from the distribution Y. The two distributions X and Y are different according to which of the two hypothesis is accepted. In case H_0 then $X_i \sim C_X, Y_j \sim U$. Alternatively if H_1 is true then $X_i \sim U$ and $Y_j \sim C_Y$. Without losing generality we will demonstrate when to accept hypothesis H_0. The derivations are the same in the other case.

In case the hypothesis H_0 is correct, $E\left[\log C_X(X)\,|\,H_0 : X_i \sim C_X\right]$ converges to the entropy of the probability distribution $C_X(t)$, denoted $\mathcal{E}[C_X(t)]$, since the probabilities assigned to each value of the random variable $\log C_X(X)$ follow the distribution C_X.

$$E\left[\log C_X(X)\,|\,H_0 : X_i \sim C_X\right] = \int_0^T C_X(t)\log C_X(t)dt = \mathcal{E}[C_X(t)] \qquad (29)$$

On the other hand $E\left[\log C_Y(Y)\,|\,H_0 : Y_j \sim U\right]$ converges to the expectation of C_Y namely $E\left[\log C_Y(t)\right]$.

$$E\left[\log C_Y(Y)\,|\,H_0 : Y_j \sim U\right] = \int_0^T u\log C_Y(t)dt = E\left[\log C_Y(t)\right] \qquad (30)$$

Therefore in case we accept hypothesis H_0 the expected value of the decision rule $\log \mathcal{L}_{H_0/H_1}$ (28) is μ_{H_0}:

$$\mu_{H_0} = E\left[\sum_{i=1}^{n}\log C_X(X_i) - \sum_{j=1}^{m}\log C_Y(Y_j) + (m-n)\log u \;|\; H_0\right]$$
$$= nE\left[\log C_X(X)\,|\,H_0\right] - mE\left[\log C_Y(Y)\,|\,H_0\right] + (m-n)\log u$$
$$= n\mathcal{E}[C_X(t)] - mE\left[\log C_Y(t)\right] + (m-n)\log u \qquad (31)$$

The variance can be calculated using the above observations:

$$V\left[\log C_X(X)\,|\,H_0\right] = \int_0^T C_X(t)(\log C_X(t) - \mathcal{E}\left[C_X(X)\right])^2 dt \qquad (32)$$

$$V\left[\log C_Y(Y)\,|\,H_0\right] = \int_0^T u(\log C_Y(t) - E\left[\log C_Y(Y)\right])^2 dt \qquad (33)$$

Using these we will calculate the variance $\sigma_{H_0}^2$ of the decision rule $\log \mathcal{L}_{H_0/H_1}$ (28) which is:

$$\sigma_{H_0}^2 = V\left[\sum_{i=1}^{n}\log C_X(X_i) - \sum_{j=1}^{m}\log C_Y(Y_j) + (m-n)\log u \;|\; H_0\right]$$
$$= nV[\log C_X(X) \;|\; H_0] + mV\left[\log C_Y(Y) \;|\; H_0\right] \qquad (34)$$

Using Chebyshev's inequality[2] we can derive the condition necessary in order to accept hypothesis H_0 with confidence p. We require the log-likelihood not to

---

[2] If a random variable x has a finite mean μ and finite variance σ^2, then $\forall k \geq 0 \quad \Pr[|x - \mu| \geq k] \leq \frac{\sigma^2}{k^2}$.

deviate, with probability greater than p, from its expected value (the mean) more than its mean (which would invalidate our decision rule (28)).

$$p = \Pr\left[\left|\log \mathcal{L}_{H_0/H_1} - \mu_{H_0}\right| \geq \mu_{H_0}\right] \leq \frac{\sigma^2_{H_0}}{\mu^2_{H_0}} \quad \Rightarrow \quad p \leq \frac{\sigma^2_{H_0}}{\mu^2_{H_0}} \qquad (35)$$

An equivalent test can be derived to assess our confidence when accepting hypothesis H_1.

3.4   Traffic Analysis of Networks

We modify slightly the simple techniques described above to perform traffic analysis against a mix network composed of continuous-time mixes. Instead of performing a hypothesis test on two links, we compare all the links in the network with the pattern extracted from the input stream that we want to trace. This way each link is assigned a degree of similarity with the traced input. This can be used to infer some information about the intermediate and final nodes on the path.

To illustrate our techniques we use a mix network made of 50 nodes with 10 links each. The network is sparse, which is consistent with quite a few fielded systems, such as Freedom [4]. Five hundred streams (500) are routed through this network, using a random path of 4 nodes (the same node cannot appear twice in the path). Each stream contains 400 packets during the period the network is under observation, which is 10000 simulation ticks. Mixes delay packets individ-

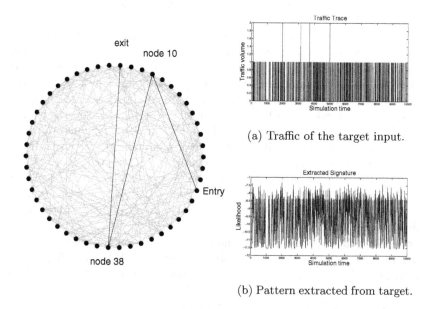

(a) Traffic of the target input.

(b) Pattern extracted from target.

Fig. 3. Network, route and stream traced

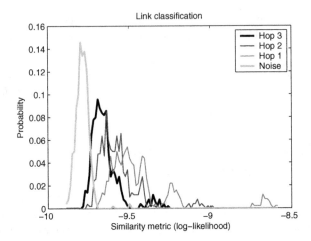

Fig. 4. Classification of the link (false positive and false negative curves)

ually using an exponential mix with mean 10 simulation ticks. Figure 3 presents a view of the network, along with the route that the stream under observation takes. The attacker's objective is to uncover the route of this stream, knowing only its input pattern and entry point, and the traffic on the network links.

As before a pattern (figure 3(b)) is extracted for the input under observation (figure 3(a)) that is compared with each link in the network. The convolution of the input traffic with the exponential delay characteristic, has been used to compute the pattern, but there has been no attempt to model the noise on each channel.

The pattern is compared to the traffic on each link of the network. This returns a measure of similarity of the link to the input traced. This in turn can be used to classify the link, as containing the target input on its way to the second mix (hop 1), the third mix (hop 2) or the final mix (hop 3). Alternatively the link might be unrelated to the target input, and simply contain noise. We choose the decision rule in such a way that we avoid false negatives. Figure 4 shows the classification curves that have been compiled after simulations.

The classification of each link as 'noise' or 'candidate link' allows us to simplify the graph of the network. Information can also be extracted relating to how likely the link is to contain the signal traced, and therefore a weighted graph (figure 5(a)) and its corresponding matrix (figure 5(b)) can be extracted. The intensity of the links or the entries in the matrix represents the likelihood a link contains the stream under observation.

A random walk is performed for one to three hops on the resulting graph, starting that the entry point of the observed stream. This provides us with the likely second, third or final nodes of the path (figures 6(a), 6(b) and 6(c) respectively). The stars on the graphs indicate the actual nodes that relay the target stream. In the example shown the final node is not guessed correctly, but is within the three nodes with highest probability. In the presence of longer delays

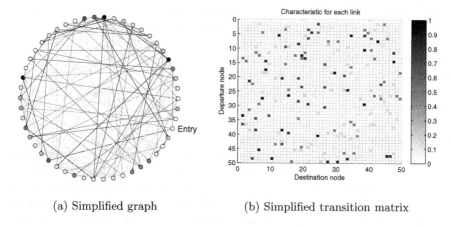

(a) Simplified graph   (b) Simplified transition matrix

Fig. 5. Simplified network (intensity is the likelihood of containing the target input)

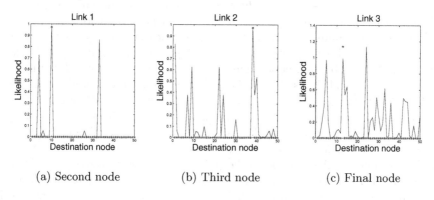

(a) Second node   (b) Third node   (c) Final node

Fig. 6. Likely second, third and final nodes on the path

or more traffic the correct nodes might not be the ones with highest likelihood but the attack still yields a lot of information and significantly reduces the effective anonymity provided to the users.

4   Further Considerations and Future Work

Measuring Anonymity. The work presented measures the average anonymity provided by a mix strategy. One of the important assumptions is that the expected number of messages is received in any time interval t, namely $\lambda_\alpha t$. The actual number of messages received in any interval may vary according to the Poisson distribution. Should a mix be flooded by the attacker's messages the rate needs to be adjusted to the level of genuine traffic.

Mix strategies that take into account the number of messages queueing or that adapt their parameters according to the rate of arrival of messages have not been explicitly studied. The metric proposed should still be usable with them, although their delay characteristic function may be dependant of additional factors such as the rate of arrival of messages λ_α. We expect the functions that depend upon the delay characteristic, such as the mean and variance of the latency, to still be usable.

Traffic Analysis. More work needs to be done on how far the traffic analysis attack presented against stream-based anonymity systems can be exploited. Techniques from transient signal detection, as surveyed in [21], can be used as the foundation for a theory of traffic analysis. Some straightforward extensions of the work presented could be to simplify the extracted patterns, by retaining only the parts that are good at discriminating well the target stream, or at making the matching quicker. An experimental evaluation of how the length of the stream, or a more realistic distribution of packets, affects anonymity should also be easy to perform.

The attack assumes that an adversary can observe a "naked" stream somewhere in the network, in order to build a model later used for detection. An attacker might acquire the knowledge that a series of messages belong to the same stream by observing unpadded links at the edges of the mix network or by the means of subverted nodes. This assumption might be invalidated if cover traffic is used on all links, but variants of the attack might still work. Some preliminary results suggest that good models can be created despite this.

The attack can be performed by a passive adversary, without any knowledge of the relationships between packets on the attacked links. When an attacker knows the relationship between packets in the same stream, as a subverted node would, it is much easier to perform the statistical tests since the cover traffic can be discarded. In other words we expect most of the anonymity provided, up to the point where the path goes through a corrupt node, to be easily cancelled if the node applies our attack.

Furthermore the attacks are passive, in the sense that the attacker does not modify in any way the characteristics of the traffic. An active attacker would modulate the input traffic in order to maximise the chances of detecting it. They could introduce periodicity, allowing for periodic averaging for noise cancellation or injecting patterns of traffic specially designed to be easily detected. Unless the anonymity system takes special steps beyond delaying the traffic to destroy such structure, traffic streams will quickly be traceable.

5   Conclusions

The information theoretic anonymity metric is adapted to describe the properties of mixes that simply delay individual packets. We proved that the optimal delaying strategy is the exponential mix, for which we calculate the anonymity and latency.

A very powerfully attack is then presented that traces streams of messages following the same path through a delaying mix network. We present the conditions under which it is possible, and derive expressions that an adversary can use to assess his confidence. The attack is efficient enough to to be applied against whole networks by a global passive adversary. When performed by an adversary controlling subverted nodes or with the ability to shape traffic on the links, its effects are even more devastating. This attack is applicable to systems that provide real-time anonymous communications and leaves us very sceptical about the possibility of secure and efficient such constructions, in the absence of heavy amounts of cover traffic or delay.

Acknowledgements. This work has been substantially improved after discussions with Ross Anderson, Markus Kuhn, Piotr Zielinski and Andrei Serjantov.

References

1. Adam Back, Ulf Möller, and Anton Stiglic. Traffic analysis attacks and trade-offs in anonymity providing systems. In Ira S. Moskowitz, editor, *Information Hiding workshop (IH 2001)*, volume 2137 of *LNCS*, pages 245–257. Springer-Verlag, April 2001.
2. Oliver Berthold and Heinrich Langos. Dummy traffic against long term intersection attacks. In Roger Dingledine and Paul Syverson, editors, *Privacy Enhancing Technologies workshop (PET 2002)*, volume 2482 of *LNCS*, pages 110–128. Springer-Verlag, 2002.
3. Oliver Berthold, Andreas Pfitzmann, and Ronny Standtke. The disadvantages of free MIX routes and how to overcome them. In H. Federrath, editor, *Designing Privacy Enhancing Technologies*, volume 2009 of *LNCS*, pages 30–45. Springer-Verlag, July 2000.
4. Philippe Boucher, Adam Shostack, and Ian Goldberg. Freedom systems 2.0 architecture. White paper, Zero Knowledge Systems, Inc., December 2000.
5. David Chaum. Untraceable electronic mail, return addresses, and digital pseudonyms. *Communications of the ACM*, 24(2):84–88, February 1981.
6. Claudia Diaz and Andrei Serjantov. Generalising mixes. In Roger Dingledine, editor, *Privacy Enhancing Technologies workshop (PET 2003)*, volume 2760 of *LNCS*, pages 18–31, Dresden, Germany, March 2003. Springer-Verlag.
7. Michael J. Freedman and Robert Morris. Tarzan: A peer-to-peer anonymizing network layer. In Vijayalakshmi Atluri, editor, *ACM Conference on Computer and Communications Security (CCS 2002)*, pages 193–206, Washington, DC, November 2002. ACM.
8. Ceki Gülcü and Gene Tsudik. Mixing E-mail with Babel. In *Network and Distributed Security Symposium — NDSS '96*, pages 2–16, San Diego, California, February 1996. IEEE.
9. Dogan Kesdogan, Dakshi Agrawal, and Stefan Penz. Limits of anonymity in open environments. In Fabien A. P. Petitcolas, editor, *Information Hiding workshop (IH 2002)*, volume 2578 of *LNCS*, pages 53–69, Noordwijkerhout, The Netherlands, 7-9 October 2002. Springer-Verlag.

10. Dogan Kesdogan, Jan Egner, and Roland Büschkes. Stop-and-Go MIXes: Providing probabilistic anonymity in an open system. In David Aucsmith, editor, *Information Hiding workshop (IH 1998)*, volume 1525 of *LNCS*, pages 83–98, Portland, Oregon, USA, 14-17 April 1998. Springer-Verlag.

11. Brian N. Levine, Michael K. Reiter, Chenxi Wang, and Matthew Wright. Timing attacks in low-latency mix systems. In *Finacial Cryptography (FC'04)*, 2004.

12. Jean-François Raymond. Traffic Analysis: Protocols, Attacks, Design Issues, and Open Problems. In Hannes Federrath, editor, *Designing Privacy Enhancing Technologies*, volume 2009 of *LNCS*, pages 10–29. Springer-Verlag, July 2000.

13. Michael G. Reed, Paul F. Syverson, and David M. Goldschlag. Anonymous connections and onion routing. *IEEE Journal on Selected Areas in Communications*, 16(4):482–494, May 1998.

14. Marc Rennhard and Bernhard Plattner. Introducing MorphMix: Peer-to-Peer based Anonymous Internet Usage with Collusion Detection. In *workshop on Privacy in the Electronic Society (WPES 2002)*, Washington, DC, USA, November 2002.

15. Andrei Serjantov and George Danezis. Towards an information theoretic metric for anonymity. In Roger Dingledine and Paul Syverson, editors, *Privacy Enhancing Technologies workshop (PET 2002)*, volume 2482 of *LNCS*, pages 41–53, San Francisco, CA, USA, 14-15 April 2002. Springer-Verlag.

16. Andrei Serjantov, Roger Dingledine, and Paul Syverson. From a trickle to a flood: Active attacks on several mix types. In Fabien A. P. Petitcolas, editor, *Information Hiding workshop (IH 2002)*, volume 2578 of *LNCS*, pages 36–52, Noordwijkerhout, The Netherlands, 7-9 October 2002. Springer-Verlag.

17. Andrei Serjantov and Richard E. Newman. On the anonymity of timed pool mixes. In *workshop on Privacy and Anonymity Issues in Networked and Distributed Systems*, pages 427–434, Athens, Greece, May 2003. Kluwer.

18. Andrei Serjantov and Peter Sewell. Passive attack analysis for connection-based anonymity systems. In *European Symposium on Research in Computer Security (ESORICS 2003)*, Gjovik, Norway, 13-15 October 2003.

19. Claude E. Shannon. A mathematical theory of communication. *The Bell System Technical Journal*, 27:379–423, 623–656, 1948.

20. Paul F. Syverson, Gene Tsudik, Michael G. Reed, and Carl E. Landwehr. Towards an analysis of onion routing security. In Hannes Federrath, editor, *Designing Privacy Enhancing Technologies*, volume 2009 of *LNCS*, pages 96–114, Berkeley, CA, USA, 25-26 July 2000. Springer-Verlag.

21. Zhen Wang and Peter Willett. A performance study of some transient detectors. *IEEE transactions on signal processing*, 48(9):2682–2685, September 2000.

22. Robert Weinstock. *Calculus of variations*. Dover publications, 1974. ISBN: 0486630692.

Reputable Mix Networks

Philippe Golle

Palo Alto Research Center, 3333 Coyote Hill Road,
Palo Alto, CA 94304
pgolle@parc.com

Abstract. We define a new type of mix network that offers a reduced form of robustness: the mixnet can prove that every message it outputs corresponds to an input submitted by a player without revealing which input (for honest players). We call mixnets with this property *reputable mixnets*. Reputable mixnets are not fully robust, because they offer no guarantee that distinct outputs correspond to distinct inputs. In particular, a reputable mix may duplicate or erase messages. A reputable mixnet, however, can defend itself against charges of having authored the output messages it produces. This ability is very useful in practice, as it shields the mixnet from liability in the event that an output message is objectionable or illegal.

We propose three very efficient protocols for reputable mixnets, all synchronous. The first protocol is based on blind signatures. It works both with Chaumian decryption mixnets or re-encryption mixnets based on ElGamal, but guarantees a slightly weaker form of reputability which we call near-reputability. The other two protocols are based on ElGamal re-encryption over a composite group and offer true reputability. One requires interaction between the mixnet and the players before players submit their inputs. The other assumes no interaction prior to input submission.

Keywords: Mix Network, Privacy, Anonymity.

1 Introduction

The motivation for this paper lies in the following question: Why is it so difficult to recruit volunteers willing to operate remailers? We identify two answers to that question:

1. The *overhead* of setting up and operating a remailer deters potential volunteers. This issue appears on the verge of resolution. Newly developed infrastructures for anonymous communication such as Mixminion [DDM03] offer remailing clients that are fast becoming as easy to set-up and operate as some hugely popular Peer-to-Peer clients.
2. The *risk and liability* (both real and perceived) of operating a remailer deters potential volunteers. Remailers may unwittingly relay illegal or objectionable messages (e.g. a death threat, child pornography), but can neither filter

D. Martin and A. Serjantov (Eds.): PET 2004, LNCS 3424, pp. 51–62, 2005.
© Springer-Verlag Berlin Heidelberg 2005

those messages (since they are encrypted) nor defend themselves effectively against accusations of having authored them. Potential volunteers thus shy away from the risks and liability that come with operating a remailer or mix server.

This paper addresses the second problem (the risk and liability of operating a remailer), which we now examine in more detail. We note first that any legal protection that remailers might enjoy, while useful as an ultimate recourse, will not be sufficient to convince a lot of volunteers that it is safe to run a remailer. Few volunteers will run remailers if they must face the threat and inconvenience of lawsuits, even if they were guaranteed to win in court every time. To spur the deployment of remailers on a large scale, what is needed instead is a simple technological solution that allows a remailer to prove beyond a doubt that it did not author a certain message.

We review first briefly two possible approaches to this problem and explain why they are unsatisfactory:

- **Robust mixnets.** A first approach is to base anonymous communication on robust mix networks [OKST97, Nef01, JJR02]. A robust mixnet can prove that the set of output messages it produces is exactly a permutation of the set of input messages it received from players, without revealing anything about the correspondence between inputs and outputs. Thus in particular, a robust mixnet can prove that it did not produce any output that was not already present in the input. This proof is given without compromising the privacy of any player. But robust mixnets are computationally expensive and require many rounds of interaction between mix servers. This makes them unsuitable for a general-purpose anonymous communication system.
- **Keeping Logs.** Another approach is for each mix server (or remailer) to keep logs of the relationships between the input messages it has received and the output messages it has produced (if the mix derives its randomness from a seed, it only needs to remember that seed, since the log can be reconstructed from it). If a mix server is accused of delivering an offensive or illegal email, it can defend itself by breaking the privacy of the message in question and revealing the corresponding input message. The mix servers are exonerated, but at the price of exposing the player who submitted the message. This approach is extremely undesirable. Indeed, the existence of logs leaves mixnets vulnerable to threats and makes them maybe more willing to compromise the privacy of their users to avoid trouble for themselves. Keeping logs thus weakens the privacy of all users.

The contribution of this paper is to propose a new type of mixnet, called *reputable mixnet*, which offers a limited form of robustness. A reputable mixnet can prove that every message it outputs corresponds to an input submitted by a player, without revealing which input (at least as long as players obey the protocol: see discussion below). Reputable mixnets thus offer a simple and effective defense against accusations of authoring objectionable outputs.

Reputable mixnets are much more computationally efficient than even the fastest robust mixnets [JJR02, BG02]. However, reputability is a weaker property than robustness, because the mix can not prove that distinct outputs correspond to distinct inputs. In particular, a malicious server in a reputable mix can erase or replicate inputs with impunity. In Chaumian mixnets, servers can easily detect and eliminate multiple fraudulent copies of the same input. In re-encryption mixnets on the other hand, the ability to make copies of inputs goes undetected and potentially allows a malicious server to trace selected inputs [PP89, Pfi94].

For this attack to be successful, the adversary must control a non-negligible fraction of remailers. This is easier to achieve when the total number of remailers is small. If reputable mixnets lead to a large increase in the number of volunteers who operate remailers, reputable mixnets will offer much better anonymity in practice than systems with fewer remailers, in spite of the attack just described. Indeed, we believe that the small number of remailers currently constitutes a much graver threat to players' privacy than the risk of a dishonest remailer tracing a message by making copies of it.

We propose three very efficient protocols for reputable mixnets, all synchronous. The first protocol is based on blind signatures. It works both with Chaumian decryption mixnets or ElGamal-based re-encryption mixnets, but guarantees a slightly weaker form of reputability which we call near-reputability (defined below in section 1.1). The other two protocols are based on ElGamal re-encryption over a composite group and offer true reputability. One requires interaction between the mixnet and the players before players submit their inputs. The other assumes no interaction prior to input submission.

Organization of the Paper. In the rest of this section, we present our model, define near-reputable and reputable mixnets and review related work. In section 2, we present a near-reputable mixnet protocol based on blind signatures. We present our two reputable protocols in section 3, and conclude in section 4.

1.1   Model and Definition

We review first briefly how mix networks are used for private communication. To send an anonymous message to Bob, Alice encrypts her message (including Bob's email address) under the public key of the mixnet. The mixnet collects ciphertexts submitted by different senders to form a batch. It decrypts (or re-encrypts, then decrypts) all these ciphertexts and delivers them (in a random order) to their recipients. The identity of the sender of the message is hidden from the recipient of the message.

We define a reputable mixnet as follows. Let $\mathcal{A}$ be the set of input ciphertexts submitted to a mixnet, and let $\mathcal{B}$ be the corresponding set of output plaintexts produced by the mixnet (for re-encryption mixnets, we assume that the outputs are jointly decrypted after having been re-encrypted by ever server, hence the outputs are always plaintext). Since we consider synchronous mixes throughout this paper, $\mathcal{A}$ and $\mathcal{B}$ are simply the inputs and outputs of a batch.

Definition 1. (Reputable Mixnet) *A mixnet $\mathcal{M}$ is f-reputable if for every batch output $\mathcal{B}$ there exists a subset $f(\mathcal{B}) \subseteq \mathcal{B}$ such that the mixnet can prove to a third party that unless all mix servers collude, every output in $f(\mathcal{B})$ is a decryption of an input in $\mathcal{A}$ without revealing which one.*

Example. Let f_0 be the function that maps every set to the empty set. Every mixnet is trivially f_0-reputable. Let f_1 be the identity function. A mixnet that is f_1-reputable can prove that every output it produces is the decryption of an input received from a player.

Definition 2. (Near-reputable Mixnet) *A mixnet $\mathcal{M}$ is f-near-reputable if for every batch output $\mathcal{B}$ there exists a subset $f(\mathcal{B}) \subseteq \mathcal{B}$ and a set of players $\mathcal{P}_{\mathcal{B}}$ such that the mixnet can prove to a third party that unless all mix servers collude, every output in $f(\mathcal{B})$ was authored by one of the players in $\mathcal{P}_{\mathcal{B}}$ without revealing which one.*

Example. If we define $\mathcal{P}_{\mathcal{B}}$ to be the set of players who submitted the inputs in $\mathcal{A}$, then f-near-reputable and f-reputable are the same. But near-reputation is more general than reputation, because the set of players $\mathcal{P}_{\mathcal{B}}$ need not be the players who submitted the inputs in $\mathcal{A}$. For example, the set $\mathcal{P}_{\mathcal{B}}$ could be a set of players who committed themselves to submit at a later time.

Our definitions of reputation and near-reputation make no assumption about whether the players execute the submission protocol correctly or about whether the servers execute the mixing protocol correctly (although, as we shall explain, the function f depends on the behavior of players and servers). The only assumption we make is that the number of servers that collude is below a certain threshold. As long as the number of colluding servers is below the threshold, servers gain nothing by colluding. But if the number of colluding servers reaches or exceeds the threshold, they may falsely convince a third party that they are f-reputable or f-near-reputable even though they are not.

A reputable or near-reputable mixnet makes no claim about how messages are processed between the time they are input and the time they are output. In particular, reputable mixnets do not guarantee that messages are correctly mixed, nor even that messages will go through every server along the mixing route that was set for them. Recall that the goal of reputable mixnets is to let servers defend themselves against accusation of having authored their output, without breaking the privacy of the outputs. This indirectly enhances the privacy of players, but it does not offer privacy where there is none (e.g. if servers do not mix correctly).

Finally it should be made clear that, naturally, an f-reputable mixnet does not prove that messages in $f(\mathcal{B})$ did not originate with a mix server. Indeed, servers may submit messages in the input of the mix like any other player. What a reputable mixnet can prove however is that every message in $f(\mathcal{B})$ was submitted by a player in the input (or a player in $\mathcal{P}_{\mathcal{B}}$ for near-reputable mixnets). That fulfills our stated goal of shielding the servers from liability related to the outputs they produce. We do not and can not shield servers from liability related to other activities they may choose to engage in, such as for example being a player as well as a server.

An analogy might help clarify this last point. A reputable mixnet is akin to a postal mail sorting facility where workers are searched before reporting for work to make sure they do not smuggle letters from outside into the sorting facility. This search procedure shields the sorting facility from liability in case illegal pieces of mail are found to have passed through the facility. Indeed, those pieces of mail may have been sorted at the facility, but were provably not created there. Of course, nothing can prevent a worker at the facility from mailing illegal material from home while off-duty. The search procedure proves the innocence of the facility and of the workers while on-duty at the facility, but need not and does not account for what workers do when they are off-duty. Similarly, a reputable mixnet proves only the innocence of the mixing operation (which is all we care about).

1.2   Related Work

Chaum defined mix networks in his seminal paper [Cha81] in the context of an anonymous email system. Chaum's mixnet, based on RSA decryption, is not robust. His paper inspired a long line of work on non-robust private communication, from Type I Cypherpunk remailers [Par96] to Onion Routing [GRS99], Babel [GT96] and most recently Mixminion [DDM03]. We refer the interested read to [FHP] for a complete annotated bibliography of the most significant results in anonymity.

A parallel but separate line of work is the development of robust mixnets based on ElGamal re-encryption. The first techniques for robust mixing were based on cut-and-choose zero-knowledge proofs [SK95, OKST97] that are very computationally expensive . A number of recent schemes [FS01, Nef01, JJR02] offer more efficient proofs of robust mixing but they remain very expensive compared to Chaumian mixes. As already noted, robust mixnets can prove to a third party that the set of output they produce is a permutation of the set of inputs without revealing the correspondence between inputs and outputs. This implies that robust mixnets are Id-reputable (where Id is the identity function), but the converse is not true. An Id-reputable mixnet does not guarantee that distinct messages in the output correspond to distinct messages in the input. The near-reputable and reputable mixnet protocols described in this paper are much more computationally efficient than robust mixnets.

In our protocols, we use blind signature to authenticate messages. This approach is similar to the work on hybrid mixes by Jakobsson and Juels [JJ01].

2   Near-Reputable Mixnet with Blind Signatures

In this section, we present a protocol for a near-reputable mixnet based on blind signatures [Cha82]. Our protocol works both with decryption or re-encryption mixnets. We assume throughout that messages are mixed synchronously in batches.

Recall first that a blind signature scheme allows a player to obtain a signature S on a message m without revealing m to the entity that produces the signature. The RSA signature scheme and the Schnorr signature scheme for example have blind variants. For concreteness, we base our presentation on RSA blind signatures. Let N be an RSA modulus, e a public verification key and d a private signing key such that $ed = 1 \mod \varphi(N)$. To obtain a blind signature on message m, a player chooses at random a blinding factor $r \in \mathbb{Z}_N$ and submits $mr^e \mod N$ to the signer. Let S' be a signature on mr^e. It is easy to see that the signer learns nothing about m, yet $S = S'/r$ is a signature on m.

We show how to use blind signatures to convert a mixnet into a near-reputable mixnet. Let $\mathcal{M}$ be a mixnet protocol (either decryption or re-encryption mix) that processes messages synchronously. The description of $\mathcal{M}$ consists of a public encryption function E and a mixing protocol MIX. Players submit encrypted inputs $E(m)$ to the mixnet. The protocol MIX takes a batch of encrypted inputs and produces as output the corresponding plaintexts in random order.

Near-reputable Mixnet. In a setup phase, the near-reputable mixnet publishes the encryption function E. In addition, the mix servers jointly generate an RSA modulus and a shared signing key d and they publish the corresponding verification key e (see [BF01] for detail on shared generation of RSA parameters). These parameters may be replaced at any time, but they are meant to be long-lived and reused to mix many batches. In what follows, the symbol $\|$ denotes string concatenation. The mixnet processes a batch in two phases:

1. **Signature phase.** All mix servers jointly generate a random (say, 160-bit) value b. This value serves as a unique identifier for the current batch. The value b is published. To submit a message m for processing in batch b, a player obtains from the mixnet a blind signature S on $m\|b$ and submits as input $E(m\|b\|S)$. We denote by $\mathcal{P}_b$ the set of players who request a blind signature during batch b. Note that a player may cheat and obtain a signature on an improperly formatted message (for example, a message with the wrong batch identifier).

2. **Mixing phase.** At some point (e.g. when enough inputs have been submitted), the mixnet stops issuing signatures and starts mixing the batch. The mixnet executes the protocol MIX on the batch of inputs and outputs in random order the set of plaintexts $m\|b\|S$. The mixnet need not verify that the signature S on $m\|b$ is valid.

When mixing is over, the mixnet returns to the signature phase. It generates a new random batch identifier b' and starts accepting messages for that new batch.

Proposition 1. *We define the function f as follows. The set $f(\mathcal{B})$ contains every message in $\mathcal{B}$ that was (1) submitted by an honest player and (2) processed correctly by the mix. The mixnet defined above is f-near-reputable for the set of players $\mathcal{P}_b$.*

Given the definition of the set $f(\mathcal{B})$, it comes as no surprise that every output in $f(\mathcal{B})$ was authored by a player. The property of being near-reputable lies not in the truth of that statement, but in the ability to *prove* to a third party that the statement is true.

Proof. (Proposition 1) By definition of the set $f(\mathcal{B})$, every output $m||b||S$ in $f(\mathcal{B})$ contains a valid signature S on $m||b$. This signature allows the mixnet to convince a third party that the author of message $m||b$ belongs to the set of players $\mathcal{P}_b$ who requested signatures during batch b. Indeed, the only window of opportunity for a player to obtain with non-negligible probability a valid signature for a message submitted in batch b is after the value b is published, and naturally before submission is closed for batch b. Furthermore since the signature is blind, it reveals nothing about the correspondence between outputs in $f(\mathcal{B})$ and players in $\mathcal{P}_b$. Note that a regular signature would afford players no privacy precisely because it would expose the correspondence between $f(\mathcal{B})$ and $\mathcal{P}_b$. □

If accused of authoring a message that is not in $f(\mathcal{B})$ (e.g. a message that contains an invalid signature, or no signature at all), the mixnet has no other option but to break the privacy of that message and trace it back either to an input, or to a malicious server who introduced the input into the batch fraudulently. In either case, honest servers are exonerated. It is consequently in the best interest of players and servers to execute the protocol correctly.

Efficiency. The protocol is efficient: the only additional overhead comes from the shared signing of messages, at a cost of one exponentiation per server per message.

3   Reputable Mixnet Protocols

In this section, we propose two reputable mixnet protocols. These protocols are based on synchronous ElGamal re-encryption mixnets over composite groups. The section is organized as follows. We review first briefly the properties of the ElGamal cryptosystem. We present next a reputable mixnet protocol. We end with a variant protocol that eliminates the need for interaction between mix servers and players prior to input submission.

3.1   Preliminaries: The ElGamal Cryptosystem

We review briefly the ElGamal cryptosystem and introduce two properties of this cryptosystem that underpin the design of our reputable mixnets: the re-encryption and ciphertext-signing operations. The first property, re-encryption, is well-known and has long been used in the design of mixnets [OKST97]. The second property, ciphertext-signing, is used here for the first time to guarantee the reputation of the mixnet.

ElGamal is a probabilistic public-key cryptosystem, defined by the following parameters: a group G of order n, a generator g of G, a private key x and the corresponding public key $y = g^x$. To encrypt a message $m \in G$, a player chooses a random element $s \in \mathbb{Z}_n$ and computes the ciphertext $E(m) \in G \times G$

as the pair $E(m) = (g^s, my^s)$. To decrypt, one uses the private key x to compute $my^s/(g^s)^x = m$. ElGamal is semantically secure under the assumption that the Decisional Diffie Hellman (DDH) problem is hard in the group G.

Re-encryption. Re-encryption mixnets exploit the fact that the ElGamal cryptosystem allows for *re-encryption* of ciphertexts. Given an ElGamal ciphertext $C = (g^r, my^r)$ and the public key y under which C was constructed, anyone can compute a new ciphertext $C' = (g^{r+s}, my^{r+s})$ by choosing a random s and multiplying the first and second element of the pair by g^s and y^s respectively. Note that C and C' decrypt to the same plaintext m. Furthermore, without knowledge of the private key x, one cannot test if C' is a re-encryption of C if the DDH problem is hard in G.

Signatures. In typical implementations of ElGamal, the group G is a multiplicative subgroup of $\mathbb{Z}_p$ of prime order q. We will instead be working with ElGamal over a composite group. Let p, q be two large primes (say, 1024 or 2048 bits) and let $N = pq$. We define G to be the group $\mathbb{Z}_N^*$. The ElGamal encryption, decryption and re-encryption operations are exactly the same over a composite group as over a group of primer order. See [McC88, FH96] for more detail on the security of ElGamal over composite groups.

We can define an RSA signature scheme for ElGamal ciphertexts over a composite group G as follows. We choose a public exponent e and compute the corresponding secret key d such that $ed = 1 \mod \varphi(N)$, where $\varphi(N) = (p-1)(q-1)$. Let $E(m) = (g^r, my^r)$ be an ElGamal ciphertext over G. We define the signature on $E(m)$ to be $S = ((g^r)^d, (my^r)^d) = (g^{rd}, m^d y^{rd})$. The signature S is itself an ElGamal encryption of the plaintext m^d in the cryptosystem defined by the public parameters (G, g^d, y^d) and private key x. The signature S can therefore be re-encrypted like any other ElGamal ciphertext.

Signatures and Re-encryption. Let S be a signature on $E(m)$. We have already noted that both S and $E(m)$ can be re-encrypted. It remains to show how to verify signatures. The common strategy to verify a signature fails: raising both elements of the ciphertext S to the power e yields nothing recognizable after S or $E(m)$ have been re-encrypted. Instead, we verify the signature by first decrypting S (we get plaintext a) and $E(m)$ (we get plaintext b) and verifying that $a^e = b$. This verification is compatible with re-encryption.

3.2   A First Reputable Mixnet

The reputable mixnet protocol presented here is based on a re-encryption mixnet with ElGamal over a composite group. While our presentation is self-contained, readers unfamiliar with re-encryption mixnets may consult [OKST97] for more detail.

Setup. The mix servers jointly generate an RSA modulus N, a shared signing key d and the corresponding public verification key e. See [BF01] for an efficient protocol to generate shared RSA parameters. The mix servers publish the modulus N and the public key e. The mix servers then jointly generate the parameters of an ElGamal cryptosystem over the composite group $\mathbb{Z}_N^*$. Each mix server holds a share of the private key x. The corresponding public key $y = g^x$ is published. See [Ped91, GJKR99] for efficient protocols to generate shared El-Gamal keys. Finally, the mix servers jointly compute and publish g^d and y^d. All these parameters can be changed at any time, but they are meant to be long lived and reused to process a number of batches.

Creation of a Batch of Inputs. The creation of a batch of inputs proceeds in 2 steps.

1. **Submission of inputs.** All mix servers jointly generate a random (say, 160-bit) value b. This value serves as a unique identifier for the current batch. The value b is published. Players submit their input m to the batch as follows. A player encrypts $m||b$ under the ElGamal public key of the mixnet to create the ciphertext $E(m||b) = (g^r, (m||b)y^r)$ and posts this ciphertext to a bulletin board. Note that players may submit inputs that are improperly formatted.

2. **Signing.** When all ciphertexts have been posted to the bulletin board, the mix servers jointly compute for every ciphertext $E(m||b)$ a threshold signature $S = ((g^r)^d, ((m||b)y^r)^d)$ and append this signature to the ciphertext. The bulletin board now contains pairs of the form $(E(m), S)$.

Mixing. Each server in turn mixes and re-encrypts the set of messages in the batch. The first server takes as input the list of pairs $(E(m), S)$ posted on the bulletin board. Let $E(m) = (a, b)$ and $S = (\alpha, \beta)$ be one particular input. To re-encrypt this input, the server chooses independently at random $r, r' \in \mathbb{Z}_N$ and computes two new pairs (ag^r, by^r) and $(\alpha g^{dr'}, \beta y^{dr'})$. Every pair is re-encrypted in the same way. Finally, the first server outputs these pairs of values in a random order. These outputs become the input to the second server, who processes them in the same way. More generally, mix server M_i receives as input the set of pairs of ElGamal ciphertexts output by mix server M_{i-1}. Server M_i permutes and re-randomizes (i.e. re-encrypts) each element of all these pairs of ciphertexts, and outputs a new set of pairs of ciphertexts, which is then passed to M_{i+1}.

Decryption. The mix servers jointly decrypt the final output. Note that the servers need not provide a zero-knowledge proof of correctness for decryption (we are not aiming for robustness). The servers need not verify the validity of signatures either.

Proposition 2. *We define the function f as follows. The set $f(\mathcal{B})$ contains every message in $\mathcal{B}$ that was (1) submitted by an honest player and (2) processed correctly by the mix. The mixnet defined above is f-reputable.*

Proof. Signatures ensure that every output in $f(\mathcal{B})$ corresponds to an input, assuming that the number of colluding servers is below the threshold required to generate a fake signature.   □

Efficiency. The computational and communication cost of our reputable mixnet is exactly twice that of the mixing cost of a standard plain-vanilla re-encryption mixnet, since every input consists of a pair of ElGamal ciphertexts. All exponentiations for re-encryption depend only on fixed public parameters and can therefore be pre-computed before the batch is processed.

3.3 A Reputable Mixnet with Non-interactive Submission of Inputs

The near-reputable and reputable protocols described so far both rely on the ability of the mix servers to interact with players *before* they encrypt and submit their inputs. Indeed, the mix servers must communicate the batch identifier b to the players. In some circumstances, this requirement may be too restrictive. A mix server may be given as input a set of ciphertexts, without the ability to interact with the players who created these ciphertexts.

Consider for example the last k servers in a mix cascade that consists of $K > k$ servers. These k servers may decide to form a reputable sub-cascade and prove that every ciphertext they output corresponds to one of their input ciphertexts. The protocol of the previous sections do not work in this case. In this section, we describe a variant of the reputable protocol of section 3.2 that allows a reputable mixnet to work with already encrypted inputs.

Variant protocol. In a setup phase, the mix servers jointly generate and publish an RSA modulus N, then jointly generate the parameters of an ElGamal cryptosystem over the composite group $\mathbb{Z}_N^*$. The secret key x is shared among the servers while the corresponding public key $y = g^x$ is published. The submission of inputs involves the following 2 steps:

1. **Generation of a signing/verification key pair.** All mix servers jointly generate a shared RSA signing key d and the corresponding public verification key e over the group $\mathbb{Z}_N$. New keys d and e are generated for each batch.
2. **Submission and signing of inputs.** Players submit their input m encrypted under the ElGamal public key of the mixnet as $E(m) = (g^r, my^r)$. The mix servers jointly compute for every ciphertext $E(m)$ a threshold signature $S = ((g^r)^d, (my^r)^d)$ and append this signature to the ciphertext. The bulletin board now contains pairs of the form $(E(m), S)$.

From here onwards, the mixing and decryption proceed as in the protocol of section 3.2. In essence, the signatures in this protocol are tied to a batch not via a batch identifier appended to the plaintext, but rather by using a new and different signing/verification key pair for every batch.

Proposition 3. *We define the function f as follows. The set $f(\mathcal{B})$ contains every message in $\mathcal{B}$ that was processed correctly by the mix. The variant mixnet defined above is f-reputable.*

Observe that here the set $f(\mathcal{B})$ depends only on the honesty of the servers, not that of the players. This is arguably a small difference, since we have already shown that it is in the best interest of players to execute the protocol correctly. Nevertheless, this variant protocol offers the strongest guarantee of reputability.

4   Conclusion and Future Work

We defined a new property of mix network: reputability. Reputable mixnets can prove to a third party that every output they produce is a decryption of an input submitted by a player without revealing which input for honest players (dishonest players forfeit their own privacy). In practice, reputable mixnets offer a twofold advantage.

- First, reputable mixnets are almost as efficient as non-robust mixnets, yet they offer better privacy than non-robust mixnets because they are not vulnerable to accusations of having authored the outputs they produce. For private communication systems, we believe that such accusations constitute a much graver threat to players' privacy than the risk of a mix server cheating in the execution of the mixing protocol.
- Second, reputable mixnets may spur the development of anonymous email systems as volunteers need not fear the threats and liability to which non-robust non-reputable mixnets are exposed.

We proposed three very efficient protocols for near-reputable and reputable mixnets, all synchronous. An interesting direction for future work would be to look into the design of reputable protocols for asynchronous mixnets.

Acknowledgements

The author would like to thank the anonymous referees for valuable comments that helped improve the presentation of this paper.

References

[BF01]   D. Boneh and M. Franklin. Efficient generation of shared RSA keys. In *Journal of the ACM (JACM)*, Vol. 48, Issue 4, pp. 702–722, July 2001.

[BG02]   D. Boneh and P. Golle. Almost entirely correct mixing with applications to voting. In *Proc. of the 9th ACM Conference on Computer and Communications Security,* pp. 68–77. ACM Press, 2002.

[Cha81]   D. Chaum. Untraceable electronic mail, return addresses, and digital pseudonyms. In *Communications of the ACM,* 24(2):84-88, 1981.

[Cha82]   D. Chaum. Blind signatures for untraceable payments. In *Proc. of Crypto '82,* pp. 199–203. Plenum Press, N.Y., 1983.

[CFN88]   D. Chaum, A. Fiat, M. Naor. Untraceable electronic cash. In *Proc. of Crypto'88,* pp. 319–327. Springer-Verlag, LNCS 403.

[DDM03]   G. Danezis, R. Dingledine and N. Mathewson. Mixminion: design of type III anonymous remailer protocol. In *Proc. of the 2003 IEEE Symposium on Security and Privacy*, pp. 2-15. On the web at `http://mixminion.net/`

[FH96]   M. Frankling and S. Haber. Joint encryption and message-efficient secure computation. In *Journal of Cryptology*, pp. 217–232, Vol. 9, No. 4, Autumn 1996.

[FHP]   The Free Haven Project. On the web at `http://www.freehaven.net/anonbib/`

[FS01]   J. Furukawa and K. Sako. An efficient scheme for proving a shuffle. In *Proc. of Crypto '01*, pp. 368-387. Springer-Verlag, 2001. LNCS 2139.

[GJKR99] R. Gennaro, S. Jarecki, H. Krawczyk and T. Rabin. Secure Distributed Key Generation for Discrete-Log Based Cryptosystems. In *Proc. of Eurocrypt '99*, pp. 295-310. LNCS 1592.

[GRS99]   D. Goldschlag, M. Reed and P. Syverson. Onion routing for anonymous and private internet connections. In *Communications of the ACM*, 42(2):39-41, 1999.

[GJJS03] P. Golle, M. Jakobsson, A. Juels and P. Syverson. Universal re-encryption for mix networks. In *Proc. of the 2004 RSA Conference, Cryptographer's track.*

[GT96]   C. Gulcu and G. Tsudik. Mixing E-mail with Babel. In *Proc. of Network and Distributed Security Symposium - NDSS '96*. IEEE, 1996.

[JJ01]   M. Jakobsson and A. Juels. An optimally robust hybrid mix network. In *Proc. of PODC '01*, pp. 284–292. ACM Press, 2001.

[JJR02]   M. Jakobsson, A. Juels and R. Rivest. Making mix nets robust for electronic voting by randomized partial checking. In *Proc. of USENIX'02.*

[McC88]   K. McCurley. A key distribution system equivalent to factoring. In *Journal of Cryptology*, pp. 95–105, Vol. 1, No. 2, Autumn 1988.

[Nef01]   A. Neff. A verifiable secret shuffle and its application to E-Voting. In *Proc. of ACM CCS'01*, pp. 116-125. ACM Press, 2001.

[OKST97] W. Ogata, K. Kurosawa, K. Sako and K. Takatani. Fault tolerant anonymous channel. In *Proc. of ICICS '97*, pp. 440-444, 1997. LNCS 1334.

[Par96]   S. Parekh. Prospects for remailers. *First Monday,* 1(2), August 1996. On the web at `http://www.firstmonday.dk/issues/issue2/remailers/`

[Ped91]   T. Pedersen. A Threshold cryptosystem without a trusted party. In *Proc. of Eurocrypt'91*, pp. 522-526, 1991.

[PP89]   B. Pfitzmann and A. Pfitzmann. How to break the direct RSA-implementation of mixes. In *Proc. of Eurocrypt '89*, pp. 373-381. Springer-Verlag, 1989. LNCS 434.

[Pfi94]   B. Pfizmann. Breaking an Efficient Anonymous Channel. In *Proc. of Eurocrypt'94*, pp. 332–340. Springer-Verlag, LNCS 950.

[SK95]   K. Sako and J. Kilian. Receipt-free mix-type voting scheme. In *Proc. of Eurocrypt '95*. Springer-Verlag, 1995. LNCS 921.

Secure Outsourcing of Sequence Comparisons*

Mikhail J. Atallah and Jiangtao Li

CERIAS and Department of Computer Sciences, Purdue University,
250 N. University Street, West Lafayette, IN 47907
{mja, jtli}@cs.purdue.edu

Abstract. Large-scale problems in the physical and life sciences are being rev-
olutionized by Internet computing technologies, like grid computing, that make
possible the massive cooperative sharing of computational power, bandwidth, storage, and data. A weak computational device, once connected to such a grid, is no
longer limited by its slow speed, small amounts of local storage, and limited bandwidth: It can avail itself of the abundance of these resources that is available elsewhere on the network. An impediment to the use of "computational outsourcing"
is that the data in question is often sensitive, e.g., of national security importance,
or proprietary and containing commercial secrets, or to be kept private for legal requirements such as the HIPAA legislation, Gramm-Leach-Bliley, or similar
laws. This motivates the design of techniques for computational outsourcing in
a privacy-preserving manner, i.e., without revealing to the remote agents whose
computational power is being used, either one's data or the outcome of the computation on the data. This paper investigates such secure outsourcing for widely
applicable sequence comparison problems, and gives an efficient protocol for a
customer to securely outsource sequence comparisons to two remote agents, such
that the agents learn nothing about the customer's two private sequences or the
result of the comparison. The local computations done by the customer are linear
in the size of the sequences, and the computational cost and amount of communication done by the external agents are close to the time complexity of the best
known algorithm for solving the problem on a single machine (i.e., quadratic,
which is a huge computational burden for the kinds of massive data on which such
comparisons are made). The sequence comparison problem considered arises in a
large number of applications, including speech recognition, machine vision, and
molecular sequence comparisons. In addition, essentially the same protocol can
solve a larger class of problems whose standard dynamic programming solutions
are similar in structure to the recurrence that subtends the sequence comparison
algorithm.

1 Introduction

Internet computing technologies, like grid computing [8], enable a weak computational
device connected to such a grid to be less limited by its inadequate local computational,

---

* Portions of this work were supported by Grants IIS-0325345, IIS-0219560, IIS-0312357, and
IIS-0242421 from the National Science Foundation, Contract N00014-02-1-0364 from the
Office of Naval Research, by sponsors of the Center for Education and Research in Information
Assurance and Security, and by Purdue Discovery Park's e-enterprise Center.

D. Martin and A. Serjantov (Eds.): PET 2004, LNCS 3424, pp. 63–78, 2005.

storage, and bandwidth resources. However, such a weak computational device (PDA, smartcard, sensor, etc) often cannot avail itself of the abundant resources available on the network because its data is sensitive. A prime example of this is DNA sequence comparisons: They are expensive enough to warrant remotely using the computing power available at powerful remote servers and super-computers, yet sensitive enough to give pause to anyone concerned that some unscrupulous person at the remote site may leak the DNA sequences or the comparison's outcome, or may subject the DNA to a battery of unauthorized tests whose outcome could have such grave consequences as jeopardizing an individual's insurability, employability, etc. Techniques for outsourcing expensive computational tasks in a privacy-preserving manner, are therefore an important research goal. This paper is a step in this direction, in that it gives a protocol for the secure outsourcing of the most important sequence comparison computation: The "string editing" problem, i.e., computing the edit-distance between two strings. The edit distance is one of the most widely used notions of similarity: It is the least-cost set of insertions, deletions, and substitutions required to transform one string into the other. Essentially the same protocol can solve the larger class of comparisons whose standard dynamic programming solution is similar in structure to that of string editing. The generalizations of edit distance that are solved by the same kind of dynamic programming recurrence relation as the one for edit distance, cover an even wider domain of applications. We use string editing here merely as the prototypical solution for this general class of dynamic programming recurrences.

In various ways and forms, sequence comparisons arise in many applications other than molecular sequence comparison, notably, in text editing, speech recognition, machine vision, etc. In fact the dynamic programming solution to this problem was independently discovered by no fewer than fourteen different researchers [22], and is given a different name by each discipline where it was independently discovered (Needleman-Wunsch by biologists, Wagner-Fischer by computer scientists, etc). For this reason, these problems have been studied rather extensively in the past, and form the object of several papers [13, 14, 17, 21, 24, 22, 27], to list a few). The problems are typically solved by a serial algorithm in $\Theta(mn)$ time and space, through dynamic programming (cf. for example, [27]). When huge sequences are involved, the quadratic time complexity of the problem quickly becomes prohibitively expensive, requiring considerable power. Such super-computing power is widely available, but sending the data to such remote agents is problematic if the sequence data is sensitive, the outcome of the comparison is to be kept private, or both. In such cases, one can make a case for a technology that makes it possible for the customer to have the problem solved remotely but without revealing to the remote super-computing sites either the inputs to the computation or its outcome.

In other words we assume that Carol has two private sequences λ and μ, and wants to compute the similarity between these two sequences. Carol only has a weak computational device that is incapable of performing the sequence comparison locally. In order to get the result, Carol has to outsource the computation task to some external entities, the agents. If Carol trusted the agents, she could send the sequences directly to the external agents and ask them to compute the similarity on her behalf. However, if Carol is concerned about privacy, it is not acceptable to send the sequences to external agents because this would reveal too much information to these agents – both the sequences and the result. Our result is a protocol that computes the similarity of the sequences yet inherently safeguards the privacy of Carol's data. Assuming the two external agents do not conspire with each other against Carol by sharing the data that she sends to them, they learn nothing about the actual data and actual result.

The dynamic programming recurrence relation that subtends the solution to this problem, also serves to solve many other important related problems (either as special cases, or as generalizations that have the same dynamic programming kind of solution). These include the longest common subsequence problem, and the problem of approximate matching between a pattern sequence and text sequence (there is a huge literature of published work for the notion of approximate pattern matching and its connection to the sequence alignment problem). Any solution to the general sequence comparison problem could also be used to solve these related problems. For example, our protocol can enable a weak PDA to securely outsource the computation of the Unix command

$$\texttt{diff } \textit{file1 file2 } | \texttt{ wc}$$

to two agents where the agents learn nothing about *file1*, *file2*, and the result.

We now more precisely state the edit distance problem, in which the cost of an insertion or deletion or substitution is a symbol-dependent non-negative weight, and the edit distance is then the *least-cost* set of insertions, deletions, and substitutions required to transform one string into the other. More formally, if we let λ be a string of length n, $\lambda = \lambda_1 \ldots \lambda_n$ and μ be a string of length m, $\mu = \mu_1 \ldots \mu_m$, both over some alphabet Σ. There are three types of allowed *edit operations* to be done on λ: insertion of a symbol, deletion of a symbol, and substitution of one symbol by another. Each operation has a cost associated with it, namely $I(a)$ denotes the cost of inserting the symbol a, $D(a)$ denotes the cost of deleting a, and $S(a, b)$ denotes the cost of substituting a with b. Each sequence of operations that transforms λ into μ has a *cost* associated with it (which is equal to the sum of the costs of the operations in it), and the least-cost of such sequence is the *edit-distance*. The *edit path* is the actual sequence of operations that corresponds to the edit distance. Our outsourcing solution allows arbitrary $I(a)$, $D(b)$, and $S(a, b)$ values, and we give better solutions for two special cases: (i) $S(a, b) = |a - b|$, and (ii) unit insertion/deletion cost and $S(a, b) = 0$ if $a = b$ and $S(a, b) = +\infty$ if $a \neq b$ (in effect forbidding substitutions).

The rest of paper is organized as follows. We begin with a brief introduction of previous work in Section 2. Then we describe some building blocks in Section 3. In Section 4, we present the secure outsourcing protocol for computing string edit distance. Section 5 extends the protocol so as to compute the edit path. Section 6 concludes.

2   Related Work

Recently, Atallah, Kerschbaum, and Du [2] developed an efficient protocol for sequence comparisons in the secure two-party computation framework in which each party has a private string; the protocol enables two parties to compute the edit distance of two sequences such that neither party learns anything about the private sequence of the other party. They [2] use dynamic programming to compare sequences, but in an additively split way – each party maintains a matrix, the summation of two matrices is the real matrix implicitly used to compute edit distance. Our protocol directly builds on their work, but is also quite different and more difficult in the following ways:

- We can no longer afford to have the customer carry out quadratic work or communication: Whereas in [2] there was "balance" in that all participants had equal computational and communication power, in our case the participant to whom all of the data and answer belong is asymmetrically weaker and is limited to a *linear* amount of computation and communication (hence cannot directly participate or help in each step of the quadratic-complexity dynamic programming solution).
- An even more crucial difference is the special difficulty this paper's framework faces in dealing with the costs table, that is, the table that contains the costs of deleting a symbol, inserting a symbol, and substituting one symbol by another: There is a quadratic number of accesses to this table, and the external agents cannot be allowed to learn which entry of the table is being consulted (because that would leak information about the inputs), yet the input owner's help cannot be enlisted for such table accesses because there is a quadratic number of them (recall that the owner is limited to linear work and communication – which is unavoidable).

Secure outsourcing of sequence comparisons adds to a growing list of problems considered in this framework (e.g. [4, 10, 12, 15, 19, 3], and others). We briefly review these next. In the server-aided secret computation literature (e.g. [4, 10, 12, 15, 19], to list a few), a weak smartcard performs public key encryptions by "borrowing" computing power from an untrusted server, without revealing to that server its private information. These papers deal primarily with the important problem of modular exponentiations. The paper [3] deals primarily with outsourcing of scientific computations.

In the the privacy homomorphism approach proposed in [20], the outsourcing agent is used as a permanent repository of data, performing certain operations on it and maintaining certain predicates, whereas the customer needs only to decrypt the data from the agent to obtain the real data; the secure outsourcing framework differs in that the customer is not interested in keeping data permanently with the external agents, instead, the customer only wants to temporarily use their superior computational power.

Du and Atallah have developed several models for secure remote database access with approximate matching [6]. One of the models that is related to our work is the secure storage outsourcing model where a customer who lacks storage space outsources her database to an external agent. The customer needs to query her database from time to time without revealing to the agent the queries and the results. Several protocols for other distance metrics were given, including Hamming distance, the L_1 and L_2 distance metrics. All these metrics considered in [6] were between strings that have *the same length* as each other – it is indeed a limitation of the techniques in [6] that they do not extend to the present situation where the strings are of different length and insertions and deletions are part of the definition. This makes the problem substantially different, as the edit distance algorithm is described by a dynamic program that computes it, rather than as a simple one-line mathematical expression to be securely computed.

3 Preliminaries

Giving the full-fledged protocol would make it too long and rather hard to comprehend. This section aims at making the later presentation of the protocol much crisper by presenting some of the ideas and building blocks for it ahead of time, right after a brief review of the standard dynamic programming solution to string edit.

3.1 Review of Edit Distance via Dynamic Programming

We first briefly review the standard dynamic programming algorithm for computing edit distance. Let $M(i,j)$, $(0 \leq i \leq n,\ 0 \leq j \leq m)$ be the minimum cost of transforming the prefix of λ of length i into the prefix of μ of length j, i.e., of transforming $\lambda_1 \ldots \lambda_i$ into $\mu_1 \ldots \mu_j$. Then $M(0,0) = 0$, $M(0,j) = \sum_{k=1}^{j} I(\mu_j)$ for $1 \leq j \leq m$, $M(i,0) = \sum_{k=1}^{i} D(\lambda_i)$ for $1 \leq i \leq n$, and for positive i and j we have

$$M(i,j) = \min(M(i-1,j-1)+S(\lambda_i,\mu_j),\ M(i-1,j)+D(\lambda_i),\ M(i,j-1)+I(\mu_j))$$

for all i,j, $1 \leq i \leq n$ and $1 \leq j \leq m$. Hence $M(i,j)$ can be evaluated row-by-row or column-by-column in $\Theta(mn)$ time [27]. Observe that, of all entries of the M-matrix, only the three entries $M(i-1,j-1)$, $M(i-1,j)$ and $M(i,j-1)$ are involved in the computation of the final value of $M(i,j)$.

Not only does the above dynamic program for computing M depend on both λ and μ, but even if M could be computed without knowing λ and μ, the problem remains that M itself is too revealing: It reveals not only the overall edit distance, but also the edit distance from every prefix of λ to every prefix of μ. It is required in our problem that the external agents should learn nothing about the actual sequences and the results. The matrix M should therefore not be known to the agents. It can of course not be stored at the customer's site, as it is a requirement that the customer is limited to $O(m+n)$ time and storage space.

3.2 Framework

We use two non-colluding agents in our protocol. Both the input sequences (λ and μ) and the intermediate results (the matrix M) are additively split between the two agents, in such a way that neither one of the agents learns anything about the real inputs and results, but the two agents together can implicitly use the matrix M without knowing it, that is, obtaining additively split answers "as if" they knew M. They have to do so without the help of the customer, as the customer is incapable of quadratic computation time or storage space. More details, about how this is done, are given below.

In the rest of the paper, we use following notations: We use $\mathcal{C}$ to denote the customer, $\mathcal{A}_1$ the first agent, and $\mathcal{A}_2$ the second agent. Any items superscripted with $'$ are known to $\mathcal{A}_1$ but not to $\mathcal{A}_2$, those superscripted with $''$ are known to $\mathcal{A}_2$ but not to $\mathcal{A}_1$. In what follows, we often *additively split* an item x between the two agents $\mathcal{A}_1$ and $\mathcal{A}_2$, i.e., we assume that $\mathcal{A}_1$ has an x' and $\mathcal{A}_2$ has an x'' such that $x = x' + x''$; we do this splitting for the purpose of hiding x from either agent. If arithmetic is modular, then this kind of additive splitting of x hides it, in an information-theoretic sense, from $\mathcal{A}_1$ and $\mathcal{A}_2$. If, however, arithmetic is not modular, then even when x' and x'' can be negative and are very large compared to x, the "hiding" of x is valid in a practical but not in an information-theoretic sense.

Splitting λ and μ. Let λ and μ be two sequences over some finite alphabet $\Sigma = \{0, \ldots, \sigma - 1\}$. This could be a known fixed set of symbols (e.g., in biology $\Sigma = \{A, C, T, G\}$), or the domain of a hash function that maps a potentially infinite alphabet into a finite domain. $\mathcal{C}$ splits λ into λ' and λ'' such that λ' and λ'' are over the same alphabet Σ, and their sum is λ, i.e., $\lambda_i = \lambda_i' + \lambda_i''$ mod σ for all $1 \leq i \leq n$. To split λ, $\mathcal{C}$ can first generate a random sequence λ' of length n, then set $\lambda_i'' = \lambda_i - \lambda_i'$ mod σ for all $1 \leq i \leq n$. Similarly, $\mathcal{C}$ splits μ into μ' and μ'' such that $\mu_i = \mu_i' + \mu_i''$ mod σ for all $1 \leq i \leq m$. In the edit distance protocol, $\mathcal{C}$ sends λ' and μ' to $\mathcal{A}_1$ and sends λ'' and μ'' to $\mathcal{A}_2$.

Splitting M. Our edit distance protocol computes the same matrix as the dynamic programming algorithm, in the same order (e.g., row by row). Similar to [2], the matrix M in our protocol is additively shared between $\mathcal{A}_1$ and $\mathcal{A}_2$: $\mathcal{A}_1$ and $\mathcal{A}_2$ each hold a matrix M' and M'', respectively, the sum of which is the matrix M, i.e., $M = M' + M''$; the protocol will maintain this property as an invariant through all its steps. The main challenge in our protocol is that the comparands and outcome of each comparison, as well as the indices of the minimum elements, have to be shared (in the sense that neither party individually knows them).

Hiding the Sequences' Lengths. Splitting a sequence effectively hides its content, but fails to hide its length. In some situations, even the lengths of the sequences are sensitive and must be hidden or, at least, somewhat obfuscated. We now briefly sketch how to pad the sequences and obtain new, longer sequences whose edit distance is the same as that between the original sentences. Let $\hat{m}$ and $\hat{n}$ be the respective new lengths (with padding); assume that randomly choosing $\hat{m}$ from the interval $[m, 2m]$ provides enough obfuscation of m, and similarly $\hat{n}$ from the interval $[n, 2n]$.

We introduce a new special symbol "$" to the alphabet Σ such that the cost of insertion and deletion of this symbol is 0 (i.e., $I(\$) = D(\$) = 0$), and the cost of substitution of this symbol is infinity (i.e., $S(\$, a) = S(a, \$) = +\infty$ for every symbol a in Σ). The customer appends "$"s to the end of λ and μ to turn their respective lengths into the target values $\hat{n}$ and $\hat{m}$, before splitting and sending them to the agents. This padding has following two properties: 1) the edit distance between the padded sequences is the same as the edit distance between the original sequences, 2) the agents cannot figure out how many "$"s were padded into a sequence because of the random split of the sequence.

To avoid unnecessarily cluttering the exposition, we assume λ and μ are already padded with "$"s before the protocol, thus we assume the lengths of λ and μ are still n and m respectively, and the alphabet Σ is still $\{0, \ldots, \sigma - 1\}$.

3.3   Secure Table Lookup Protocol for Split Data

Recall that the $\sigma \times \sigma$ size cost table S is public, hence known to both $\mathcal{A}_1$ and $\mathcal{A}_2$; we make no assumptions about the costs in the table (they can be arbitrary, not necessarily between 0 and $\sigma - 1$). Recall that $\mathcal{A}_1$ and $\mathcal{A}_2$ share additively each symbol α from

λ and β from μ, i.e., $\alpha = \alpha' + \alpha''$ mod σ, and $\beta = \beta' + \beta''$ mod σ where $\mathcal{A}_1$ has α' and β', $\mathcal{A}_2$ has α'' and β''. $\mathcal{A}_1$ and $\mathcal{A}_2$ want to cooperatively look up the value $S(\alpha, \beta)$ from the cost table S, but without either of them knowing which entry of S was accessed and what value was returned by the access (so that value itself must be additively split). The protocol below solves this lookup problem in one round and $O(\sigma^2)$ computation and communication; note that naively using the protocol below $O(mn)$ times would result in an $O(\sigma^2 mn)$ computation and communication complexity for the overall sequence comparison problem, not the $O(\sigma mn)$ performance we claim (and that will be substantiated later in the paper).

Protocol 1. Secure Table Lookup Protocol

Input. $\mathcal{A}_1$ has α' and β' and $\mathcal{A}_2$ has α'' and β'', such that $\alpha = \alpha' + \alpha''$ mod σ and $\beta = \beta' + \beta''$ mod σ.

Output. $\mathcal{A}_1$ obtains a number a, and $\mathcal{A}_2$ obtains a number b, such that $a + b = S(\alpha, \beta)$.

The protocol steps are:

1. $\mathcal{A}_1$ generates a key pair for a homomorphic semantically-secure public key system and sends the public key to $\mathcal{A}_2$ (any of the existing systems will do, e.g., [16, 18]). In what follows $E(\cdot)$ denotes encryption with $\mathcal{A}_1$'s public key, and $D(\cdot)$ decryption with $\mathcal{A}_1$'s private key. (Recall that the homomorphic property implies that $E(x) * E(y) = E(x + y)$, and semantic security implies that $E(x)$ reveals nothing about x, so that $x = y$ need not imply $E(x) = E(y)$.)
2. $\mathcal{A}_1$ generates a $\sigma \times \sigma$ size table $\hat{S}$ with entry $\hat{S}(i, j)$ equal to $E(S(i + \alpha'$ mod $\sigma, j + \beta'$ mod $\sigma))$ for all $0 \leq i, j \leq \sigma - 1$, and sends that table $\hat{S}$ to $\mathcal{A}_2$.
3. $\mathcal{A}_2$ picks up the (α'', β'')th entry from the table received in the previous step, which is $\hat{S}(\alpha'', \beta'') = E(S(\alpha, \beta))$. $\mathcal{A}_2$ then generates a random number b, then computes $\theta = E(S(\alpha, \beta)) * E(-b) = E(S(\alpha, \beta) - b)$, and sends it back to $\mathcal{A}_1$.
4. $\mathcal{A}_1$ decrypts the value received from $\mathcal{A}_2$ and gets $a = D(E(S(\alpha, \beta) - b)) = S(\alpha, \beta) - b$.

As required, $a + b = S(\alpha, \beta)$, and $\mathcal{A}_1$ and $\mathcal{A}_2$ do not learn anything about the other party from the protocol. The computation and communication cost of this protocol is $O(\sigma^2)$.

4 Edit Distance Protocol

We now "put the pieces together" and give the overall protocol. We begin with the general case of arbitrary $I(a)$, $D(b)$, $S(a, b)$. Then two special cases are considered. One is the case of arbitrary $I(a)$ and $D(b)$, but $S(a, b) = |a - b|$. The other is the practical case of unit insertion/deletion cost and forbidden substitutions (i.e., $S(a, b)$ is 0 if $a = b$ and $+\infty$ otherwise). For all the above cases, the cost of computation and communication by the customer is linear to the size of the input. The cost of computation and communication by agents is $O(\sigma mn)$ for the general case and $O(mn)$ for the two special cases.

4.1   The General Case: Arbitrary $I(a)$, $D(b)$, $S(a, b)$

In this section, we begin with a preliminary solution that is not our best, but serves as a useful "warmup" to the more efficient solution that comes later in this section.

A Preliminary Version of the Protocol. Recall that $\mathcal{C}$ splits λ into λ' and λ'' and μ into μ' and μ'', then sends λ' and μ' to $\mathcal{A}_1$, and sends λ'' and μ'' to $\mathcal{A}_2$. $\mathcal{A}_1$ and $\mathcal{A}_2$ each maintains a matrix M' and (respectively) M'', such that $M = M' + M''$. $\mathcal{A}_1$ and $\mathcal{A}_2$ compute each element $M(i, j)$ in additively split fashion; this is done as prescribed in the recursive edit distance formula, by $\mathcal{A}_1$ and $\mathcal{A}_2$ updating their respective M' and M''. After doing so, $\mathcal{A}_1$ and $\mathcal{A}_2$, send their respective $M'(n, m)$ and $M''(n, m)$ back to $\mathcal{C}$. $\mathcal{C}$ can then obtain the edit distance $M(n, m) = M'(n, m) + M''(n, m)$.

During the computation of each element $M(i, j)$, $S(\lambda_i, \mu_j)$ has to be computed by $\mathcal{A}_1$ and $\mathcal{A}_2$ in additively split fashion and without the help of $\mathcal{C}$, which implies that the substitution table S should be known by both $\mathcal{A}_1$ and $\mathcal{A}_2$. Hence, $\mathcal{C}$ needs to send the table to both of the agents during the initialization phase of the protocol. The content of the table is not private, and need not be disguised.

Initialization of Matrices. M' and M'' should be initialized so that their sum M has $M(0, j)$ and $M(i, 0)$ equal to the values specified in Section 3.1. The $M(i, j)$ entries for nonzero i and j can be random (they will be computed later, after the initialization). The following initializes the M' and M'' matrices:

1. $\mathcal{C}$ generates two vectors of random numbers $a = (a_1, \ldots, a_n)$ and $b = (b_1, \ldots, b_m)$. Then $\mathcal{C}$ computes two vectors $c = (c_1, \ldots, c_n)$ and $d = (d_1, \ldots, d_m)$ where
   (a) $c_i = \sum_{k=1}^{i} D(\lambda_k) - a_i$ for $1 \leq i \leq n$,
   (b) $d_j = \sum_{k=1}^{j} I(\mu_k) - b_j$ for $1 \leq j \leq m$.
   $\mathcal{C}$ sends to $\mathcal{A}_1$ the vectors b, c, and to $\mathcal{A}_2$ the vectors a, d.
2. $\mathcal{A}_1$ sets $M'(0, j) = b_j$ for $1 \leq j \leq m$, and sets $M'(i, 0) = c_i$ for $1 \leq i \leq n$. All the other entries of M' are set to 0.
3. $\mathcal{A}_2$ sets $M''(i, 0) = a_i$ for $1 \leq i \leq n$, and sets $M''(0, j) = d_j$ for $1 \leq j \leq m$. All the other entries of M'' are set to 0.

Note that the above does implicitly initialize $M(i, j)$ in the correct way, because it results in

- $M'(0, 0) + M''(0, 0) = 0$.
- $M'(0, j) + M''(0, j) = \sum_{k=1}^{j} I(\mu_j)$ for $1 \leq j \leq m$.
- $M'(i, 0) + M''(i, 0) = \sum_{k=1}^{i} D(\lambda_i)$ for $1 \leq i \leq n$.

Neither $\mathcal{A}_1$ nor $\mathcal{A}_2$ gain any information about λ and μ from the initialization of their matrices, because the two vectors they each receive from $\mathcal{C}$ look random to them.

Mimicking a Step of the Dynamic Program. The following protocol describes how an $M(i, j)$ computation is done by $\mathcal{A}_1$ and $\mathcal{A}_2$, i.e., how they modify their respective $M'(i, j)$ and $M''(i, j)$, thus implicitly computing the final $M(i, j)$ without either of them learning which update was performed.

1. $\mathcal{A}_1$ and $\mathcal{A}_2$ use the secure table lookup protocol with inputs λ_i' and μ_j' from $\mathcal{A}_1$, and inputs λ_i'' and μ_j'' from $\mathcal{A}_2$. As a result, $\mathcal{A}_1$ obtains γ' and $\mathcal{A}_2$ obtains γ'' such that

$$\gamma' + \gamma'' = S(\lambda_i' + \lambda_i'' \bmod \sigma, \mu_j' + \mu_j'' \bmod \sigma) = S(\lambda_i, \mu_j).$$

$\mathcal{A}_1$ then forms $u' = M'(i-1, j-1) + \gamma'$ and Bob forms $u'' = M''(i-1, j-1) + \gamma''$. Observe that $u' + u'' = M(i-1, j-1) + S(\lambda_i, \mu_j)$, which is one of the three quantities involved in the update step for $M(i, j)$ in the dynamic program.

2. $\mathcal{A}_1$ computes $v' = M'(i-1, j) + M'(i, 0) - M'(i-1, 0) = M'(i-1, 0) + D(\lambda_i) - a_i + a_{i-1}$, $\mathcal{A}_2$ computes $v'' = M''(i-1, j) + M''(i, 0) - M''(i-1, 0) = M''(i-1, j) + a_i - a_{i-1}$. Observe that $u_A + u_B = M(i-1, j) + D(\lambda_i)$, which is one of the three quantities involved in the update step for $M(i, j)$ in the dynamic program.

3. $\mathcal{A}_1$ computes $w' = M'(i, j-1) + M'(0, j) - M'(0, j-1) = M'(i, j-1) + b_j - b_{j-1}$, $\mathcal{A}_2$ computes $w'' = M''(i, j-1) + M''(0, j) - M''(0, j-1) = M''(i, j-1) + I(\mu_j) - b_j + b_{j-1}$. Observe that $w' + w'' = M(i, j-1) + D(\mu_j)$, which is one of the three quantities involved in the update step for $M(i, j)$ in the dynamic program.

4. $\mathcal{A}_1$ and $\mathcal{A}_2$ use the minimum finding protocol for split data (described in [2]) on their respective vectors (u', v', w') and (u'', v'', w''). As a result, $\mathcal{A}_1$ gets an x' and $\mathcal{A}_2$ gets an x'' whose sum $x' + x''$ is

$$\min(u' + u'', v' + v'', w' + w'') =$$

$$\min(M(i-1, j-1) + S(\lambda_i, \mu_j), M(i-1, j) + D(\lambda_i), M(i, j-1) + I(\mu_j)).$$

5. $\mathcal{A}_1$ sets $M'(i, j)$ equal to x', and $\mathcal{A}_2$ sets $M''(i, j)$ equal to x''.

Performance Analysis. The local computations done by $\mathcal{C}$ in the above protocol consist of splitting λ and μ and sending the resulting shares to the agents, and computing and sending the vectors a, b, c, d. These are done in $O(m + n)$ time and communication.

Each agent mimics mn steps of the dynamic program. During each step, two agents run the secure table lookup protocol once and the minimum finding protocol once. Thus, the communication between $\mathcal{A}_1$ and $\mathcal{A}_2$ for each such step is $O(\sigma^2) + O(1)$. Therefore the total computation and communication cost for each agent is $O(\sigma^2 mn)$.

An Improved Version of the Protocol. A bottleneck in the above protocol is the split computation of $S(\lambda_i, \mu_j)$: Running the secure table lookup protocol at each step of the dynamic program costs an expensive $O(\sigma^2)$. In this subsection, we present a solution that is more efficient by a factor of σ.

Recall that in the dynamic program, M is constructed row-by-row or column-by-column. We assume, without loss of generality that M is computed row-by-row. We will compute $S(\lambda_i, \mu_j)$ row-by-row exploiting the fact that all (λ_i, μ_j) in row i have the same λ_i: We will "batch" these table accesses for row i, as we describe next.

Protocol 2. Batched Secure Table Lookup Protocol

Input. $\mathcal{A}_1$ has λ_i' and $\mu' = \mu_1', \ldots, \mu_m'$, and $\mathcal{A}_2$ has λ_i'' and $\mu'' = \mu_1'', \ldots, \mu_m''$, all symbols being over alphabet Σ.

Output. $\mathcal{A}_1$ and $\mathcal{A}_2$ each obtains a vector γ' and γ'' of size m, such that $\gamma'_j + \gamma''_j = S(\lambda_i, \mu_j)$ for $1 \leq j \leq m$.

The protocol is:

1. $\mathcal{A}_1$ generates a key pair for a homomorphic semantically-secure public key system and sends the public key to $\mathcal{A}_2$. As before, $E(\cdot)$ denotes encryption with $\mathcal{A}_1$'s public key, and $D(\cdot)$ decryption with $\mathcal{A}_1$'s private key.
2. $\mathcal{A}_1$ generates a $\sigma \times \sigma$ table $\hat{S}$ with $\hat{S}(k, l)$ equal to $E(S(k + \lambda'_i \bmod \sigma, l))$ for all $0 \leq k, l \leq \sigma - 1$, and sends that table to $\mathcal{A}_2$.
3. For each $j = 1, \ldots, m$, the next 5 sub-steps are carried out to compute the (γ'_j, γ''_j) pair.
   (a) $\mathcal{A}_2$ creates a σ size vector v equal to the λ''_ith row of the table $\hat{S}$ received in the previous step. Observe that $v_l = E(S(\lambda''_i + \lambda'_i \bmod \sigma, l)) = E(S(\lambda_i, l))$ for $0 \leq l \leq \sigma - 1$.
   (b) $\mathcal{A}_2$ circularly left-shifts v by μ''_j positions, so that v_l becomes $E(S(\lambda_i, \mu''_j + l \bmod \sigma))$ for $0 \leq l \leq \sigma - 1$.
   (c) $\mathcal{A}_2$ generates a random number γ''_j, he then updates v by setting $v_l = v_l * E(-\gamma''_j) = E(S(\lambda_i, \mu''_j + l \bmod \sigma) - \gamma''_j)$ for $0 \leq l \leq \sigma - 1$. Note that the μ'_jth entry of the resulting v is now $E(S(\lambda_i, \mu_j) - \gamma''_j)$.
   (d) $\mathcal{A}_1$ uses a 1-out-of-σ oblivious transfer protocol to obtain the μ'_jth entry of v from $\mathcal{A}_2$ without revealing to $\mathcal{A}_2$ which v_l he received (see, e.g., [23] for many detailed oblivious transfer protocols).
   (e) $\mathcal{A}_1$ decrypts the value he obtained from the oblivious transfer of the previous step, and gets $\gamma'_j = S(\lambda_i, \mu_j) - \gamma''_j$. Observe that $\gamma'_j + \gamma''_j = S(\lambda_i, \mu_j)$, as required.

Neither $\mathcal{A}_1$ nor $\mathcal{A}_2$ learned anything about which entry of S was implicitly accessed, or what the value obtained in split fashion is. The communication cost of the above scheme is $O(\sigma^2) + O(\sigma m)$. The size of the alphabet is much smaller than the length of a sequence (e.g., in bioinformatics $\sigma = 4$ whereas a sequence's length is huge). Therefore the dominant term in the complexity of the above is $O(\sigma m)$.

The new outsourcing protocol for sequence comparisons is same as the preliminary protocol in the previous subsection, except for some modifications in the first step of the protocol, titled "mimicking a step of the dynamic program". Recall that the aim of Step 1 is to produce a u' with $\mathcal{A}_1$ and a u'' with $\mathcal{A}_2$ such that $u' + u'' = M(i - 1, j - 1) + S(\lambda_i, \mu_j)$. In the improved protocol, we first run the above batched lookup protocol for row i to produce a γ' for $\mathcal{A}_1$ and a γ'' for $\mathcal{A}_2$, such that $\gamma'_j + \gamma''_j = S(\lambda_i, \mu_j)$ for $1 \leq j \leq m$. Then, during Step 1 of the modified protocol, $\mathcal{A}_1$ sets $u' = M'(i - 1, j - 1) + \gamma'_j$ and $\mathcal{A}_2$ sets $u'' = M''(i - 1, j - 1) + \gamma''_j$. Note that, at the end of the new Step 1, $u' + u''$ equals to $M(i - 1, j - 1) + S(\lambda_i, \mu_j)$, as required. The computational task for the customer in this protocol is the same as in the preliminary version. The computational and communication cost for the agents in this protocol are $\Theta(\sigma m n)$.

4.2   The Case $S(a, b) = |a - b|$

The improvement in this case comes from a more efficient way of computing the split $S(\lambda_i, \mu_j)$ values needed in Step 1 of the protocol. Unlike previous sections of the paper, each symbol in λ and μ is split into two numbers that are not modulo σ, and can in fact be arbitrary (and possibly negative) integers. The protocol is otherwise the same as in section 4.1.

The main difference is in the first step of sub-protocol "mimicking a step of the dynamic program". Note that

$$S(\lambda_i, \mu_j) = |\lambda_i - \mu_j|$$
$$= \max(\lambda_i - \mu_j, \mu_j - \lambda_i)$$
$$= \max((\lambda_i' - \mu_j') + (\lambda_i'' - \mu_j''), (\mu_j' - \lambda_i') + (\mu_j'' - \lambda_i''))$$

The $S(\lambda_i, \mu_j)$ can be computed as follows: $\mathcal{A}_1$ forms a two-entry vector $v' = (\lambda_i' - \mu_j', \mu_j' - \lambda_i')$, $\mathcal{A}_2$ forms a two-entry vector $v'' = (\lambda_i'' - \mu_j'', \mu_j'' - \lambda_i'')$, then $\mathcal{A}_1$ and $\mathcal{A}_2$ use the split maximum finding protocol (described in [2]) to obtain γ' and γ'' such that

$$\gamma' + \gamma'' = \max(v' + v'') = |\lambda_i - \mu_j| = S(\lambda_i, \mu_j).$$

Then the first step of the dynamic program can be replaced by $\mathcal{A}_1$ setting $u' = M'(i - 1, j - 1) + \gamma'$, and $\mathcal{A}_2$ setting $u'' = M''(i - 1, j - 1) + \gamma''$. As required, $u' + u''$ equals $M(i - 1, j - 1) + S(\lambda_i, \mu_j)$. Since the communication cost of Step 1 is now $O(1)$, the total communication cost for the agents is $O(mn)$.

4.3   The Case of Unit Insertion/Deletion Costs and Forbidden Substitutions

The improvement in this case directly follows from a technique, given in [2], that we now review. Forbidden substitutions means that $S(a, b)$ is $+\infty$ unless $a = b$ (in which case it is zero because it is a "do nothing" operation). Of course a substitution is useless if its cost is 2 or more (because one might as well achieve the same effect with a deletion followed by an insertion). The protocol is then:

1. For $i = \sigma, \ldots, 1$ in turn, $\mathcal{C}$ replaces every occurrence of symbol i by the symbol $2i$. So the alphabet becomes effectively $\{0, 2, 4, \ldots, 2\sigma - 2\}$.
2. $\mathcal{C}$ runs the protocol given in the previous section for the case of $S(a, b) = |a - b|$, using a unit cost for every insertion and every deletion.

The reason it works is that, after the change of alphabet, $S(a, b)$ is zero if $a = b$ and 2 or more if $a \neq b$, i.e., it is as if $S(a, b) = +\infty$ if $a \neq b$ (recall that a substitution is useless if its cost is 2 or more, because one can achieve the same effect with a deletion followed by an insertion).

5   Computing the Edit Path

We have so far established that the edit distance can be computed in linear space and $O(\sigma mn)$ time and communication. This section deals with extending this to computing, also in split form, the *edit path*, which is a sequence of operations that corresponds to the edit distance (that is, a minimum-cost sequence of operations on λ that turns it into μ). We show that the edit path can be computed by the agents in split form in $O(mn)$ space and in $O(\sigma mn)$ time and communication.

5.1   Review: Grid Graph View of the Problem

The interdependencies among the entries of the M-matrix induce an $(n+1)\times(m+1)$ *grid directed acyclic graph* (grid DAG for short) associated with the string editing problem. It is easy to see that in fact the string editing problem can be viewed as a shortest-paths problem on a grid DAG.

Definition 1. *An $l_1 \times l_2$ grid DAG is a directed acyclic graph whose vertices are the $l_1 l_2$ points of an $l_1 \times l_2$ grid, and such that the only edges from grid point (i, j) are to grid points $(i, j + 1)$, $(i + 1, j)$, and $(i + 1, j + 1)$.*

Note that the top-left point of a grid DAG has no edge entering it (i.e., is a *source*), and that the bottom-right point has no edge leaving it (i.e., is a *sink*). We now review the correspondence between edit scripts and grid graphs. We associate an $(n+1) \times (m+1)$ grid DAG G with the string editing problem in the natural way: The $(n + 1)(m + 1)$ vertices of G are in one-to-one correspondence with the $(n + 1)(m + 1)$ entries of the M-matrix, and the *cost* of an edge from vertex (k, l) to vertex (i, j) is equal to $I(\mu_j)$ if $k = i$ and $l = j - 1$, to $D(\lambda_i)$ if $k = i - 1$ and $l = j$, to $S(\lambda_i, \mu_j)$ if $k = i - 1$ and $l = j - 1$. We can restrict our attention to edit paths which are not wasteful in the sense that they do no obviously inefficient moves such as: inserting then deleting the same symbol, or changing a symbol into a new symbol which they then delete, etc. More formally, the only edit scripts considered are those that apply at most one edit operation to a given symbol occurrence. Such edit scripts that transform λ into μ or vice versa are in one-to-one correspondence to the weighted paths of G that originate at the source (which corresponds to $M(0, 0)$) and end on the sink (which corresponds to $M(n, m)$). Thus, any complexity bounds we establish for the problem of finding a shortest (i.e., least-cost) source-to-sink path in an $(n + 1) \times (m + 1)$ grid DAG G, extends naturally to the string editing problem.

At first sight it looks like "remembering" (in split form), for every entry $M(i, j)$, which of $\{M(i-1, j-1), M(i-1, j), M(i, j-1)\}$ "gave it its value" would solve the problem of obtaining the source-to-sink shortest path we seek. That is, if we use $P(i, j)$ (where P is mnemonic for "parent") to denote that element $(k, l) \in \{(i - 1, j - 1), (i - 1, j), (i, j - 1)\}$ such that the edit path goes from vertex (k, l) to vertex (i, j) in the $(n + 1) \times (m + 1)$ grid graph that implicitly describes the problem, then all we need to do is store matrix P in split fashion as $P' + P''$. However, this does not work because it would reveal the edit path to both agents: To get that edit path would require starting at vertex (n, m) and repeatedly following the parent until vertex $(0, 0)$ is reached, which appears impossible to do without revealing the path to the agents. To get around this difficulty, we use a different approach that we develop next.

5.2   The Backward Version of the Protocol

The protocol we presented worked by computing (in split form) a matrix M such that $M(i, j)$ contains the length of a shortest path from vertex $(0, 0)$ to vertex (i, j) in the grid graph. We call this the *forward protocol* and henceforth denote the M matrix as M_F where the subscript F is a mnemonic for "forward".

One can, in a completely analogous manner, give a protocol that computes for every (i, j) the length of a shortest path from vertex (i, j) to the sink vertex (n, m). We denote the length of such a path as $M_B(i, j)$ where the subscript B is a mnemonic for "backward". The edit distance is $M_B(0, 0)$ $(= M_F(n, m))$. The protocol for M_B is similar to the one for computing M_F and is omitted for reason of space limitations (the details will be given in the journal version).

Note that $M_F(i, j) + M_B(i, j)$ is the length of a shortest source-to-sink path *that is constrained to go through vertex (i, j)* and hence might not be the shortest possible source-to-sink path. However, if the shortest source-to-sink path goes though vertex (i, j), then $M_F(i, j) + M_B(i, j)$ is equal to the length of shortest path. We use M_C to denote $M_F + M_B$ (where subscript C is mnemonic for "constrained").

The protocol below finds (in split fashion), for each row i of M_C, the column $\theta(i)$ of the minimum entry of that row, with ties broken in favor of the rightmost such entry; note that $M_C(i, \theta(i))$ is the edit distance $M_F(n, m)$. Computing (in split fashion) the θ function is an implicit description of the edit path:

- If $\theta(i + 1) = \theta(i) = j$ then the edit path "leaves" row i through the vertical edge from vertex (i, j) to vertex $(i + 1, j)$ (the cost of that edge is, of course, the cost of deleting λ_{i+1}).
- If $\theta(i + 1) = \theta(i) + \delta$ where $\delta > 0$ then the client can "fill in" in $O(\delta)$ time the portion of the edit path from vertex $(i, \theta(i))$ to vertex $(i + 1, \theta(i) + \delta)$ (because such a "thin" edit distance problem on a $2 \times \delta$ sub-grid is trivially solvable in $O(\delta)$ time). The cumulative cost of all such "thin problem solutions" is $O(m)$ because the sum of all such δ's is $\leq m$.

5.3   Edit Path Protocol

The steps of the protocol for computing the edit path are:

1. C, A_1, and A_2 conduct the edit distance protocol as described in Section 4 to compute M_F in split fashion, i.e., A_1 gets M'_F and A_2 gets M''_F such that $M_F = M'_F + M''_F$.
2. Similarly, A_1 and A_2 conduct the backward version of the edit distance protocol and compute M_B in split fashion. As a result, A_1 gets M'_B and A_2 gets M''_B.
3. A_1 computes $M'_C = M'_F + M'_B$ and A_2 computes $M''_C = M''_F + M''_B$. Note that $M'_C + M''_C$ is equal to M_C.
4. For $i = 1, \ldots, n$ in turn, the following steps are repeated:
   (a) A_1 picks ith row from M'_C, denoted as $(v'_0, \ldots, v'_m)$, and A_2 picks ith row from M''_C, denoted as $(v''_0, \ldots, v''_m)$.
   (b) For $0 \leq j \leq m$, A_1 sets $v'_j = (m + 1) * v'_j$ and A_2 sets $v''_j = (m + 1) * v''_j + (m - j)$; note that $v'_j + v''_j = (m + 1) * M_C(i, j) + (m - j)$. Also observe that, if $M_C(i, j)$ is the rightmost minimum entry in row i of M_C, them $v'_j + v''_j$ is now the *only* minimum entry among all $j \in [0..m]$; in effect we have implicitly broken any tie between multiple minima in row i in favor of the rightmost one (which has the highest j and therefore is "favored" by the addition of $m - j$). Note, however, that breaking the tie through this addition of $m - j$ without the

prior scaling by a factor of $m + 1$ would have been erroneous, as it would have destroyed the minima information.

(c) $\mathcal{A}_1$ and $\mathcal{A}_2$ run the minimum finding protocol for split data (described in [2]) on their respective $(v'_0, \dots, v'_m)$ and $(v''_0, \dots, v''_m)$. As a result, $\mathcal{A}_2$ gets an x' and $\mathcal{A}_2$ gets and x'' whose sum $x' + x''$ is $\min(v'_0 + v''_0, \dots, v'_m + v''_m)$.

(d) $\mathcal{A}_1$ and $\mathcal{A}_2$ send x' and (respectively) x'' to $\mathcal{C}$. $\mathcal{C}$ computes

$$
\begin{aligned}
p_i &= x' + x'' \bmod (m + 1) \\
&= ((m + 1) * M_F(i, \theta(i)) + (m - \theta(i))) \bmod (m + 1) \\
&= m - \theta(i),
\end{aligned}
$$

therefore obtains $\theta(i) = m - p_i$.

5. As mentioned earlier, given $\theta(0), \dots, \theta(m)$, $\mathcal{C}$ can compute the edit path in $O(m)$ additional time.

Performance Analysis. The computation by the client includes initializing the edit distance protocol (step 1) and computing the edit path from the $\theta(i)$s (step 5). It can be done in $O(m + n)$ time and communication.

The agents run the edit distance protocol twice (steps 1 and 2), and the minimum finding protocol n times (step 4). Each edit distance protocol can be done in $O(\sigma mn)$ time and communication, and each minimum finding protocol needs $O(m)$ time and communication. Therefore, the total computation and communication cost for each agent is $O(\sigma mn)$. The space complexity for each agent is $O(mn)$ as the agents need to store M_C in split fashion; in the journal version of this paper, we will include a solution of $O(m + n)$ space complexity for the agents (i.e., same as for the edit distance protocol rather than edit path).

6 Concluding Remarks

We gave efficient protocols for a customer to securely outsource sequence comparisons to two remote agents, such that the agents learn nothing about the customer's two private sequences or the result of the comparison. The local computations done by the customer are linear in the size of the sequences, and the computational cost and amount of communication done by the external agents are close to the time complexity of the best known algorithm for solving the problem on a single machine. Such protocols hold the promise of allowing weak computational devices to avail themselves of the computational, storage, and bandwidth resources of powerful remote servers without having to reveal to those servers their private data or the outcome of the computation.

Acknowledgement

We would like to thank the anonymous reviewers for their helpful comments.

References

1. A. V. Aho, D. S. Hirschberg and J. D. Ullman. Bounds on the Complexity of the Longest Common Subsequence Problem. *Journal of the ACM* 23, 1, pp.1–12 (1976).

2. M. J. Atallah, F. Kerschbaum, and W. Du. Secure and Private Sequence Comparisons. *Proceedings of 2nd ACM Workshop on Privacy in Electronic Society* (2003).

3. M. J. Atallah, K. N. Pantazopoulos, J. Rice, and E. H. Spafford. Secure Outsourcing of Scientific Computations. *Advances in Computers* 54, 6, pp.215–272 (2001).

4. P. Beguin and J. J. Quisquater. Fast Server-Aided RSA Signatures Secure Against Active Attacks. *CRYPTO'95*, pp.57–69 (1995).

5. C. Cachin. Efficient Private Bidding and Auctions with an Oblivious Third Party. *Proceedings of the 6th ACM Conference on Computer and Communications Security*, pp.120-127 (1999).

6. W. Du and M. J. Atallah. Protocols for Secure Remote Database Access with Approximate Matching. *Proceedings of the 1st ACM Workshop on Security and Privacy in E-Commerce* (2000).

7. M. Fischlin. A Cost-Effective Pay-Per-Multiplication Comparison Method for Millionaires. RSA Security 2001 Cryptographer's Track, *Lecture Notes in Computer Science* 2020, pp.457–471 (2001).

8. I. Foster and C. Kesselman, editors. *The Grid: Blueprint for a New Computing Infrastructure.* Morgan Kaufmann Publishers (1999).

9. O. Goldreich. Secure Multi-party Computation (working draft). Available at *http://www.wisdom.weizmann.ac.il/home/oded/public_html/pp.html* (2001).

10. S. I. Kawamura and A. Shimbo. Fast Server-Aided Secret Computation Protocols for Modular Exponentiation. *IEEE Journal on Selected Areas in Communications*, 11(5), pp. 778–784 (1993).

11. G. Landau and U. Vishkin. Introducing Efficient Parallelism into Approximate String Matching and a new Serial Algorithm. *Proceedings of the 18-th ACM STOC,* pp. 220–230 (1986).

12. C. H. Lim and P. J. Lee. Security and Performance of Server-Aided RSA Computation Protocols. *CRYPTO'95*, pp. 70–83 (1995).

13. H. M. Martinez (ed.) Mathematical and Computational Problems in the Analysis of Molecular Sequences. *Bulletin of Mathematical Biology* (Special Issue Honoring M. O. Dayhoff), 46, 4 (1984).

14. W. J. Masek and M. S. Paterson. A Faster Algorithm Computing String Edit Distances. *Journal of Computer and System Science* 20, pp.18–31 (1980).

15. T. Matsumoto, K. Kato and H. Imai. Speeding Up Secret Computations with Insecure Auxiliary Devices. *CRYPTO'88*, pp. 497–506 (1988).

16. D. Naccache and J. Stern. A New Cryptosystem based on Higher Residues. *Proceedings of the ACM Conference on Computer and Communications Security* 5, pp.59-66 (1998).

17. S. B. Needleman and C. D. Wunsch. A General Method Applicable to the Search for Similarities in the Amino-acid Sequence of Two Proteins. *Journal of Molecular Biology* 48, pp.443–453 (1973).

18. T. Okamoto and S. Uchiyama. A New Public-Key Cryptosystem as Secure as Factoring. *EUROCRYPT'98*, Lecture Notes in Computer Science 1403, pp.308-318 (1998).

19. B. Pfitzmann and M. Waidner. Attacks on Protocols for Server-Aided RSA Computations. *EUROCRYPT'92*, pp. 153–162 (1992).

20. R. L. Rivest, L. Adleman, and M. L. Dertouzos. On Data Banks and Privacy Homomorphisms. In Richard A. DeMillo, editor, *Foundations of Secure Computation*, Academic Press, pp. 169–177 (1978).

21. D. Sankoff. Matching Sequences Under Deletion-insertion Constraints. *Proceedings of the National Academy of Sciences of the U.S.A.* 69, pp.4–6 (1972).

22. D. Sankoff and J. B. Kruskal (eds.). Time Warps, String Edits and Macromolecules: The Theory and Practice of Sequence Comparison. *Addison-Wesley*, Reading, PA (1983).

23. Bruce Schneier. Applied cryptography : protocols, algorithms, and source code in C (Second Edition). John Wiley & Sons, Inc (1995).

24. P. H. Sellers. An Algorithm for the Distance between two Finite Sequences. *Journal of Combinatorial Theory* 16, pp.253–258 (1974).

25. P. H. Sellers. The Theory and Computation of Evolutionary Distance: Pattern Recognition. *Journal of Algorithms* 1, pp.359–373 (1980).

26. E. Ukkonen. Finding Approximate Patterns in Strings. *Journal of Algorithms* 6, pp.132–137 (1985).

27. R. A. Wagner and M. J. Fischer. The String to String Correction Problem. *Journal of the ACM* 21,1, pp.168–173 (1974).

28. C. K. Wong and A. K. Chandra. Bounds for the String Editing Problem. *Journal of the ACM* 23, 1, pp.13–16 (1976).

29. A. Yao. Protocols for Secure Computations. *Proceedings of the Annual IEEE Symposium on Foundations of Computer Science* 23, pp.160–164 (1982).

An Improved Construction for Universal Re-encryption

Peter Fairbrother

10 Sheepcote Barton,
Trowbridge BA14 7SY UK
peter@m-o-o-t.org

Abstract. Golle et al recently introduced universal re-encryption, defining it as re-encryption by a player who does not know the key used for the original encryption, but which still allows an intended player to recover the plaintext. Universal re-encryption is potentially useful as part of many information-hiding techniques, as it allows any player to make ciphertext unidentifiable without knowing the key used.

Golle et al's techniques for universal re-encryption are reviewed, and a hybrid universal re-encryption construction with improved work and space requirements which also permits indefinite re-encryptions is presented. Some implementational issues and optimisations are discussed.

1 Introduction

Golle et al [1] recently introduced universal re-encryption, defining it as re-encryption by a player who does not know the key used for the original encryption, but which still allows an intended player to recover the plaintext.

Golle et al proposed using universal re-encryption in mixnets and anonymous bulletin boards, but it has many other potential uses in anonymous communications and untraceable messaging. It can also be used to provide cover against observation-based attacks on the plausible deniability of steganographic filing systems [2]. It is generally a useful addition to the toolkit of information hiding technologies.

The constructions of Golle et al, while secure and effective, have some important drawbacks. Their simple system increases the ciphertext to four times the plaintext size, and is computationally very expensive, requiring two El Gamal encryptions with the four associated large modular exponentiations per block. This can be improved for large files, but it remains expensive both computationally and in terms of ciphertext size.

Their hybrid system has the disadvantages of taking significant effort and space in managing the keys, often more effort than their simple system, but more importantly of limiting the number of re-encryptions possible before the plaintext becomes unrecoverable; further, it leaks information about the history of the underlying plaintext, making the system unuseable in many situations.

The construction presented here reduces the computational requirements to a single modular exponentiation per block, with no increase in file size (excepting

D. Martin and A. Serjantov (Eds.): PET 2004, LNCS 3424, pp. 79–87, 2005.
© Springer-Verlag Berlin Heidelberg 2005

a single key storage block per file). It imposes no limit to the number of possible re-encryptions, and no historical information is leaked, so it can be used in situations where Golle et al's construction cannot. However it's usefulness is limited in that it is not semantically secure in the presence of an active attacker who can "tag" texts.

2   Universal Cryptosystems

2.1   Golle et al's Simple System

In Golle et al's simple system plaintext is encrypted as a pair of El Gamal ciphertexts. The first is a standard encryption of the plaintext to an El Gamal public key, the second is an El Gamal encryption of unity to the same public key - a "unit" - but encrypted with a different random x.

A "unit" has the following properties, as far as the holder of the relevant secret key is concerned: any player can generate new "units" from a known "unit", without knowing the public key used to generate the "unit". A part-by-part multiplication of an El Gamal ciphertext by a "unit" encrypted with the same public key does not change the underlying plaintext.

Without knowledge of the secret keypart, it is presumed (under the Decisional Diffie-Hellman assumption) to be difficult to identify a ciphertext multiplied by an unknown "unit" with the original ciphertext. It is also presumed to be difficult to identify a generated "unit" as being generated from another "unit".

In Golle et al's system on re-encryption two new "units" are generated from the original "unit"; the player part-wise multiplies one with the standard ciphertext, the second replaces the "unit" ciphertext in the exposed ciphertext pair. The original "unit" is discarded.

The holder of a secret keypart can ascertain whether the constructed pair is encrypted to it by decrypting the second ciphertext using his secret keypart. If the decrypted value is one, he can then decrypt the re-encrypted ciphertext; else the ciphertext is not encrypted to his public key.

A player who does not have the El Gamal secret keypart cannot identify a ciphertext as a "unit" encrypted to a specific key; and he cannot identify a ciphertext multiplied by an unknown "unit" with the unmultiplied ciphertext.

Problems. A pair of El Gamal ciphertexts is four times the size of the corresponding plaintext file, requiring four times the computation, storage and transport of ordinary, non-universal, cryptosystems.

Each pair will take $4 \times k$-bit data blocks to store a single k-bit block of information, where k is the first security parameter, the size of the El Gamal modulus. k will be at least 1024 bits for present-day security. Files will typically be many times that size, and split into blocks.

A small improvement on Golle's construction, for larger files, reducing the size requirements to approaching twice file size, would be splitting the file into chunks and encrypting them as simple El Gamal ciphertexts with different "units", concatenating, and appending only a single "unit" to the whole. On re-encryption as many "units" as needed can be generated from the single "unit" and used to camouflage the individual blocks. This does not change the overall workload however.

- **Key Generation:** Output is an El Gamal keypair $p, g, x, y \ (= g^x)$. p and g are usually used and held in common.

- **Encryption:** Input is a file F of f k-bit blocks; an El Gamal public key (y, g, p); and random $k_1 \ldots k_f, k_u \in Z_p$
  Output is a ciphertext $C = [(\alpha_1, \beta_1); (\alpha_2, \beta_2) \ldots (\alpha_f, \beta_f)]; [(\alpha_u, \beta_u)]$
  $= [(F_1 y^{k_1}, g^{k_1}); (F_2 y^{k_2}, g^{k_2}) \ldots (F_f y^{k_f}, g^{k_f})]; [(y^{k_u}, g^{k_u})]$.

- **Re-encryption:** Input is a ciphertext C; and random $k'_1 \ldots k'_f, k'_u \in Z_p$.
  Output is a ciphertext $C' = [(\alpha'_1, \beta'_1); (\alpha'_2, \beta'_2) \ldots (\alpha'_f, \beta'_f)]; [(\alpha'_u . \beta'_u)]$
  $= [(\alpha_1 \alpha_u^{k'_1}, \beta_1 \beta_u^{k'_1}); (\alpha_2 \alpha_u^{k'_2}, \beta_2 \beta_u^{k'_2}) \ldots (\alpha_f \alpha_u^{k'_f}, \beta_f \beta_u^{k'_f})]; [(\alpha_u^{k'_u} . \beta_u^{k'_u})]$.

- **Decryption:** Input is a ciphertext C (or C'); and a private key x.
  If $\alpha_u / \beta_u^x = 1$ then the output is $[(\alpha_1 / \beta_1^x); (\alpha_1 / \beta_1^x) \ldots (\alpha_1 / \beta_1^x)]$. If not, the file is not decryptable by (or meant for) the holder of that private key.

The computational requirements remain at the same very high level, and the ciphertext size is still over twice file size $(2M + 4k)$; while this is an improvement, it is still very costly overall.

2.2   Golle et al's Hybrid System

Golle et al also proposed a hybrid universal cryptosystem, where the file is conventionally encrypted with a symmetric cipher and the key is appended, stored using a simple universal cryptosystem. To allow re-encryption extra "blank" re-encryptable keys are appended. On re-encryption the ciphertext is re-encrypted with the conventional cipher, using a random key which is then stored in one of the "blank" keys, and the position of the "blank" keys is rotated.

Problems. This adds $4k$ bits per "blank" key to the file; if a typical 4kB message is considered, with 1024-bit security parameter k, then only eight "blank" keys will double message size. A more realistic number of "blank" keys will make this system actually worse in terms of traffic requirements than a simple system.

Furthermore, the "blank" keys must be re-encrypted or decrypted as appropriate. In many situations the hybrid system will also end up needing more work than a simple system.

The number of re-encryptions a message has undergone is available to any observer, and this significantly impacts the untraceability properties of the system. Only messages with the same number of re-encryptions can be grouped for anonymity.

Possibly the worst drawback of this hybrid system however is that only a limited number of re-encryptions can be performed before the plaintext becomes unrecoverable.

3   An Improved Hybrid Construction

We present this improved construction. It is similar to Golle et al's hybrid construction, but the file is encrypted using the Pohlig-Hellman secret key algorithm [3], and only a single key-block is appended to hold the secret key.

Pohlig-Hellman is chosen as the symmetric algorithm because on re-encryption a player can, using the group multiplicative properties of Pohlig-Hellman keys, create a new "overall" key - and using similar multiplicative properties of El Gamal keys (properties preserved in a simple universal cryptosystem based on it), a player can calculate and store this new "overall" symmetric key in the single key-block without knowing (or being able to calculate) either the initial key, the calculated "overall" key, or the public key used to store it in the key-block.

Pohlig-Hellman, as used here, works like this:

- **Encryption:** $C = M^e \bmod p$

- **Re-encryption:** $C' = C^{e'} \bmod p$

- **Decryption:** First find d, the inverse of $ee'e'' \ldots \bmod p$, such that $de = 1$ mod $(p\text{-}1)$: then $M = C^d \bmod p$.

(C - ciphertext: M - message)

A k-bit "safe" $(= 2q + 1, q$ prime$)$ prime is chosen for p. p is not secret, and would normally be shared by all players in a system.

Generating suitable Pohlig-Hellman keys is simply a matter of concatenating a random number of suitable size with 1 in order to ensure the key is odd, and thus that a unique inverse of the "overall" key exists mod $\phi(p)$. This is essential for decryption. A solution to $de = 1 \bmod (p - 1)$ only exists if e and $p - 1$ are relatively prime. $p - 1$ is even for prime p, so e must be odd. q is the only odd number $< p$ which is not relatively prime to $p - 1$, and should not be used as a key, but the probability of that happening if the key is generated this way is so low that we ignore it.

The encryption key e is stored in a simple universal re-encryption block appended to the ciphertext; but we use q, not p, as the El Gamal modulus. On re-encryption we generate at random a new key e', and exponentiate the main ciphertext to that value. We also multiply the first part of the first of the El Gamal ciphertext pairs in the universal block by e', modulo q. Then we do a simple re-encryption of the El Gamal universal block, again modulo q. The value stored in the universal block is now $ee' \bmod q$.

If we know the secret El Gamal keypart, to find the relevant Pohlig-Hellman decryption key d we need to know the "overall" encryption key, which is equal to $ee' \bmod (p - 1)$, $= ee' \bmod (2q)$.

To find $ee' \bmod (2q)$ let $v = ee' \bmod q$, the value stored in the universal key block, ie $ee' = [n].q + v$ where $[n]$ is some integer (we'll use square brackets to denote integer values in this paragraph). As all the intermediate keys are odd, so ee' must be odd. If v is odd then $[n]$ is even and $ee' = [n/2].2q + v$, ie ee' mod $(2q) = v$. If v is even then $[n]$ is odd, $ee = [(n-1)/2].2q + q + v$, and ee' mod $(2q) = v + q$.

We find the modular inverse of the value of ee' mod $(2q)$, and use it to decrypt the main file.

- **Setup:** Output is p, q $(= (p\text{-}1)/2)$, g; such that p, q are prime, and g is a generator of q (or of a subgroup of q; q may be of special form, see below). p and g are usually used and held in common.

- **Key Generation:** Output is an El Gamal keypair x, y $(= g^x$ mod $q)$.

- **Encryption:** Input is a file F of f k-bit blocks; an El Gamal public key (y, g, p); a random Pohlig-Hellman key $e \in Z_p$, e mod $2 = 1$; and random k_0, $k_u \in Z_q$.

Output is a ciphertext $C = [\psi_1, \psi_2 \ldots \psi_f]; [(\alpha_0, \beta_0); (\alpha_u, \beta_u)]$
$= [F_1^e$ mod p, F_2^e mod $p \ldots F_f^e$ mod $p]; [(ey^{k_0}$ mod q, g^{k_0} mod q); $(y^{k_u}$ mod q, g^{k_u} mod $q)]$.

- **Re-encryption:** Input is a ciphertext C (or C'); a random $e' \in Z_p$, e' mod $2 = 1$; and random k'_0, $k'_u \in Z_q$.

Output is a ciphertext $C' = [\psi'_1, \psi'_2 \ldots \psi'_f]; [(\alpha'_0, \beta'_0); (\alpha'_u, \beta'_u)]$
$= [\psi_1^{e'}$ mod p, $\psi_2^{e'}$ mod $p \ldots \psi_f^{e'}$ mod $p]; [(e'\alpha_0 \alpha_u^{k'_0}$ mod q, $\beta_0 \beta_u^{k'_0}$ mod q); $(\alpha_u^{k'_u}$ mod q, $\beta_u^{k'_u}$ mod $q)]$.

- **Decryption:** Input is a ciphertext C (or C') $= [\psi_1, \psi_2 \ldots \psi_f]; [(\alpha_0, \beta_0); (\alpha_u, \beta_u)]$; and a secret key x.

If α_u / β_u^x mod $q = 1$ then calculate $E = (\alpha_1 / \beta_1^x$ mod $q)$; iff E even, $E = E + q$; find d, the inverse mod p of E.

Output is a file $F = (\psi_1^d$ mod p; ψ_2^d mod p; $\ldots \psi_f^d$ mod $p)$.

If α_u / β_u^x mod $q \neq 1$, the file is not decryptable by (or meant for) the holder of that private key.

This construction is reasonably computationally efficient, increases the ciphertext by only $4k$ bits, permits unlimited re-encryptions, and gives no information about the number of re-encryptions undergone, greatly increasing useability.

4   Some Implementation Issues

4.1   Security

The security parameter, k, is the size in bits of the primes used for the Pohlig-Hellman ($k - 1$ bit primes for the El Gamal) moduli. k should be chosen so that finding discreet logarithms and DHP is hard. Typical minimum values are 1,024 bits.

4.2   Encryption Mode

The Pohlig-Hellman cipher is presented here in what is effectively ECB mode, with all the malleability and other problems that that mode can have. These can easily be overcome with standard modes and techniques - one solution is to use OAEP [5] or its variants on the plaintext. A fast solution, as used by the author in his online SFS work, is to pre-encrypt the plaintext using a symmetric cipher in CBC mode with a random IV.

4.3   Speed

Pohlig-Hellman is much slower than a modern symmetric cipher, but with modern processors and typical bandwidths this need not be a problem. A not-highly-optimised implementation re-encrypts 1024-bit blocks with 160-bit exponents at 512 kb/s using 60-65% cpu utilisation on an Athlon 2600+.

4.4   Optimisations

There is no useful subgroup of prime order in the Pohlig-Hellman group, which means that decryption will involve exponentiation to a full k-bit exponent. However we assume that decryption will only be done once, by the recipient, and that re-encryption will be the most common operation. This is undoubtably true in a mixnet situation, and likely to be the case in all situations where re-encryption is useful.

A full-size exponentiation is not necessary for security of re-encryption. For the 1024 bit k example an exponentiation key of about 160 bits is sufficient [4].

It is eminently possible to have a subgroup of prime order in the field used for the El Gamal universal key-storage block, and this is desirable in order to speed up a potential recipient's identification of which ciphertexts are meant for him. Using a subgroup of prime order around 160 bits will give an order of magnitude performance improvement here without impact on overall security.

4.5   Semantic Security

Semantic Security of the Construction - Active Tagging Attacks. After this paper was presented we discovered two related classes of attacks on the construction, exemplified by this attack:

The exponential relationship between any two Pohlig-Hellman blocks survives re-encryption. If an adversary knows any such relationship in a "before" ciphertext, he can test to see whether the relationship exists in candidate "after" ciphertexts, and if it does he will know with near-certainty that the candidate is a re-encryption of the "before" ciphertext.

The only efficient method for an attacker to know such a relationship is if he can insert a calculated value in a block; to find such a relationship by passive inspection would require finding discreet logarithms, which we presume to be hard. The real value of all the new attacks is as active tagging attacks, and they are practical only to an active attacker.

Passive versions of all the attacks in the two new classes exist, but all require work equivalent to finding a discreet logarithm. We believe the new attacks do not affect the semantic security of the construction against passive attackers.

The particular attack mentioned can be defeated by a small modification of the construction, but it is not clear that all attacks in the two new classes can be so defeated; we are presently investigating this point.

In consequence, although secrecy is preserved, the construction must be regarded as semantically insecure in the face of an active attacker. For this reason the construction should not be used in mixnets.

Semantic Security of the Universal Re-encryption Block. For general security it is essential that the order of g mod q be large and prime. 160 bits would be a typical size when used with 1024-bit k. As an attacker can tell whether or not a candidate block is a member of the subgroup, for semantic security it is essential that only members of that subgroup be accepted - an attacker can identify whether blocks are members of that subgroup both before and after re-encryption. It is normally essential that a re-encryptor tests all blocks that are presented to him for membership of the relevant subgroup.

As the re-encrypter is going to re-encrypt the presented block unless it fails the test, and as most blocks can be expected to pass the test, it is convenient to combine the testing and re-encryption. The first 160 intermediate modular squarings will be calculated in order to do the re-encrypting modular exponentiation, and these values can also be used to calculate the value of the presented value exponentiated to the order of the subgroup. This will equal 1 iff the presented value is a member of the subgroup.

The order of the subgroup could be chosen with a low Hamming weight in order to speed up these checks. We believe that a low Hamming weight would not affect overall security, as it does not make any of the well-known attacks easier, but we would like to see more analysis before recommending it.

Semantic Security of the Pohlig-Hellman Blocks. A similar limitation applies to the plaintext encrypted in the Pohlig-Hellman blocks, but here the order of the subgroup is q. Again the re-encrypter must check that every value he is presented with is a member of the subgroup, and reject any that are not.

A full-length exponentiation would be required to calculate the presented value exponentiated to the order of the subgroup, while security would be maintained with a smaller exponent, so the method above is not so attractive when the re-encryption exponentiation is limited in size for speed. However as $p = 2q + 1$ the subgroup of order q is identical to the subgroup of quadratic residues, and the "Euclidean-like" test (e.g. [6]) for quadratic residuosity can be used to advantage.

The remaining problem is to ensure the plaintext values initially encrypted are quadratic residues mod p (QR). One method is as follows : first, choose q so that $q = 1$ mod 4. Thus $p = 3$ mod 8, and $(2/p) = -1$ (ie 2 is a quadratic non-residue mod p, or QNR). Prepend the bits 001 to the plaintext block, and test the result for QR. If it is a QR then pass to the encrypter, if a QNR then shift left before doing so. The latter has the effect of multiplying the appended plaintext by 2, and changing it into a QR (a QNR multiplied by a QNR, 2 in this case, is a QR).

On decryption, shift right if the second bit of the block is 1. Discard the first three bits.

Because the Pohlig-Hellman exponents are odd and $\neq q$ it is also possible to use the set of NQR's instead of the group of QR's.

4.6   Future Directions

While it would be computationally advantageous to replace Pohlig-Hellman with a faster symmetric cipher, no suitable well-reviewed secure fast cipher with the required properties exists, and developing one is a formidable task. Such a cipher would of necessity be a group, requiring a doubled keysize because of possible birthday and cycling attacks [7] based on the group property.

Such a cipher would potentially have other uses, in Atomic Proxy Cryptography [8], trusted parties, general re-encryption, and elsewhere, so perhaps one may be developed.

5   Conclusions

The hybrid construction presented here improves on the previous constructions, being almost optimal in size requirements and considerably more efficient computationally. It's use is somewhat limited by it's susceptibility to active tagging attacks, but the removal of public information about the number of re-encryptions undergone, the absence of limitations on the number of possible re-encryptions, and it's better efficiency make it useful in situations where the previous hybrid system was unuseable.

Acknowledgements. Discussions with Debra Cook, George Danezis, Ari Juels, John Malley, David Martin, Paul Rubin and Andrei Serjantov have improved the paper, and made me aware of other research and the accepted names for some wheels I reinvented. I thank them for their time and kindness.

References

1. P. Golle, M. Jakobsson, A. Juels and P. Syverson, "Universal Re-encryption for Mixnets". RSA conference 2004, cryptographer's track. http://citeseer.nj.nec.com/golle02universal.html
2. P. Fairbrother, "Observation-Based Attacks on Steganographic File Systems". In preparation.
3. M Hellman, M Pohlig, "Exponentiation cryptographic apparatus and method". US Patent 4,424,414 (Expired).
4. NIST. Special Publication 800-57: Recommendation for Key Management. Part 1: General Guideline. Draft, January 2003.

5. M. Bellare and P. Rogaway, "Optimal asymmetric encryption", Advances in Cryptology - Eurocrypt '94, Springer-Verlag (1994), 92-111.
6. V. Shoup, "A Computational Introduction to Number Theory and Algebra" beta3, ch.13 s.1 p274 http://shoup.net/ntb/ntb-b3.pdf
7. Burton S. Kaliski Jr,. Ronald L. Rivest, and Alan T. Sherman, "Is the Data Encryption Standard a Group?" Eurocrypt '85.
8. M. Blaze and M. Strauss, "Atomic Proxy Cryptography", Technical report 98.5.1, AT&T research laboratories, http://citeseer.nj.nec.com/blaze98atomic.html

Electromagnetic Eavesdropping Risks of Flat-Panel Displays

Markus G. Kuhn

University of Cambridge, Computer Laboratory,
15 JJ Thomson Avenue, Cambridge CB3 0FD, United Kingdom
http://www.cl.cam.ac.uk/~mgk25/

Abstract. Electromagnetic eavesdropping of computer displays – first
demonstrated to the general public by van Eck in 1985 – is not restricted
to cathode-ray tubes. Modern flat-panel displays can be at least as vulnerable. They are equally driven by repetitive video signals in frequency
ranges where even shielded cables leak detectable radio waves into the
environment. Nearby eavesdroppers can pick up such compromising emanations with directional antennas and wideband receivers. Periodic averaging can lift a clearly readable image out of the background noise. The
serial Gbit/s transmission formats used by modern digital video interfaces in effect modulate the signal, thereby making it even better suited
for remote reception than emanations from analog systems. Understanding the exact transmission format used leads to new attacks and defenses.
We can tune screen colors for optimal remote readability by eavesdroppers. We can likewise modify text-display routines to render the radio
emanations unreadable.

1 Introduction

Electronic equipment can emit unintentional signals that allow eavesdroppers
to reconstruct processed data at a distance. This has been a concern for the
design of military hardware for over half a century. Some governments handle
highly confidential information only with equipment that is especially shielded
against such compromising electromagnetic emanations. The exact "TEMPEST"
emission limits and test procedures applied in the procurement of these systems are still secret. Anecdotal evidence suggests that they are several or-
ders of magnitude stricter than, for example, civilian radio-interference
regulations.

Electromagnetic radiation as a potential computer security risk was mentioned in the open literature as early as 1967 [1]. The concept was brought to
the attention of the broader public in 1985 by van Eck [2], who showed that
the screen content of a cathode-ray tube (CRT) display can be reconstructed
at a distance using a TV set whose sync pulse generators are replaced with
manually controlled oscillators. Several more studies of the compromising video
emanations of late 1980s CRT displays appeared [3, 4, 5, 6, 7], with advice on

D. Martin and A. Serjantov (Eds.): PET 2004, LNCS 3424, pp. 88–107, 2005.

electromagnetic shielding as a countermeasure. Steganographic embedding of information into CRT emissions and the use of low-pass filtered fonts as a simple software countermeasure have been demonstrated as well [8].

Display technologies have evolved rapidly since then. Additional shielding has become standard, not only to meet stricter international electromagnetic compatibility requirements [9], but also to address health worries associated with non-ionizing radiation [10]. Pixel frequencies and video bandwidths have increased by an order of magnitude since [2, 3, 4, 5, 6, 7] and analog signal transmission is in the process of being replaced by Gbit/s digital video interfaces. Various flat-panel display (FPD) technologies are well on their way of replacing the cathode-ray tube (CRT) monitor. All these developments make it necessary to reevaluate the emission-security risks identified in the 1980s.

A new form of compromising emanations from video displays was discovered more recently. The high-frequency variations of light emitted by a CRT can carry enough information about the video signal to permit the reconstruction of readable text [11]. Under low background illumination, this is practical even after diffuse reflection from nearby surfaces. LCDs are not vulnerable to this particular risk, not only because their pixels react much slower than CRT phosphors, but also because these technologies update all pixels in a row simultaneously. This makes it impractical to separate the contribution of individual pixels in a row to the overall light emitted.

Discussions following the publication of [11] suggest that flat-panel displays are widely believed to pose no electromagnetic eavesdropping risk either. Two facts may contribute to such an assumption. Firstly, FPDs lack deflection coils, which makes them – compared to CRTs – "low radiation" devices in the frequencies below 400 kHz, where field strengths are limited by a Swedish ergonomic standard [10]. Secondly, LCDs operate with low voltages and – unlike CRTs – do not amplify the video signal by a factor of about 100 to drive a control grid that modulates an electron beam.

The experiments reported here demonstrate that some types of flat-panel display do pose a realistic eavesdropping risk. In particular, with some modern video interfaces, it is quite easy to configure the display of text in a way that maximizes the leaking signal strength. This makes emanations from these displays even easier to receive than those of modern CRTs. We begin with a brief description of video, eavesdropping and measurement technology in Sect. 2 and 3. The two case studies presented in Sect. 4 and 5 analyze the compromising radio emanations first from a laptop LCD and then from a desktop LCD that is connected to its PC graphics card with a *Digital Visual Interface (DVI)* cable. In both cases, the video cable used to connect the display panel with the graphics controller turned out to be the primary source of the leaking signal. An understanding of the digital transmission format used helped to optimize the choice of screen colors to raise or reduce the feasibility of an eavesdropping attack significantly.

2   Video Display Interfaces

Early video terminals contained the frame buffer and CRT in a single unit, avoiding the need for a user-visible video interface. With the modular PC architecture introduced by the IBM PC, displays and graphics cards turned into exchangeable components, available from multiple vendors with standardized connectors. The signalling techniques used on these interfaces were initially parallel digital interfaces. With 1, 4, and 6 TTL-level lines, respectively, the IBM PC's MDA, CGA, and EGA video controllers signalled the color of each pixel to the monitor. With the 15-pin VGA connector introduced in 1987, the dominant personal computer display interface turned to using three analog voltages (0–0.7 V), one to control each primary color.

More recently, the industry moved back to digital video signalling for two reasons. The first is related to signal quality limits. The geometry of the old 15-pin VGA connector was not designed for very-high-frequency signals. The 640×480@60Hz video mode used by the original VGA card had a pixel clock frequency of merely 25 MHz, whereas more recent high-end displays use pixel rates of 300 MHz or more. As signal wavelengths drop below typical cable lengths, the lack of a properly impedance-matched coaxial feedthrough in the VGA connector causes increased inter-pixel interference.

The second reason is the advent of flat-panel technologies, such as liquid-crystal, plasma, or organic electroluminescence displays. These devices have to sample the video signal, in order to assign to each discrete pixel on the display surface its current color via row and column access lines. They maximize contrast by buffering an entire line of the video signal, to drive all pixels in a row concurrently.

As flat-panel displays have to store video lines in digital memory, they require video information not only as binary encoded color shades, but also as a sequence of discrete pixel values. All recent digital interface standards therefore include a pixel clock line, avoiding the reconstruction of the pixel clock signal that has to be performed in FPDs with VGA input.

Current flat-panel displays buffer digitally only a few pixel rows. The entire image is still stored only in the frame buffer of the video controller. Modern flat-panel video interfaces therefore still have to continuously refresh the entire image content between 60 and 85 times per second, just as with CRTs. This continuous refresh ensures that the signals on the video interface are periodic, at least between changes in the displayed information. A periodic signal has a frequency spectrum that consists of narrow lines spaced by the repetition frequency. A receiver can attenuate all other spectral content by periodic averaging with the exact same repetition frequency.

3   Eavesdropping Instrumentation

Any signal carried by a conductor can, at least in principle, be eavesdropped electromagnetically, by simply connecting a nearby antenna to an amplifier and recording device, for example a digital storage oscilloscope. While this approach can be useful in attempts to record a waveform in the largest possible bandwidth, it is in practice not feasible, unless the signal is strong, or the experiment is performed with very low background noise. Outside special shielded chambers, waveforms picked up by antennas will be dominated by the many radio broadcast services that populate the spectrum from below 10 kHz to above 10 GHz, not to mention numerous other sources of radio noise.

An eavesdropper of compromising emanations, therefore, must selectively amplify only those parts of the radio spectrum that provide the best signal-to-noise ratio. Unlike radio transmissions, most compromising RF emanations are baseband signals, that is, they are not modulated with a carrier frequency to shift them into a narrow and reserved frequency slot of the radio spectrum. However, digital signals consist of discrete symbols (bits, pixels, etc.) transmitted at some rate f. From the sampling theorem we know that the frequency spectrum up to $f/2$ contains already all information carried by the signal. If the individual symbols have spectral energy beyond that frequency, for example because they contain sharp edges with a raise time much shorter than the bit or pixel duration, then the information in the signal will be repeated in several $f/2$ wide bands at higher harmonic frequencies. It is therefore sufficient for an eavesdropper to find any frequency range with good signal-to-noise ratio that is merely at least half as wide as the bit or pixel rate.

The frequency range with the best signal-to-noise ratio depends equally on the targeted device and on the background noise, both of which can vary significantly with the device, video mode and location. Building good analog bandpass RF filters that can be adjusted over a wide range of frequencies is not easy. A more practical approach than direct filtering is the use of a superheterodyne AM receiver that multiplies the input signal with a sine wave of adjustable frequency to shift the frequency band of interest to a fixed intermediate frequency where it can then be filtered easily to the required bandwidth. The subsequent rectification and low-pass filtering in the AM demodulator will destroy some phase information and with it valuable information, such as the difference between positive and negative edges in the eavesdropped signal. But it will also lead to a much lower frequency signal that can be digitized comfortably with a sampling rate of not much more than twice the bandwidth.

The particular receiver used to acquire the example images shown in this paper was a *Dynamic Sciences R1250*, an instrument that was specifically designed to meet the (confidential) requirements of the "TEMPEST" measurement standard NACSIM 5100A. Its center frequency can be tuned from 100 Hz to 1 GHz and it offers intermediate-frequency (IF) filters with bandwidths ranging from 50 Hz to 200 MHz. The length of the shortest impulse that can be recognized at a receiver output is the inverse of the IF filter bandwidth, which therefore has to be comparable to the pixel clock frequency of modern displays. Most other commercially available AM radio receivers (including TV tuners) are not designed for bandwidths larger than about 8 MHz. Another important feature of the R1250 is that its automatic gain control can be disabled. This makes it possible to compare the amplitude of any input signal with that of a reference sine-wave generator. This way, it was possible to provide an antenna input voltage scale for all the received video images shown here. The output of the AM receiver was for adjustment purposes displayed in real-time on a normal computer monitor, whose sync lines were driven by a programmable arbitrary-waveform generator, to reproduce the line and frame rate of the targeted display. Special care was necessary to set up the sync-pulse generators such that the refresh rate they generated was adjustable to match that of the targeted display with less than 10^{-7} relative error, which is smaller than the stability and sometimes even resolution of many standard function generators.

The images shown in this paper were recorded with a digital storage oscilloscope (8-bit resolution, 16 MB acquisition memory, up to 1 GHz sampling frequency) directly from the output of the AM demodulator and converted with specially written software into raster images. The antenna used was a log-periodical broadband antenna designed for a frequency range of 200–1000 MHz, as it is commonly used for electromagnetic compatibility measurements. All recordings were performed without any shielding in a normal modern office building in a semi-urban environment with over a hundred other computers operating in the same building. Further details about the instrumentation are given in [18].

4   Case Study: Laptop Display

Figure 1 shows an amplitude-demodulated and rastered signal as it was received from the first example target, a Toshiba Satellite Pro 440CDX laptop that shows a Linux boot screen in an 800×600@75Hz video mode. The antenna was located at 3 m distance in the same room as the target device. A quick scan through different frequencies in the 50–1000 MHz range showed that setting the AM receiver to a center frequency of 350 MHz and an intermediate-frequency bandwidth of 50 MHz gave one of the clearest signals. The image shown is the average of 16 recorded frames, in order to reduce noise. For comparison, the lower right corner shows one of these frames without any averaging. Even there, readable text stands out clearly from the background noise. The frames were recorded with a sampling frequency of 250 MHz.

A number of observations distinguish the signal seen Fig. 1 from those typical for CRTs:

- The low-frequency components of the video signal are not attenuated. Horizontal bright lines appear in the reconstructed signal as horizontal lines and not just as a pair of switching pulses at the end points, as would be the case with CRTs.
- Font glyphs appear to have lost half of their horizontal resolution, but are still readable.
- In the 800×600@75Hz video mode used, the clearest signal can be obtained at a center frequency of about 350 MHz with 50 MHz bandwidth, but weaker signals are also present at higher and lower frequencies, in particular after every step of 25 MHz.

350 MHz center frequency, 50 MHz bandwidth, 16 (1) frames averaged, 3 m distance

magnified image section

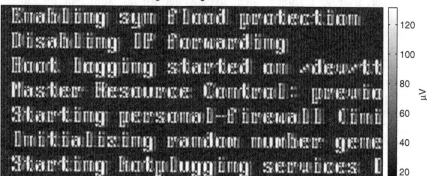

Fig. 1. Eavesdropped Linux boot screen visible on the LCD of a Toshiba 440CDX laptop (log-periodic antenna, vertical polarization)

- The mapping between displayed colors and the amplitude of the signal received for a pixel turned out to be highly non-monotonic. A simply gray-bar image resulted in a complex barcode like display, as if the generated signal amplitude were somehow related to the binary representation of the pixel value.
- Using a simple improvised near-field probe (a coaxial cable whose ends are shaped into a 50 mm dipole) instead of an antenna, to scan the immediate vicinity of the laptop, it became clear that no significant emissions came from the display module itself, but that the source appeared to be the interconnect cable between the LCD module and the mainboard.

A closer examination of the laptop reveals a digital video link as the origin of these emanations. The display module (Sharp LM12S029 FSTN) used in this laptop is connected to the video controller via eight twisted pairs, each about 30 cm long. They originate on the mainboard in two integrated parallel-to-serial converters and LVDS transmitter chips designed for linking to flat-panel displays (NEC DS90CF581 [12]). The 18-bit color data that the video controller provides for each pixel on its parallel output port has to be serialized into fewer lines, to fit through the hinges, which is exactly the task that these two "FPD-Link" chips perform. They multiply the clock signal supplied from the video controller by seven, and each transmits per clock cycle on three twisted-pair channels $3 \times 7 = 21$ data bits, which consist here of 18 data bits for the pixel color and three bits for horizontal sync, vertical sync and a control signal. The fourth pair carries the clock.

The video controller outputs 50 million pixels per second. However, since it transmits the data for two consecutive pixels simultaneously over two independently operating FPD-Link chips, each of these receives a clock frequency of only 25 MHz, which it multiplies to a data rate of 175 MHz, resulting in an overall data rate of 1.05 Gbit/s transmitted on all six channels through the hinges.

LVDS (low voltage differential signaling [13]) is a generic interface standard for high-speed data transmission (up to 655 Mbit/s). It uses symmetric twisted transmission lines and was designed to minimize RF interference.

However, as Fig. 1 shows, such precautions are not sufficient for emission security. The approximately 100 μV amplitude that the log-periodic antenna receives for the BIOS default colors used in this screen at 3 m distance corresponds to a field strength of 57 dBμV/m (50 MHz bandwidth) and an equivalent isotropic radiating power would be about 150 nW.

A signal of this amplitude is strong enough to permit a simple and realistic eavesdropping demonstration across several rooms. In the next experiment, the same laptop and antenna are located about 10 m apart in different office rooms, separated by two other offices and three 105 mm thick plaster-board walls.

In this setup 12 consecutive frames were acquired with a sampling rate of 50 MHz in one single recording of 160 ms (eight million samples). The exact frame rate necessary for correctly aligned averaging was determined with the necessary precision of at least seven digits from the exact distance of the first and last of the recorded frames. It was determined with an algorithm that calculated starting from a crude estimate of the frame rate the cross-correlation of these two frames, and then corrected the estimate based on the position of the largest peak found there (Fig. 2). (The process is not fully automatic, as due to other video signals in the vicinity, echos, and multiple peaks, it can sometimes be necessary to manually chose an alternative peak.)

Figure 3 shows the result, an easily readable view of an `xterm` window that shows some test text. The received signal amplitude of about 12 μV corresponds with this antenna to a field strength of 39 dBμV/m. This drop by 18 dB compared to the 57 dBμV/m in the previous 3 m line-of-sight measurement can in part be attributed to the 10 dB free-space loss to be expected when tripling the

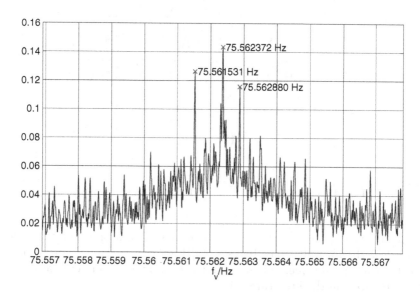

Fig. 2. Determination of the frame rate f_v for the multi-frame signal recorded in Fig. 3 through crosscorrelation between the first and last frame in the recorded series

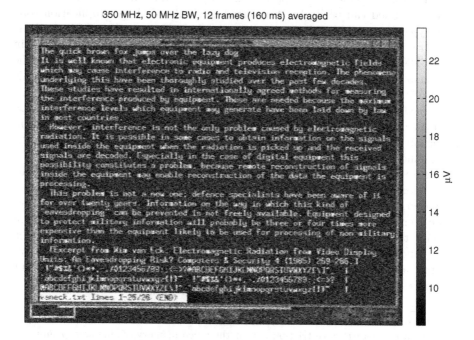

Fig. 3. Text signal received from a 440CDX laptop at 10 m distance through two intermediate offices (3 plasterboard walls)

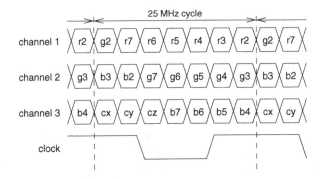

Fig. 4. Bit assignment in the FPD-Link transmission cycle

distance between emitter and antenna. The remaining drop suggests that each of the plasterboard walls contributes 2–3 dB additional attenuation, which appears to be a typical value, judging from the UHF building-material attenuation values described in the literature [14].

In order to better understand the relationship between the signal displayed on the target device and that seen on the rastered output of an AM receiver, it is worth having a closer look at the exact transmission format. The details are very specific to the particular product targeted here, but the principles explained can easily be transferred to similar designs. Application software typically provides the display driver with 24-bit color descriptions of the form $(r_7 \ldots r_0, g_7 \ldots g_0, b_7 \ldots b_0)$. Figure 4 shows, how these bits are packed in a 440CDX laptop into the pixel cycle of three FPD-Link channels[1]. One of the FPD-Link chips transmits all pixels in odd-numbered columns, the other one the pixels in even-numbered columns.

Armed with an understanding of what choice of colors elicits which waveform from the channel drivers, we can now experiment with various combinations, in particular those that promise to maximize or minimize the contrast between the foreground and background of text in the emitted signal.

Figure 5 shows a test text in various color combinations, together with the corresponding RGB values specified by the application program and the resulting bit patterns on the three transmission channels. Line 1 is simply the black-on-white combination commonly used in word processing software. Line 2 is an attempt to find the signal with the largest number of bit transitions in the foreground and the smallest number in the background, in order to maximize contrast and readability for the eavesdropper. Line 3 attempts the same, but maximizes the visible contrast in favor of having identical signal polarity on

---

[1] Being an 18-bit per pixel interface, the two least significant bits of each byte are not represented. A further restriction is that the video memory of this laptop supports the 800×600@75Hz video mode only with a 16 bits per pixel encoding (5 red, 6 green, 5 blue), in which the video controller hardware fills in the values $r_2 = r_7 \wedge \ldots \wedge r_3$ and $b_2 = b_7 \wedge \ldots \wedge b_3$ automatically.

line	description	foreground		background	
		RGB	signal	RGB	signal
1	black on white	00 00 00	000000x 0x00000 xxx0000	ff ff ff	111111X 1X11111 xxx1111
2	maximum contrast	a8 50 a0	010101x 0x01010 xxx1010	00 00 00	000000x 0x00000 xxx0000
3	maximum contrast (gray)	a8 a8 a8	010101x 1x10101 xxx1010	00 00 00	000000x 0x00000 xxx0000
4	minimum contrast	78 00 00	001111x 0x00000 xxx0000	00 f0 00	000000x 0x11110 xxx0000
5	minimum contrast	78 60 00	001111x 0x01100 xxx0000	30 f0 00	000110x 0x11110 xxx0000
6	minimum contrast (phase shift)	70 70 00	001110x 0x01110 xxx0000	38 e0 00	000111x 0x11100 xxx0000
7	text in most significant bit, rest random	—	r1rrrrx rx1rrrr xxx1rrr	—	r0rrrrx rx0rrrr xxx0rrr
8	text in green two msb, rest random	—	rrrrrrx rx11rrr xxxrrrr	—	rrrrrrx rx00rrr xxxrrrr
9	text in green msb, rest random	—	rrrrrrx rx1rrrr xxxrrrr	—	rrrrrrx rx0rrrr xxxrrrr

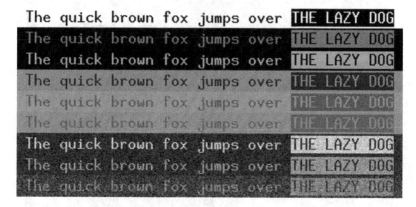

Fig. 5. Test text to compare the emission characteristics of selected foreground and background color combinations

all three lines for the foreground pixels. (In a symmetric transmission channel, signal polarity should in principle not make a difference for an eavesdropper.)

Line 4 is a first attempt to find a combination of two colors whose radio signature is difficult to distinguish under the assumption that the eavesdropper can evaluate only the total number of bit transitions that happen on all channels together. The idea is to let bit transitions always happen at the same time during the cycle, but in different channels.

Line 5 is a variant that keeps even the total number of transitions in each line constant and line 6 keeps in addition the length of positive pulses constant and encodes the difference between foreground and background color only as a one-bit phase shift in two of the channels.

The last three lines finally demonstrate what happens if most of the bits are filled randomly, in order to jam the eavesdropper's periodic averaging process with a meaningless signal of exactly the same period. This jamming should be particularly effective if the neighbor bits of each data carrying bit are selected

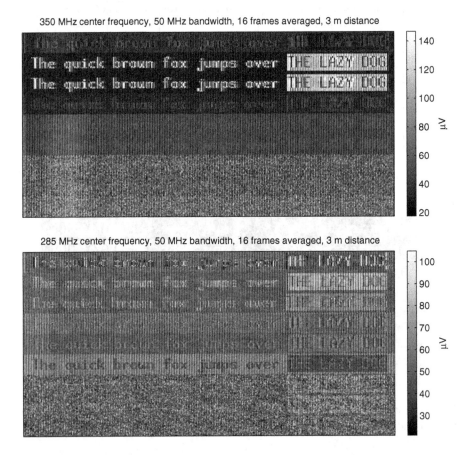

Fig. 6. Signals received from the test display in Fig. 5

randomly, as this will randomize whether the data bit will contribute a transition pulse to the compromising emanations or not.

Figure 6 shows the signal received with 50 MHz bandwidth at two frequencies. The first at 350 MHz is the one where the maximum-contrast colors in lines 2 and 3 offer the strongest signal. They result in a $175/2 = 87.5$ MHz square wave, but this particular frequency and its first harmonic collide in Cambridge with signals from local broadcasting stations. 350 MHz is one of the first harmonics in a quieter band, and a $\lambda/4$ monopole for that frequency is with 40 cm also quite close to the length of the twisted pair, leading to more efficient far-field emissions. In this band, the maximum bit-transition patterns in lines 2 and 3 generate field levels of 59 dBμV/m at 3 m (240 nW EIRP). The black-on-white text in line 1 causes a significantly weaker signal, because only a single bit transition is generated in each channel by a transition between full black and white levels (except for the blue channel which also contains control bits).

The first attempt at finding a protective color combination in line four is not fully effective, which suggests that edges in different transmission lines cause noticeably different electromagnetic pulses and can therefore be distinguished. This could be caused either by tolerances in LVDS driver parameters or by impedance differences between conductor pairs. Lines 5 and 6, which use a constant number of bit transitions in each channel and vary only their relative phases, provide the eavesdropper at this frequency band practically no usable contrast, as do all the test lines in which random-bit jamming is applied.

Even though a 50 MHz wide band captures enough information to resolve horizontally pixel pairs accurately, it does not quite cover the entire $175/2 = 87.5$ MHz wide spectrum that contains (according to the sampling theorem) the full information present in the 175 Mbit/s bitstream. Tuning to a different center frequency provides a different extract of the entire signal to the demodulator, effectively applying a different filter to the video signal. The bottom half of Fig. 6 shows one center frequency (285 MHz), where the low-contrast color combinations suddenly become readable.

We can conclude that the only effective software protection technique against compromising emanations of FPD-Links, as used in numerous laptops, appears to be the addition of random bits to the color combinations used for text display. When implementing such a technique, it is critical to understand that these random bits must be randomly selected each time a new character is placed on the screen.

If the random bits were selected, for example, in a glyph rendering routine that is connected to a glyph cache, to ensure that an already generated bitmap is reused whenever the same character is used multiple times on the screen, then this merely assists the eavesdropper. If the addition of random bits were done identically at each location where a glyph is used, then the random bits merely increased the values in a glyph-signal distance matrix, which would only reduce the error probability during automatic radio character recognition.

5   Case Study: Digital Visual Interface

The NEC FPD-Link interface technology appears to be mainly used in embedded display systems, such as laptops. For connecting flat-panel displays to desktop computers, three other interface standards that define connector plugs have been defined: VESA Plug & Display (P&D) [15], VESA Digital Flat Panel (DFP) [16], and Digital Visual Interface (DVI) [17].

These three standard connectors differ only in auxiliary interfaces (USB, IEEE 1394, VGA) that are carried on the same cable, but that are not relevant here. All three interfaces use, in mutually compatible ways, a digital video transmission technology called *Transition Minimized Differential Signaling (TMDS)*, also known as *PanelLink*, developed by Silicon Image Inc.

A TMDS link consists of three channels, similar to the FPD-Link system described in the previous section. Each is formed by a symmetric twisted-line pair and carries 8-bit values for one of the three primary colors. A fourth twisted-pair channel provides a byte clock for synchronization.

What distinguishes TMDS most from FPD-Link is the encoding used. Each 8-bit value transmitted over a channel is first expanded into a 10-bit word. The encoding process consists of two steps, each of which has one of two options to change the eight data bits, and each signals its choice to the receiver by appending another bit.

In the first step, the number of "one" bits in the 8-bit data value $d_7 d_6 \ldots d_0$ is counted. A new 9-bit value q is generated by setting $q_0 = d_0$ and

$$q_i = q_{i-1} \oplus d_i \qquad \text{for } 1 \leq i \leq 7$$
$$q_8 = 1$$

if there are more zeros in d ($\oplus$ is *exclusive or*), and

$$q_i = \neg q_{i-1} \oplus d_i \qquad \text{for } 1 \leq i \leq 7$$
$$q_8 = 0$$

if there are more ones in d. In case of four zeros and ones each, only d_0 is counted.

In the second step, either the bits $q_7 q_6 \ldots q_0$ are all inverted and $q_9 = 1$ is added, or all bits remain as they are and $q_9 = 0$ is added instead. The decision is made by taking into account how many "zero" and "one" bits have been transmitted so far and the choice is made that leads to a more equal count.

The first step aims at reducing the maximum number of bit transitions that can occur per value on the channel, as the following examples illustrate (d_0 and q_0 are at the right end, respectively):

$$10101010 \longrightarrow 0\,11001100, \qquad 01010101 \longrightarrow 1\,00110011,$$
$$00000000 \longrightarrow 1\,00000000, \qquad 11111111 \longrightarrow 0\,11111111.$$

While an 8-bit word can contain up to eight bit transitions, after this recoding, only a maximum of five transitions is possible in any of the resulting 9-bit words (including one transition between consecutive words). This is, because the less frequent bit can only appear up to four times in a byte, and each presence of it is signalled by a transition in the generated 9-bit word.

The purpose of the second step is to limit the difference between the total number of "zero" and "one" bits. This keeps the signaling scheme DC balanced, which simplifies the use of transformers for galvanic separation of transmitter and receiver. For an exact description of the encoding algorithm see [17–p. 29].

The following examples show how in the full encoding the DC-balancing mechanism adds longer repetition cycles to sequences of identical bytes. The binary words are this time shown in Littleendian order (q_0 and d_0 at the left end), in order to match transmission order, which is least significant bit first. For example, encoding a sequence of zero bytes leads to a cycle of nine 10-bit words, whereas for the byte 255, the cycle length is only seven:

$$00000000, 00000000, 00000000, 00000000, 00000000, \ldots \longrightarrow$$
$$0000000010, 1111111111, 0000000010, 1111111111, 0000000010$$
$$1111111111, 0000000010, 1111111111, 0000000010,$$
$$0000000010, 1111111111, 0000000010, 1111111111, 0000000010$$
$$1111111111, 0000000010, 1111111111, 0000000010,$$
$$\ldots$$
$$11111111, 11111111, 11111111, 11111111, 11111111, \ldots \longrightarrow$$
$$0000000001, 1111111100, 1111111100, 0000000001, 1111111100$$
$$0000000001, 1111111100$$
$$0000000001, 1111111100, 1111111100, 0000000001, 1111111100$$
$$0000000001, 1111111100$$
$$\ldots$$

To find a color combination that provides the best possible eavesdropping reception of TMDS encoded video signals, we can try to look for one with as many bit transitions as possible in one color and as few as possible in the other. A second consideration is that the extended cycles added by the DC-balancing algorithm might reduce readability and that it is therefore desirable to find maximum contrast bytes with a cycle length of one. This can only be achieved if the resulting 10-bit words do not affect the difference in the bit balance counter maintained by the DC-balancing algorithm. In other words, the 10-bit words selected should contain exactly five "one" bits, and there exist 52 byte values that will be encoded in such a DC balanced TMDS word.

For example, the bytes hexadecimal 10 and 55 fulfil these criteria:

$$00001000, 00001000, \ldots \longrightarrow 0000111110, 0000111110, \ldots$$
$$10101010, 10101010, \ldots \longrightarrow 1100110010, 1100110010, \ldots$$

These TMDS bit patterns will be used irrespective of the previous bit balance, because the full encoding algorithm specified in [17–p. 29] contains a special case.

line	description	foreground RGB	background RGB
1	black on white	00 00 00	ff ff ff
2	maximum bit transition contrast	00 00 00	aa aa aa
3	half bit transition contrast	00 00 00	cc cc cc
4	balanced word, max contrast	10 10 10	55 55 55
5	minimum signal contrast	ff 00 00	00 ff 00
6	low nybble random	0r 0r 0r	fr fr fr
7	text in msb, rest random	—	—
8	text in green two msb, rest random	—	—
9	text in green msb, rest random	—	—

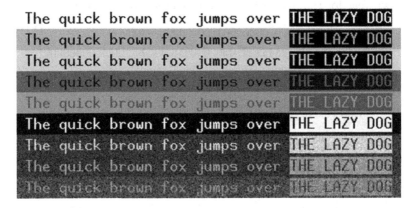

Fig. 7. Test image for text contrast in compromising emanations from DVI cables

It sets $q_9 = \neg q_8$ whenever the rest of q contains exactly four "zero" and four "one" bits, which is the case here. The encoding of any pixels encoded with one of the 52 balanced words will therefore remain unaffected by any other screen content.

Figure 7 shows a number of different foreground/background color combinations, including the black-on-white text in line 1 and two naïve approaches to obtain maximum reception contrast in lines 2 and 3. The color combination for high-contrast reception just suggested is used in line 4, and the rest represents a number of attempts to find minimum contrast signals and to add random bits for jamming.

Figure 8 shows the signals received from a DVI display system that shows the test display of Fig. 7. The graphics card in this setup was an "ATI Rage Fury Pro" and the display a "Samsung SyncMaster 170T". The 1280×1024@60Hz video mode used in this setup has a pixel clock frequency of 108 MHz.

While an excellent signal can be obtained with the 55/10 color combination, other color combinations, including black/white are either considerably weaker or provide a noticeable reception contrast only on a different frequency. The tran-

324 MHz center frequency, 50 MHz bandwidth, 5 frames averaged, 3 m distance

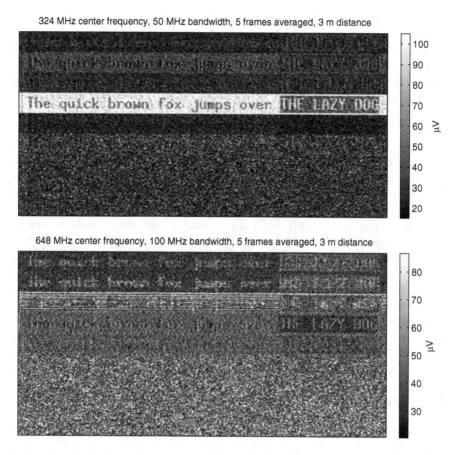

648 MHz center frequency, 100 MHz bandwidth, 5 frames averaged, 3 m distance

Fig. 8. Received emanation in two frequency bands from a DVI cable transmitting the text image of Fig. 7

sitions and DC-balancing cycles added by the TMDS encoding are not sufficient to make emanations from DVI cables entirely unreadable, but the signal quality is noticeably degraded compared to simpler transmission formats. In particular, thanks to the TMDS encoding, a much smaller number of least-significant random bits added for jamming already is sufficient to eliminate even weakest traces of the displayed text in the received signal.

An additional property of the TMDS encoding that might be of use for a radio-frequency eavesdropper is that during blanking intervals, four special 10-bit words 0010101011, 1101010100, 0010101010 and 1101010101 represent the four possible combinations of the horizontal and vertical sync signals. These words contain eight bit transitions each and can this way be distinguished from any normal color.

It might be worth noting that the DVI standard is prepared for two optional extensions that, even though not intended for this purpose, might also be of use for reducing emanation security concerns. The first is *selective refresh*, a mode of operation in which the display has its own frame buffer and refreshes the display with the desired frequency, without overloading the transmission capacity of the DVI link. The DVI link can then operate at a lower speed and might even become active only when data in the display's frame buffer needs to be updated. The absence of a continuous periodic signal would be likely to make radio-frequency eavesdropping on the interface cable impractical.

The second option under development is *High-bandwidth Digital Content Protection (DVI/HDCP)*, an encryption and key negotiation layer designed to be used over the DVI interface between digital video players and television sets. Intended to prevent unauthorized copying of uncompressed video signals by placing the decryption step into the display device, it would also render interface cable emanations unreadable.

Even a cryptographically weak key exchange protocol is likely to provide sufficient protection against a passive compromising-emanations eavesdropper, who can see the communication only in a noisy and restricted form. In the presence of significant noise, a computationally secure key negotiation scheme can be built using simple anti-redundancy techniques. One party sends out a several thousand bits long random string R. Both sides then use a hash $h(R)$ as the session key to encrypt the remaining communication. Even a moderate amount of bit errors in an eavesdropped copy of R will make it computationally infeasible to find from that the key $h(R)$.

6   Conclusions

The eavesdropping risk of flat-panel displays connected via Gbit/s digital interfaces to their video controller is at least comparable to that of CRTs. Their serial transmission formats effectively modulate the video signal in ways which provide eavesdroppers with even better reception quality. A detailed understanding of the encoding algorithms and bit arrangement used in digital video links allows programmers fine-grained control over the emitted signal. In a simple serial transmission system, like NEC's FPD-Link, the strongest signal can be obtained by choosing colors that result in alternating bits on the transmission line. In interfaces involving TMDS encoding, only a careful analysis of the encoding algorithm leads to a maximum contrast color combination. Using colors that result in bit-balanced code words prevents a state change in the encoder. This avoids distortions to the transmitted signal and can be used to improve the quality of intentional emissions. Combinations of foreground and background colors can be selected to reduce the readability of text in the compromising emanations. Much better protection can be achieved by randomizing the less-significant bits of the transmitted RGB values. This emits a jamming signal that cannot be eliminated via periodic averaging, because it has exactly the same period as the text signal.

References

1. Harold Joseph Highland: Electromagnetic Radiation Revisited. Computers & Security, Vol. 5, pp. 85–93 and 181–184, 1986.
2. Wim van Eck: Electromagnetic Radiation from Video Display Units: An Eavesdropping Risk? Computers & Security, Vol. 4, pp. 269–286, 1985.
3. Anton Kohling: TEMPEST – eine Einführung und Übersicht zu kompromittierenden Aussendungen, einem Teilaspekt der Informationssicherheit [TEMPEST – an introduction and overview on compromising emanations, one aspect of information security]. In H.R. Schmeer (ed.): Elektromagnetische Verträglichkeit/EMV'92, Stuttgart, February 1992, pp. 97–104, VDE-Verlag, Berlin, ISBN 3-8007-1808-1.
4. Erhard Möller, Lutz Bernstein, Ferdinand Kolberg: Schutzmaßnahmen gegen kompromittierende elektromagnetische Emissionen von Bildschirmsichtgeräten [Protective measures against compromising electromagnetic emissions of video displays]. 1. Internationale Fachmesse und Kongreß für Datensicherheit (Datasafe '90), Karlsruhe, Germany, November 1990.
5. Gerd Schmidt, Michael Festerling: Entstehung, Nachweis und Vermeidung kompromittierender Strahlung [Origin, detection and avoidance of compromising radiation]. MessComp '92, 6. Kongreßmesse für die industrielle Meßtechnik, Wiesbaden, 7–9 September 1992.
6. Sicurezza Elettromagnetica nella Protezione dell'Informazione, ATTI SEPI'88, Rome, Italy, 24–25 November 1988, Fondazione Ugo Bordoni.
7. Symposium on Electromagnetic Security for Information Protection, SEPI'91, Proceedings, Rome, Italy, 21–22 November 1991, Fondazione Ugo Bordoni.
8. Markus G. Kuhn, Ross J. Anderson: Soft Tempest: Hidden Data Transmission Using Electromagnetic Emanations. Information Hiding, IH'98, Portland, Oregon, 15–17 April 1998, Proceedings, LNCS 1525, Springer-Verlag, pp. 124–142.
9. Information technology equipment – Radio disturbance characteristics – Limits and methods of measurement. CISPR 22, International Electrotechnical Commission (IEC), Geneva, 1997.
10. TCO'99 – Mandatory and recommended requirements for CRT-type Visual Display Units (VDUs). Swedish Confederation of Professional Employees (TCO), 1999. http://www.tcodevelopment.com/
11. Markus G. Kuhn: Optical Time-Domain Eavesdropping Risks of CRT Displays. Proceedings 2002 IEEE Symposium on Security and Privacy, Berkeley, California, 12–15 May 2002, IEEE Computer Society, pp. 3–18, ISBN 0-7695-1543-6.
12. LVDS Transmitter 24-Bit Color Flat Panel Display (FPD) Link, National Semiconductor Cooperation, 1998. http://www.national.com/pf/DS/DS90CF581.html
13. Electrical characteristics of low voltage differential signaling (LVDS) interface circuits, ANSI/TIA/EIA-644, Electronic Industries Alliance, 1996.
14. Homayoun Hashemi: The Indoor Radio Propagation Channel. Proceedings of the IEEE, Vol. 81, No. 7, July 1993, pp. 943–968.
15. VESA Plug and Display Standard. Version 1, Video Electronics Standards Association, 11 June 1997.
16. VESA Digital Flat Panel (DFP). Version 1, Video Electronics Standards Association, 14 February 1999.
17. Digital Visual Interface – DVI. Revision 1.0, Digital Display Working Group, April 1999. http://www.ddwg.org/
18. Markus G. Kuhn: Compromising emanations: eavesdropping risks of computer displays. Technical Report UCAM-CL-TR-577, University of Cambridge, Computer Laboratory, December 2003.

A   Spectral Analysis of TMDS Signals

Fourier theory and the convolution theorem can be used to explain the spectral composition of the signal on a TMDS channel in the example from Sect. 5. Let the function t_{55} denote the waveform that we obtain if we repeat the 10-bit word representing the byte value hexadecimal 55 with 108 MHz. The Fourier transform $\mathcal{F}\{t_{55}\}$ is a line spectrum with lines at 108 MHz, 216 MHz, 324 MHz, ..., 972 MHz. Let v be a binary video signal with a pixel frequency of 108 MHz, which equals 1 during bright pixels and 0 while a dark pixel is transmitted. So if we transmit bright pixels as the value 55 and dark pixels as a value 10, the resulting waveform is

$$w = v \cdot t_{55} + (1 - v) \cdot t_{10} = v \cdot (t_{55} - t_{10}) + t_{10} \ . \tag{1}$$

Multiplication in the time domain corresponds to convolution in the frequency domain, hence we end up for the waveform transmitted on the TMDS channel

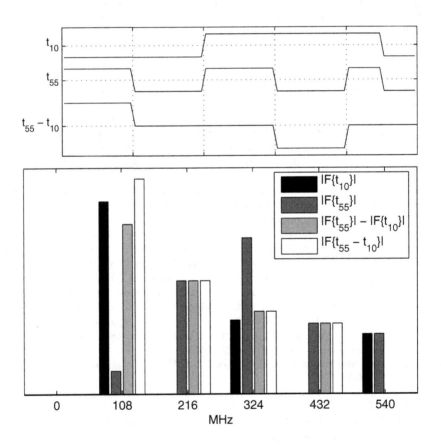

Fig. 9. Time and frequency domain representation of the TMDS-encoded maximum contrast byte combination hexadecimal 10 and 55 as well as their difference signal

with the spectrum

$$W = V * \mathcal{F}\{t_{55} - t_{10}\} + \mathcal{F}\{t_{10}\} \ . \tag{2}$$

In other words, the spectrum of the pixel-value waveform V will be copied in W centered around each of the spectral lines of the Fourier transform of the difference between the two data words. The signal intensity of the various frequency-shifted incarnations of V depends on the amplitude of the respective spectral lines of $\mathcal{F}\{t_{55} - t_{10}\}$. Figure 9 illustrates the relative intensity of the spectral lines of $|\mathcal{F}\{t_{10}\}|$, $|\mathcal{F}\{t_{55}\}|$, and $|\mathcal{F}\{t_{55} - t_{10}\}|$. It also shows the line spectrum $|\mathcal{F}\{t_{55}\}| - |\mathcal{F}\{t_{10}\}|$, which better approximates the contrast that an AM demodulating receiver can see, as it discards phase information received. Since w is a discretely sampled waveform, its spectrum will be copied at all multiples of the sampling frequency (1.08 GHz here), attenuated by the spectrum of a single bit pulse.

The center frequency of 324 MHz used in Figure 8 is not the strongest line in the spectrum of $|\mathcal{F}\{t_{55}\}| - |\mathcal{F}\{t_{10}\}|$, but it was the strongest located in a quieter part of the background-noise spectrum during this measurement. It still results in a signal strength in the order of 100 μV at the receiver input, comparable to what was measured earlier in Sect. 4 for the laptop.

On the Anonymity of Banknotes

Dennis Kügler

Federal Office for Information Security,
Godesberger Allee 185-189,
53175 Bonn, Germany
Dennis.Kuegler@bsi.bund.de

Abstract In this paper we analyze the anonymity of banknote based payments. We show how to model intermediary-chains and present statistical methods that can be used by banks to extract information on the length of the chain from deposited banknotes. If the bank has discovered a chain of length zero, the anonymity of the payment is immediately revoked. To protect against such deanonymizations, customers have to be very careful when spending banknotes.

1 Introduction

Banknotes are clearly considered as an anonymous payment system. But as every banknote is uniquely identified by a serial number printed on the banknote itself, they are actually non-anonymous. Nevertheless, tracking banknotes is claimed to be difficult, because handing on banknotes from person to person is unobservable in general.

First worries that in the forseeable future banknotes probably may no longer provide a sufficient degree of anonymity were given by Juels and Pappu [JP03]. Their concerns are based on the rumors that the next generation of Euro banknotes will be equipped with an additional RFID chip [Yos01]. Serial numbers of such RFID-enabled banknotes can be read out at some distance without optical contact.

In this paper we will focus on another banknote related but different and potentially more dangerous threat to privacy: The anonymity of ordinary banknote based payments with respect to the bank. We will show that in principle banks can observe spending habits of their customers. We like to make absolutely clear that our attack does *not* require RFID-enabled banknotes. The only assumption we make is that banks store the serial numbers of withdrawn and deposited banknotes along with the identity of the withdrawer and depositor, respectively, in a common database. As we will show later, law enforcement will benefit from such a database. Therefore, we claim that the existence of such a database is not too unrealistic.

Processing serial numbers is possible with both conventional banknotes using optical character recognition and RFID-enabled banknotes. Using optical character recognition to read the banknotes' serial numbers is common practice

D. Martin and A. Serjantov (Eds.): PET 2004, LNCS 3424, pp. 108–120, 2005.

today as this is required for criminal investigation to detect blacklisted banknotes. However, with RFID-enabled banknotes processing serial numbers will be simplified even more.

The straightforward application of such a database is to deanonymize payments where high denominated banknotes have been used. As it is unlikely that a merchant returns a high denominated banknote as change to another customer, with high probability this banknote will be deposited immediately. Therefore, the withdrawer is exposed by a simple database lookup.

We do not think that the deanonymization of high value payments is a big threat to privacy, as such payments need not or even must not be anonymous at all. Preserving anonymity is most important for low value payments. The goal of this paper is to show that statistical methods can be used by banks to revoke the anonymity of some low value payments. To preserve the privacy of customers, we propose some very simple methods to prevent such deanonymizations. As a minor note, we also show that the same statistical methods can be used by collaborating merchants to link several payments.

The remainder is structured as follows. The next section explains the role of banknote serial numbers in criminal investigation. Then in Section 3 we model intermediary-chains and show some similarities to MIX networks. This model is the foundation for Section 4, which presents statistical methods to deanonymize payments. The deanonymization mechanism is discussed and some countermeasures are sketched in Section 5. Finally, we conclude our paper in Section 6.

2   Investigating Crimes

It is a well known fact that anonymous payments can be misused by criminals. Therefore, it is necessary for law enforcement to be able to restrict the anonymity of some payments. Two types of anonymity are distinguished, which can both be abused by criminals:

Withdrawer Anonymity: The withdrawer does not want the bank to know where the withdrawn banknotes have been spent. Withdrawer anonymity can be abused for blackmailing, bankrobberies, and money theft.

Depositor Anonymity: The depositor does not want the bank to know from where the deposited banknotes have been received. Depositor anonymity can be abused for money laundering, which also includes tax evasion, drug trafficking etc.

Both types of anonymity are related as they require intermediary-chains of length greater than zero, as shown in Figure 1. The intermediary-chain starts with the withdrawal of a banknote, followed by at least one payment, and finally ends with a deposit.

In the following, we sketch how law enforcement can restrict withdrawer and depositor anonymity of suspicious payments with conventional banknotes, with RFID-enabled banknotes, or with electronic cash.

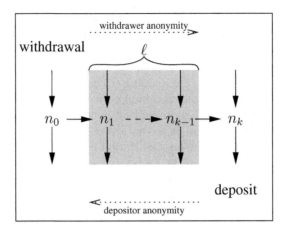

Fig. 1. Intermediary-chain of length ℓ. Arrows denote cash flows

2.1   Conventional Banknotes

With conventional banknotes withdrawer and depositor anonymity cannot be restricted actively by law enforcement. To restrict anonymity, law enforcement has to find short intermediary-chains, which enable linkage of withdrawals and deposits.

Restricting Withdrawer Anonymity. To restrict withdrawer anonymity the serial numbers of illegally obtained banknotes are blacklisted. As blacklisting requires knowledge of serial numbers in advance, this can only be used in case of blackmailing and bank robberies. In case of money theft, merchants in general do not know the serial numbers of the stolen banknotes.

Furthermore, blackmailers often demand low denominated, not consecutively numbered banknotes. Although this increases the physical size of the ransom, it counteracts blacklisting. Due to the size of the list, providing merchants with blacklisted serial numbers becomes impractical. Thus, blacklisted banknotes will not be detected until deposit, where banknotes are automatically verified.

Restricting Depositor Anonymity. Money laundering is the process by which a large amount of illegally obtained money is given the appearance of having originated from a legitimate source. The deposit of those illegally obtained banknotes is where the launderer is most vulnerable to detection.

To make money laundering more difficult, banks are obliged to notify law enforcement when large amounts of cash are deposited, s.a. [Fin03]. Unfortunately, the serial numbers of banknotes obtained e.g. from drug trafficking or terrorist activity are not known and thus cannot be detected easily.

2.2   RFID-Enabled Banknotes

As RFID-enabled banknotes are still not existant it is highly speculative how they might be used for criminal investigation. It is assumed that very small chips will be used (e.g. the Hitachi μ chip [Hit03]). Those chips have very restricted capabilities, e.g. the range of the transmission is not only very limited (1 mm without external antenna, up to 25 cm with an external antenna), but the transmission is also not collision resistant: to read out serial numbers, banknotes must not be too close together.

Due to those restrictions we do not share the worries of Juels and Pappu [JP03] that RFID chips on banknotes are a threat to privacy. With RFID-enabled banknotes, law enforcement can more actively restrict withdrawer and depositor anonymity. Instead of remotely reading serial numbers we expect that law enforcement will use different methods to restrict the anonymity of payments with RFID-enabled banknotes:

Restricting Withdrawer Anonymity. The simplified reading of serial numbers can be used by merchants to read the serial numbers of received banknotes. This has two consequences:

1. Merchants can easily check for blacklisted banknotes. Thus, it becomes more difficult for criminals to spend illegally obtained banknotes.
2. Merchants can store the serial numbers of received banknotes. This enables law enforcement to blacklist stolen banknotes.

Note also that reception of a blacklisted banknote could also trigger a silent alarm or e.g. activate video surveillance, to catch the criminal while spending the blacklisted banknotes.

Restricting Depositor Anonymity. As it becomes possible for banks to store the identity of the withdrawer along with the serial numbers of the withdrawn banknotes, the original withdrawer of a deposited banknote can always be found out easily. Thus, in case of suspicious deposits, the identified withdrawer can be watched closer, which enables law enforcement to investigate drug trafficking etc. more easily.

Additional Notes. For criminal investigation the advantage of RFID-enabled banknotes is the simplified reading of serial numbers. It is therefore self-evident that criminals may try to circumvent this by destroying the RFID chips in their banknotes. This is however not very helpful: Banknotes without a working RFID chip are particularly suspicious, but the serial number can still be read out optically.

On the other side, the solution proposed by Juels and Pappu prevents merchants from reading the serial number from the RFID. Therefore, merchants cannot check received banknotes against blacklisted serial numbers, unless merchants read serial numbers optically.

2.3   Electronic Cash

Electronic cash based on Chaum's blind signature primitive [Cha83] is very different from conventional cash: The serial numbers of the electronic banknotes (for some reason often called coins), are chosen randomly by the withdrawer and are not known to the bank. Furthermore, such a banknote is only valid for one payment, where the bank immediately checks that the serial number of the received payment has not been used yet.

It has been shown by von Solms and Naccache [vSN92] that this kind of electronic cash provides more anonymity than conventional cash, which can be misused by criminals for untraceable blackmailing, the "perfect crime". Since this discovery a lot of research has been done on how to realize electronic cash providing a more restricted form of anonymity. Most proposals are based on a trusted third party that is always able to revoke the anonymity upon request.

Other proposals try to mimic conventional cash more closely by providing anonymity through intermediary-chains (e.g. [Sim96, Jak99]). This close relation to conventional banknotes leads in principle to the same solution for criminal investigation. But as the bank is involved in every payment, the withdrawer and depositor anonymity can be restricted even more than with RFID-enabled banknotes.

While [Jak99] gives a short analysis of the "chain privacy" provided by their payment system, this analysis does not cover statistical methods at all. The methods presented in the following can be used as well to deanonymize those electronic payment systems. Furthermore, as those payment systems additionally leak the length of the intermediary-chain to the bank, our methods might be improved even more.

3   Modeling Intermediary-Chains

In this section we explain how banks can derive information on the length of the intermediary-chain from deposited banknotes. We show how to model intermediary-chains and point out some similarities to anonymity degradation in MIX networks.

We would like to point out that the model is only valid for conventional banknotes. For RFID-enabled banknotes some restrictions apply: Merchants must not provide additional tracking information to the bank or even publish the serial numbers of received banknotes for voluntary tracking purposes (e.g. www.myeuro.info already provides such a database). Serial numbers should only be read to protect against money theft and to check for blacklisted banknotes.

3.1   Participants

There are three types of participants: Banks, customers, and merchants. In a nutshell, customers withdraw banknotes from their accounts and spend subsets of those banknotes at merchants. Merchants deposit banknotes to their accounts but also return change to customers. Banks keep the accounts of customers and merchants. We assume that banks store the serial numbers of withdrawn and deposited banknotes together with the identity of the withdrawer or depositor, respectively, in a common database. Thus, in principle there is only one bank.

Next, we will have a closer look on customers and merchants. For simplicity, we assume that transactions are always between a customer and a merchant, i.e. there are no transactions between customers or between merchants.

Customers. Customers use wallets to keep their banknotes. To pay a merchant, the customer randomly selects the banknotes to be used from all available banknotes of the denomination to be used. This certainly is a simplification, as the number and denomination of used banknotes depends on the amount to be payed and thus influences the selection process. On the other side, we are especially interested in low denominated banknotes, and in this case random selection is indeed a good approximation.

Merchants. Merchants keep received banknotes in cash desks[1]. Only a small subset of the received banknotes is returned as change to other customers, the remaining banknotes are deposited at the bank in regular intervals, e.g. once a day. Making change is a deterministic process, as banknotes in the cash desk are kept in a stack for each denomination, i.e. a "last in first out" order is used when making change.

3.2   Relation to MIX Networks

The role of a merchant is somehow comparable to a MIX [Cha81] used for anonymous communication. There are some similarities, but there are also some differences:

Anonymous Communication. A MIX is an intermediary transforming a number of encrypted input messages to output messages by decrypting them. The output messages are then delivered to the intended recipients. A single MIX provides anonymous communication, because due to the transformation, it is computationally infeasible to correlate single incoming and outgoing messages. Multiple MIXes are only necessary if the single MIX is not trusted.

If, however, an adversary is able to link multiple messages, then he can use statistical methods to degrade the anonymity over time. Attacks exploiting linkability are e.g. the intersection attack [BPS01] and the predecessor attack [WALS02, Shm02].

Anonymous Payments. In the setting of anonymous payments, the bank is both the sender and the receiver of banknotes. Customers are transporting the banknotes to merchants. A merchant receiving a banknote can either return it to the bank or to another customer, but cannot transform the serial number of received banknotes. Anonymity with respect to the bank requires that a banknote has been transported to several merchants prior to its deposit.

---

[1] It should be noted that merchants sometimes also make use of wallets, e.g. waitresses keep banknotes in wallets.

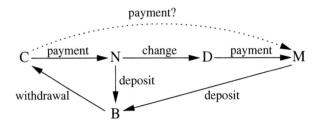

Fig. 2. Determining the length of the intermediary-chain

Anonymous payments also suffer from linkability. When a customer spends several banknotes at the same merchant, some of them are returned to the bank while others are returned to customers as shown in Figure 2. Thus, a payment often leaks some information to the bank.

3.3   Sets of Linked Banknotes

To estimate how much information is leaked to the bank, we introduce the notion of a *set of linked banknotes*:

Linked Banknotes: All banknotes that have recently been withdrawn by a single customer form a set of linked banknotes.

Banks can learn a lot from linked sets due to the way merchants process received banknotes according to our model:

- Merchants have to unlink sets when making change, because only a very small fraction of previously received banknotes are returned as change to other customers.
- Merchants have to keep sets when depositing, because a large fraction of previously received banknotes are returned to the bank.

Therefore, the bank may conclude from deposited linked sets of a certain size that with high probability the withdrawer indeed spent those banknotes at the merchant. Using a database containing the serial numbers of the withdrawn banknotes, the bank can not only decide whether some of the deposited banknotes form a linked set, but can also look up the identity of the withdrawer easily.

4   Deanonymization of Payments

We have identified linked banknotes as a potential method to deanonymize low value payments. In this section we present a more exact analysis of the probability to deanonymize payments.

4.1   Anonymity with Respect to the Bank

From the banknotes deposited by a merchant the bank may try to extract information on the length of the intermediary-chains from the denomination of the banknotes or from the size of a detected set of linked banknotes:

- High denominated banknotes are likely to be deposited by the first merchant.
- Sets of linked banknotes are likely to be unlinked when returned as change.

Note that when a customer withdraws a certain amount from his account, the denominations and the number of banknotes for each used denomination is usually determined by the bank, especially when an ATM is used. The bank calculates something in between the two extreme cases: a single high denominated banknote or several low denominated banknotes.

A Single High Denominated Banknote. High denominated banknotes are with high probability directly deposited after the first payment as such banknotes are rarely used as change. Therefore, high denominated banknotes are likely to have a short intermediary-chain.

As the length of the intermediary-chain depends on the denomination of a spent banknote, we can assign an empirically determined deposit-probability p_d to every denomination d. This probability refers to the likelihood that a banknote of denomination d received by a merchant as payment is deposited.

Lemma 1 (Single Banknote). *Let L_d be a random variable representing the length of the intermediary-chain for a banknote of denomination d. The probability that a banknote of denomination d is involved in n transactions is $P(L_d = n) = p_d^n$ and we expect an average intermediary-chain of length $E(L_d) = 1/(1 - p_d)$.*

Several Low Denominated Banknotes. We consider the following scenario. Customer $\mathcal{A}$ has withdrawn a set of low denominated banknotes. Afterwards, merchant $\mathcal{M}$ deposits a subset of size s of the banknotes withdrawn by customer $\mathcal{A}$. We are interested in the probability of the following event: $\mathcal{A}$ has spent some linked banknotes at another merchant $\mathcal{N}$, who has returned a subset of those banknotes as change to customer $\mathcal{B}$, and finally $\mathcal{B}$ has spent a subset of the received linked change at merchant $\mathcal{M}$.

To assign probabilities to this event, we make use of the following lemmas:

Lemma 2 (Wallet Model). *Let X and Y be random variables representing the number of linked banknotes used for a payment and the number of linked banknotes contained in the wallet of the customer, respectively. Let U and V be random variables representing the total number of banknotes used for a payment and the total number of banknotes contained in the wallet of the customer, respectively. Then the probability to pay with i linked banknotes is*

$$P(X = i | Y = j \cap U = n \cap V = t) = \frac{\binom{j}{i}\binom{t-j}{n-i}}{\binom{t}{n}}.$$

Lemma 3 (Cash Desk Model). *Let Y be a random variable representing the number of linked banknotes returned as change to a customer. Due to the small number of returned banknotes Y can be assumed to be Poisson distributed. Thus, the average number of received linked banknotes can be determined empirically as $E(Y) = c$ and the probability to receive j linked banknotes as change is*

$$P(Y = j) = \frac{c^j}{j!} \exp(-c).$$

Note that the number of linked banknotes returned to a customer as change is independent of the merchant and the number of banknotes contained in the cash desk.

4.2   Hypothesis Testing

Whenever the bank has discovered a set of $s > 1$ linked banknotes within a deposit, the bank can test whether the linked set has been spent by the withdrawer (event A) or by another customer (event B). The null hypothesis H_0 is that event A has happend. Depending on the size of s the null hypothesis is either accepted or rejected.

In more detail the bank calculates the probability for event B, and rejects H_0 if this event is unlikely to happen. Therefore, the bank chooses a probability p_{reject} that influences the error that the bank is willing to tolerate and accepts H_0 if $P(B) < p_{reject}$. In the following, we will argue that H_0 is likely to be accepted, even for very small deposited linked sets, e.g. for sets of size $s > 2$.

We are using lemma 2 and 3 to calculate the probability of event B. Assuming that the that the payer has used n banknotes for the payment ($U = n$) and has t banknotes in his wallet ($V = t$), where $n \leq t$, the bank can calculate the probability that the payer has received at most t linked banknotes as change ($Y \leq t$) and has spent between s and n of them ($s \leq X \leq n$):

$$P(s \leq X \leq n \cap Y \leq t | U = n \cap V = t) = \sum_{i=s}^{n} \sum_{j=i}^{t} \frac{\binom{t-j}{n-i}}{\binom{t}{n}} \cdot \frac{c^j}{i!(j-i)!} \exp(-c)$$

In addition, it is important to be able to calculate

$$P(U = n \cap V = t) = P(U = n | V = t) \cdot P(V = t).$$

Those distributions have to be determined empirically. From our own experience, we can make two observations on the distributions $P(V)$ and $P(U|V)$:

Table 1. Probabilities of event A for deposited sets of size s and $c = 2$

t	2	3	3	4	4	4	5	5	5	5	6	6	6	6	6
n	2	2	3	2	3	4	2	3	4	5	2	3	4	5	6
$s = 2$	0.27	0.27	0.99	0.23	0.54	0.9	0.17	0.37	0.54	0.76	0.13	0.27	0.41	0.53	0.66
$s = 3$			0.18		0.14	0.63		0.09	0.27	0.49		0.06	0.15	0.26	0.39
$s = 4$						0.09			0.05	0.31			0.03	0.11	0.21

1. We assume that V is Poisson distributed, as the probability for having t banknotes in the wallet decreases with t.
2. For higher numbers of banknotes, we assume that it is very unlikely that (almost) all banknotes contained in a wallet are used for a single payment, i.e. $P(U = i | V = i) \approx 0$ for some i not too small.

4.3   An Example

Even without assigning probabilities to $P(U = n \cap V = t)$, we can argue that whenever a set of size $s > 2$ is deposited, it is in general quite likely that the withdrawer of this set has indeed spent those banknotes at the depositing merchant. Table 1 shows the probabilities for event A for some values of U and V given that the average number of linked banknotes returned as change is $c = 2$, which we assume is very high.

As it turns out, event A is only likely to happen, if it were likely that the payer has spent all banknotes contained his wallet at the merchant ($U = V$). But this is exactly what we have observed is unlikely. Thus, even without calculating $P(B)$ exactly, we conclude that $P(B)$ will be very low for $s > 2$. Depending on the value of p_{reject} chosen by the bank, the bank will accept H_0 for very small deposited linked sets ($s > 2$ or $s > 3$).

5   Discussion

The presented deanonymization mechanism is based on the number of banknotes used for a payment, not on the value of the payment. Consequently for the deanonymization of low value payments the availability of low denominated banknotes is required. While most currencies have such low denominated banknotes, some currencies don't. For example for US Dollars banknotes 1\$ and 2\$ banknotes exist, but the smallest denomination for Euro banknotes is 5€. Thus, unless 1€ and 2€ banknotes are additionally introduced, our attacks probably do not work very well for *low value* payments. Nevertheless, the deanonymization mechanism also works for medium and high value payments, but for those payments, lemma 1 can also be applied, to increase the bank's confidence even more.

This directly leads to the positive aspect of the deanonymization mechanism. As we will show in the following, honest customers can protect themselves against possible deanonymization of their payments very well. For criminals, however, it is very difficult to apply similar countermeasures, because illegally obtained banknotes (especially blackmailed banknotes) should always form a huge set of linked banknotes. Spending those banknotes will therefore leak a lot of information to the bank which can be used to support criminal investigation.

5.1   How to Use Banknotes Correctly

Our deanonymization mechanism exploits sets of linkable banknotes. To protect against possible deanonymization, concerned customers should avoid using linked sets of banknotes for payments as far as possible. In the following we will propose some simple suggestions how to lower the risk of being deanonymized.

- When withdrawing banknotes customers should prefer to withdraw a single high denominated banknote instead of several low denominated banknotes. Although high denominated banknotes are more likely to be deanonymizable (see also Lemma 1), it is easily possible to "launder" this banknote: The returned change can be used for payments that are indeed anonymous with respect to the bank.
- To pay anonymously, customers should use as few banknotes as possible. Although it is possible to spend a single (perhaps up to two) low denominated, non-anonymous banknotes anonymously, recurring payments should be avoided, as the number of linked banknotes deposited by the merchants accumulate over time.

In addition to those countermeasures, customers may additionally use other and perhaps more impractical methods to avoid using sets of linked banknotes, e.g. by exchanging banknotes directly with other customers.

5.2   Collaborating Merchants

Our analysis is based on the assumption that merchants only return a few banknotes as change to their customers. In this last section we show that by returning an unnecessary high number of small denominated banknotes instead of few higher denominated banknotes some collaborating merchants may link payments. To some extent, this attack limits the countermeasures presented above. However, to make this attack practical, RFID-enabled banknotes are required as merchants have to process serial numbers of received and returned banknotes.

Collaborating merchants store the serial numbers of banknotes returned as change in a common database. Assigning an unique identifier to each set of returned banknotes allows the merchants to identify a banknote spent at another merchant. Thus, returned banknotes are linked by the unique identifier.

As we have already learned, the likelihood that a customer spends more than one banknote from a received set increases with the size of the set. Therefore, if a customer spends at least two banknotes of the same set at another merchant, those merchants can link both payments with a certain probability. If either payment is non-anonymous, the other is also. But even if both payments are anonymous, the linkage of both payments is valuable for statistical purposes.

6   Conclusion

We have shown that banknotes are *not* an unconditionally anonymous payment system. Careless use of banknotes leaks in principle a lot of information to the bank that can be used to deanonymize many payments. Those deanonymizations are always probabilistic; in most cases the withdrawer will be correctly identified as the payer, but in some (rare) cases a successful deanonymization can be completely wrong due to some limitations of our model, which does not cover e.g. pocket-money.

To our knowledge, a such a deanonymization mechanism is currently not in use. From a technical viewpoint implementing the described mechanism is not very difficult, as the required infrastructure already is almost available. As a consequence we also have presented some simple rules how to use banknotes to guarantee payments to be anonymous.

References

[BPS01]   Oliver Berthold, Andreas Pfitzmann, and Ronny Standtke. The disadvantages of free MIX routes and how to overcome them. In *Designing Privacy Enhancing Technologies – International Workshop on Design Issues in Anonymity and Unobservability 2000*, Lecture Notes in Computer Science 2009, pages 30–45. Springer-Verlag, 2001.

[Cha81]   David Chaum. Untraceable electronic mail, return adresses and digital pseudonyms. *Communications of the ACM*, 24(2):84–88, 1981.

[Cha83]   David Chaum. Blind signatures for untraceable payments. In *Advances in Cryptology – CRYPTO '82*, pages 199–203. Plenum, 1983.

[Fin03]   Financial Action Task Force on Money Laundering. The fourty recommendations, 2003. Online available at http://www.oecd.org/fatf/.

[Hit03]   Hitachi μ solutions, 2003. Online available at http://www.hitachi-eu.com/mu/.

[Jak99]   Markus Jakobsson. Mini-cash: A minimalistic approach to e-commerce. In *Public Key Cryptography – PKC'99*, Lecture Notes in Computer Science 1560, pages 122–135. Springer-Verlag, 1999.

[JP03]   Ari Juels and Ravianth Pappu. Squealing euros: Privacy protection in RFID-enabled banknotes. In *Financial Cryptography – FC 2003*, Lecture Notes in Computer Science 2742, pages 103–121. Springer-Verlag, 2003.

[Shm02]   Vitaly Shmatikov. Probabilistic analysis of anonymity. In *15th IEEE Computer Security Foundations Workshop*, pages 119–128. IEEE Computer Society Press, 2002.

[Sim96]   Daniel R. Simon. Anonymous communication and anonymous cash. In *Advances in Cryptology – CRYPTO '96*, Lecture Notes in Computer Science 1109, pages 61–73. Springer-Verlag, 1996.

[vSN92]   B. von Solms and David Naccache. On blind signatures and perfect crimes. *Computers and Security*, 11(6):581–583, 1992.

[WALS02]   Matthew Wright, Micah Adler, Brian N. Levine, and Clay Shields. An analysis of the degradation of anonymous protocols. In *Network and Distributed System Security Symposium – NDSS 2002*. Internet Society, 2002.

[Yos01]   Junko Yoshida. Euro bank notes to embed RFID chips by 2005. *EE Times*, December 2001. Online availabe at http://www.eetimes.com/story/OEG20011219S0016.

FLASCHE – A Mechanism Providing Anonymity for Mobile Users*

Alf Zugenmaier

Microsoft Research Cambridge, UK
alfz@microsoft.com

Abstract. The protection goal anonymity helps to preserve the privacy of users by ensuring that their identity remains unknown. Many mechanisms enabling anonymity exist. However, these mechanisms work inefficiently when used in mobile wireless networks. This contribution shows how anonymity can be provided efficiently for mobile users by exploiting the fact that they are mobile. A possible realization, called FLASCHE, is described.

1 Introduction

Computer users' increasing urge to communicate even while on the move has led to a proliferation of systems for mobile communication into everyday life. Nowadays it is possible to sit in a park and connect wirelessly to the internet using GPRS or a public wireless LAN. For the future, many more services, especially local services are envisioned. These include information kiosks with information on nearby places of interest, train or plane timetable services, today's specials in stores, etc., which can be accessed with all kinds of devices, ranging from highly powerful laptop to low power embedded devices. The networks these local services are offered on may not necessarily allow connection to the internet.

Sometimes the users of these services may want to communicate anonymously. They may want to do so because of legal reasons or simply because of an uncomfortable feeling when considering the amount of data that can be attributed to them. For this purpose, the condition required by the protection goal *anonymity* is fulfilled by an action, if the attacker is not able to deduce the identity of the originator, in this paper called user, from that action or its context. The identity is the set of all personal data and uniquely identifying subsets thereof [1]. An action is anything the user does which takes a limited time, i.e. has a defined start and end time and has an instantaneous effect. The context of an action is all additional knowledge an attacker can gain about this action – it includes the request and reply messages, the log files of the server, etc. An action can be as granular as sending a single message, or contain a complete web transaction.

This is a more user centered definition than the one that is normally given in the literature [2-8], although it is very much in the colloquial meaning of the word. It is also

---

* Part of this work was done while the author was at the University of Freiburg

D. Martin and A. Serjantov (Eds.): PET 2004, LNCS 3424, pp. 121–141, 2005.

sufficient for this paper, as only situations in which the user is a client in a client server relationship with the service is considered.

This paper makes the following contributions: it shows why current anonymizing techniques are not suitable for use with mobile devices; and it uses a conceptual model, the Freiburg privacy diamond, to systematically deduce a suitable anonymizing mechanism. It is structured as follows: The next section details the threats to a mobile user's anonymity. Section 3 determines the requirements an anonymity mechanism for mobile users must meet and evaluates existing mechanisms against these criteria. Section 4 describes the structure of anonymity mechanisms using the Freiburg Privacy Diamond as conceptual model and deduces from it an anonymity mechanism suitable for mobile use. It also presents its architecture for a UNIX implementation. Possible attacks are shown in Section 5, a conclusion is given in the final section.

2   Usage Scenario and Threat Model

The usage model assumed for the purpose of this paper is that of a mobile user wirelessly connecting to an access points that through some network, not necessarily the Internet, connects to a service.

The danger of eavesdroppers on the link between a mobile device and the access point or base station is far greater in a mobile wireless environment than in a fixed network environment, as access to the transmission medium cannot be controlled. As the number of access providers increases and the economic dependencies between them become more complex it is possible to view the access point itself as an adversary. The attacker could also be listening to the traffic in the network. Finally, it could be that the service itself can not be trusted to handle information which would identify a person (cf. Figure 1).

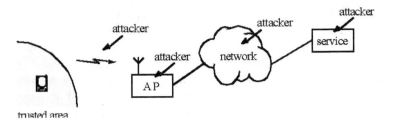

Fig. 1. Usage scenario and possible locations for the eavesdrop-per(s) (arrows) of the attacker model used for FLASCHE. AP: access point (base station)

The following are the sources of information for an attacker when no anonymizing[1] techniques are employed. The attacker can attack the physical communication layer, being able to access the wireless medium; attack within the local network, being able to

---

[1] The Oxford English Dictionary defines "anonymous" as "nameless, having no name". "Anonymity" is "the state of being anonymous, used of an author or his writings".

access the link layer; attack within the Internet, being able to gather information from the network layer upwards; and attack the service, being able to retrieve the data on the application layer (cf. Figure 2). Unless encryption is employed in the higher layers, the information of the higher layers is also accessible in the lower layers.

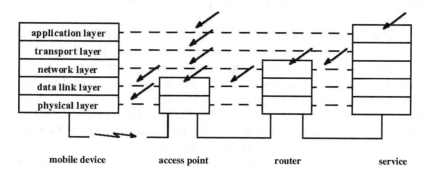

Fig. 2. Possible points of attack within the communication are depicted with arrows. There is a wireless link between the mobile device and the access point

A *physical* attacker can observe the physical activity of a device. He is, thus, able to locate activity on the medium, i.e. detect that a device is active, as well as physically determine the location of an active device.

An attacker on the local network can read packets on the link layer. For a broadcast medium it is necessary to have a sender and destination address attached to every packet. These addresses can be used by a local attacker to determine who communicates with whom. If the attacker is located within the access point or at the link between mobile device and access point, he can also read any management messages which may be required at link layer.

An attacker on the network layer, e.g. on the Internet, can read the network layer address used for routing and use this address to deduce information about the location of the device. This location information is, of course, much less precise than the information that can be gained by the physical attacker. The smallest area to which the location of the device can be pinpointed covers the area served by the last router on the way to the mobile device. An attacker having access to the network layer protocols between the mobile device and the router, or within the router, can gain even more information. The correlation of link layer address and network layer address is usually accessible to him.

The transport layer address contains information about which service is used. If the attacker is able to access this information, his knowledge about the action becomes much more detailed.

An attacker reading the application layer protocol can gain very detailed information about the action. An attacker within the service is able to read all data on the application layer, i.e. this attacker is even able to decrypt cryptographically protected content that is addressed to the service. Whereas the attackers eavesdropping on the communication as previously described can be confined to observing the action *communication between mobile device and service* by using cryptography, an attacker who subverts or collaborates with the service is always able to observe the action in the most detailed fashion. If a service is provided locally, a single attacker may be able to gain all of the above information, thus assuming the role of an omnipresent attacker.

3 Requirements on Mobile Anonymity Mechanisms

According to the definition of anonymity given in Section 1, anonymity mechanisms must try to hide the identity of a user performing an action. Information about the user of a service can be gathered from the content of the messages between service and user, the source and destination addresses of these messages, and the traffic flow. To protect content information from an attacker in the communication system, the messages can be encrypted. If possible, omitting all references to the user in the content of the messages serves to protect the user's identity from the communication partner and everyone else who is able to access the content of the message.

It is more difficult to conceal the source and destination addresses of the messages. If a broadcast communication is possible, as in television, the intended recipient of a message can be concealed. Nevertheless, the sender of a message can still be determined, in this case the broadcasting company. Sender anonymity can be achieved with DC-net-works [9],[10].

For networks that do not have the broadcast property a number of anonymizing techniques exist at the application and network level. An overview is provided, e.g., in [11] or in [12]. The simplest anonymizing technique is to use a relay, also called a proxy, for requests and replies. The relay removes identifying information from the headers of the request. This way the web server does not receive the address of the user; the user is anonymous to the communication system apart from the relay. But the communication is still vulnerable to traffic analysis.

To overcome the limitations of proxy based solutions, it is possible to use the Mix concept [13]. Several mixes are integrated into the network and messages are routed through these mixes. Every mix collects messages, waits for a certain number of messages to arrive, shuffles them, and then sends them to their next destination. Variants of this concept are Onion Routing [14], SG mixes [15], Web-mixes [16], and Mixminion [17]. They try to overcome performance limitations while still trying to provide resistance to attacks in which a number less than the total number of mixes are collaborating with the attacker. To some extent the system *Crowds* [18] can also be seen as a variant of this concept.

To evaluate whether these mechanisms are adequate in a mobile setting, it is necessary to examine the characteristic features of mobile devices [19]. These can then be translated into the following requirements for mobile anonymity mechanisms:

r1 Mobile devices usually run on battery power. To make it last as long as possible, they usually run at slower speeds, therefore offering less computational power than devices running on mains power. This is even more so with embedded devices. Asymmetric cryptography requires intensive computations. The RSA algorithm requires long integer calculations with numbers of 1000 to 2000 bit length. Although elliptic curve cryptography can achieve the same level of security with integers of 100 to 200 bit length, the computational burden on the device is still of the same order of magnitude. Therefore, the use of asymmetric cryptography should be kept to a minimum.

r2 A mobile device does not know in advance whether the network it connects to provides connectivity to a global network. Therefore, all supporting services it requires should be in the proximity of the device. The anonymizing system should not require connections to one central instance, especially if only local services is used; the anonymizing mechanism should be able to act locally.

r3 Wireless connections are not as reliable as ones over wires. Disconnections and network segmentations may occur. In addition to central services being unavailable from time to time, mobile nodes can join and drop out of the network at any time. Thus, the anonymity mechanism should not rely on a fixed set of participants.

r4 Available bandwidth over wireless connections is lower than over a wire. The mobile device should send and receive data only if it is necessary for the application. The overhead necessary to provide anonymity should be minimal. Dummy traffic wastes bandwidth and should not be necessary.

r5 Wireless networks usually adapt their bandwidth depending on the environmental conditions. The anonymity mechanism should not rely on a fixed bandwidth being available to the mobile device.

r6 Mobile devices will very often leave one network and join another one. The anonymity mechanism should only require low setup costs in terms of time and resources to join a new network.

r7 Mobile users have even less time and attention available to dedicate to the anonymity mechanism. The users should not be required to make changes to the configuration while moving, e.g. additional user interaction like choice of mix cascades etc.

r8 This requirement does not originate in a characteristic of mobile use. It simply states that the anonymity mechanism should support the most widely used client server protocol in the Internet, HTTP.

With these requirements, the anonymizing mechanisms described above can be analyzed.

	r1	**r2**	**r3**	**r4**	**r5**	**r6**	**r7**	**r8**
DC-network	+	+	-	-	-	-	n/a	n/a
Relay	+	-	+	+	+	+	+	+
Chaum Mix	-	-	+	-	+	+	-	+
Onion Routing	+	-	+	-	+	-	-	+
Crowds	-	+	-	-	+	+	-	+

Fig. 3. Evaluation of existing anonymizing mechanisms. (+: fulfilled, -: not fulfilled, n/a: no implementation available)

In addition to these technical mechanisms there are *classical* anonymizing techniques such as using public pay phones or internet cafes.

In the mechanisms proposed by RFC 3041 [20] or the IEEE [21], the address of the us-er's device is replaced by a temporary address, therefore making it difficult to correlate the address of the device with the identity of the user. These mechanisms by themselves are not considered to provide anonymity in view of the threat model discussed as they only operate on one layer of the networking stack. However in terms of fulfilling the requirements imposed by mobility, they are a step in the right direction.

4 FLASCHE[2]

To deduce an anonymity mechanism suitable for mobile users, the Freiburg privacy diamond [22],[23] is used. The model tries to capture the essence of anonymity mechanisms with regard to the most important forms of mobility in mobile communications: terminal mobility and user mobility. It must, therefore, consider at least four types of entities: the action itself, the terminal, i.e. the device used for the action, the user who performs the action and the location which the device and the user are located at.

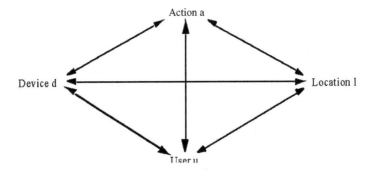

Fig. 4. The privacy diamond

The privacy diamond in Figure 4 represents the relations between these entities. With this completely interconnected graph it is possible to determine which information can be concluded from other information. The use of the privacy diamond is illustrated in a very simplified fashion by the following example. An attacker attempting to disclose the identity of a user tries to reveal the relationship between the user and an action. To do this, he could find out which device was used for this action and then find out who used this device. If the identity of the device used for the transaction is concealed, e.g. using a mix network, this deduction is not possible. Other conclusions, e.g. based on taking into consideration the location from which the action was carried out may, however, still be possible. There are five loop-free paths which can be used to deduce the identity of a user by linking this action to the user:

---

[2] The acronym FLASCHE (German for bottle) is meant to remind of an anonymous message in a bottle.

1. user to action directly
2. user via location to action
3. user via device to action
4. user via location and then device to action
5. user via device and then location to action

For anonymizing systems, all five paths have to be broken. Four minimal ways of doing this exist (cf. Figure 5). Minimal means that it is not possible to re-connect a severed relation in the privacy diamond without allowing the attacker to infer the relation of user to action through transitive closure.

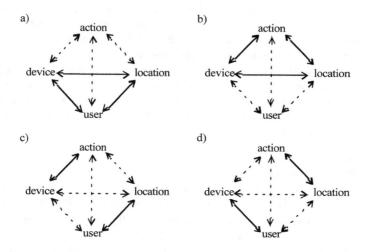

Fig. 5. Four minimal possibilities for anonymity mechanisms. Dotted arrows are relations that must be concealed by the anonymity mechanism

All of the anonymizing mechanisms described in Section 3 fall into the category described by the privacy diamond of Figure 5a. The privacy diamond b) describes anonymizing mechanisms that rely on user mobility like phone booths or Internet cafés. An anonymizing mechanism in category c) relies on broadcasts to and from a specific device. Both categories b) and c) rely on the users changing their devices. Therefore, it is not possible to employ a personal device. Category d) allows terminal mobility. The principle of this last anonymity mechanism can be demonstrated by going through the relations in Figure 5d. Two connections are preserved: the relations between user and device and between action and location. The reason for preserving the relations between action and location is that optimization based on the current location of the mobile device is possible. The networking infrastructure is able to optimize routing according to where messages associated to the action originate from and go to. In addition, the device can use supporting services in the vicinity of the device, like directory services, because its location does not have to be concealed. Not severing the relations between device and user has the advantage that the users can keep their personal devices. This gives them a trusted environment in which to store personal data.

The relations between user and location are hidden from the attacker by mobility of the user. The user performs actions from different locations which are inconspicuous, i.e. do not allow conclusion of the identity of the user from the location alone. Obscuring the relations between device and location is done in the same manner.

To ensure that the attacker is not able to directly link user to action, a tool like the identity manager prevents personally identifying data from being included in the action. To separate the relations between device and action, all communication protocols have to avoid references to the device. The device addresses are replaced by addresses derived from the location of the device only. These addresses are called location addresses in this paper. Actions may take some time to complete; the location may change during this time. During this action, the address of the device should not change. Therefore, the location is determined at the start of the action.

In addition to anonymizing one action, the mechanism must assure that an attacker can not link two privacy diamonds. This means, that following one action in which the user chooses to disclose his or her identity, it is possible for the user to perform further anonymous actions. An attacker should also be unable to link previous actions to the user after an identifiable action took place.

A. Location Addresses

Because only one device can occupy a physical space at a time, it seems natural to use the location of the device as its address. Technical limitations regarding the resolution with which the location can be determined may lead to the situation where two devices have the same address. The same problem can be caused by the fact, that actions are not atomic, they may take time during which the device may move. Therefore, an additional part to distinguish between devices that are seemingly at the same location is necessary. This part is chosen randomly.

The device address then consists of two parts: a prefix derived from the location, which can be used within the network and a random suffix, which ensures that two devices close to each other have different addresses (cf. Figure 6. The prefix may not uniquely determined by the physical location location of the device, it may also depend on which network the device attaches to.

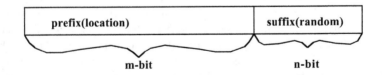

Fig. 6. Location address consisting of location dependent prefix and random suffix

Location information can be given in terms of network topology or of geography. Topological information gives information about the physical or logical arrangement of the network elements, i.e. about the configuration of the connection between the nodes. Topological information is encoded in routing tables of the routers used to send packets to the desired destination based on the network identifier.

Geographic information can be provided in two forms: symbolic or physical. The physical location can be represented by coordinates in a coordinate system, such as the WGS84 [24] system used by GPS.

The random part is used to disambiguate unicast messages between recipients having the same location dependent prefix. This can be done on all layers, from physical to application layer.

The length n of the random part of the address depends on the number of devices that simultaneously require an address within the location cell described by the location dependent part of the address. The probability p_a for an address collision can be calculated in analogy to the birthday problem [25]:

$$P_a = 1 - \frac{(2^n)!}{(2^n - k)! 2^{nk}}$$

where 2^n is the number of possible addresses and k is the number of devices in one cell. This equation can be used to determine the number of devices which can be accommodated in a cell given the size of the random part and the acceptable collision probability. Figure 7 shows that the random part must be at least 16 bits long to accommodate more than just a few device addresses at a collision probability of 1%.

n	$=0.1_{pa}$ p a	$=0.05$ pa	$=0.01$ pa	$=0.001$
2	1	1	1	1
4	3	1	1	1
8	7	5	3	1
16	117	83	37	11
24	1880	1312	581	183
32	30085	20991	9292	2932

Fig. 7. Maximum number of simultaneously active devices depending on the length of the random part (n) and the accepted collision probability (p_a)

A device may have multiple addresses, thus appearing as multiple devices. If an address collision occurs, there are two possibilities for handling this. One is to ignore the address collision and leave it to the higher layers to discard unwanted packets. The other is to resolve a collision. For example, in IPv6 this is done by broadcasting a request asking which other station uses the address in question. The address is assumed

---

[3] The birthday problem asks for the probability that in a given group of people, two have their birthday on the same day.

to be collision free, i.e. not used by another device, if there is no reply within a certain time-out interval [26]. If conservation of addresses is an issue, the device may want to use a central service for address allocation such as DHCP.

If the device address were derived only from the location of the device, together with a random part to uniquely identify the device at that location, an attacker would be able to transfer knowledge about actions from one connection to actions of another connection. Therefore, with location addressing, a device uses an address that is derived from the location it is at when establishing a connection. For each new connection, the address is derived anew. For parallel connections, this leads to simultaneous use of multiple addresses.

Client addresses are also used to assign messages from the clients to the appropriate server process connection. Therefore, a client should not change its address during a client server interaction. The address in use when a connection is set up will remain valid for this connection until the connection is torn down. An address loses its validity when the respective connection is closed.

Once the device moves out of range of the radio transmitter providing access to the cell described by the location address, all connections using this address break. The duration of connections should, therefore, be short in comparison to the duration a user stays in one place, i.e. remains in contact.

If a layer n utilizes further services at lower layers, the addresses of the services at the lower layers have to change synchronously with the address of layer n. If the addresses at the lower layer were left unchanged and an address change in layer n occurs, an attacker would be able to link instances of communications at layer n.

B. Possible Realization

A strength of location addressing is that it can be introduced into different networks which support mobile devices in which there is a client server relationship between the mobile client and the service.

The protocols in use in this network have to be examined to see whether they give information that can be used to identify the device. All fields of the protocol headers are analyzed whether the information from that field can be used to link several protocol data units to each other, or to the same device, thus allowing the attacker to recognize a device.

The addresses in use in each protocol are reviewed to determine which parts of the address should depend on the location and which part should be randomized. Interdependencies between protocols sometimes require addresses on lower layers to remain the same for the duration of a connection on the higher layer. These interdependencies are pointed out as well.

FLASCHE[34] is a design proposal to implement this concept. It is based on a TCP/IP stack with IPv6. The wireless communication follows the IEEE 802.11b standard in infrastructure mode. This decision is based on the simplicity of 802.11b radio technology compared to Bluetooth and the availability of complete documentation. FLASCHE uses HTTP at the application layer. In the following the protocols are examined in detail:

---

[4] This acronym was chosen because of its meaning in German, it stands for Freiburg Location Addressing SCHEme.

1) Physical Layer IEEE 802.11b

No addresses or other information identifying the mobile device are transmitted by the physical layer header. It may be possible to recognize a device by RF-fingerprinting [28]. However, the equipment necessary to do this is very expensive.

2) MAC Layer IEEE 802.11b

Information uniquely identifying the device is contained in the address fields. Routing is not performed at the MAC layer. Therefore the network does not require location information ithin the MAC address. To introduce location addressing, at layer 2 the source or destination MAC address representing the mobile device are replaced by a random unicast address. The complete MAC address is random, it contains no location dependent part. The lifetime of the MAC address depends on that of the address at the network layer, one MAC address is used per network layer address, leading to multiple MAC addresses to be used in parallel.

Using random addresses at the MAC layer leads to an increase in different MAC addresses within a network. For a network with an infrastructure, this may lead to problems with switches which can be used to connect networks at the data link layer, as their address tables are usually limited in size. The advantages switches have over hubs, namely to segment a network to keep the traffic between the segments minimal, may be lost. The probability of an address collision is marginal and can be neglected.

The mobility support that IEEE 802.11b offers should not be used with FLASCHE, because the reassociation of multiple MAC addresses at the same time can allow the attacker to link several connections together.

The basic service set identifier of the access point that currently handles the connection encodes the location dependent part.

In case of a mobile ad-hoc network with location aided routing, the location cell would be the cell that the positioning system, usually GPS, returns. This is because the more exactly the position of the device is determined, the better the routing algorithms can work.

3) Logical Link Control IEEE 802.2

No information identifying the device is transmitted in the header of the LLC sublayer.

4) Network Layer

The major obstacle to employing IP version 4 with location addressing is that it offers only 4 bytes of address space, leaving only a limited number of bits for the random part. IP version 6 offers a large address space of 16 bytes. For this reason it is used as an alternative to IPv4. RFC3041 [20] standardizes a mechanism which provides anonymous addresses for a device. This mechanism is used for FLASCHE, for performance reasons no duplicate address detection is carried out. The resulting address contains topological location information in the network identifier part of the address, and a random device specific part of the address. One address is required per transport layer connection, each of which is associated with one MAC address.

It may be possible to link different connections originating from the same device with different source address by the destination address, if the destination address is not a particularly popular one. The only way to avoid that would be to employ an anonymizing proxy, the existence of which may not be guaranteed in the scenario described.

The Internet control message protocol ICMPv6 is closely linked with IPv6. The neighbor solicitation and advertisement messages are used to resolve IPv6 addresses to MAC addresses. If the device's MAC and IPv6 addresses are set up correctly, neighbor solicitation and advertisement will work correctly. Router solicitation must be performed at the setup of every address, otherwise it would be possible to link IP addresses for which the router discovery has not been performed to IP addresses for which the router discovery has been performed.

5) Transport Layer UDP and TCP
Both TCP and UDP use port numbers to identify communicating entities at the application layer. In addition, the IP source and destination addresses are used at the transport layer to uniquely assign packets to connections. This violation of the layering principle is an advantage for location addressing: A connection will remain open under the IP address it was established with, even if other IP addresses are added to the same interface. The four-tuple of source port, source address, destination port and destination address is called a socket. A client uses a socket to send and receive UDP datagrams or to establish a connection. The state of the sockets on a device, therefore, indicates which addresses are in use.

Care has to be taken with the port numbering. Most implementations of TCP and UDP use only one counter for the next available client port and increase this counter by one with each connection. Therefore, with location addressing the port numbers used by the client are randomized to foil an attack which attempts to link several requests.

Additionally, the sliding window protocol of TCP uses sequence numbers. Here RFC1948 [29] must be followed to counter linking attacks using the initial sequence numbers of TCP connections.

6) Application Layer HTTP
The protocol for communication between the mobile client and the server is the hypertext transfer protocol, HTTP [30]. If the content of the communication needs to be secured from eavesdroppers outside of the server, secure HTTP, called HTTPS [31] is used. HTTPS uses public key cryptography only to negotiate a session key. This session key is then used for symmetric encryption of the communication. Sessions can be resumed across several TCP connections with the use of session IDs, foregoing the need for renegotiation.

The headers used in HTTP can be used to link requests to a device if the headers are set to unusual values, e.g. the accept charset header could show that this device also accepts unusual character sets. The from header even allows linking of a request to a user! Clearly, these fields must be stripped to a minimum, e.g. the user-agent field, or left empty, as the from field. Fortunately, most HTTP servers don't seem to mind.

This task can be performed by the identity manager [32], a proxy that runs on the mobile device which also filters the content for identifying information like cookies, names, etc.

HTTP uses TCP to connect to a server to retrieve a web page. After the page has been downloaded, the connection is closed. This ensures short connections, usually in the order of 5 to 10 seconds. Therefore, HTTP is suitable as the application layer protocol for location addressing, if the device does not move out of range of the access point or nearest neighbor during this time. If the connection breaks down, the application layer has to initiate a reload of the page. Unfortunately, breaking down of a connection can only be recognized through a time-out.

To determine the IP address of the host, the HTTP server process uses the domain name service (DNS). The hostname is sent to the DNS server with a UDP packet, the server returns the information it can find about this host name in another UDP packet. The address of the available DNS server may migrate with the locality of the mobile device. It is necessary to use DHCP to retrieve the address of a DNS server if the user and his device move to a network of a different service provider. A change of the network provider cannot generally be determined. A DHCP request should be initiated for every DNS query.

C. Architecture

There are two possibilities for implementing location addressing: either as a network layer or sublayer, or within a management plane. Implementation as a separate layer is advantageous because it does not violate the principle of layering within the communication protocol stack. However, it has the major disadvantage that all entities involved in the communication at that layer must implement a location addressing layer, e.g. necessitating changes in routers or similar intermediary devices.

Figure 8 shows how the architecture of FLASCHE implements location addressing as a management plane. This approach has the advantage of keeping the protocol stack mainly unchanged, and necessitates alterations only at the mobile device.

The examination of the protocols shows that the management plane must span transport, network and data link layers. The changes to the HTTP protocol are done with the identity manager, which runs as a proxy at the application layer. The management plane can replace all addresses unique to the device by addresses derived from the location of the device. Addresses unique to the device are used at the network layer, i.e. the IP address, and the data link layer, the Ethernet address at the media access layer. Thus, this management plane must be able to the access the data link and network layers, and be able to set the addresses at these layers. The management plane must also be able to associate addresses to TCP connections at the transport layer, and be able to determine when a connection is set up and torn down, in order to determine the lifetime of addresses. The management plane does not access connection information of the application layer, as there are too many different implementations of connection management at this layer.

The management plane has two tasks: connection supervision and address control. Determination of location is performed outside of the management plane. Connection supervision is a monitor at the service access point of the transport layer. There all requests for connection set up and connection tear down of the application layer can be seen. The management plane keeps a data structure listing all active connections.

Address control derives the device address to be used from the current location. The addresses of the device on the data link and network layers are changed simultaneously. If they were not changed synchronously, the network layer address or the data link layer address would enable linking of actions. A new network layer address could be linked to the network layer address previously used by the same device by correlating the data link layer addresses or vice versa.

Upon request for a connection establishment from the application layer to the transport layer, the monitor informs the location addressing management plane (LAMPe) of this request. LAMPe uses a locating module to determine the current location cell. It derives a prefix from this cell identifier to be used for the network layer. LAMPe also determines the random suffix to be used with this connection. The same random suffix is also used to create a unique data link layer address. This address is used for a virtual data link layer interface, to which the network layer address is assigned. Whenever the application layer sends data through this connection, the corresponding network layer and data link layer addresses are used. On termination of the connection, the virtual interface and the addresses in use by the connection are deleted to save device resources.

With TCP/IP, the monitor is implemented as a wrapper, a bump in the stack, at the socket interface. Whenever a new socket is opened by an application, LAMPe creates a virtual interface with a random MAC address. A new IP address derived from the location is bound to that interface. A socket is created using that IP address, and the socket descriptor returned to the invoking application. Periodically, the sockets are checked to determine which IP addresses are no longer used. These IP addresses and the associated interfaces are then deleted.

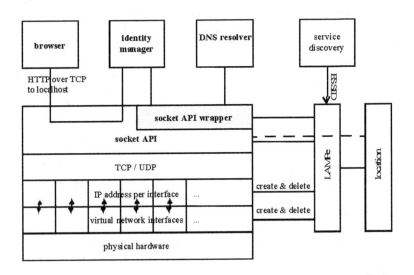

Fig. 8. Location addressing with browser and identity manager on UNIX based system

The following description applies to infrastructure networks and to mobile devices which contain only one network interface. For UNIX based systems, the monitor functionality lies at the service access point of the transport layer which is implemented in the socket API [33]. With this API, a client has to call the functions socket() and connect() and optionally bind() to connect to a server with TCP, and just socket() for UDP.

The function `socket()` opens a socket and returns a socket descriptor, which is similar to a UNIX file descriptor. `socket()` takes as arguments the protocol family, i.e. IPv4 or IPv6, the socket type, i.e. stream, datagram and raw, and a protocol argument which is used for raw sockets only. A stream type socket is used for TCP connections, and a datagram type socket for UDP connections. Raw sockets are used for other protocols, like ICMP.

For TCP type sockets, after the client application has received the socket descriptor, it must determine the starting point and end point of the connection. The starting point of the connection can be fixed using `bind()`. As arguments bind requires the socket descriptor, a socket address, consisting of an interface IP address of the device and an unused port address, as well as the address length. If the port number 0 is given, the kernel decides which unused ephemeral port to use. Usually, only servers call the function `bind()`, this enables us to exploit `bind()` for a client using location addressing.

To determine the end point, the client application calls the function `connect()`. If the starting point of a connection has not yet been determined, the kernel selects the IP address with a route to the server and an unused ephemeral port as source port and IP address. It performs connection establishment and returns a negative error number if this fails and zero if it is successful. The parameters for `connect()` are the socket descriptor returned by the socket function, the socket address, which is the address and port number of the destination, and the length of the address.

The socket can be used like a stream allowing data to be read from it and written to it. The socket can be actively closed using the function `close()` or passively closed by the server.

For TCP, location addressing implements the function `connect()` as a wrapper; the monitor sits in between the application and the transport layer and emulates one to the other. The function call `connect()` by the application calls the connect function of location addressing. If the destination's address is the local loopback address, which is the way the browser communicates with the identity manager, the original `connect()` function is called and the result returned. If not, `locationAddress()` is called, which returns a data structure containing the BSSID of the MAC layer and a random MAC address. A virtual IEEE802.11 interface is created with this random MAC address. This interface is then configured with an IP address which is also contained in the data structure returned by `locationAddress()`. The function `bind()` is called to bind this local interface with a random ephemeral port to the socket descriptor. The original connect, now named `connect_orig()`, is then called with the identical parameters that the connect function was called with. If `connect_orig()` returns an error, the virtual interface is deleted again. After that, or if `connect_orig()` succeeds, `connect()` returns with the return value of `connect_orig()`.

For an UDP client, it is not necessary to call connect before using the socket. Therefore, the function `socket()` is modified, so that for an UDP type socket, the original socket function is first called, then a new interface is created as described above, and the socket is bound to that local address using `bind()`.

The function call `close()` is also modified. It first calls the original function `close_orig()`, and then deletes the unused virtual device. In addition, a watchdog process periodically checks the active sockets with the UNIX command `netstat` and removes virtual devices that are no longer in use.

The socket interface offers a function that is used to translate host names into IP addresses: `gethostbyname()`. This function takes as argument the host name as character string and returns a pointer to a structure containing all IPv4 or IPv6 addresses of this host. `gethostbyname()` uses a program called resolver to perform a DNS query. Every time gethostbyname is called, the DNS server address is requested anew from the location module with the function `locationDNSAddress()` and the resolver is configured accordingly.

The location module offers two functions to LAMPe: `locationAddress()` and `locationDNSAddress()`. The function `locationAddress()` takes as parameter the ESSID of the network and returns a data structure containing a BSSID, a random MAC address and an IP address consisting of the local network's address and a random device address. To determine the BSSID, first the field strength of the current BSS is checked. If it is too low, it scans for a new BSS belonging to the same ESS. The local network's address is determined by router solicitation that is sent from an interface with a random link local address and the router advertisement that is received through a broadcast.

The function `locationDNSAddress()` also takes as argument an ESSID. After checking which BSS is available for this ESS, it creates a virtual interface with a random link local IP address. With the unchanged socket function call an UDP socket is opened and a DHCP request for the DNS server is broadcast to the network.

One drawback of this approach is that the use of link local addresses by the application is not supported for TCP or UDP.

In addition to implementing the wrapper and the location module, small changes have to be made to the implementation of the protocol stack. In the TCP and UDP implementations the code determining the next available free port uses a random number generator. The TCP initial sequence number is also randomized. The parameter ESSID that is required for both functions of the location module is given to the management plane by the service discovery.

This architecture is flexible enough to accommodate infrastructure less networks as well. `locationAddress()` will then use a positioning system such as GPS to determine the position and from that deduce the IP address. The MAC address is random. An unsolved problem is the determination of the DNS server's address. As a DHCP server cannot be assumed to be in the vicinity of the mobile device, the DNS server address must be propagated through the network somehow, e.g. by diffusion or proxy DHCP, in which the neighbors forward the DHCP messages.

5   Evaluation of Possible Attacks

An action is performed anonymously if an attacker is not able to draw conclusions about the identity of the originator from the action itself or its context. FLASCHE is designed to provide a mechanism to conceal identifying information in the protocol headers. In this subsection, the privacy diamond is examined again to determine which types of attacks for the purpose of determining the identity of the user performing an action are possible. In this section, active attacks are considered, as well as passive attacks.

D. Attacking User-Action

The attacker can try to gain information about the identity of the user from the action itself. This can be done with an intersection attack, in which one privacy diamond contains the action for which the attacker knows the user who performed the action, and one privacy diamond in which the user is concealed in an anonymity set. For this intersection attack, a piece of context information is required which can be used to correlate the diamonds. If the action under consideration is at the network layer, this context information could be the address of the server. If it can be assumed that only one person uses this server at a time, then the server address can be used to find corresponding actions. If an action at application level is considered, e.g. a web transaction, the information for linking two actions could be embedded in hidden variables or in dynamic links on the web pages.

Countermeasures would be not supporting hidden variables. Dynamic links on web pages cannot be countered. The only way for the user to protect his identity in this case is not to reveal it in any action. This would prevent the attacker from gaining knowledge by means of an intersection attack.

E. Attacking Device-Action

The behavior of the device, especially in response to non-standard protocol data units, can be implementation specific. This can also be used to create a fingerprint of the device. This type of fingerprinting only requires software that is available for free on the Internet. This kind of attack leads to no useful information, if the implementation of the protocol stack is employed for a great number of devices. Fingerprints on higher network layers can also be based on timing, e.g. a device currently running many applications simultaneously or having a slow processor might respond differently to echo requests than a device running only one application or having a fast processor. Another way of fingerprinting a device could be the use of management packets to set parameters that influence the behavior of the whole device. The implementation of the networking software has to ensure that parameters affect only one connection and one interface at a time.

An attack could also be aimed directly at the trusted area. A trojan horse could force applications on the device to bypass FLASCHE. Virus scanners may be able to detect some of these trojan horses. They will not be able to counter a directed attack.

The knowledge of the connection of device and action by itself is of no value to the attacker, unless at the same time the attacker knows who uses the device.

F. Attacking User-Device

Although the concept of the anonymizing mechanism location addressing permits the use of personal devices and thus assumes this knowledge is available to the attacker, he may still be interested in finding out which user uses a particular device. To find out which user performed an action, it is also necessary to attack the relation action to device.

A user who reveals his identity in an action in which the device also is identifiable provides enough information for the attacker to discover who uses this device. The attacker may also gain this information by non-technical means, e.g. physically observing which user uses which device.

G. Attacking Device-Location

Typically, more than one device can be expected to be able to operate at a given location. An attack of this nature would be to simulate a specific location for a certain device, e.g. if a device is recognizable by its fingerprint. Returning a special network identifier in response to router solicitation will make this device recognizable by the location; only one device will be at this location.

An attacker can gain such information if he can assume collocation with another device, e.g. a mobile phone. Then an intersection attack can provide information about whichdevice could be where.

H. Attacking User-Location

Concealing this relation is important because, even if the technology works flawlessly, this relation can reveal the identity of the user. The location from which the action takes place, is known to an attacker, as the location is encoded in the address. It can be presumed that the device is a personal device of the user, and that static information must only become known to the attacker once.

The attacker can guess the user's identity from the location of the user. This could be at home or at the office. Several further attacks on this relation are possible. The simplest is a physical attack. A camera could be used to identify the person at the location of the device. Collocation of devices registered to the user could also help the attacker.

Location addressing should only be used if a sufficient number of users are likely to be at the same place. This is usually not the case at places like home or at the office, but is at public places like train stations or airports.

If a user identifies himself during a transaction, his whereabouts become known. In subsequent transactions this knowledge may be used for an attack. It may also be used to determine the identity of the user for previous actions. The confidence of the observer about the relation between location of the user will decrease over the course of time, as the user may move to a different location and because a different user may move to the original location.

The movement of the user who has identified himself can be modeled by *spreading* of a confidence parameter over neighboring cells. However low the confidence value is, until a sufficient probability exists that other users are within the same cell, actions of this user are still attributable to him. To ensure anonymity for the actions preceding and following an identifying transaction there must be a chance of another user entering the same location cell in which he performs the next action.

6 Conclusions

The anonymity mechanism FLASCHE exploits a user's mobility to provide anonymity for an action of the mobile user under the condition that the user does not identify himself in the action, the device used to perform that action can not be uniquely identified, and the location of the user and the device does not offer any clues about the identity of the user. The mechanism is resilient to traffic analysis attacks, as they provide information about the location of the device, which by design does not have ot be kept secret. The most serious attack on location addressing is physically observing the location where the action takes place. However, proliferation of the surveillance of public places, coupled with person recognition systems, may make it generally impossible to remain anonymous outside one's own home. In addition to recognizing the person the surveillance system may also capture the content of the screen of the mobile device.

All requirements specific to employing an anonymity mechanism for mobile devices are fulfilled by FLASCHE. The anonymity provided by FLASCHE is a trade-off between suitability for mobile applications, provided by including the location of the device, and confidentiality of this location. Theoretical studies show that the overhead per TCP connection is approximately 2kB.

Proof of concept implementations for all aspects of the described implementation exist, however an efficient implementation of the complete system is not yet realized. Future work also includes anonymous service discovery.

References

[1]   Uwe Jendricke and Daniela Gerd tom Markotten. Usability meets Security - The Identity-Manager as your Personal Security Assistant for the Internet. In: Proceedings of the 16th Annual Computer Security Applications Conference. pp 344-353, December 2000.

[2]   Common Criteria for Information Technology Security Evaluation. Part 2: Security Func tional Requirements. Version 2.1, August 1999.

[3]   Kai Rannenberg, Andreas Pfitzmann, and Günter Müller. Sicherheit, insbesondere mehrseitige IT-Sicherheit. In: Günter Müller and Andreas Pfitzmann, editors, Komponenten, Integration, volume 1, Mehrseitige Sicherheit in der Kommunikationstechnik, pp 21-29. Addison Wesley Bonn, 1997.

[4]   Kai Rannenberg. Zertifizierung mehrseitiger IT-Sicherheit: Kriterien und organisatorische Rahmenbedingungen. Vieweg Wiesbaden, 1998.

[5]   Roger Clarke. Identified, Anonymous and Pseudonymous Transactions: The Spectrum of Choice. In: Proceedings of the User Identification & Privacy Protection Conference, September 1999. Accessed at http://www.ana.edu.au/people/Roger.Clarke/DV/ UIPP99. html, on March1, 2002.

[6]   Andreas Pfitzmann and Marit Köhntopp. Anonymity, Unobservability, and Pseudonymity A Proposal for Terminology. In: Hannes Federrath (Ed.): Designing Privacy Enhancing Technologies; Proc. Workshop on Design Issues in Anonymity and Unobservability; LNCS 2009; pp 1-9, 2001 .

[7]   Vitaly Shmatikov and Dominic Hughes. Defining Anonymity and Privacy(extended abstract). In: Workshop on Issues in the Theory of Security (WITS '02), 2002.

[8]   Pierangela Samarati and Latanya Sweeney. Protecting Privacy when Disclosing Information: k-Anonymity and its Enforcement through Generalization and Suppression. Technical Report SRI-CSL-98, Computer Science Laboratory, SRI, 1998.

[9]   David Chaum. The dining cryptographers problem: unconditional sender and recipient un-traceability. Journal of Cryptology, pp 65-75, 1 (1) 1988.

[10] Michael Waidner and Birgit Pfitzmann. Unconditional Sender and Recipient Untraceabil-
      ity in spite of Active Attacks - Some Remarks. Fakultät für Informatik, Universität Karl-
      sruhe, Interner Bericht 5/89, March 1989. Accessed at http://www.semper.org/sirene/publ/
      WaPf_89IB_DCandFailStop.ps.gz on May 24, 2002.
[11] David Martin. *Local Anonymtiy in the Internet*. Ph. D. Thesis, Boston University of
      Computer Science, 1999.
[12] Mark Borning, Dogan Kesdogan, and Otto Spaniol. Anonymität und Unbeobachtbarkeit
      im Internet (Anonymity and Untraceability in the Internet). In: *it+ti Informationstechnik
      und Technische Informatik*, pp 246-253, 5 (43) 2001.
[13] David Chaum. Untraceable Electronic Mail, Return Addresses, and Digital Pseudonyms.
      In: *Communications of the ACM*, pp 84-88, 2 (24) 1981 .
[14] David M. Goldschlag, Michael G. Reed, and Paul F. Syverson. Hiding Routing Informa-
      tion. In: R. Anderson, editor, *Information Hiding*, LLNCS 1174, pp 137-150.
      Springer-Verlag, May 1996.
[15] Dogan Kesdogan, Jan Egner, and Roland Büschkes. Stop-and-Go-MIXes Providing
      Probabilistic Anonymity in an Open System. In: *Information Hiding 1998*, LNCS 1525, pp
      8398, Springer Heidelberg, 1998.
[16] Oliver Berthold, Hannes Federrath, and Stefan Köpsell. Web MIXes: A System for
      Anonymous and Unobservable Internet Access. In: Hannes Federrath, editor, *Designing
      Privacy Enhancing Technologies*, LNCS 2009, pp 115-129, 2001.
[17] George Danezis, Roger Dingledine, and Nick Mathewson. Mixminion: Design of a Type
      III Anonymous Remailer Protocol. In *IEEE Security and Privacy Symposium,* 2003.
[18] Michael Reiter, Aviel Rubin. Crowds: Anonymity for Web Transactions. In: *ACM Trans-
      actions on Information and Systems Security,* pp 66-92, 1 (1) 1998.
[19] George H. Foreman and John Zahorjan. The Challenges of Mobile Computing. In: *IEEE
      Computer*, 6 (27) 1994.
[20] T. Narten and R. Draves. Privacy Extensions for Stateless Autoconfiguration in IPv6.
      January 2001. Accessed at http://www.ietf.org/rfc/rfc3041.txt on June 21, 2002.
[21] Pekko Orava, Henry Haverinen, Jukka-Pekka Honkanen, Jon Edney. Temporary MAC
      Addresses for Anonymity. Document 02/261 of the 802.11i working group, 2002. Ac-
      cessed at: http://grouper.ieee.org/groups/802/11/Documents/D2T251-300.html on June 6,
      2003.
[22] Alf Zugenmaier. The Freiburg Privacy Diamond - A Conceptual Model for Mobility in
      Anonymity Mechanisms. *Proceedings of IEEE Globecom 2003*, 2003.
[23] Alf Zugenmaier, Michael Kreutzer, Günter Müller. The Freiburg Privacy Diamond: An
      Attacker Model for a Mobile Computing Environment, Kommunikation in Verteilten
      Systemen, KIVS '03, Leipzig, 2003.
[24] Department of Defense MIL-STD-2401. World Geodetic System WGS84. Accessed at
      ht-tp://164.214.2.59/publications/specs/printed/WGS84/wgs84.html, on March 7, 2002.
[25] Ulrich Krengel. *Einführung in die Wahrscheinlichkeitstheorie und Statistik*. 4th edition,
      Vieweg Braunschweig/Wiesbaden, 1998.
[26] Herbert Wiese. *Das neue Internetprotokoll IPv6*. Hanser Verlag München, 2002.
[27] T. Narten and R. Draves. Privacy Extensions for Stateless Autoconfiguration in IPv6.
      January 2001. Accessed at http://www.ietf.org/rfc/rfc3041.txt on June 21, 2002.
[28] Ross Anderson. *Security Engineering: A Guide to Building Dependable Systems*. Wiley,
      2001.
[29] Steve Bellovin. Defending Against Sequence Number Attacks, May 1996. Accessed at
      ht-tp://www.ietf.org/rfc/rfc1948.txt on July 30, 2002.

[30] R. Fielding, J. Gettys, J. Mogul, H. Frystyk, L. Masinter, P. Leach, and T. Berners-Lee. Hypertext Transfer Protocol -- HTTP/1.1. June 1999. Accessed at http://www.ietf.org/rfc/rfc2616.txt on May 21, 2002.

[31] R. Khare and S. Lawrence. Upgrading to TLS Within HTTP/1.1. May 2000. Accessed at http://www.ietf.org/rfc/rfc2817.txt on May 21, 2002

[32] Uwe Jendricke. *Der Identitätsmanager*. Doctoral Thesis, Rhombos Verlag, 2002.

[33] Richard Stevens. *Programmierung von UNIX-Netzwerken*, 2nd edition, Hanser, 2000.

Cryptographically Protected Prefixes for Location Privacy in IPv6

Jonathan Trostle[1], Hosei Matsuoka[2], Muhammad Mukarram Bin Tariq[3], James Kempf[3], Toshiro Kawahara[3], and Ravi Jain[3]

[1] DoCoMo Communications Laboratories USA, Inc.,
181 Metro Dr. Suite 300. San Jose, CA 95110
jtrostle@world.std.com
[2] Multimedia Laboratories, NTT DoCoMo, Inc.,
3-5, Hikari-no-oka, Yokosuka, Kanagawa, 239-8536, Japan
matsuoka@spg.yrp.nttdocomo.co.jp
[3] DoCoMo Communications Laboratories USA, Inc.,
181 Metro Dr. Suite 300. San Jose, CA 95110
{tariq, kempf, kawahara, jain}@docomolabs-usa.com

Abstract. There is a growing concern with preventing unauthorized agents from discovering the geographical location of Internet users, a kind of security called location privacy. The typical deployments of IPv6 in mobile networks allow a correspondent host and any passive eavesdroppers to infer the user's rough geographical location from the IPv6 address. We present a scheme called *Cryptographically Protected Prefixes (CPP)*, to address this problem at the level of IPv6 addressing and forwarding. CPP randomizes the address space of a defined topological region (privacy domain), thereby making it infeasible to infer location information from an IP address. CPP can be deployed incrementally. We present an adversary model and show that CPP is secure within the model. We have implemented CPP as a pre-processing step within the forwarding algorithm in the FreeBSD 4.8 kernel. Our performance testing indicates that CPP pre-processing results in a 40–50 percent overhead for packet forwarding in privacy domain routers. The additional end to end per packet delay is roughly 20 to 60 microseconds.

1 Introduction

IPv6 addressing, as it is typically deployed, can reveal information about the geographical location of hosts because there is a correlation between the topological location and geographical location of an address. Concern has been increasing about ways to prevent unauthorized agents from using this information to determine the geographical location of fixed users, or to track the geographical location of mobile users as they move [AK, WM]. Protection against such activity is called location privacy. There are regulations in some countries which mandate that network operators protect their user's location privacy. The need for this protection is likely to grow as Voice over IP (VoIP) and other applications become more prevalent.

D. Martin and A. Serjantov (Eds.): PET 2004, LNCS 3424, pp. 142–166, 2005.

The problem is particularly evident with wireless networks. A common deployment pattern for wireless networks is to assign a specific subnet prefix to a collection of wireless cells in a fixed geographical area. For IPv6, this corresponds to having a fixed subnet prefix, typically 64 bits in length, with the form $P0, Q^1$, where P_0 is the ISP identifier, and Q is the subnet identifier within that ISP [DH2, DH3]. Users without proper authorization credentials can determine which area a host occupies by simply inspecting the IP address.

An attacker can use such information to track the location of a host in the following way. Since the subnet prefix appears in the IPv6 source address and the IPv6 source address appears in plaintext in the packet header, the eavesdropper can easily obtain the prefix and use it as an index into the mapping table to determine where the sender is located. Every host is vulnerable to this attack regardless of whether it is mobile or non-mobile.

In this paper, we present a new technique, called Cryptographically Protected Prefixes (CPP), which solves this problem by eliminating any obvious correlation between the topological and geographic location. CPP encrypts parts of the IP address prefix in order to provide location privacy. In the next section, we review existing work in this area. Section 3 describes the basic CPP scheme. In Section 4, we discuss security considerations. In Section 5, we present the CPP adversary model, and prove that CPP is secure within the model. We also obtain a probability bound that limits an adversary's ability to obtain location information about a CPP address. Our extension for intradomain (BGP (Border Gateway Protocol) domain) location privacy is included in this section as well. Section 6 discusses performance results from our implementation. In Section 7, we discuss CPP with respect to network integration and also compare it with some of the other approaches. In Section 8, we draw some conclusions. Appendix A gives additional techniques for defending against a global adversary as well as protecting the first prefix bit from attacks.

2   Related Work

Prior work on location privacy can be separated into IETF protocol work including Mobile IPv6 [Mipv6] and HMIPv6 [SC] (which are the location privacy equivalent of an anonymizing proxy), anonymity techniques that also provide location privacy, and a technique that modifies the basic underlying IPv6 routing, IP^2 [YH]. Onion routing [Onion], Freedom [Go1], and Tarzan [Tarzan] are examples of overlay approaches specifically developed for providing generic privacy that are discussed here as location privacy solutions. The review in [SK] contains more information on existing generic network level privacy approaches that are not specifically mobility related.

Mobility management protocols like Mobile IPv6 [Mipv6] provide means whereby the geographical location of the mobile node can remain hidden to the

---

[1] Through the rest of this paper, we will use the notation x, y, z to refer to concatenation of bitstrings x, y, and z.

correspondent and some eavesdroppers, though that is not its primary purpose. The basic location management technique of Mobile IP requires correspondent hosts to tunnel traffic to and from a mobile host through a home address in the mobile host's home network.

A similar overlay routing approach is HMIPv6 [SC]. In HMIPv6, the network operator deploys a collection of home agent-like servers around the topological periphery of the wireless network, near the border routers to the Internet. These servers manage traffic through a regional care-of- address for the mobile node. A mobile node within the topological span covered by such a server is assigned a regional CoA on the server, in addition to its local CoA on its subnet. As the mobile node moves, it sends local CoA change updates to its current regional CoA server rather than to the home agent or correspondent hosts. If an adversary can map a regional CoA to a larger geographical region than the local CoA, the adversary is still able to obtain some information about the location of the mobile host. Thus HMIPv6 blurs the geographical to topological mapping without breaking it.

Both Mobile IP and HMIPv6 force all the traffic to/from a mobile host to traverse via the home agent or a regional CoA server. This includes the traffic within the coverage area of the regional CoA server for HMIP, thus enforcing suboptimal routes within the region and making the home agent or regional CoA server into traffic concentration points. Also, these approaches are vulnerable to host attacks, against both mobile nodes and the CoA server. The regional CoA server is a stateful single point of failure, and is vulnerable to denial of service attacks as well. Both HMIPv6 and Mobile IP are vulnerable to intersection attacks, including in the case where IPsec encryption is used. These attacks occur when an attacker matches up outgoing packets on the internal network with outgoing packets between the regional CoA server, or home agent, and the Internet. Multiple associated sets of packets can be intersected which then yields the mapping between CoA and HoA.

Crowds [RR] is an example of an application specific (web browsing) anonymity service. Other application specific approaches include [Ch1, BF, GT, DD]. Some of these introduce additional network latency making them unsuitable for real time applications.

Onion routing [Onion] is an example of a generic privacy approach that secondarily provides location privacy. Anonymity is provided by an overlay network of onion routers that proxy TCP traffic through a series of TCP connections. Although onion routing provides a good privacy/performance trade-off for many real time applications, the overhead (especially when recovering from a failed onion router) may be problematic for some real-time applications (e.g., Voice over IP). Onion routing was originally designed for communication between two secure sites, and it is optimized for TCP based applications. Onion routing does not protect against host attacks aimed at obtaining a host's location, and it does not furnish an easily scaleable means for removing source IP addresses from application layer data. Since it is a system of proxies, it cannot coexist with end to end IPsec [Kent]. Therefore, Onion Routing does not provide an easily scaleable means of achieving location privacy for all applications.

The Freedom Network [Go1, EH] consisted of a private overlay network containing proxies called Anonymous Internet Proxies (AIP). Freedom creates random routes in the private overlay network and associates them with the client's real identity or a pseudo-identity. User host operating specific changes are required; the Freedom network filter removes the client's IP address. Using Freedom to provide location privacy raises some of the same issues as Onion Routing (as described above).

Tarzan [Tarzan] is a general purpose anonymity system that operates at the IP layer. In that sense, it closer to our approach than some of the higher layer techniques. Tarzan uses layers of encryption through a relay network, similar to Onion Routing. Although Tarzan is more application transparent than Onion Routing or Freedom, it is still problematic in some aspects. Since the PNAT must perform a source IP address NAT operation, end to end encryption/integrity protection protocols such as TLS/SSL cannot be used (e.g. when application data is encrypted, the source IP address cannot be rewritten in a packet payload, as is required by some protocols such as FTP). Also, the NAT operations are problematic in the sense that they are application specific; thus a NAT module is required for each application that includes source addresses in packet payloads. Existing NAT code will not always be sufficient, since some protocols include these addresses but the responder does not make use of them. For location privacy, however, it is not acceptable to leak arbitrary source IP addresses to the responder. As with Onion Routing and Freedom, Tarzan does not protect against host attacks aimed at obtaining a user's location from its IP address. But this information cannot necessarily be associated with anonymous traffic from the host. The latter depends on whether the local operating system exposes the PNAT address to untrusted applications.

An approach that requires modifying the border routers and access routers is IP^2 [YH]. IP^2 requires that servers in the control plane maintain the mapping between the home address and the CoA in a logically centralized manner. This approach may lead to scalability and performance issues. Additionally, the approach assumes that all routers and operators in the IP^2 network are trusted.

3   The CPP Scheme

3.1   Requirements and Design Considerations

We discuss some design considerations in this section. We suppose a public access network and users that are usually (but not always) mobile users. Onion Routing [Onion] is seminal work but is aimed as a general anonymity solution between two secure sites for a relatively fixed set of applications. We require application transparent location privacy for a full set of IPv6 applications in a wider variety of scenarios. A key design point is how addresses are handled. We discuss three approaches: address rewriting/proxies, home address/care of address, and obfuscated addresses.

Many existing solutions rewrite addresses using NAT schemes [Tarzan], or proxies [Onion]. One of our requirements is to support application level encryption schemes including TLS/SSL. Since some applications include addresses in application layer protocol data (e.g., FTP, H.323, and many others), it is not possible to rewrite these addresses when application encryption is used. For the purposes of location privacy, all source addresses must be rewritten. Depending on which entity rewrites the address, identifying a particular application protocol is not always straightforward. The only truly reliable way of communicating this information is through API changes which requires changes to applications. The cost of misidentifying one of these applications is a loss in location privacy for the affected host.

Another approach is for a host to use two IP addresses: a home address which is used as the host source address by the transport (TCP, UDP, etc.) and application layers, and a care of address (CoA) which is used by the network layer. The CoA can be rewritten by proxies or a HMIP MAP server [SC]. The disadvantages here are that the IPsec Authentication Header (AH) protocol cannot be used, significant changes must be made to user hosts, and an untrusted local process may be able to obtain the CoA and thus the location of the end host. It is desirable to avoid determining all the possible ways that the CoA might be obtained by an untrusted local process and to also minimize modifications to user hosts.

The third approach is the one we have selected, which is to obfuscate the IP address (through encryption). We avoid the problems mentioned above. Routers perform encryption operations as part of the CPP forwarding algorithm. As an additional extension we provide a hybrid solution, Enhanced Router Security Extension (ERS), using elements of both the second and third approaches in a way that still protects against host attacks.

3.2   CPP Overview

CPP IP addresses are designed to hide the location of nodes in an IP access network. The basic idea is that only routers with the proper keys are able to determine how to forward a packet with a CPP destination address to the next hop. The location of a CPP address is the IPv6 subnet that packets destined for the address will be forwarded to. At a high level, CPP protects against attacks that attempt to determine a user's geographical location from their CPP IP address. Since a user identity is, in most cases, an application level entity, attacks against location privacy require the cooperation of an application running on a correspondent host and other entities. These other entities can take the following forms:

1. host based attacks - with CPP, any local process, even if trusted, is unable to determine the location of a host from its CPP address,
2. network attacks - an eavesdropper in some location other than the CPP host's local link is unable to determine the location of the CPP host, (although additional protection is required against more advanced traffic analysis attacks)
3. compromised routers - a router in the CPP access network is only able to determine enough information to forward the packet to its next hop. A

malicious router is unable, by itself, to determine the location of the CPP host (except when the next hop is the access router for the CPP host). CPP routers closer to the Internet will be able to obtain limited information about CPP address location, for a large number of hosts (the hosts attached to routers in subtrees below them). CPP access routers will be able to obtain a lot of information about a smaller number of CPP addresses (the hosts directly attached to them).

4. prefix correlation attacks - since CPP users in the same subnet have IP addresses with uncorrelated prefixes, an attacker cannot build a prefix table that determines the location of all users from the known location of a few users.

In other words, determining the location of a CPP address by itself does not disclose a user's location. The combination of CPP address location and a mapping between a user and that CPP address does disclose a user's location. CPP requires limited modifications to access network routers. Routers outside the CPP network (identified by a global prefix identifier P_0), or privacy domain, are not modified. (But this privacy domain may span multiple BGP domains). Routing protocols are not modified either. CPP uses a new forwarding algorithm (but not all access network routers need be CPP capable). An IPv6 address is of the form (P0, Q, M) where P0 is the global routing prefix, Q is the subnet prefix, and M is the host identifier. When forwarding packets, each CPP capable router decrypts a piece of the destination IP address subnet prefix, or prefix component, corresponding to its depth in the routing graph. The router concatenates the prefix components corresponding to the higher routers that were included in a hop by hop option with the prefix component that it decrypts. This concatenated prefix is then used as an input into the longest prefix matching forwarding algorithm. CPP does not hide or obscure the global routing prefix, but we do discuss an extension in Section 5 for intradomain location privacy.

The segmentation of prefixes into prefix components is accomplished through route aggregation. Route aggregation occurs when a router advertises a single prefix in place of multiple prefixes, where the new prefix is a proper prefix substring of all of the replaced prefixes.

Since each router is only able to decrypt a piece of the prefix, the higher level routers only obtain the information they need to forward the packet. They are unable to determine the subnet where the user host is located.

A CPP access network requires a CPP key/address server in order to provide symmetric keys to the routers for CPP forwarding. The CPP server also provides CPP addresses to DHCP servers which can then assign addresses to user hosts. These DHCP servers may be co-located with access routers for performance reasons. The next section will explain how the CPP server creates a CPP address, using cryptographic operations.

We will present the CPP address structure, a forwarding example, rekeying, and describe how CPP addresses are created.

3.3   CPP Address Structure

IPv6 addresses are divided into a network identifier prefix, P, and a host identifier suffix, M, so the address has the form P, M [DH2]. A host's first hop router uses M to map between the IPv6 address of a received packet and the link layer address, so it can deliver the packet to a host. P is used to route packets within the ISP's routing domain and on the Internet.

P can be further divided into two parts, $P0, Q$, with $P0$ being a global routing prefix and Q being a subnet identifier [DH3]. $P0$ remains unchanged within the ISP's routing domain and is used on the public Internet to identify packets that must be routed to the ISP. Q is a subnet identifier and is used by routers within the ISP's routing domain to determine the first hop router to which a packet is delivered. A full IPv6 address can therefore be represented as $P0, Q, M$.

The set of CPP access network routers is partitioned according to their depth in the aggregated routing graph; these subsets are called levels. All the routers in (or at) the same level share a secret symmetric key with each other and the CPP key server. This key is used by the CPP forwarding algorithm to decrypt the piece of the IP address needed for routing at the level.

Suppose the IP address prefix is the concatenation of prefix components corresponding to route aggregations:

$$Q = P_1, P_2, \ldots, P_k$$

The CPP IP address has the format described in Figure 1. Let

$$X_j = P_j \oplus h(L_j, M), 1 \leq j \leq k.$$

where h is a one-way cryptographic hash function. The keys $L_1, \ldots, L_k$ are symmetric keys such that each key L_j is shared by the routers at the same level j. Suppose the current router is at level d in the routing graph. It obtains the prefix component P_d by computing

$$P_d = h(L_d, M) \oplus X_d.$$

The current router obtains the prefix components $P_1, \ldots, P_{d-1}$ from the previous hop router; $P_1 \ldots, P_{d-1}$ is forwarded in an IPv6 hop by hop option. The

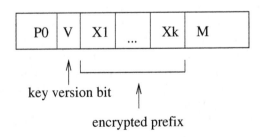

Fig. 1. CPP IPv6 Address Showing Prefix Encryption

current router now forwards the packet using the longest prefix matching algorithm, with the prefix $Q = P_1, \ldots, P_{d-1}$, P_d as the input. It also includes the prefix Q in an IPv6 hop by hop option. The next hop will use this prefix Q concatenated with the prefix P_{d+1}, which it will obtain in the same way that the current router obtains P_d; the next hop uses $Q|P_{d+1}$ as an input into the longest prefix matching algorithm. In this way, the packet is forwarded to the destination access router. We note that each packet is completely encrypted as it traverses the link (tunnel encrypted).

A CPP address uses one bit, v, to toggle the key version, for smooth updating of keys. The router uses this bit to determine the key version to be used for decrypting the subnet identifier. Rekeying will be described later in the paper. An additional bit is used to distinguish between CPP addresses and non-CPP addresses.

An outgoing packet is forwarded up the default route until it hits a border router. The border router forwards locally destined packets using the algorithm described above.

3.4   CPP Forwarding Examples

The following example illustrates the CPP forwarding algorithm. Figure 2 depicts the example CPP access network (but not all links are shown). R1 is a border router. A link is denoted by Ri - Rj where Ri is the upstream router and Rj is the downstream router (so the link labeled with the prefix P1 is denoted by R1 - R2). The user host, host H, is attached to the access router R5. The optimal path for packets from a border router to host H is R1 - R2, R2 - R3, R3 - R5.

There are also a set of level keys: R1 has level key L_1, R7 and R2 share level key L_2, R8, R3, and R4 share level key L_3, and R5 and R6 share level key L_4. The CPP IP address for host H is:

$$P_0|X_1|X_2|X_3|M$$

where $X_j = P_j \oplus h(L_j, M)$ denotes P_j exclusive or'd with the truncation of $h(L_j, M)$ to the same number of bits as P_j, $j = 1, 2, 3$.

The forwarding algorithm for an inbound packet in the case where link R2 - R3 is down is now described: Since R1 is a border router, it decrypts the first prefix component, P_1 using key L_1:

$$P_1 = h(L_1, M) \oplus (P_1 \oplus h(L_1, M)).$$

R1 then computes the next hop for the packet by inputting $P_0 P_1$ into the longest prefix matching forwarding algorithm. The packet is forwarded to R2, and it includes a hop by hop option with the prefix P_1.

R2 uses key L_2 to obtain $P_2 = h(L_2, M) \oplus (P_2 \oplus h(L_2, M))$. R2 also obtains P_1 from the hop by hop option. R2 now uses the longest prefix matching algorithm, with $P_0|P_1|P_2$ as input, to forward the packet to R4. R2 includes the prefix $P_1|P_2$ in a hop by hop option. R4 receives the packet and uses key L_3 to obtain $h(L_3, M)$ and

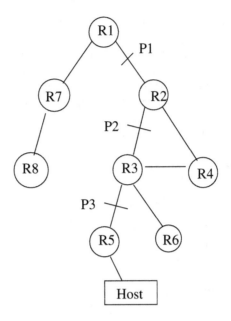

Fig. 2. CPP Forwarding Example

$$P_3 = h(L_3, M) \oplus (P_3 \oplus h(L_3, M)).$$

R4 then uses the longest prefix matching algorithm to match $P_0|P_1|P_2|P_3$ and forwards the packet to R3. The prefix $P_1|P_2|P_3$ is included in a hop by hop option. R3 then uses the longest prefix matching algorithm on $P_0|P_1|P_2|P_3$ to forward the packet to R5. The hop by hop option also includes the next level which must decrypt the prefix; in this last case, R3 will not decrypt any parts of the prefix since the prefix is completely decrypted.

The following pseudocode summarizes the CPP forwarding algorithm:

```
M = destination_address.suffix;
    if (we are a border router)
        use level key L to obtain
        initial prefix component.
        Forward packet using this
        prefix in longest prefix
        match algorithm;
        include prefix in hop by hop
        option
    else
        if (no hop by hop option is
            present)
            forward packet up the
            default route;
        else
```

```
concatenate hop by hop
prefix with prefix
obtained by decrypting
with key L and input into
longest prefix match
forwarding algorithm,
include concatenated
prefix in hop by hop
option. Forward packet
to next hop.
```

The full paper contains a more formal desription of the CPP forwarding algorithm, along with a proof of resilience in the presence of network failures.

3.5   Rekeying

CPP routers periodically obtain new keys for forwarding CPP addresses. CPP addresses include a key version bit to allow CPP routers to select the correct key. For example, the key period could be 8 hours. During the last half of a key period, CPP routers would obtain keys for the next period. Addresses would expire within 8 hours of being issued. Therefore, a CPP router would never encounter an address that was issued more than one period before the current key period, thus ensuring that a single key version bit is sufficient.

3.6   Creating the CPP IP Address

There are a variety of ways that CPP addresses can be mapped onto the 128 bit IPv6 address. The most common address structure expected for general IPv6 addresses [IPv6-Alloc] is that P_0 is 48 bits, Q is 16 bits, and M is 64 bits, two bits of which are reserved as the 'universal', u, and 'group', g, bits to designate whether the host identifier is derived from an EUI-64 address [DH2]. However, P_0 can be smaller if a particular ISP requires more address space, with 32 bits being a recommended minimum. In addition, the IPv6 addressing architecture supports addresses with no fixed boundary between P and M. These addresses begin with the special bit pattern 000.

From Figure 1, the $X_i's$ require about 16 bits in the address, and P0 requires 48 bits, if IPv6 address blocks are assigned according to [DH3] The bit v is used for key versioning (see Section 3.5). An additional bit may be required to distinguish CPP addresses from non-CPP addresses (for CPP capable routers) within the domain. So there are 62 bits available for M in the address.

3.7   Aggregation and Incremental Deployment

The encryption scheme for the subnet prefix Q requires that route advertisements distributed by the ISP's interior gateway protocol be aggregated into distinct levels. A route is fully aggregated when it summarizes all the routers under it using a reduced size prefix. For example, consider the privacy domain shown in

Figure 2. Here, the Ri are routers. A fully aggregated routing table means that no routes for R3 through R6 and R8 occur in R1's routing table, since these routes are aggregated by R2 and R7. All routers in the domain contain a default route to R1, since it is the border gateway router to the Internet.

CPP can be deployed incrementally. For example, an overlay network can be used. The CPP routers use IPsec tunneling to tunnel packets to other CPP routers. The non-overlay CPP routers do not have to be CPP capable (one possible exception is the border routers which we discuss below). Therefore, CPP can be used for location privacy, even if the majority of routers do not support CPP. Additionally, the CPP overlay network can be set up to maximize the number of aggregated routes (all CPP overlay routers can aggregate routes). The aggregation can be done automatically, without administrator intervention.

In overlay CPP, border routers must either be CPP routers, or they must be set up to forward CPP traffic to CPP routers and non-CPP traffic to other routers. For example, this forwarding can be accomplished through the use of two distinct global routing prefixes, one for CPP traffic, and the other for non-CPP traffic.

Although CPP routers use tunneling, tunneling is not required between first hop routers and hosts. Many of the other location privacy solutions, such as HMIP also require tunneling, but these require tunneling to the user host which is more problematic due to limited wireless network bandwidths.

4   Security Considerations

4.1   Eavesdropping

CPP does not necessarily prevent an eavesdropper on the same network link from obtaining the host's location and IP address. If local link encryption combined with some host modifications are employed, then some protection against local eavesdroppers can be provided.

If protection against local eavesdroppers is desired, than hosts and routers in the location privacy domain must not use link local addresses, do not perform local link address resolution [NN], and do not perform duplicate address detection on the local link [TN] as most IPv6 hosts typically do. Receipt of a packet with a link local address or any of the messages associated with local link address resolution, which are partially multicast, can provide a hint to an eavesdropper that a particular address is on the local link, and thus within the geographic area covered by the local link. In order to prevent the router on a link from performing local link address resolution, CPP requires hosts to include their link layer address in unicast Router Solicitation messages to routers. This message informs the router of the mapping between the hosts' link layer address and CPP IPv6 address. In some cases, routers with co-located DHCP servers can keep track of the mapping through requests to renew the lease on a DHCP address, and the release of an address by a mobile host that has moved. First hop routers are therefore the only nodes on the link that have any knowledge of a host's presence on the link.

CPP does not by itself protect against eavesdroppers on multiple links. A multiple link eavesdropper can obtain information from each link, and ultimately obtain the location of a CPP address. For example, the attacker can follow the packet from a border router to the access router that the victim host is attached to. CPP uses IPsec tunnels between CPP routers to prevent such an attack. (Alternatively, link encryption can be used to protect all the access network links). However, more sophisticated attackers can still obtain information (e.g. through timing, etc.), especially in a network that is lightly loaded. More powerful countermeasures can also be employed to defeat these attacks (e.g., one of the mechanisms from [Onion, Tarzan]) at the cost of increased performance impact. For these high privacy environments, CPP should be deployed in combination with other techniques to prevent traffic analysis.

4.2   Guessing Attacks and the CPP Extended Address

We now describe a guessing attack against the CPP address. An attacker on a subnet in the CPP access network desires to obtain the location of a victim host, somewhere else in the access network. The suffix of the victim host's CPP address is M_v. The attacker makes guesses G_i at each of the values $h(L_i, M_v)$ and then XORs these with the prefix components in his own IP address. The attacker then sends a ping packet (or uses some other protocol for which a response is expected), using a source address of the form:

$$P_0, P_1 \oplus G_1, P_2 \oplus G_2, ..., P_k \oplus G_k, M_v,$$

(where the attacker's location is $P_0, P_1, P_2, ..., P_k$).

If a response is received, the attacker has guessed the $h(L_i, M_v)$ values correctly. If the attacker does guess these correctly, it can obtain the location of the victim host. (Since the subnet prefix is often only 16 bits long, the expected number of queries for the attack is 32000 - which is not a problem for an attacker with even modest resources.) The attacker user host must send a neighbor solicitation for each address guess, to its local access router. This behaviour is not out of the ordinary, since the user host needs to inform its local access routers of the mapping between its CPP IP address and its link layer address.

The following address structure, the CPP extended address, prevents this attack. The prefix is $Q = X_1, \ldots, X_k$ where

$$X_k = P_k \oplus h(L_k, M, P_1, \ldots, P_{k-1})$$
$$X_{k-1} = P_{k-1} \oplus h(L_{k-1}, M, P_1, P_2, \ldots, P_{k-2}, X_k)$$
$$\ldots$$
$$X_3 = P_3 \oplus h(L_3, M, P_1, P_2, X_4, \ldots, X_k)$$
$$X_2 = P_2 \oplus h(L_2, M, P_1, X_3, X_4, \ldots, X_k)$$
$$X_1 = P_1 \oplus h(L_1, M, X_2, X_3, \ldots, X_k)$$

We discuss the security of the extended CPP address further in the next section.

If an attacker has the resources to simultaneously send neighbor solicitations on all subnets, then the attacker can locate a target address. For example, when the attacker is on the same subnet as the target address, the attacker will start receiving traffic for the address after sending the solicitation. We prevent this last attack from occurring, by requiring that CPP access routers set the neighbor cache lifetime for a CPP address to link layer address binding equal to the lifetime of the CPP address. With this countermeasure, an attacker cannot create a new mapping in the router neighbor cache with the CPP address of the victim and the attacker's link layer address. Therefore, the attacker cannot directly mount a subnet search attack.

4.3   ICMP

ICMP messages are often used by routers to signal certain error conditions to a sending host. If the router uses a non-CPP address in the IPv6 header containing an ICMP header, and the ICMP message is in response to a packet that contained a CPP destination address, then an attacker can use this information to help localize the CPP address.

Therefore, a router must always use a one-time random source IP address as the source address in an ICMP error message packet, if the original packet that caused the response contained a CPP destination address. An exception is when IPsec is being used and the peer is authorized to view the real IP address. Per the IETF specifications, nodes do not reply to ICMP error messages.

An instructive example is traceroute. Traceroute is a standard IP tool used for determining the path taken by packets. Traceroute can compromise location privacy unless router sending of ICMP messages is modified. Traceroute determines the topological location of a client by sending out packets with gradually increasing time to live (TTL) values until the correspondent on the other end of the connection is reached. TTLs that are smaller than required to reach the correspondent are decremented to zero enroot. If the TTL value is decremented to zero, the router doing the decrementing sends an ICMP Time Exceeded message back to the source. The source address on this packet is the router where the TTL = 0 was detected. An attacker could use such information to build up a location map of IP addresses.

An exception to the above rule is to send ICMP error packets with real source addresses when the sender has authenticated using IPsec [Kent], and the sender is authorized to request topological information. For example, only a user with administrative privileges should be able to successfully run traceroute and obtain real IP address route information.

5   Security of CPP Extended Address

In this section, we present an approach for using CPP extended addresses in a way that prevents guessing attacks. We present an adversary model and prove security against guessing attacks in the model. We also present an extension that provides location privacy across BGP domains. Although correspondents can obtain the global prefix identifier (P_0) from an address, it is possible to use the same P_0 across multiple, geographically distributed BGP domains.

5.1   CPP Adversary Model

We now give the intuition behind the CPP adversary model. The adversary can move to different subnets in the CPP access network, register a CPP address of its choosing (but this address must meet neighbor cache restrictions), and receive packets at the address. The adversary is a multi-location entity (may consist of multiple hosts/users in different locations). There is no limit to the number of packets that may be sent and received by the adversary. There is a restriction on the number of subnets that the adversary can move to in a given key period, s, (the motivation here is that moving takes some amount of time, and the key period may be only 6-7 hours long).

The adversary can send packets to any destination address. It will receive any packets sent to it by the other adversary components, providing the neighbor cache restrictions are met. In particular, if the adversary chooses a source address on a subnet where the same source address has already been used, then the adversary cannot receive packets destined to that address. A CPP router neighbor cache will not allow the same CPP address to be reused with multiple different link layer address mappings. Furthermore, the neighbor cache entry will become stale after some period of inactivity, preventing that address from being reused again, even with the same link layer address. Finally, the adversary can move to a new subnet at any time. The following model now formalizes this construction.

Definition: The CPP adversary model is the tuple (G, F, Adv, s, T_1, T_2, ..., T_k), where G is a CPP routing graph with aggregated prefixes, F is the function described below, Adv is an adversary that can query F, s is the number of different locations that Adv can receive packets in, and T_i is the number of prefix components for the ith prefix component. Adv selects an address $A = Q_1 \oplus G_1, \ldots, Q_k \oplus G_k, M$ and a location $Q = Q_1, \ldots, Q_k$. $F(A, Q)$ returns 1 if the following equations are satisfied

$$G_1 = h(L_1, M, (Q_2 \oplus G_2), \ldots, (Q_k \oplus G_k))$$
$$G_2 = h(L_2, M, Q_1, (Q_3 \oplus G_3), \ldots, (Q_k \oplus G_k))$$
$$G_3 = h(L_3, M, Q_1, Q_2, (Q_4 \oplus G_4), \ldots, (Q_k \oplus G_k))$$
$$\cdots$$
$$G_{k-1} = h(L_{k-1}, M, Q_1, \ldots, Q_{k-2}, (Q_k \oplus G_k))$$
$$G_k = h(L_k, M, Q_1, \ldots, Q_{k-1})$$

and A has not already been used on the subnet Q. Otherwise $F(A, Q)$ returns no answer. Adv is allowed to select up to s different locations Q in its series of queries. The adversary is adaptive in the sense that the next query is allowed to depend on the results of previous queries.

The CPP adversary model assumes that additional countermeasures prevent traffic analysis attacks on the links of the access network, and that access network routers are not compromised. We will also rule out hash function specific attacks.

We now give a bound for the security of the CPP extended address against guessing attacks. The CPP extended address does not completely prevent guessing attacks; rather, it makes these attacks unlikely to succeed. We let $|S| =$ length of the bit string S.

Theorem 1. *Given the CPP adversary model* $(G, F, Adv, s, T_1, T_2, \ldots, T_k)$ *as described in the above definition. Let* $B = P_0, X_1, \ldots, X_k, M$ *be a CPP address with location* $P_1, \ldots, P_k$. *Let*

$$p_1 = 1 - [(2^{|P_1|} - 1)/2^{|P_1|}]2^{-(|P_2|+\ldots+|P_k|)}$$
$$p_2 = 1 - [(2^{|P_2|} - 1)/2^{|P_2|}]2^{-(|P_3|+\ldots+|P_k|)}$$
$$p_3 = 1 - [(2^{|P_3|} - 1)/2^{|P_3|}]2^{-(|P_4|+\ldots+|P_k|)}.$$

Then the probability that Adv obtains the prefix components P1, P2, and P3 of address B is bounded by

$$q = (1/2)\alpha[x(s - 2)p^{s-2} - x(0)],$$

where $p = max\{p_1, p_2, p_3\}$, $\alpha = (1 - p_1)(1 - p_2)(1 - p_3)$, *s is the number of subnets searched, and* $x(s) = x_2 s^2 + x_1 s + x_0$ *where*

$$x_2 = 1/(p - 1), x_1 = (3 - 2px_2)/(p - 1),$$

$$x_0 = [2 - px_2 - px_1]/(p - 1)$$

Proof: We can assume that a received packet D has the same host identifier M as B, else the adversary cannot learn any information about B's address (we are ruling out hash function specific attacks as described above, and M is part of the hash computation). Suppose Adv is located on the subnet with subnet prefix $Q_1, \ldots, Q_k$. Then Adv's address has the form $Q_1 \oplus G_1, \ldots, Q_k \oplus G_k$, for some Gi's. D is forwarded to this subnet, so the following equations are satisfied:

$$G_1 = h(L_1, M, (Q_2 \oplus G_2), \ldots, (Q_k \oplus G_k))$$
$$G_2 = h(L_2, M, Q_1, (Q_3 \oplus G_3), \ldots, (Q_k \oplus G_k))$$
$$G_3 = h(L_3, M, Q_1, Q_2, (Q_4 \oplus G_4), \ldots, (Q_k \oplus G_k))$$

$$\ldots$$

$$G_{k-1} = h(L_{k-1}, M, Q_1, \ldots, Q_{k-2}, (Q_k \oplus G_k))$$
$$G_k = h(L_k, M, Q_1, \ldots, Q_{k-1})$$

$G_1, \ldots, G_k$ are completely determined by the above equations. The attacker uses the following equations to determine its guesses $G_2, \ldots, G_k$: $Q_2 \oplus G_2 = X_2, \ldots, Q_k \oplus G_k = X_k$; in order to obtain the value $h(L_1, M, X_2, X_3, \ldots, X_k)$. The attacker can guess G_1 such that the first equation above is satisified, but all of the equations must be satisfied in order to receive the reply D. If $P_1 = Q_1$, then $P_2 = Q_2, \ldots, P_k = Q_k$ in order for D to be received. Therefore, either A is on the same subnet as B, or P_1 is not equal to Q_1 (see the definition of the CPP extended address in Section 4). In the first case, A will not receive a response packet, since we require that A not be able to create an entry in the neighbor cache with its own link layer address and the CPP address B. (The CPP router will also consider a neighbor cache entry to be stale if no packets have utilized the entry in the recent past; therefore, the attacker will not be able to observe packets sent to address B unless it is on the same link as the victim at the same time, or close to the same time. We ignore this case, since there are other ways of detecting the victim's physical location at this point, including physical recognition of the victim.)

In the latter case (P_1 not equal to Q_1), the above equations (1) are satisfied with probability $1 - p_1$. But A learns only $h(L_1, M, X_2, X_3, \ldots, X_k)$, and P_1, from the above equations in this case. The attacker must now repeat the search using $Q_1 = P_1$, in order to learn $h(L_2, M, P_1, X_3, X_4, \ldots, X_k)$. The attacker can guess G_1 and G_2; the probability that the remaining equations can be satisfied is bounded by $1 - p_2$. The same argument holds for $1 - p_3$. Therefore the success probability is

$$\alpha \sum_{i_1+i_2+i_3 \leq s-3} p_1^{i_1} p_2^{i_2} p_3^{i_3} \leq$$

$$\alpha \sum_{i_1+i_2+i_3 \leq s-3} p^{i_1+i_2+i_3} =$$

$$\alpha \sum_{i=0}^{s-3} [(i+2)(i+1)/2] p^i$$

where $\alpha = (1 - p_1)(1 - p_2)(1 - p_3)$. The last quantity is equal to

$$q = \alpha(1/2)[x(s-2)p^{s-2} - x(0)].$$

For guessing attacks where the attacker moves to multiple subnets, we assume that some time is required to physically traverse between the multiple subnets. For example, if we assume a traversal time of four minutes, then less than 100 subnets can be covered during a key period of 6.67 hours. We compute some probabilities in the next subsection.

5.2   CPP Prefix Component Segmentation

Although the above proof shows the difficulty of obtaining the first three components of a CPP address, in some cases it is desirable to prevent an adversary from obtaining any prefix components of an address. The first subnet prefix component P_1 can be segmented into multiple single bit prefix components, $W_1, W_2, \ldots, W_m$, where W_1 consists of the first bit of P_1, W_2 consists of the second bit in P_1, and so on. The first CPP router (CPP border router) will use m separate encryption keys and decrypt all of $W_1, W_2, \ldots, W_m$ before forwarding the packet. This additional segmentation is independent of, and has no affect on, the forwarding tables and prefix aggregation. We expect m to be between 3 and 6, typically.

With P_1 segmentation, the above probability bounds show that it is highly unlikely for an adversary to obtain more than two bits of information about the prefix component P_1. We will now show that it is very unlikely for an adversary to obtain more than a single bit of information about P_1, when P_1 segmentation is used. From the argument in the theorem proof above, the probability that the adversary obtains the first two bits (W_1 and W_2) is bounded by

$$\alpha \sum_{i_1+i_2 \leq s-2} p_1^{i_1} p_2^{i_2} \leq \alpha \sum_{i=0}^{s-2} (i+1)p^i =$$
$$\alpha[\frac{(1-p^s) - (s)p^{s-1}(1-p)}{(1-p)^2}]$$

where $\alpha = (1-p_1)(1-p_2)$, $p = \max\{p_1, p_2\}$, and p_1 and p_2 are defined above. In this case, $1 - p_1 = 1/2^{16}$, and $1 - p_2 = 1/2^{15}$. We obtain a bound less than $1/434187$, when $s = 100$. In other words, the probability that the adversary obtains more than one bit of information about P_1 is less than $1/434187$.

To this point we have not considered any hash function specific attacks; more precisely, we are assuming that the hash function outputs are uniform. The uncertainty in the outputs obscures the prefix values in the CPP address. We now relax this assumption. In particular, we consider attacks where the adversary attempts to determine partial information about prefixes. We relabel $W_1, \ldots, W_m, P_2, \ldots, P_k$ as $P_1, \ldots, P_k$. Instead of trying to learn the value of the victim's P_1, the adversary notes the values G_2 in (1) when a response packet is returned. These are potential covering values for the prefix component P_2. The adversary obtains one of the values in the set of all possible covering values for P_2, each time a response packet is returned. Let Y be the random variable which takes the value of the prefix component under attack, from the victim's CPP address. V denotes the random variable which the adversary observes (the value G_2 in this case). More precisely, the adversary observes

$$G_2 = h(L_2, M, Q_1, X_3, \ldots, X_k)$$

for various values of Q_1, where M and $X_3, \ldots, X_k$ are from the victim's CPP address. Then the adversary obtains $I(Y, V) = H(Y) - H(Y|V)$, or the information about Y that V gives (mutual information), where $H(X)$ denotes the entropy of the random variable X.

We have computed bounds for these values for a typical example. The example graph has a 3 bit first prefix component which is segmented into P_1, P_2, and P_3, with one bit each. P_4 has 3 bits, P_5 has 4 bits, and P_6 has 6 bits. Our results indicate very small leakage for the higher prefix components (P_2, P_3, etc.), with some increase in leakage towards the bottom of the tree. To compute the leakage for P_2, we set $n = 2$, $p = 3/2^{16}$, and $q = 1 - p$. We obtain

Table 1. Leakage for Prefix Components

prefix component	leakage
P_2	$< 1/1150$
P_3	$< 1/1500$
P_4	$< 1/139$
P_5	$< 1/51$
P_6	< 0.188

$$I(Y, V) =$$
$$H(Y) - H(Y|V)$$
$$= \log(n) - \sum Pr(V = v_i)H(Y|V = v_i)$$
$$\leq 1 - Pr(0 \; response)(1) -$$
$$Pr(1 \; response)H(Y|V = 1 \; response) -$$
$$Pr(2 \; responses)H(Y|V = 2 \; responses)$$
$$= 1 - q^{100} -$$
$$100(q^{99})p[3/4 \log(4/3) + 1/4 \log(4)] -$$
$$100(99)(p^2)(q^9 8)/2[1/2]$$
$$\approx 0.000864915$$
$$< 1/1150$$

Table 1 shows the leakages for the example graph. We note that each leakage value assumes the adversary has moved through 100 distinct subnets; therefore, the adversary may only obtain leakage from one of the prefix components. Also, the average leakage for P_6 will be much less than 0.188 bits.

Appendix A gives additional techniques for defending against a global adversary as well as protecting the first prefix bit from attacks.

5.3   CPP Intradomain Location Privacy Extension

CPP is designed for protecting location privacy within a CPP domain. This section introduces an extension to protect the location over multiple CPP domains.

Our approach is to use the same global identifier P_0 across multiple CPP domains, regardless of their geographic location. Each domain has a different AS number and distributes routing information with BGP messages to indicate that packets destined for P_0 should be delivered to its domain. The outside domains receive the BGP messages which have the same set of destinations P_0 from different ASes. According to the specification of BGP-4 (RFC1771), when an AS receives BGP messages for the same destinations from different ASes, it uses the message with the highest routing metrics. Therefore, the packet destined for P_0 would be delivered to the nearest CPP domain. The border gateway of each domain can decrypt P_1, which indicates the individual CPP domain, and

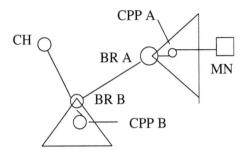

Fig. 3. CPP Forwarding with ERS

if the decrypted P_1 is not for its own domain, it has to forward the packet to the other border gateway of the domain identified by the decrypted P_1. In order to forward packets to the other CPP domains, each CPP domain needs to have another individual global prefix identifier that is routable to the individual CPP domain. Each CPP domain advertises both P_0 and its own individual global prefix identifier. The border gateway encapsulates the packet (possibly using an IPsec tunnel) and forwards it to the other border gateway through the addition of tunneling header in which the destination address contains the domain-dedicated prefix of that domain. (With the segmentation of the first prefix component P_1 into three segments as described above, the border gateway would decrypt all three pieces before forwarding the packet to the destination CPP domain).

Figure 3 shows an example topology with the CPP intradomain extension. When hosts CH and MN communicate, CH packets are forwarded to domain B since domain B is the closest domain, advertising P_0, to CH. CH is not aware of which domain MN actually resides in, amongst the multiple domains that advertise P_0.

The intradomain extension that we have presented so far is vulnerable to timing/triangulation attacks. In particular, a correspondent node can determine how many hops away a user host is. Multiple cooperating malicious correspondent nodes can exchange information and make a reasonable guess about the location of a user host. In order to prevent these attacks, a CPP border gateway can queue packets for flows for an amount of time equal to the round trip time to a remote CPP domain. All of the packets for a particular flow would be queued, prior to forwarding, for an amount of time corresponding to a round trip time. The particular remote CPP domain is selected randomly. In this way, the location of a CPP user, with respect to these attacks, is not visible to correspondent nodes, either within remote CPP domains or within the same CPP domain. The performance impact of this countermeasure should be minimal, since no extra traffic is introduced into the network, and the extra delay time is fairly consistent for a selected flow.

The full paper includes an example showing how CPP can be combined with an encrypting border router to give enhanced protection against compromised routers, maintain limited state on routers, and provide intradomain location privacy in an incremental deployment.

6   Implementation and Performance Results

6.1   CPP Preprocessor Performance

CPP includes a preprocessing step prior to the conventional forwarding algorithm. We implemented the modifications to the router downward path forwarding algorithm for CPP in the FreeBSD 4.8 kernel to measure the performance of packet forwarding for CPP addresses. The process of computing P_i, the cleartext prefix, was added prior to the process of forwarding table lookup. To compute the true prefixes, each router obtains the prior prefix components and the bit position from which to begin decryption, from the hop-by-hop option. Fig. 4 shows the format of the hop-by-hop option header. The prefix component for the current route aggregation level is obtained by decrypting the current level's component of X.

The first 16 bits of the hop by hop option, Type and Length, are compliant with the IPv6 specification [DH1]. The Offset field (8 bits) identifies the bit position to begin decryption of this level's prefix component. The Prefix Components of Higher Routers field (32 bits) identifies the prefix components to be concatenated with the target prefix component after decryption. The rest of the parameters are preconfigured.

Two different algorithms were tried for $h()$: SHA-1 and AES (Advanced Encryption Standard) [AES]. The input variables to $h()$ are the router's secret key L_i and M, with 64 bits zero-padding satisfying the input size (128bits) in the case of AES since AES is a block cipher algorithm. After the table lookup, the hop-by-hop option field is modified by adding the target prefix component to the prefix components of higher routers field and overwriting the offset field.

The hop-by-hop option of the CPP scheme is processed in the ip6_input() function. The prefix decryption and routing table lookup are also processed in this function. If the packet hasn't reached its final destination, the ip6_input() function forwards the packet to the ip6_forward() function and then the packet goes into the output process.

To measure the packet forwarding time, the timestamp at the time of dequeuing the packet from the input queue is attached to the forwarding packet and the timestamp is checked when the packet is enqueued for forwarding. The elapsed time is measured as the packet forwarding time.

We measured the packet forwarding time of unmodified FreeBSD forwarding, and also measured the CPP packet forwarding time for SHA-1 and AES

01234567890123456789012345678901

Type	Length	Offset	Target Level
Prefix components of higher routers			

Fig. 4. CPP Hop by Hop Option Format

Table 2. Forwarding Time Performance for Unmodified and CPP Forwarding

Type of Router	unmodified	SHA-1	AES
Time to route one packet	6 μsec.	11 μsec.	9 μsec.

encrypted Q. The performance measurements were made on a PC with single Intel Pentium III processor running at 1.0GHz (IBM ThinkPad T23); the FreeBSD 4.8 system contained our implemented kernel. The time in this system can be measured to an accuracy of 1 microsecond. The results are shown in Table 1. With additional work, it is likely that the CPP forwarding times can be improved.

CPP performance impact will be offset when packets are forwarded based on an entry in the router cache; in this case, no cryptographic processing is required. Also, when MPLS [RoR] is used, CPP cryptographic processing is typically only required for the first packet with a given CPP address during the address period.

7   Discussion

CPP routers perform cryptographic processing on each inbound CPP packet and intra-domain packet, at a cost of one hash operation per packet. There is no performance impact for outgoing packets destined outside the privacy domain (if ERS is not used), since the default routes simply forward outbound packets to the border routers. Given the above performance results, CPP does not appear to impact performance excessively, especially for non-border routers. Lower level routers are more likely to be limited by the bandwidth of links than by CPU capability, so CPP can be viewed as leveraging unused CPU capacity. Border routers are likely to more heavily loaded. Hardware assist can be of help in reducing the overhead.

CPP configuration is simplest if either all advertised routes are fully aggregated, or overlay CPP is used. In general, route aggregation is considered to be beneficial for good network engineering, because it reduces the size of the routing tables. In CPP, protection against compromised routers is partly facilitated through route aggregation.

CPP continues to allow ISPs to institute simple first order security practices. Access routers can still perform ingress filtering if they additionally act as DHCP servers for handing out addresses. If the routers are handing out the addresses, they can check the source addresses on outgoing packets to determine whether they match an assigned address. Instead of filtering on the /64 subnet prefixes, the routers need to filter based on the full /128 address.

ISPs commonly delegate blocks of address space to enterprise customers and allow routing through the ISP to the Internet. This practice is still possible with CPP, except network administrators for delegated address blocks must make sure that the global routing prefix indicates that the address is not a CPP address. The delegated network achieves no location privacy protection, but the addresses can be forwarded using the standard algorithm. Alternatively, if the enterprise network administrator wants location privacy, the ISP can delegate a separate plaintext prefix P0 to the enterprise, allowing the enterprise to set up its own location privacy domain.

The encoding of addresses in CPP causes addresses in the same subnet to be uncorrelated. Network operators often use correlations between addresses to diagnose problems. CPP requires a set of tools that would allow authorized network administrators to access the plaintext address of packets, for such diagnostic purposes. By using IPsec as described above (ICMP discussion), we should be able to use existing tools without modification.

7.1   Comparison with Other Approaches

CPP gives up some location privacy when compared with [Onion, Go1, Tarzan], since with these approaches, the user's location can be anywhere on the Internet. With CPP, the user is located on some access network associated with the global prefix identifier P_0. The latter can still be a large set of geographically distributed locations (especially for a large ISP). Compromise of first hop routers is a problem for CPP, but the ERS extension helps here. Compromise of first hop routers or relays is also problematic for [Onion, Go1, Tarzan] in varying degrees (but [Go1, Tarzan] also do encryption on the user host resulting in more protection).

In exchange for giving up some privacy, CPP gains some advantages over the above schemes. CPP network devices maintain no connection specific state; therefore, it is much easier to recover from failures of network elements. Fast recovery is essential for real time applications such as VoIP. CPP can leverage existing IP based protocols to facilitate recovery.

CPP is well suited for lightweight wireless clients. In [Tarzan], each outgoing (incoming) packet must be encrypted (decrypted) several times (corresponding to the multiple layers). CPP requires either no cryptographic operations on the client or a single layer of encryption for the ERS extension described above. CPP has better resistance to host attacks aimed at disclosing location privacy from an IP address then [Onion, Go1, Tarzan], since the CPP address can be used as the host's IP address. Due to the way CPP handles addresses, a larger set of applications can be transparently supported. [Onion, Go1, Tarzan] have limits with respect to the number of applications due to encryption and NAT issues.

CPP offers less protection against traffic analysis than [Onion], and much less than [Tarzan]. But Tarzan's approach of making user hosts into relays is not currently practical for lightweight wireless clients due to the significant latency of the wireless link. Integration of CPP with the appropriate traffic analysis countermeasures is an area for future research. CPP can be potentially combined with one of these other techniques. If combined with Onion Routing, CPP helps to solve the application layer leakage of information in IP addresses, as well as giving protection against host attacks aimed at location privacy.

8   Conclusions

We have presented an approach to location privacy in IPv6 networks, Cryptographically Protected Prefixes (CPP), which directly disrupts the ability of an attacker to map between a mobile host's IPv6 subnet identifier and the geographical location of the access router. CPP does this by encrypting the subnet identifier in the IP address. The encryption is done in a way that only the routers within the routing domain can decrypt. Other approaches to location privacy work by tunneling across parts of the network, including the wireless network, or by masking the IP address. These methods are subject to attacks at various points in the network where the address appears in plaintext, or they result in heavy routing inefficiencies, making them inappropriate for real-time traffic. CPP involves modifications to the basic IP forwarding algorithm, and our implementation results indicate that a modest performance penalty is incurred.

From a security standpoint, CPP achieves a high level of security, when compared to other approaches that facilitate real time traffic, such as Mobile IP and HMIP. The cost is a small performance penalty in forwarding, and the addition of the CPP server. However, as with all cases of security, the main issue is addressing the threat probability. While the current deployment of IPv6 networks is low (and practically non-existent for Mobile IPv6 networks), the situation could change quite rapidly should IPv6 start being deployed for essential services.

References

[AK]   Ackerman, L., Kempf, J., Miki, T.: Wireless Location Privacy: Current State of U.S. Law and Policy. Proceedings of the Workshop on Privacy, Washington DC. (2003)

[BF]   Berthold O., Federrath H., Kospell S.: Web Mixes: A System for Anonymous and Unobservable Internet Access. Designing Privacy Enhancing Technologies: International Workshop on Design Issues in Anonymity and Unobservability. LCNS vol. **2009** (2001)

[Ch1]   Chaum D.: Untraceable Electronic Mail, Return Addresses, and Digital Pseudonyms. Communications of the ACM **24** (1981)

[DD]   Danezis G., Dingledine R., and Mathewson N.: Mixminion: Design of a Type III Anonymous Remailer Protocol. IEEE Symposium on Security and Privacy (2003) 2–15

[DH1]   Deering, S., Hinden, R.: Internet Protocol Version 6 (IPv6) Specification. RFC 2460 (1998)

[DH2]   Hinden, R., and Deering, S.: Internet Protocol Version 6 (IPv6) Addressing Architecture. RFC 3513 (2003)

[DH3]   Hinden, R., Deering, S., and Nordmark, E.: IPv6 Global Unicast Address
             Format. Internet draft, *work in progress*

[DHCPv6]   Droms, R. (editor): Dynamic Host Configuration Protocol for IPv6
             (DHCPv6). Internet Draft, *work in progress*

[Dj1]   Dijkstra. E.: A Note on Two Problems in Connection with Graphs. Nu-
             merische Mathematic, **1** (1969) 269–271

[EH]   Escudero, A., Hedenfalk, M., Heselius, P.: Flying Freedom: Location Pri-
             vacy in Mobile Interworking. Proceedings of INET (2001)

[Tarzan]   Freedman, M., Morris R.: Tarzan: A Peer-to-Peer Anonymizing Network
             Layer. CCS (2002)

[Go1]   Goldberg, I.: A Pseudonymous Communications Infrastructure for the
             Internet. PhD dissertation, University of California, Berkeley (2000)

[GT]   Gulcu C., Tsudik G.: Mixing E-mail with Babel. Network and Distributed
             Systems Security Conference (1996) 2–16

[IPv6-Alloc] IAB, IESG.: IAB/IESG Recommendations on IPv6 Address Allocations
             to Sites. RFC 3177 (2001)

[Mipv6]   Johnson, D., Perkins, C., and Arkko, J.: Mobility Support in IPv6. Inter-
             net draft, *work in progress*

[Kent]   Kent, S., and Atkinson, R.: Security Architecture for the Internet Proto-
             col. RFC 2401 (1998)

[Ospf]   Moy, J.T.: OSPF: Anatomy of an Internet Routing Protocol. Addison
             Wesley (1998) 345.

[NN]   Narten, T., Nordmark, E., Simpson, W.: Neighbor Discovery for IP Ver-
             sion 6 (IPv6). RFC 2461 (1998)

[AES]   National Institute of Standard and Technology.: Specification for the Ad-
             vanced Encryption Standard (AES). FIPS **197** (2001)

[RR]   Reiter, M. Rubin, A.: Crowds: Anonymity for Web Transactions. ACM
             Transactions on Information and System Security. Vol. **1**, No. **1** (1998)
             66–92

[RoR]   Rosen, E., and Rekhter Y.: BGP/MPLS VPNs. RFC 2547 (1999)

[SC]   Soliman, H., Castelluccia, C., El-Malki, K., and Bellier, L.: Hierarchical
             Mobile IPv6 mobility management (HMIPv6). Internet draft, *work in
             progress*

[SK]   Song, R., and Korba, L.: Review of Network-based Approaches for Pri-
             vacy. 14th Annual Canadian Technology Security Symposium. (2002)

[Onion]   Syverson, P.F., Goldschlag, D.M., and Reed, M.G.: Anonymous Connec-
             tions and Onion Routing. IEEE Symposium on Security and Privacy.
             IEEE CS Press. (1997) 44–54

[TN]   Thomson, S., and Narten, T.: IPv6 Stateless Address Autoconfiguration
             RFC 2462 (1998)

[WM]   Warrior, J., McHenry, E., and McGee, K.: They Know Where You Are.
             IEEE Spectrum, Vol. **50**, No. **7** (2003) 20–25

[YH]   Yabusaki, M., Hirata, S., Ihara, T., and Kawakami, H.: IP^2 Mobility
             Management. NTT DoCoMo Technical Journal, Vol. **4**, No. **4** (2003) 16–
             22

A   Defending Against A Global Adversary

In this section, we focus on preventing the first attack from Section 5, where prefix segmentation of the first prefix component is used, and the adversary attempts to determine the first bit. The technique is then extended to protect against an adversary who listens on more than 100 subnets.

We prepend a randomly generated bit to each possible first level prefix component. Thus in the example from the preceding subsection, we would now have 16 possible prefix components for the first prefix component (prior to segmentation). Then after segmentation, we obtain four single bit prefix components. The adversary must now obtain both P_1 and P_2 in order to obtain any location information, using the first attack. Such an event occurs with extremely low probability, as shown above. Thus the first attack is not a good strategy for the adversary. The cost of this countermeasure is the additional bit that is taken from the host identifier part of the IPv6 address.

More generally, we can drop prefix segmentation and make both P_1 and P_2 be randomly generated prefix components that are independent of the packet forwarding path. The first "real" prefix component is now P_3. The border router uses three decryption keys to obtain all of P_1, P_2, and P_3. With this approach, the attack from the theorem in the preceding subsection is eliminated. As we increase the number of bits in P_1 and P_2, we also decrease the amount of information that the adversary can gain through an information-theoretic attack, as in the previous subsection. This decrease occurs for two reasons: (1) the number of subnets that must be covered increases (2) the probability of encountering highly skewed hash outputs for a given prefix component drops.

We also can select M at address creation time such that the leakage for P_3 (the most vulnerable prefix component in this scheme) is known and is less than a predefined bound. In other words, the address server can compute the entropy for $h(L_3, M, P_1, P_2, X_4, \ldots, X_k)$ where P_1 and P_2 vary. If the entropy is not large enough, a new M is randomly selected, and the entropy is recomputed for this new M and $X_4, \ldots, X_k$. Table 3 gives loose upper bounds on the number of expected hash operations for a couple of cases. For the second case, we expect the average number of hash operations to be much less, perhaps around $1/3$ times the bound or less. This last countermeasure (selecting M to minimize leakage for P_3) is independent of selecting P_1 and P_2 randomly. The cost of each of these countermeasures is approximately 6-8 bits from M.

Table 3. Loose Upper Bounds on Number of Hash Operations To Create Address in Global CPP Scheme

domain size $P_1 + P_2$ into range of size P_3	leakage	bound
$P_1 + P_2 = 5, P_3 = 3$	$< .046$	1641 hashes
$P_1 + P_2 = 6, P_3 = 4$	$< .0814$	10158 hashes

Protecting User Data in Ubiquitous Computing: Towards Trustworthy Environments

Yitao Duan and John Canny

Computer Science Division,
University of California, Berkeley,
Berkeley, CA 94720, USA
{duan, jfc}@cs.berkeley.edu

Abstract. In a Ubiquitous Computing environment, sensors are actively collecting data, much of which can be very sensitive. Data will often be streaming at high rates (video and audio) and it must be dealt with in real-time. Protecting the privacy of users is of central importance. Dealing with these issues will be a central challenge for ubicomp for some time to come. Here we propose some simple design principles which address several of these issues. We illustrate them through the design of a smart room capture system we are building. The main design principle is "data discretion:" users should have access and control of data about them, and should be able to determine how it is used. We show how data discretion supports both personal *and* collaborative uses. In our implementation, the data discretion principle is enforced with cryptographic techniques. Unlike ACL based access control systems, our scheme embeds access rights of legitimate users *within* the data. An important property of the method is that it hides meta-information about data access: no user can determine who (else) has access to any given datum. Access information is sensitive because it discloses information about which and when users were in the room. We have implemented a prototype system in the smart room equipped with several cameras, and we give data throughput rates under various degrees of protection. Finally we describe ongoing work towards a trustworthy ubicomp environment whose discretion is realistically checkable.

1 Introduction

A ubiquitous computing (ubicomp) or pervasive computing environment is typically envisioned as a space populated with large number of invisible, collaborating computers, sensors and actuators interacting with user-worn gadgets. Data about individuals who are in the environment is constantly being generated, transmitted and stored. Much of the data can be quite sensitive. Protecting private data is a major concern for users. There are a few challenges that make data security in such settings different from other system protection:

1. The environment is often unfamiliar to the users. They will not have a trust relationship with the owners of the environment as they might with their local system administrator appropriate for handling their private information.

D. Martin and A. Serjantov (Eds.): PET 2004, LNCS 3424, pp. 167–185, 2005.

2. Data are often generated dynamically and streaming at high rates (video and audio) and must be processed in real-time.
3. Users' access rights change dynamically. For example, a group of users can record a meeting using a camera and audio in the smart room. They should only have access to the video produced during the meeting period but not others. The system must be able to associate data with the correct set of users while it is being produced.
4. The system is typically decentralized, with multiple data sources/sinks. Data caching or replication can be common. There is usually no single point where access control can be enforced.
5. Data usage often involves sharing among a group of people [1]. Any protection scheme must allow efficient sharing among legitimate users.

Users will often be uncomfortable trusting such recordings to unfamiliar infrastructure. Our goal is to create protection schemes that are backed up by clearly stated policies, that can help mitigate users concerns. In the long run, users generally become comfortable with technologies that do not cause significant harm (e.g. online credit card purchases and e-banking became common after initial user apprehension). In the long run we would like to work toward automatic verification to bolster these basic safeguards, which rely on trustworthiness of the environment.

For the data that are generated by the user (e.g., documents produced on users' laptops), protection is relatively easy. Clients can generate proper keys and encrypt the files by themselves and upload the encrypted files to the server. They can also store the keys on the server using a variant of the scheme that will be described in Section 5. Since the server never sees the keys or the clear data, it has no way to leak them.

In ubiquitous computing settings, however, the data are often generated by another party. In this paper we are concerned with protection of user data that are generated by the infrastructure. This case is tricky because the users have to trust the system to some degree (e.g. the fidelity of the sensor data) since they rely on the system to perform certain operations (e.g. data generation, transmission, and encryption). We do not want to encourage "blind trust" from the user. Rather, we would like to design the system in such a way that it promotes user trust and confidence. We consider a typical ubicomp environment, in this case a smart room augmented with a variety of sensors.

The smart room (modeling a smart office) is chosen as a "canonical" ubicomp environment. We also chose it because we see it as the locus of significant future privacy risks. Employers exercise strong control over the workplace, and most large employers use electronic monitoring (web and email) routinely. In fact almost all Fortune-500 companies have *dismissed* employees because of discoveries from routine electronic surveillance. Lawrence Lessig has called this the "most serious violations of privacy by anyone's standard." Cameras and mics in offices and meeting rooms are useful for conferencing, collaboration, recording (memory aids), and "pro-active" computing applications. They are greatly increasing in number. With this growth of high-end sensing come many obvious privacy risks (e.g. of the same kind of routine monitoring as for email and web use). This motivates our approach and our testbed. The specific issues we address in this paper are:

1. Protection of the user data generated and maintained by the environment.
2. Privacy of individuals who use the environment.
3. Ability of legitimate users to make use of data recorded in the environment.
4. Dealing with high-speed streams of data.
5. Trustworthiness of the environments. (This is work in progress)

We argue that traditional access control schemes employed by stand-alone computers and small networks don't provide the right protection models for ubiquitous computing, and propose an approach to protecting user data in a dynamic and ad hoc environment. Our scheme makes use of both symmetric and public-key cryptography and can achieve efficiency high enough to be implemented using today's commodity hardware and software, and deal with streams of audio and video data. Our scheme embeds access rights in the *data* and offers a simpler and more efficient alternative to ACLs and provides a natural model for defining access policies and mechanisms for enforcing them. It also makes it impossible for observers to determine who has access to the data, thereby protecting the information about who was using the room and when. Our work takes a technological approach, and looks for policy or legal incentives for employers to adopt it.

1.1   Privacy Principles

User data protection is closely related to privacy. Not only can protection techniques be used to ensure privacy, but privacy considerations can influence protection policy and implementation. This is especially true in a fluid setting like ubiquitous computing. For instance, before we design any protection scheme, we need to determine who should have the access right to what data under what conditions, and this will be drastically shaped by privacy considerations. Here we state some privacy principles for ubiquitous computing that motivate our approach to data protection. Later we will derive design principles of our own that support these privacy principles and directly dictate our protection scheme.

In [2], Marc Langheinrich laid out some principles for design of privacy-respecting ubicomp systems. Langheinrich stresses the importance of including privacy considerations in the early stage of system design process. He develops six principles for guiding privacy-aware ubiquitous system design:

1. Notice: users should always be aware of what data is being collected.
2. Choice and Consent: users should be able to choose whether it is used.
3. Anonymity, Pseudonymity: should apply when identity is not needed.
4. Meeting Expectations: systems should mimic real-world norms.
5. Security: different amounts of protection depending on the situation.
6. Access and Recourse: users should have access to data about them.

Langheinrich's principles provide very specific guidance for our work. They are in good agreement with other frameworks including FIP (Fair Information Practices). Later, we describe our design approach that supports several of the principles directly, and makes it easy to build systems which support all of them.

The rest of the paper is organized as follows. In Section 2 we survey related work on ensuring user privacy and data protection in ubicomp environments. In Section 3 we describe personal and collaborative applications of smart spaces which leverage our protection system to ensure privacy. Section 4 illustrates a smart room setting that we are using as a testbed for our principles and implementations. In Section 5 we present the data discretion principle and describe the protection scheme that enforces this principle and how it is applied to our smart room. Section 6 gives performance evaluation of our prototype system. Section 7 discusses the issue of trustworthiness of ubicomp environments and presents extensions and possible techniques for improving and validating privacy compliance in such environments. It also describes directions for future research. Finally we give summarizing remarks in Section 8.

2   Related Work

User privacy has been a major concern in the design of many ubicomp systems. Several recent projects seek to protect user anonymity in communication and data capturing [3, 4]. They basically follow the rules and practice established in Internet Privacy [5, 6], which focus on obscuring user's IP address, and extend them into ubiquitous computing context. The Mist Project at UIUC strives to anonymize users' communication in ubicomp environments [4]. It utilizes a hierarchy of "Mist Routers" that perform "handle-based routing" to preserve privacy and hide information about the source and destination. Users will expose their identities to part of the system, but their locations will be concealed. The EuroPARC's RAVE [7] presents a networked node model where interactions are defined by connections established between nodes. It emphasizes two principles in preserving privacy: control and feedback. The former empowers users to stipulate what information they project and who can access it while the latter allows the users to be informed of the capturing and usage of their information. Privacy preserving is achieved by controlling connection capabilities. While this is a reasonable model for protecting transient information, it is not clear how permanent data is protected. Also it represents an "untrustworthy" environment for visitors who have no knowledge of how it works.

Motivated by user privacy, as well as system security, concerns, data protection in ubicomp systems is attracting more attention. Among the many types of information, user location is the focus of many studies probably due to its close tie to user privacy. In [8] Mike Spreitzer and Marvin Theimer describe their design of an architecture for providing, and controlling access to, location information in a ubiquitous computing environment. In their architecture, each user owns an "User Agent" that collects and controls all personal information pertaining to its user (including location) and any request for such information must be routed through the "User Agent" which enforces predetermined access policies. One problem with their architecture, however, is that location, and other personal information, can be derived from a variety of sources (e.g. a camera owned by a mall) and it is infeasible for an user's agent to have control over all of them.

Another location data protection scheme described in [9, 10] anonymizes user location in sensor network by reducing the spatial accuracy of sensor readings and perturbing the count of users in the covered area. In addition, [11] describes the protection of user location information based on policies that are defined to reflect various privacy requirements of users and spaces. The implementation is based on digital certificate. This scheme provides a framework for protecting user location data as an output of the People Locator service in their system.

All these schemes assume that requests for user location information are directed towards some *service* or *agent* where access control can be naturally enforced. However, in many distributed system applications, especially in ubiquitous/pervasive computing environments, user location information can be derived from raw data (e.g. sensor data or images taken by a camera in a room) in a variety of ways that bypass the service. For example, by gaining access to an image taken by a camera in a particular room and checking the time stamp of the file, one can easily obtain the location of some user(s) at certain time. And this unauthorized access could be quite often in a fluid environment like ubicomp (e.g. a stolen or lost device). This shows that existing schemes for controlling access to user location are inadequate without proper data protection. Our scheme can be used to complement existing ones to make them more secure. For example, our scheme can safeguard the image data so that no one except the owner(s) of that data can decipher them thus protecting the user(s) location information against illegitimate access.

Some access control architectures were proposed specifically for ubiquitous computing [12, 13, 14, 15]. Most of them focus on formalizing and automating policies and their enforcement. For example, Role Based Access Control (RBAC), introduced in 1992 by Ferraiolo and Kuhn [16], is probably one of the best-known method for access control for distributed systems and is attracting increasing attention because it reduces the complexity and cost of security administration in large networked applications [17, 18, 19]. In RBAC systems, entities are assigned roles and access rights are associate with each role. Similar to the location systems described earlier, these schemes are primarily concerned with controlling access to the *services* provided by the system and many are based on authentication/authorization models which are used extensively in traditional centralized systems. This model is inadequate for ubiquitous computing in a number of ways: (1) it is difficult to specify the security policies in a fluid environment in a way that matches the dynamic access relationship users can have with the data; (2) it is difficult to make data sharing, which can be essential in collaborative ubicomp applications, efficient and safe; (3) data are not protected if the authorization agent is down or faulty, or bypassed. And such situations can be quite common in ubiquitous computing environments (e.g. a lost device).

In contrast, both our design principle and the enforcing scheme focus on data protection. The security of our scheme does not rely on any access control. Rather, it uses cryptographic techniques to make data safe by themselves. Even if an adversary gains access to the data, he cannot take advantage of them because they are encrypted and are not different from random data to those who don't have access right. Access control policies are useless if the code enforcing them is compromised or bypassed. As we argued, such situations can be common in ubicomp settings. Given this circumstance, our approach seems to be the only solution.

3   Applications

Our scheme can enable new ubicomp applications, or enhance existing ones with privacy. In this section we describe two types of applications, one stand-alone and one collaborative, that can leverage our scheme to ensure privacy.

3.1   Personal History

A number of researchers have explored the idea of lifetime personal histories collected electronically. Gelernter's "Mirror Worlds" is an early example [20]. More recently, wearable computing researchers Steve Mann [21] and Bradley Rhodes [22] (the "remembrance agent") built systems to record and retrieve their daily histories. Other current explorations of lifetime history include "Stuff I've seen" and Cyberall (resp. Susan Dumais, Gordon Bell, Microsoft), and the "Personal Server" (Roy Want, Intel).

A wearable computer provides one source of lifetime history. Wearables may or may not be adopted by most users. Sensor-equipped spaces provide an alternative. Data recorded in the space can be sent to all the users who are in the space at the time. In this way, the room becomes a "virtual personal recorder". As the user moves, they carry an ID tag, which might include their encryption key and the URI of a server to which the space should send their recorded data. If they enter another sensor-equipped space, it takes over the task of recording and shipping data to their server. Advantages of this approach are that the room may include more sensors, e.g. cameras in many positions, that the data may be streamed over a high-bandwidth fixed link to the users server, and that this server can have higher storage capacity (and backup) than a wearable.

We are implementing a simple video recording service along these lines in a smart room. We use RFID tags to determine who is in the room, although because of memory limits we use a lookup table to map from the tag number to an encryption key and target URI.

3.2   Collaborative Applications

Surprisingly, individual private data collection also allows some important *collaborative* applications that support privacy. In other words, users can share their information without losing privacy. We explain how briefly.

Collaboration is a major challenge to privacy. By its nature, collaboration involves exchange of information between collaborators. It may also involve automation – the best example of which is collaborative filtering [23]. We also have several ongoing projects which make use of history data from several individuals to support other types of collaboration. In particular, we are using personal history data to compute collaborative "activities". Activities are shared patterns of communication, document and web access which are mined using a clustering algorithm from histories of the participants.

Normally, collaborative computation would require user data to be stored and processed on a single server computer. This could raise serious privacy concerns. As mentioned before, in ubicomp settings, users generally do not have strong trust relationships with the individuals who manage the hardware. This lack of strong trust applies also between individuals and the owners of community-based services. The problem exists already on the web - many sites monitor users' progress around their sites, and their electronic purchases. The problem is at least limited to the scope of a particular web site. But ubicomp provides much richer and more invasive data.

To deal with this problem we explored encrypted computation. The idea is that raw user data should remain accessible only to the user in question. When collaborative computation is needed, it should be done only on encrypted data, thereby protecting individual privacy to the maximum extent possible. This approach is indeed feasible, and in [1] Canny showed that it is practical for interesting collaborative tasks. That paper described a new collaborative filtering (CF) algorithm based on encrypted computation that matched the accuracy of the best-performing algorithms at that time. It also showed that basic clustering (based on SVD) is possible on encrypted data.

Subsequent work on collaborative filtering [24] showed that encrypted computation need not penalize either performance or accuracy. A second collaborative filtering algorithm, based on sparse factor analysis (SFA), was introduced in [24]. Not only does that algorithm support encrypted computation, but through several experiments it showed that it is the most accurate CF algorithm to date and one of the most efficient. This method also supports *community creation and maintenance* of collaborative groups, and so addresses the needs for social participation emphasized by the social sciences perspectives on privacy.

A very interesting application of CF in ubicomp is to location data. For instance, by tracking their location and aggregating with others, users can obtain recommendations about restaurants, shops, places to see and things to do. But gathering such information creates great risks to privacy and, as mentioned before, existing protection schemes for protecting location information are insufficient for ubicomp. The general thread of our work is to explore cryptographic and AI techniques to compute from user data only the information needed for a particular task, and to protect the rest of the data. And the scheme presented in this paper is the basis of such computation.

Note that not all data are suitable for encrypted computation. In the rest of the paper we will describe a prototype system that uses video data to represent user data that are generated by a ubicomp environment. The purpose of such prototype system is to demonstrate the feasibility and efficiency of our scheme. We are not proposing performing computation on encrypted video data. However, we stress that such computation is possible with some user data (e.g. user location, activity log, etc.) that are protected with our scheme [1]. In other words, our scheme does not hinder collaborative use of the data. On the contrary, because the data are properly protected, with access rights embedded in themselves, our scheme makes collaborative use of sensitive data privacy preserving.

4   Smart Room Testbed

We have begun building a smart room equipped with sensing and able to record user activity. The room is a small meeting room with a conventional whiteboard, a Smart Technologies Smartboard^{TM} with projector, four video cameras, and a Philips I-CODE^{TM} RFID tag reader. There is a single entrance to the room, and the tag reader antenna is mounted around this entrance so that it can record entry and exit by any user carrying an I-CODE tag. The tags provide reliable recognition of users entering the room, although users without tags will not be noticed by the tag reader. It can of course be fooled by tags which move through the doorway when not attached to their users. The cameras capture images from the room continuously, and send them to a data server. Another computer drives the Smart-board, and this computer runs a logging program that records all significant user activity using the board.

Fig. 1. Smart room testbed

The smart room is representative of typical ubicomp environments and serves as a good testbed for our privacy principles. As we described earlier, knowledge workplaces are the site of the "most serious violations of privacy by anyone's standard" (Lessig) due to email and web monitoring. Physical workplaces involve a mixture of individual and collaborative work. As those spaces are fitted out with sensing and recording devices, workplace monitoring is likely to extend to the physical world. To us therefore, smart workplaces are an excellent candidate for the most serious future privacy violations in ubicomp. The images and log data represent the dynamically generated user data that we seek to protect. We will provide a simple playback application that explores the privacy protections. Figure 1 shows a photo of the smart room testbed. Section 6 will give more details about the prototype system and the experiments we conducted on the smart room testbed.

5   System Design: The Data Discretion Principle

If we take Langheinrich's principles 4 and 6 together, meeting expectations and access and recourse, we derive a principle we call data discretion:

Data Discretion: Users should always have access to, and control of (recorded or live) information that would be available to them in "real-world" situations. They should not have direct access in other situations.

So for instance, users should have access to information recorded in a smart room that while they were in the room. They should not have access to information recorded in that room while they were not present. They should also have control of this information, and be able to use it however they please.

By making access to the user a requirement, we can make it easier to satisfy the other privacy principles 1, 2, 3 and 5. That is because we can require all accesses to user data to be routed to the user, and therefore we involve the user in all decisions about use of their data. However, this does not mean that users literally participate in every decision about their data. They can certainly establish policies, use agents or proxies etc., as others have proposed. Our goal was rather to make sure that others do not override the user's current or earlier intentions regarding their data. Our proposal is a low-level architecture on which applications and user-centered information management systems can sit.

There is some subtlety in making the discretion principle work. Particularly in a smart room setting, we would like to keep the identity of the people who were in the room a secret from those who were not in the room at that time. This means that users who were not in the room at the time should not have access to information recorded in the room at that time, nor should they be able to find out who does have access, because that is equivalent to knowing who was in the room. This rules out many access control methods, which expose the set of users who have access to files to system administrators or others who can penetrate the operating system. We prefer methods based on cryptography which make it impossible to gain access to sensitive information even with control of the machine and operating system.

5.1   Basics

Our method makes use of both symmetric and public-key encryption. We assume that all data are stored in files that represent short time intervals. For instance, each video file contains a short sequences of images of one second or so, or logs from the Smartboard in files that span about a second, etc. Every user file is encrypted with a randomly generated secret key. This secret key is then encrypted by the public keys of the file owners. We will describe the scheme in details in section 5.3.

A user joins our system by registering his or her public key [1] and choosing a recognition tag that the system can detect once it is within the vicinity of a sensor. The recognition tag is used by the system to detect user's presence so that it can retrieve related information (e.g., user's public key). The user is assumed to wear the recognition tag. Those who fail to wear the tags will not have access to the data, which is a safe default from privacy point of view.

Note this approach is different from access control lists (ACL) that are typically used to protect user data whose owner is predeterminable. Our system only needs to know the association between user data and its access key(s) and can function perfectly well without knowing identification of the holder of a particular tag. No attempt is made to connect a tag with a user's real-world identity, or even his or her system-wide electronic identity. User anonymity is therefore protected and users can maintain multiple pseudo-identities with multiple tags. This of course is limited by their visible presence to other users in the space who may know them by name.

5.2   Establishing Information Ownership

The first step in protecting user data is to ascertain the natural owners of the information. In a dynamic context such as ubiquitous computing, this has to be done while the information is being generated. We assume that the system has the ability to detect a user's recognition tag when they are present in the environment. Other identification technologies (e.g., face and fingerprint recognition) are expanding rapidly, and there already exist several that are mature enough to offer non-intrusive detection at reasonable cost. However, some of these technologies rely on recognition of information that are unique to a user (e.g., fingerprint) and are not suitable for privacy. RFID tags are good technologies from a privacy perspective because they have no unique attributes of particular users. The decoupling of user's identity and their recognition tag provides anonymity. A user can also have several pseudonyms via multiple tags. Biometric data is more sensitive because if it were extracted from the system, it

---

[1] We hope to eliminate this step in future. We would prefer the user's public key to be carried in their tag, along with (possibly) a URL to which their data should be sent. Our current tags do not have enough writeable bits.

would provide outsiders with cues to this individual's identity. RFID tags also allow users who are not interested in using the system a way to opt out by not carrying a tag.

The issue of who should be the rightful owner of data is a controversial one and the legal dispute involved has not been resolved. While some believe that the party that invests in gathering personal data has a right on it, we have taken an ideological stance (based in part on European law and on principles provided by many researchers) that users have first rights to this data, as they would in real-world use of a collaborative space. This is in accordance with our "data discretion" principle.

The smart room is equipped with an ambient display that always shows the number of users in the room, according to readings of the tag reader. If this does not match what the users see, then users know there is a rogue tag in the room. This prevents an attacker from hiding his tag in the room to obtain access to data recorded while he is not present.

5.3   Encryption Scheme

The basic output of the system is a sequence of files and key-tuples. File F_i is the data logged at time i. Associated with F_i is a tuple of user keys $(k_{i1}, ..., k_{in})$, denoted as *key set*, which determine who has access to this file. The length of the tuple of user keys, n, is always fixed for that environment. The value of n is larger than the maximum number of users who could plausibly be in the environment at the same time. Using a fixed number of keys is necessary if we would like to hide the number of users who are actually in the room at a given time. This many keys may seem extravagant, but in our smart room application, the key set is much smaller than its data file.

Changes of access right are modelled by the system through transitions between *sessions*. A session is defined as a short duration of activities with a fixed set of users. Users' access rights to the data generated at that time remain invariant during one session but would change across sessions. The system is responsible for detecting events that, according to "data discretion" principle or other considerations, may trigger session change (e.g. a user entering or exiting the room, or a periodic timer expires). A session is assigned a unique ID.

Encryption on user data is performed in the following steps:

1. The system performs appropriate key generation algorithm such as ANSI X9.17 [25] and obtains a sequence of pseudorandom keys $d_1, d_2, ...$. One key, denoted d_i, will be selected from the sequence to be used to encrypt files generated in current session. Symmetric key encryption is used for efficiency. Each key will be used only for one session and a new key will be selected for new session. The system will perform key generation periodically when the pool of keys is exhausted.

2. d_i is then encrypted with the public keys of the m people in the room (determined by recognition tag reader). These encrypted keys are placed in m

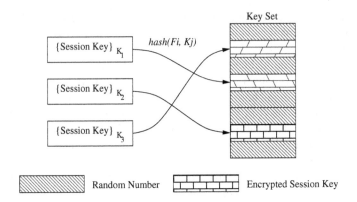

Fig. 2. Key set construction

locations among the n key positions in the key set, in pseudo-random fashion.
The other $n - m$ key positions are filled with random numbers.

3. Users who were in the room can recover the keys and review the video while
   they were in the room.

Although there are n possible keys associated with each file, it is not necessary
to search through them all in steps 2 and 3. We use a family of n hash functions
$h_1, \ldots, h_n$ to perform a pseudo-random search. At step 2, the system places user
j's key in the position specified by one of the hash functions applied to the
encrypted file and the user's public key. The first hash function which hashes to
a free key location is used. If we assume that n is at least twice the maximum
number of people in the room at one time, then at least half these locations
will be free, and on average only $\log_2 m$ such steps will be needed to find a free
location. The same method is used to retrieve the key at step 3. This scheme is
illustrated in Figure 2, where $hash \in \{h_1, \ldots, h_n\}$.

This scheme grants equal access to all users involved. This might not be
appropriate in some applications. A more general version would specify a general
access structure among the users, which can easily be done by secret-sharing the
session key among the occupants and embedding the shares in the key set. This
is left as an option for applications.

5.4   Master Key Escrow

It is sometimes necessary for a few privileged parties, e.g., police, to access data
stored in the system. However, it is not desirable that a single party be granted
full access right to the data since there is a danger of a malicious power party
misusing his privilege and compromising users' privacy. Our solution to this
dilemma is a shared master key and threshold decryption scheme. The master
key consists of a globally known El-Gamal public key and a matching private key
that is not held by any single party but instead secret shared among a number of
authorized "masters". Masters would normally be distributed to people like the

local police department, the building security manager, the corporate president or safety officer, etc. Threshold decryption allows a subset of those individuals (say any two of them) to retrieve data for safety or law enforcement reasons. But it avoids the risks of single individuals accessing data inappropriately.

Each file's key d_i is encrypted with the public master key. A group of masters whose number must exceed a pre-specified threshold can collaborate to retrieve d_i and access the data[2]. Pedersen's key generation protocol [26] or its variants/enhancements [27, 28] can be used to securely generate the public key and distribute the secret shares of the private key among participants

5.5   Unlinkability

Assuming both encryption algorithms used for encrypting the data files and the keys are secure, our scheme is "zero knowledge" in that it reveals no information about the data, not even the number of users who have access. It enforces the "data discretion" principle, i.e. only the rightful owners have access to, and control of the information.

One possible attack is on "unlinkability". I.e. an attacker may observe the public keys read by the tag readers installed at different places and link the data produced by these spaces to the same user(s). This enables the attacker to potentially track users. However, such an attack is only possible by compromising the system. The data themselves reveal no information about who have access and are totally unlinkable. Protecting the system is another issue that is orthogonal to the scheme we propose. Assuming the system is well protected with techniques such as firewall and the communication between tag readers and the server is secure, the unlinkability attack is impossible by scrutinizing the data.

6   Performance Evaluation

We have implemented a prototype system on the smart room testbed to carry out our protection scheme. Our smart room has four cameras as well as one tag reader. Images are typically captured at several images per second.

Our prototype system consists of the following four pieces of software:

1. An FTP server that receives image data from the four video cameras and saves them to disk.
2. A data encryption process that constantly checks for new data on disk and encrypts it.
3. A user data server that serves the encrypted data to users upon request.
4. A proof-of-concept client program that continuously requests the most up-to-date data from the user data server, tries to decrypt them on the fly, and

---

[2] Note that since the encryption keys are one-time only and only valid for one session, it is safe to reveal it to the collaborating "masters".

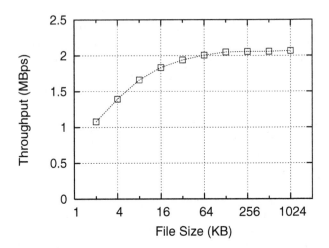

Fig. 3. System throughput

displays the recovered images on the screen (if the decryption is successful); thus if the user has legitimate access to the data, he should be able to see a smooth video replay of what's being captured in the room.

Conceptually the first two programs should be merged into one; we did not implement this due to time constraint. Instead, we simulated the effects of one single integrated data receiving/encryption server by deleting the plaintext files after we have generated the encrypted version. Nevertheless, we believe that an integrated server is more in line with our security principles and will be implemented in future versions of our system. We used Crypto++ Library^{TM} 5.0 [29], an open source crypto library written in C++, for our cryptographic functions.

The encryption server is the crucial part of the system and will be discussed in detail below. Logically it consists of two parallel modules: 1) session control and 2) data encryption. The session control module, a.k.a. the session manager, monitors the users (and their public keys) in the current session and generates session keys. It is notified of user arrivals and departures by the RFID tag reader. Whenever the session changes, the session manager destroys the old session and its associated state, and creates a new session and chooses a new session key.

The data encryption module monitors the arrival of new image data from the cameras, and encrypts those data with the current session key. We chose Triple-DES with 192-bit keys as our data encryption algorithm. In addition, the module encrypts the session key with the public key of each user in the current session. We used RSA public key encryption algorithm for this purpose. The encrypted keys are hidden in the fixed-size key set as described in Section 5 and stored together with data.

We have run several tests on our system. One involves multiple users simultaneously requesting the latest video captures while they are moving in and out of the room randomly. Our system can detect the changes of their presence in the room on time and reflect them with the changes of access rights. Thus the users could see the images while they are in the room but are unable to decrypt them when they are not. To determine the throughput of our system, we feed the system with a stream of files of fixed sizes arriving at high speed and measure the time it takes to process them. The experiments were run on a PIII 900MHz machine running Linux 2.4.18 Kernel. The code was compiled with gcc3.2. We did not account for the cost of generating and encrypting session keys in our experiments because these operations are performed only once per session and are dominated by the cost of encrypting the data files. Figure 3 shows the system throughput with different image file size. As our processing time includes two disk I/Os (one read and one write) as well as the encryption, the throughput improves as the file size increases. With a 1MB file size, the system can achieve a throughput of 2.07MBps while with 8KB file size the throughput is about 1.66MBps. Assuming a capture rate of 20 files per second, our system can support up to 10 cameras. Although these are more than enough for our current needs, there is plenty of room for improvement. First, the encryption algorithm we use, Triple-DES, is quite strong and expensive. Other symmetric encryption algorithms exist that can yield much higher throughput. As documented in the Crypto++ 5.0 Benchmarks (http://www.eskimo.com/~weidai/benchmarks.html), DES yields almost 3 times throughput as Triple-DES, Blowfish 4 times, Twofish 6 times, and ARC4 more than 13 times. In cases where the strong property of Triple-DES is not required, these algorithms can be used for higher throughput. Second, we expect the throughput to go up with an integrated receiving/encryption server, as we can eliminate one disk I/O from the critical path. mnvThird, the hardware we are using is only mediocre or even archaic according to today's standard. There are plenty of high end systems available in the market with reasonable cost. And finally code optimization has yet to be done.

7   Towards Trustworthy Environments

Our scheme provides a flexible protection method for user data in ubiquitous computing environments and can be used to complement other architectures to achieve higher level of security. However, the scheme as described so far suffers from a significant weakness: the security of the scheme is conditioned upon the assumption that the server is honest and the data are safe only after the server performs the encryption scheme *faithfully*. Ubiquitous computing systems, ours and others, suffer from the trust problems we described at the beginning of the paper. In future, users will move through a procession of sensor-equipped spaces, all of which can record their actions. Some of the owners of those spaces will be incentivized to collect and use that data. But the user about whom the data is recorded, who we argued is the rightful owner of the data, may not wish this to happen (recall Langheinrich's principle 1 against covert monitoring). The law will almost certainly have a say in this state of affairs. But laws have no potency unless they can be enforced, which means unauthorized monitoring must be detectable at reasonable cost. Bits flowing around the Internet can be extremely difficult to trace, so this is certainly a challenge. It creates a technical problem: How do we monitor and verify that a smart room or space is compliant with stated privacy policies and transmitting only the data it is supposed to?

We are approaching this problem from the framework of trusted computing. That is, we assume that most of the hardware in the environment is untrusted, but that a small and inexpensive trusted device (a tamper-proof device like a smart card, but more powerful) is incorporated into the infrastructure in a way that it can verify that the system is satisfying particular constraints. This device would need to be inserted and inspected as part of certification of the space by a third party or government, much like a GFCI receptacle (ground-fault detectors required near water). In our case, the constraints are that the system should send only messages encrypted with keys of users who are in the room, and that the system should not leak information in the messages encrypted with authorized keys. The first guarantee can be given with ZKP (Zero-Knowledge Proof) techniques [30]. The second (leakage) is quite subtle and is the subject of our ongoing work. In both cases though, the system should obey a key principle, described next.

7.1   Data Transparency Principle

Paradoxically, the first step in making an ubicomp environment trustworthy is to make sure all the data flowing out of it is encrypted, but can be seen by other users or by the inspection subsystem (which is trusted component within the infrastructure).

Data Transparency: Encrypted data recorded or transmitted by a ubicomp system should be easily observable. Where possible, the data itself should demonstrate compliance with stated principles.

The information protections provided by well-implemented cryptography are much more reliable than access restrictions using the operating system or network routing. Once data *are* encrypted, ZKP techniques allow us to prove things about it without disclosing any new information about the data. In particular, we can show that it is encrypted with particular keys. And we can attempt to show the absence of leakage.

7.2   Verification Mechanisms

How to verify the environment's compliance with privacy policies is the subject of our current research. We already noted the value of ZKPs for this step. ZKPs allow an agent A to prove to an agent B that A has information that would be very hard for B to compute, without disclosing that information ([30]). More concretely in [1], ZKPs are used to prove that private user data was validly generated without disclosing the data. In our case ZKP can be used to prove that access rights of legitimate users are indeed embedded in the data [3]. The challenge

---

[3] Please note that we are using ZKP to reason about the properties of the *key set*, not the actual data, which can be anything from video to audio and it may not be possible to apply ZKP.

with the leakage property is that there are many ways to leak information. Each leakage mechanism defines a property of the encrypted data. So proving non-leakage appears to be proving that the data does *not* have an open set of properties. This is not feasible with ZKP. To this problem we take another approach. Namely the non-leakage property is enforced by introducing verifier devices from a third party or the government and forcing the system to first fix its data by bit-commitment, and then encrypt using a security parameter created by the (trusted) verifier. That means that the system has no way to anticipate what the encrypted data will look like, and it will appear highly random.

It is unlikely that any scheme can prevent all types of cheating. We believe ours could certainly raise the technical bar for cheating, and possibly impose strong constraints on the rate of information leakage. This should be enough to reduce the frequency of non-compliance significantly.

8 Conclusion

As many researchers in ubiquitous computing have noted, in order for ubiquitous computing to be really beneficial and socially acceptable, user privacy has to be considered carefully at early stage of system design. In this paper, we argue that the essence of preserving user privacy is protecting user data and propose two design principles and an enforcing protection scheme. The "data discretion" principle stipulates that access to information stored in a system should only be granted to individuals who would have access to the data in the "real-world". Explicit notion of ownership should be established as the information is generated to determine access right. The "data transparency" principle states that, rather than trying to enhance privacy by hiding the existence of information or communication, a system should rely on well-implemented cryptography for data protection and make the recording and transmitting of encrypted data observable. Only when the usage of data is made open can the system perform effective monitoring to enforce compliance with privacy policies. We consider this to be a very important step towards building trustworthy environment.

Acknowledgements. The authors would like to thank Alessandro Acquisti and the anonymous reviewers for their valuable comments. This work was supported in part by National Science Foundation award #EIA-0122599 (Title: "ITR/SI: Societal Scale Information Systems: Technologies, Design, and Applications").

References

1. Canny, J.: Collaborative filtering with privacy. In: IEEE Symposium on Security and Privacy, Oakland, CA (2002) 45–57
2. Langheinrich, M.: Privacy by design – principles of privacy-aware ubiquitous systems. In Abowd, G., Brumitt, B., Shafer, S., eds.: Proceedings of Ubicomp 2001. Volume 2201 of Lecture Notes in Computer Science., Springer (2001) 273–291

3. Abowd, G.D., Mynatt, E.D.: Charting past, present, and future research in ubiquitous computing. ACM Trans. on Computer-Human Interaction **7** (2000) 29–58
4. Al-Muhtadi, J., Campbell, R., Kapadia, A., Mickunas, D., Yi, S.: Routing through the mist: Privacy preserving communication in ubiquitous computing environments. In: International Conference of Distributed Computing Systems (ICDCS 2002), Vienna, Austria (2002)
5. Cranor, L., Langheinrich, M., Marchiori, M., Reagle, J.: The platform for privacy preferences 1.0 (p3p1.0) specification. W3C Recommendation (2002)
6. Anonymizer Inc.: Anonymizer. http://www.anonymizer.com (2003)
7. Bellotti, V., Sellen, A.: Design for Privacy in Ubiquitous Computing Environments. In: Proceedings of the Third European Conference on Computer Supported Cooperative Work (ECSCW'93), Kluwer (1993) 77–92
8. Spreitzer, M., Theimer, M.: Providing location information in a ubiquitous computing environment. In: Proceedings of the 14th ACM Symposium on Operating Systems Principles), ACM Press (1993) 270–283
9. Gruteser, M., Schelle, G., Jain, A., Han, R., Grunwald, D.: Privacy-aware location sensor networks. In: Proceedings of the 9th Workshop on Hot Topics in Operating Systems (HotOS IX), Lihue, Hawaii, USA (2003)
10. Gruteser, M., Grunwald, D.: Anonymous usage of location-based services through spatial and temporal cloaking. In: Proceedings of the First International Conference on Mobile Systems, Applications, and Services (MobiSys 2003), San Francisco, CA, USA (2003)
11. Hengartner, U., Steenkiste, P.: Protecting access to people location information. In: Proceedings of First International Conference on Security in Pervasive Computing (SPC 2003), Boppard, Germany (2003)
12. Gribble, S.D., Welsh, M., von Behren, J.R., Brewer, E.A., Culler, D.E., Borisov, N., Czerwinski, S.E., Gummadi, R., Hill, J.R., Joseph, A.D., Katz, R.H., Mao, Z.M., Ross, S., Zhao, B.Y.: The ninja architecture for robust internet-scale systems and services. Computer Networks **35** (2001) 473–497
13. Kagal, L., Undercoffer, J., Perich, F., Joshi, A., Finin, T.: A security architecture based on trust management for pervasive computing systems. In: Proceedings of Grace Hopper Celebration of Women in Computing 2002. (2002)
14. Kagal, L., Cost, S., Finin, T., Peng, Y.: A framework for distributed trust management. In: Proceedings of IJCAI-01 Workshop on Autonomy, Delegation and Control. (2001)
15. Hengartner, U., Steenkiste, P.: Access control to information in pervasive computing environments. In: Proceedings of the 9th Workshop on Hot Topics in Operating Systems (HotOS IX), Lihue, Hawaii, USA (2003)
16. Ferraiolo, D., Kuhn, R.: Role based access control. In: Proceedings of the 15th National Computer Security Conference. (1992)
17. Lupu, E., Sloman, M.: A policy-based role object model. In: Proceedings of the 1st IEEE Enterprise Distributed Object Computing Workshop (EDOC'97), Gold Coast, Australia (1997) 36–47
18. Sandhu, R.S., Coyne, E.J., Feinstein, H.L., Youman, C.E.: Role based access control models. IEEE Computer **29** (1996) 38–47
19. Sampemane, G., Naldurg, P., Campbell, R.H.: Access control for active spaces. In: Proceedings of the 18th Annual Computer Security Applications Conference, Las Vegas, Nevada (2002)
20. Gelernter, D.H.: Mirror Worlds: Or the Day Software Puts the Universe in a Shoebox: How It Will Happen and What It Will Mean. Oxford University Press (1992)

21. Mann, S.: Smart clothing, turning the tables. In: ACM Multimedia Conf. (1996)
22. Rhodes, B.: The remembrance agent: A continuously running automated information retrieval system. In: The Proceedings of The First International Conference on The Practical Application of Intelligent Agents and Multi Agent Technology (PAAM '96), London, UK (1996) 487–495
23. Goldberg, D., Nichols, D., Oki, B., Terry, D.: Using collaborative filtering to weave an information tapestry. Comm. ACM **35** (1992) 51–60
24. Canny, J.: Collaborative filtering with privacy via factor analysis. In: Proceedings of the 25th Annual International ACM SIGIR Conference on Research and Development in Information Retrieval, Tampere, Finland, ACM Press (2002) 238–245
25. Menezes, A.J., Oorschot, P.C.V., Vanstone, S.A.: Handbook of Applied Cryptography. CRC Press Series on Discrete Mathematics and Its Applications. CRC Press (1996)
26. Pedersen, T.: A threshold cryptosystem without a trusted party. In: Proceedings of EUROCRYPT '91. Volume 547 of Springer-Verlag LNCS., Springer (1991) 522–526
27. Gennaro, R., Jarecki, S., Krawczyk, H., Rabin, T.: Secure distributed key generation for discrete-log based cryptosystems. LNCS **1592** (1999) 295–310
28. Fouque, P.A., Stern, J.: One round threshold discrete-log key generation without private channels. Public Key Cryptography (2001) 300–316
29. Wei, D.: Crypto++ Library^{TM} 5.0 (2002)
30. Goldreich, O., Oren, Y.: Definitions and properties of zero-knowledge proof systems. Journal of Cryptology **7** (1994) 1–32

Synchronous Batching:
From Cascades to Free Routes

Roger Dingledine[1], Vitaly Shmatikov[2], and Paul Syverson[3]

[1] The Free Haven Project
arma@freehaven.net
[2] SRI International
shmat@csl.sri.com
[3] Naval Research Lab
syverson@itd.nrl.navy.mil

Abstract. The variety of possible anonymity network topologies has spurred much debate in recent years. In a synchronous batching design, each batch of messages enters the mix network together, and the messages proceed in lockstep through the network. We show that a synchronous batching strategy can be used in various topologies, including a free-route network, in which senders choose paths freely, and a cascade network, in which senders choose from a set of fixed paths. We show that free-route topologies can provide better anonymity as well as better message reliability in the event of partial network failure.

1   Introduction

Modern deployed mix networks, including Mixmaster [21] and its successor Mixminion [8], are subject to partitioning attacks: a passive adversary can observe the network until a target message happens to stand out from the others [3], and an active adversary can manipulate the network to separate one message from the others via blending attacks [24]. Berthold et al. argue [3] that partitioning opportunities arise because the networks use a *free-route* topology—one where the sender can choose the mixes that make up her message's path. They suggest instead a *cascade network* topology, where all senders choose from a set of fixed paths through the mix network.

In this paper we argue that the cascade design resolves these attacks because it uses a *synchronous batching* strategy, not because it uses a particular network topology. We show that synchronous batching prevents these attacks even when free routes are used. Further, we explore three topologies with synchronous batching—cascades, stratified (a restricted-route hybrid topology), and free-route—and find that the free-route network provides the highest expected anonymity as well as the best robustness to node failure.

In Section 2 we describe the synchronous batching model. Section 3 relates previous work to synchronous batching, including a response to each of the

D. Martin and A. Serjantov (Eds.): PET 2004, LNCS 3424, pp. 186–206, 2005.

arguments from [3]. Section 4 presents the three topologies, and Section 5 describes their entropy (average anonymity the sender expects from the network). We use a model checker to compute entropy for networks with 16 nodes: we present our results and assess the assumptions behind them in Section 6. Section 7 considers other metrics such as bandwidth requirements, latency, and robustness.

2   Synchronous Batching

Chaum proposed hiding the correspondence between sender and recipient by wrapping messages in layers of public-key cryptography, and relaying them through a path composed of *mixes* [4]. Each mix in turn decrypts, delays, and re-orders messages, before relaying them toward their destinations.

A mixnet design groups messages into batches and chooses paths; its design choices affect the degree of anonymity it can provide [24]. We might define ideal anonymity for a mixnet to be when an attacker can gain no information (beyond prior knowledge) about the linkage between messages entering and leaving the network, other than that the maximum time between them is equal to the maximum network latency.

This ideal is not achieved by protocols like Mixminion that use locally computed random delays: if the maximum latency of such a network is t, the probability that an output message corresponds to a particular input message might be considerably higher than for other messages that have entered over that time. (In principle, because of its pool mode, a message's maximum latency could be infinite, but that's not a significant improvement in practice: if the probability of a given latency t drops off exponentially with t, then so does the probability that a message leaving the network could have been sent that long ago [23].) Also, because Mixminion is both *asynchronous* (messages can enter and leave the network at any time) and uses free routes, it is subject to the attacks from [3] described in Section 3.2 below.

A network that uses *synchronous batching* has a fixed *batch period*, t_{batch}, which is related to the maximum desired latency, for example 3 hours. Messages entering the network in each batch period are queued until the beginning of the next period. They are then sent through the mixnet synchronously, at a rate of one hop per *hop period*. All paths are a fixed length ℓ hops, so that if no messages are dropped, the messages introduced in a given batch will progress through their routes in lockstep, and will all be transmitted to their final destinations ℓ hop periods later. Each layer of a message, once decrypted, specifies the hop period in which it must be received, so that it cannot be delayed by an attacker.

The *width w* of a mixnet using synchronous batching is the number of nodes that simultaneously process messages from a given batch in each hop period. (If this is not constant, we can still talk about the maximum, minimum, and mean width.) When $w = 1$, we have a cascade. The latency is between ℓt_{hop} and $t_{\text{batch}} + \ell t_{\text{hop}}$, depending on when the message is submitted. We might set $t_{\text{hop}} < t_{\text{batch}}/\ell$, so the latency is at most $2t_{\text{batch}}$, independent of the path length.Thus the entire batch is processed and delivered before the next batch enters the network. Under this constraint, we can give nodes the maximum opportunity to make use of the available bandwidth, and the best chance at delivery robustness, by setting $t_{\text{hop}} \simeq t_{\text{batch}}/\ell$.

3   Related Work

3.1   Synchronous Batching Timing Model and Protocol

Dingledine et al. present in [11] a mix network that uses synchronous batching. We refer to that paper for a detailed discussion of the timing model, how to handle loosely synchronized clocks, and the step-by-step instructions for senders and mixes to use the network and judge whether messages have arrived on time.

That paper also describes a receipt and witness system by which senders and mixes can prove that a given mix failed to pass on or accept a given message. These receipts allow a reputation system: senders can recognize which nodes tend to drop messages, and avoid them in the future.

3.2   The Disadvantages of Free Mix Routes

Berthold et al. argue [3] that cascades are safer than free-route mix networks against a strong adversary who watches all links and controls many of the mixes. We consider each of their attacks below and find in each case that the arguments of [3] do not apply if the free-route network is synchronous. Indeed, against some of the attacks a free-route network is much stronger than the cascade network.

Position in Mix Route: This attack partitions messages that go through a given honest node based on how many hops each message has travelled so far. If the adversary owns all other nodes in the network, he can distinguish messages at different positions in their path (say, one has traversed two mixes already, and another has traversed three), and thus learn the sender and recipient of each message. The authors note: *Eventually, a message is only unobservable in that group of messages which have this mix on the same routing position.* But in the synchronous design, that's not a problem because this group is large (if only one mix is trustworthy, $1/w$ of all messages in the batch). They conclude: *If only one mix of a route is trustworthy, then the achievable anonymity is distinctly lower in a mix network compared to a synchronously working mix cascade.* The actual conclusion should be: If only one mix of a route is trustworthy, then the achievable anonymity for a given topology is distinctly lower in an asynchronous mixnet than in a synchronous mixnet.

Determining the Next Mix: An adversary owning most nodes in the network can attack the honest mixes: he can link senders to messages entering honest mixes, and he can link receivers to messages exiting honest mixes. Thus the target messages will only be mixing with other messages that enter the mix node at that time, and not with other messages elsewhere in the network. Even if senders use the same path for multiple messages, the authors point out that *the batches always generate different anonymity groups.* Again, the important property is whether the network uses synchronous batching, not whether it uses free routes. In a synchronous batching design, all messages in a batch exit the network together after the last hop, so messages cannot be partitioned based on when they enter or exit the network.

Probability of Unobservability: The authors explain that the cascade topology optimizes for the case that only one mix node is honest. They compare a 4-node cascade (with 3 compromised nodes) to a 20-node free-route mix network (with 75% compromised nodes), and find that whereas the cascade provides complete protection, a user choosing four nodes in the free-route network has a non-trivial chance of picking an entirely compromised path. But this is a false comparison. A better comparison would consider either a free-route mix network with 4 nodes, or a network of five $\ell = 4$ cascades—so the cascade network also has a chance of fully-compromised paths. In Section 6 we show that while each cascade in a cascade network of width w only mixes $1/w$ of the messages from the batch, a free-route network can mix all the messages from the batch and thus achieves significantly stronger anonymity even with 75% compromised nodes.

Active Attacks: The authors discuss an active attack called a trickle attack [17], wherein the adversary prevents legitimate messages from entering the batch, or removes some messages from the batch, so he can more easily trace Alice's message. To make the attack less overt, he can send his own messages into the batch, or replace the messages already in the batch with his own messages. These attacks where the adversary *blends* his messages with Alice's message threaten both synchronous-batching and asynchronous-batching networks in all topologies, and a complete solution that is practical is not known [24]. The authors of [3] present some approaches to mitigating this attack in a cascade environment, but a variety of other approaches have been developed that also work in a free-route environment. We discuss them next. Other active attacks are described in Section 7.3.

3.3   Blending Attacks

Active attacks where the adversary targets a message by manipulating the other messages in the system are a widespread problem in mix-based systems. Solutions fall into three categories: attempts to *prevent* the attack, attempts to *slow* the attack, and attempts to *detect and punish* the attacker.

One prevention technique requires each sender to acquire a *ticket* for each mix in his path before joining a given batch (the senders receive blinded tickets [5] so the mixes cannot trivially link them to their messages). Mixes ensure their messages come from distinct senders, so Alice can expect good mixing at each honest node in her path [1]. For cascades this approach is clearly efficient because Alice only needs tickets for her chosen cascade [3], but her anonymity set is still limited to that one cascade. We conjecture that other topologies can give equivalent anonymity while only obtaining tickets from a fraction of the mixes, but we leave that analysis to future work. A bigger problem with the ticket scheme, however, is the feasibility of requiring all users to register with the mixes: it is hard to imagine that attackers can be excluded from being registered in an open network [13]. Other prevention techniques use complex cryptography to provide *robustness* [18] — messages are only delivered if a threshold of the mixes agree that the batch has been properly processed.

Techniques to slow the blending attack are generally designed for asynchronous mix networks. In Mixmaster and Mixminion, the goal of the batching algorithm is to hide from the adversary when an outgoing message entered the mix. Mixes 'pool' some messages from previous batches, to try to mix them as far back as possible. These approaches force the adversary to spend more time and messages on the attack [24]. Some designs allow a pool mix to commit to its choice of randomness to allow verifying its behavior [15]. Link encryption, as well as Babel's *inter-mix detours* [17] and early Onion Routing's *loose routing* [16], aim to block a limited adversary from knowing when his message has exited a mix. This also complicates blending because even the sender cannot always recognize a message he created. In stop-and-go mixes [20], each sender specifies a time window for each mix in his path: as with synchronous batching designs, messages arriving outside the time window are dropped, so the attacker cannot arbitrarily delay messages without destroying them.

Other approaches aim to detect and deter misbehavior. Chaum suggests allowing each sender to examine the output of each mix [4], but this approach scales poorly. Danezis and Sassaman propose a 'heartbeat' dummy scheme [9] for asynchronous pool mix networks: dummies are sent from a node in the network back to itself, creating an early warning system to detect if the adversary is launching a blending attack. *Reliability* mechanisms aim to improve a sender's long-term odds of choosing a mix path with well-behaving nodes. The witness-and-receipt system in [11] provides such a reputation system for synchronous-batching networks. Another reputation system for cascades [12] allows mixes to send test messages into the network to detect misbehavior. Finally, randomized partial checking [19] allows each mix to show evidence of its correctness by revealing a pseudo-randomly selected subset of its input-output relationships, while the mix network as a whole still protects linkability with high probability.

Clearly much work has been done to address blending attacks. Each topology seems to have some plausible partial solutions.

4   Threat Model and Mixnet Topologies

Our analysis considers a slight variant on the traditional powerful adversary who observes globally and controls a fraction of the nodes [3]. We assume the adversary compromises nodes at random rather than in a targeted fashion (see Section 6.1 for more discussion on this point). Along with being able to control some of the nodes, our adversary can observe messages from senders to the mixnet and from the mixnet to receivers, but our initial analysis assumes he cannot observe the links between honest nodes in the mixnet (in Section 6.4 we argue that with high probability, observing these links will not yield much new information anyway). This paper only examines sender anonymity, though many of the advantages of synchronous batching may carry over to receiver anonymity.

We assume that selective forwarding will be discovered, and either the attack will be prevented or the malfunctioning node will be removed from the network (see Section 3.3). We address the attack of intersecting individual batches in Section 3.2 (under "determining the next mix"), but unsurprisingly, we leave the long-term intersection attack [2, 7] unsolved. Further active attacks to degrade anonymity are described in Section 7.3.

We analyze a 16 node mixnet where all messages follow a four node path. Besides being a tractable size for analysis, 16 nodes also approximates deployed mixnets. (Mixminion currently has between 20 and 30 active nodes.) One might argue that a 4 node mixnet gives better security, because all messages are mixed together in any topology. We assume a larger network is needed because 1) the bandwidth of a single node may be insufficient to handle all the traffic; 2) a single path may not include as many choices for jurisdiction as some users want; and 3) a single path is not very robust, either to network attacks or to nature.

Messages proceed through the network in *layers*; all the nodes in a layer process messages of one mixnet batch at the same time. In general we describe networks as wxℓ, where w is the number of nodes at each layer and ℓ is the number of nodes in a path. We consider three basic topologies: a 4x4 cascade mixnet in which all messages pass through four cascades of length four; a 4x4 *stratified* mixnet, in which all messages pass through four layers of disjoint nodes such that messages may pass from any node at one layer to any node at the next layer; and a 16x4 free-route mixnet, in which all nodes may receive messages at all layers. Note that because free-route nodes are reused, '16x4' does not mean 64 nodes. Examples of the three topologies are illustrated below.

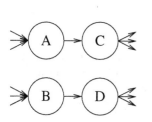

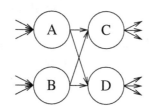

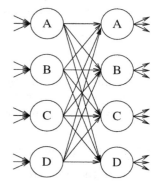

Fig. 1. A 2x2 cascade mix network (4 nodes)

Fig. 2. A 2x2 stratified network (4 nodes)

Fig. 3. A 4x2 free-route mix network (4 nodes)

5   Modeling Methodology

The basic model underlying our comparative study of mix network topologies is *mixing as probabilistic permutation*. At the cost of a few simplifying but reasonable assumptions about distribution of message traffic in the network, we obtain a tractable Markov chain model, and use a fully automated probabilistic model checking technique to compute probability distributions for different network topologies and configurations. We use *entropy* of each topology's respective distribution as our comparison metric, in the spirit of [10, 23].

5.1   Mixing as Permutation

Consider a single batch of N messages entering the mix network together. We can view each message $m_1, \dots, m_N$ as occupying a certain position in a (virtual) input array of length N. Suppose the adversary targets a particular message m in position i. Without loss of generality, assume that $i = 1$ (we can always re-number the input array so that the targeted message is in the first slot).

Having passed the network, all N messages re-appear and may be observed by the adversary again. Of course, if some of the network nodes have been compromised by the adversary, the adversary will have access to their observations, too. Let $m'_1, \dots, m'_N$ be the (virtual) output array. Due to the mixing performed by the network, it may or may not be the case that $m'_i = m_i$, *i.e.*, the messages have been probabilistically permuted by the network. We will refer to the discrete probability distribution $p_1 \dots p_N$, where $p_i = Prob(m'_i = m)$, as the *mixing distribution* of the network. Informally, each p_i is the probability that the targeted message m re-appears in the ith position of the output buffer.

In our basic model, we assume that the network doesn't lose messages (this restriction is not critical and may be relaxed, if necessary). Therefore, $\sum_{1 \leq i \leq N} p_i = 1$, and p_i form a proper discrete probability distribution. Following [23], we calculate *entropy* of this distribution as

$$\mathcal{E} = - \sum_{1 \leq i \leq N} p_i \log_2(p_i)$$

Very informally, entropy is a measure of "randomness" in a distribution. Other things being equal, network topologies that provide mixing distributions associated with higher entropy values are considered preferable.

5.2   Overview of the Model

We use the standard techniques of probabilistic verification and model the mix network as a discrete-time Markov chain. Formally, a *Markov chain* consists of a finite set of states S, the initial state s_0, the transition relation $T : S \times S \rightarrow [0, 1]$ such that $\forall s \in S \ \sum_{s' \in S} T(s, s') = 1$, and a labeling function.

In our model, the states of the Markov chain will represent the position of the targeted message m in the (virtual) buffer of N messages as m moves through the network. The initial state s_0 corresponds to the message being in the first slot

Fig. 4. Model of a good mix   **Fig. 5.** Model of a bad mix

of the input array prior to entering the mix network. Every probabilistic state transition $s \to s'$ is associated with m passing through a single mix within the network. Intuitively, s can be interpreted as m's position before passing through the mix, and s' as its position afterwards.

For the purposes of computing the mixing distribution p_i, we are interested in deadlock states, *i.e.*, those corresponding to the situation in which m has passed through all mixes in its path and exited the mix network with no further transitions possible. Suppose a special predicate *done* is true in such states. Then p_i is simply $Prob[\mathcal{U}(s = i \land done)]$ evaluated in the initial state s_0. (Informally, formula $\mathcal{U}\varphi$ holds if φ eventually becomes true.)

We use a probabilistic model checker called PRISM [14] to compute these probabilities automatically. We omit the details of the underlying model checking algorithms; a detailed explanation of how probabilistic model checking is used to analyze randomized routing protocols can be found in [25].

5.3 Single-Mix Model

Consider a single mix receiving a batch of K messages, including the targeted message m. Assume an uncompromised mix that collects all K messages before distributing them to their respective destinations. In this case, the mixing performed by the mix can be interpreted as permutation in a virtual buffer of size K. In particular, the targeted message m appears in any of the K output positions with equal probability after passing through the mix. Therefore, each honest mix can be modeled by a simple Markov chain as below (recall that state s represents the current position of message m, and let t be the sequential number of the current hop). However, the compromised mix performs no mixing at all, and thus does not change the position of any message it processes.

5.4 Network Model

We consider several mix network topologies, and compare them under various assumptions about the density of hostile mixes in the network. Instead of assuming a fixed number of hostile mixes, in each scenario we will assume a fixed *probability* that a randomly selected mix is hostile.

For each topology, the behavior of a single node is modeled as in Section 5.3. The main difference between topologies is how the targeted message moves through the network, resulting in different mixing distributions $p_1 \ldots p_N$.

We assume the adversary observes the edge of the network and thus knows the first mix chosen by the targeted message—so the randomness of mix selection is ignored for the first hop. Formally, we make probability p_i conditional on selection of a particular first mix. Instead of computing $Prob[\mathcal{U}(s = i \land done)]$, we compute $Prob[\mathcal{U}(s = i \land done \mid \text{mix } x \text{ was selected as entry point})]$.

Note that we must consider two sources of uncertainty. The first is the distribution of compromised nodes in the network, which we address by assuming a fixed probability that any given node is bad. Thus we are calculating *prior* distributions—effectively the average of all possible occurrences of compromised nodes in the network. (In contrast, [10, 23] consider *posterior* distributions, where certain nodes are known to be bad). The second uncertainty is the users' selection of message routes, which we address by treating the message load on each internal link within the network as exactly equal to the statistically expected load given a particular network topology. This assumption is approximated with very high probability when the number of messages in a single batch is significantly higher than the number of network nodes (see Section 6.4 for discussion).

Intuitively, suppose there are four mixes in the first layer of the network, and batch size is 128. We will analyze the average-case behavior of the network, *i.e.*, we will assume that each of the mixes receives exactly 32 messages, even though it is possible (albeit highly improbable) that in some batch all 128 senders will randomly choose the same entry mix.

Under the equal loading assumption, we treat the size of the input/output buffer for each mix (see Section 5.3) as a constant which is determined only by batch size and network topology, and is independent of the actual random distribution of a given batch through the network.

Appendix B provides a walk-through of calculating entropy for each topology, to help the unfamiliar reader build intuition about our assumptions and results.

6   Graphs and Analysis

Figure 6 shows the entropy Alice can expect from each of the three topologies. The cascade network immediately divides the incoming batch by the number of cascades, so it provides substantially less protection even with many compromised nodes. The stratified topology provides about the same expected entropy as the free-route topology. In this section and the next we will examine other metrics for deciding which is best. Further graphs in Appendix A indicate how much entropy is achieved after a given number of steps through each network.

6.1   Is the Adversary Really Randomly Distributed?

To keep our model tractable, we have assumed that each node has an equal chance of being controlled by the adversary. A real adversary might prefer to control certain key nodes in the topology. To justify our assumption, we might

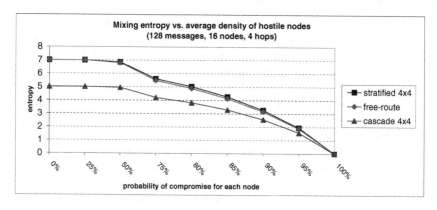

Fig. 6. Entropy vs probability of compromise for each node (16 nodes)

assume that secure nodes (or equivalently, vulnerable nodes) are randomly distributed. That is, rather than letting the adversary have his pick of nodes, we instead let the adversary control all the machines that have some security vulnerability. A related approach would be to place particularly secure and trusted (or at least jurisdictionally separate) nodes in key places in the topology: if such nodes are discouragingly secure, they are no longer an appealing target.

Alternatively, the mixes can periodically generate a communally random seed to reorganize the network [12]. Thus, being able to control or sign up a node does not allow the adversary to dictate its position in the topology. This may be a satisfactory solution, though it is not a complete solution because not all nodes are equal: e.g. nodes that refuse to deliver messages to the final recipients shouldn't be chosen as exit nodes, so they may be less appealing targets.

6.2   Choosing the Same Node Twice in a Row

Conventional wisdom (see e.g. [8]) suggests that in a free-route network, Alice should never pick the same node twice in a row: it increases her risk of picking only bad nodes. We find that for a sufficiently large network, this increased complexity in path selection has little impact on Alice's entropy.

Intuitively, when the adversary density is low, entropy will be high in either case; whereas when most nodes are owned by the adversary, the difference between picking between B and $B-1$ bad nodes is slight.

More formally, for G good nodes and B bad nodes, the chance of selecting a bad node next is $\frac{B-1}{G+B}$ if the current node is bad and $\frac{B}{G+B}$ otherwise. The difference is only $\frac{1}{G+B}$: it does not depend on what fraction of the nodes are bad. Specifically, for a 16x4 free-route mixnet (8 bad nodes), it's a 5.1% chance of an all bad path if a node cannot be picked twice in a row, and 6.3% chance if it can. With 32x4, it's 5.7% vs. 6.3%.

6.3   Reputations and Node Preferences

Most deployed systems let users choose a preferred entry or exit hop, e.g. based on trust. A skewed distribution of messages only at the entry or exit of the network should not impact entropy too much—we see from Figures 7-9 that much of each network's entropy is achieved from just a few hops.

Reputation systems, on the other hand, encourage users to prefer certain nodes at *each layer* of the network. Further, reputation information can be exploited by an adversary to reduce anonymity, for example by predicting the user's behavior based on reputation statistics, or by attracting more traffic by building a strong reputation or degrading the reputation of others. Placing nodes with similar reputation in the same layer of a stratified network, or placing them in the same cascade, might complicate these attacks, but employed naively, this can facilitate other attacks [12]. This topic merits further investigation.

6.4   Average Entropy Versus Actual Entropy

The graphs and analysis above are for average entropy—the network's behavior for very large batches. But in reality the batch size may be quite small, and each sender chooses paths independently from the others. We must consider the possible variance in entropy depending on the actual path choices.

For m messages to u buckets (nodes in a layer), we find the chance that any bucket will have less than p messages based on Maxwell-Boltzmann statistics and inclusion-exclusion:

$$\binom{u}{1} \sum_{i=0}^{p} (\frac{1}{u})^i (1 - \frac{1}{u})^{m-i} \binom{m}{i} - \binom{u}{2} \sum_{i=0}^{p} \sum_{j=0}^{p} (\frac{1}{u})^i (\frac{1}{u})^j (1 - \frac{2}{u})^{m-i-j} \binom{m}{i,j}$$

$$+ \binom{u}{3} \sum_{i=0}^{p} \sum_{j=0}^{p} \sum_{k=0}^{p} (\frac{1}{u})^i (\frac{1}{u})^j (\frac{1}{u})^k (1 - \frac{3}{u})^{m-i-j-k} \binom{m}{i,j,k} - \cdots$$

For $m = 128$ messages and $u = 4$ nodes (i.e. cascade or stratified network), the chance of any node getting less than 16 messages (compared to the 32 we expect each to get) is $6 \cdot 10^{-4}$—meaning with very high probability the average entropy represents the behavior we will see in reality. However, for $u = 16$ nodes (free-route), 48% of the time some node will get less than half the expected number; and it is not until a batch size of 480 that this metric reaches 1%.

This result makes sense: each link on a free-route network has a smaller expected number of messages, so variations have a bigger impact. Whether it is acceptable depends on a number of factors. First, how large do we expect batches to be in reality? The Mixmaster network receives more than 1000 messages an hour, which seems plenty sufficient. Second, how bad is it when a link varies by half the expected volume? If we change our metric to require at least 2 messages on each link, then for $m = 128$ we find that only 1% of the cases fall outside this value. Another significant question is how the number of layers affects the results:

the more layers, the greater the chance that some of them are well balanced. The exact relation and its effect on entropy are open questions.

Danezis also considers this issue of variance from average entropy for his mixnet design based on sparse expander graphs [6]. He argues that having at least one message on each link is sufficient for basic protection, and he uses a similar approach to show that his design achieves this distribution with high probability. He further raises the idea of padding unused links to guarantee one message on each link, with the aim of preventing trivial traffic analysis attacks. Is it worthwhile to prevent this simple attack? Are all other attacks significantly harder? Clearly more research remains.

6.5   Flooding Attacks to Degrade Anonymity or Service

In Section 3.3 we talk about techniques to discourage a mix from dropping or substituting messages in the batch. But what if the adversary simply submits *more* messages to the batch?

It turns out that as long as k of the n input messages come from honest senders, Alice will still be assured that she can expect entropy based on a batch of k messages. That is, assuming uniform distribution of messages over mixes, the entropy of a baseline network (all-honest senders) plus hostile messages is at least the entropy of the baseline network by itself. This is different from the pooling batching strategy [24], where messages from the adversary will influence the behavior (and thus entropy) of Alice's message.

On the other hand, directed floods can overflow node capacity. We might use techniques where mixes can prove that any output message was derived from an input message, which reduces the problem to detecting or stopping floods at the beginning of the batch. We might also argue that the fraction of adversary messages in the batch limits the maximum size of the flooding attack—honest messages will still be randomly distributed. In general, this flooding issue is an unsolved problem for all mixnet designs; more research remains.

7   Other Metrics for Comparison

7.1   Throughput, Delay, Capacity, Bandwidth

One parameter we cannot control is the rate that messages arrive to the mixnet. Similarly, we cannot control the latency that users will be willing to accept. To make the analysis more concrete, assume we choose $\ell = 4$, that users deliver 128 messages every 3 hours, and that users will tolerate a latency of 3–6 hours (which is on par with the latency experienced by a typical Mixmaster message, though it could be much longer in theory).

We can compute the maximum flow rate (traffic in unit time) through any given node. Assume that sending a message over a single hop consumes a fixed amount of network traffic; we can then use that as the unit for traffic. Let T_{batch} be the expected throughput in a single batch period, i.e. the number of messages that go through the network in a batch. If the available nodes are used optimally (see Section 6.4), the flow rate required through each node is $\frac{T_{\text{batch}}}{w \cdot t_{\text{hop}}} = \frac{\ell \cdot T_{\text{batch}}}{w \cdot t_{\text{batch}}}$.

If we choose $t_{\text{batch}} \simeq \ell t_{\text{hop}}$, all messages clear the mixnet before the next batch enters: we introduce a batch of 128 messages every 3 hours. We get 42.7 messages/hour for all three topologies. Latency is between 3 hours and 6 hours, depending on when Alice's message arrives. By accepting messages over a large amount of time, we get better expected entropy; make the actual behavior of the network closer to the expected behavior of the network (as in Section 6.4); and smooth spikes and troughs in the rate of incoming messages.

In the free-route network, each node needs to process 8 messages at a time and is active at each layer. The cascade and stratified networks require a larger capacity from each node: they must handle 32 messages at once ($128/w$), but they are idle for all but one hop in the batch. One could imagine a *systolic* or *pipelined* network where $t_{\text{batch}} = t_{\text{hop}}$ and 32 messages are let in every 45 minutes. In this case the capacity of nodes in cascade and stratified networks would also be 8, and indeed the latency could be cut to between 3 hours and 3 hours 45 minutes—but the expected entropy would be cut by a factor of ℓ.

Bandwidth is acceptable. Assuming a higher load of 5000 messages per batch, and 32KB per message (as in Mixminion), nodes in the free-route system use less than 4KB/s (nodes in the other topologies use 16KB/s but only 1/4 as often). That's well within the capabilities of current Mixmaster nodes.

7.2   Robustness of Message Delivery

Better entropy can be achieved by longer routes: e.g., if we form our 16 nodes into a 1x16 cascade or a 16x16 free-route, there is almost no falloff in entropy until each node has a ninety percent chance of being compromised. But this ignores robustness of message delivery. For the free-route 16x16 mixnet with only a single node failure, nearly two thirds of messages will be undelivered (because they will need to pass through it at some point). The 1x16 cascade is even worse: a single node crash blocks all message delivery. (We might take advantage of schemes to bypass a single failed node [22], but it's not clear how this works with the synchronous approach in all topologies.) Parallel cascades can be added to the network, but unlike the free-route, they will *a priori* reduce the entropy of an input message for a given size mixnet batch. We must be sure to consider robustness when comparing topologies.

Table 1 shows that 4x4 cascades and 4x4 stratified networks do roughly the same on average, but this is for very different reasons. The chance that the configuration will block all messages increases much more quickly for cascades, but the maximum possible delivery of messages remains much higher. This can be seen in the table reflecting the most favorable adversary distribution for up to four node crashes. To further illustrate, if half of the nodes are bad in the 4x4 cascade topology, then in about 1 in 6 cases a quarter of the messages get through, and in exactly 6 cases of 12870, half of the messages get through the cascades. For all other distributions, no messages get through. If half of the nodes are bad in the 4x4 stratified network, then the highest percentage of messages

Table 1. Percent of messages delivered vs number of crashed nodes

	Topology	1 crash	2 crash	3 crash	4 crash
	16x16 free	36	12	04	01
Worst possible	4x4 cascade	75	50	25	00
adversary distribution	4x4 stratif.	75	50	25	00
	16x4 free	77	59	44	32
	16x16 free	36	12	04	01
Best possible	4x4 cascade	75	75	75	75
adversary distribution	4x4 stratif.	75	56	42	32
	16x4 free	77	59	44	32
	16x16 free	36	12	04	01
Expected percentage:	4x4 cascade	75	55	39	27
rand. adversary dist.	4x4 stratif.	75	55	39	27
	16x4 free	77	59	44	32

that can pass through is 6.25. However, some messages will be passed in the majority of adversary distributions.

Of the scenarios we have considered, a 16x4 free route has the best expected chance of message delivery for random adversary distribution. It outperforms the others, unless the adversary has a particularly innocuous distribution. Cascades do better under favorable distributions, which are also much rarer for cascades than other topologies. Also note that the expected fraction of passed messages is the same for free routes regardless of which nodes fail: it is the most robust with respect to adversary distribution as well as adversary size.

7.3   Robustness of Anonymity

Robustness of anonymity against active attacks is harder to determine, as such attacks can take on a variety of forms. In the simplest case though, we can consider the effect on anonymity of simple node crash, since this is the most straightforward way to actively shrink anonymity. Also, as discussed in Section 3.3, there are techniques to detect and/or deter more selective attacks.

The threat model we consider here is an extension of the one in Section 4. As before, the adversary can watch senders and receivers. But now, besides failing to mix, hostile nodes may also crash—failing to deliver any of their input messages. A combination of active attacks and observations (including some internal observations) should prove the most devastating to anonymity. However, we leave full examination of this for future work. Here we concentrate on the effect of such intentional crash failures on entropy for a mixnet periphery observer.

Anonymity of cascades is unaffected by this threat model. Since each cascade batch is independent of the others, any node that crashes will wipe out all the messages in that anonymity set. Anonymity robustness of stratified and free-route topologies is more complex.

For a stratified network, if any entry node fails, the number of messages drops by one quarter, causing a reduction in entropy of .42. If two entry nodes fail, the entropy drops by 1. If 3 entry nodes fail, entropy drops by 2. If all fail, the adversary learns nothing more than if none fail. If a second layer node fails, assuming a balanced layer-two distribution, anonymity of all messages is unaffected since there is no change to the probability that an exiting message was any incoming message. Note this is so even if the distribution of messages across entry nodes is highly skewed. If the layer-two distribution is skewed, then a node may fail with some effect on entropy. However, the ability to affect anonymity in this way should be very small for randomly chosen routes. Ignoring the small effect of such non-entry-layer failures, we see that the anonymity of a stratified network given node crashes is usually better and at worst equal to that of the cascade topology.

Free routes are even more complex. For entry layer nodes, the initial effect of each crash is clearly smaller. However, since nodes are used at multiple layers, a message that reaches a crashed node at a given layer could not have been routed through that node at any earlier layer. Further, the attacker may gain additional information by crashing nodes only at certain layers! Even worse, as the ratio of input messages to width of a layer shrinks, it becomes more likely that nodes at a given layer will only receive messages from a subset of nodes at the previous layer or, in any case, that the layer distribution will be unbalanced between nodes to a significant degree.

On the other hand, because nodes are recycled for use at multiple layers, it is much harder to plan an attack. If nodes can't crash and then come back in a single batch (perhaps it's hard to do undetectably), crashing an entry node to reduce the anonymity of a message at another node may cause that message to be blocked when it must traverse the crashed node at a later layer. But it will generally be hard to predict when to come up beyond a few layers, because the targeted message will likely be coming from any of the remaining nodes after that much mixing.

To get some handle on this complex situation, we will consider a very lucky adversary. The adversary controls a quarter of the nodes in a 16x4 recycling free-route. Suppose a message enters the mixnet at a node not under adversary control, and the adversary crashes all of its nodes. Messages drop by a quarter. If the layer-2 distribution is such that the layer-1 node that received the target does not send any messages to the four adversary nodes, they remain crashed. Assuming that a quarter of the remaining messages are addressed to them at layer-2, remaining messages are now .56 of the original batch. Repeat for layer-3 and layer-4. Remaining messages are down to .32 of the original mixnet batch. In this case, despite all the luck of the adversary, the anonymity is thus still better than that of a message sent into a cascade processing a quarter of the original mixnet batch.

We have not considered all possible active attacks. But for those we have considered, the best choice for anonymity robustness appears to be the free route, and worst is the cascade. We invite further research.

7.4   Comparison with Asynchronous Batching Designs

We have shown synchronous free-routes can provide good anonymity, but we must also begin comparing this design to more traditional asynchronous free-route designs like Mixminion. Synchronous batching needs no replay cache (each message is labeled with its batch), weakens partitioning attacks from blending and key rotation, and generally provides clearer anonymity guarantees.

On the other hand, because Mixminion's pool batching strategy spreads out message distributions between batches, our design may fall more quickly to long-term statistical disclosure attacks [7]. Our design is also less robust to transient failures: a late Mixminion message still arrives, whereas in our system a node that is down throughout t_{hop} loses all messages going through it. (Stratified and cascade networks have the lowest chance of being down in a hop period they are needed, but free-route networks lose proportionally fewer messages from a single down node.) But our design can tell the user for sure whether his mail was delivered in the batch (and he can resend if not), whereas Mixminion's unpredictability always leaves the user wondering if it will come out sometime.

Like stop-and-go mixes [20], we may be able to get improved anonymity by allowing Alice to choose to delay her message at a given hop until the next batch. That is, the node would delay her message by t_{batch} and re-introduce it at the same point in the path. If each message is either delayed once or not delayed, that gives us a latency of 3 to 6 hours for non-delayed messages, 6 to 9 hours for delayed messages, and a 6-hour anonymity set (unless the attacker knows that someone never sends or receives delayed messages, in which case the anonymity set for those users is still 3 hours; also, if the attacker owns the node Alice chooses, he may be able to speculate about which senders would choose to delay messages). We leave further comparison to future work.

8   Summary

Previously, only cascade networks were considered secure against very powerful adversaries [3]. In this paper we show that other topologies can use the synchronous batching strategy to achieve similar protection. Further, we show that free-route topologies with synchronous batching compare favorably to cascade networks. We invite further analysis of the trade-offs between each topology.

Acknowledgments

We acknowledge David Hopwood for the ideas and arguments behind Sections 2 and 3; and we thank LiWu Chang, Camilla Fox, Rachel Greenstadt, Chris Laas, Ira Moskowitz, and Itamar Shtull-Trauring for probability discussions.

References

1. Oliver Berthold, Hannes Federrath, and Stefan Köpsell. Web MIXes: A system for anonymous and unobservable Internet access. In H. Federrath, editor, *Designing Privacy Enhancing Technologies: Workshop on Design Issue in Anonymity and Unobservability*, pages 115–129. Springer-Verlag, LNCS 2009, 2000.
2. Oliver Berthold and Heinrich Langos. Dummy traffic against long term intersection attacks. In Roger Dingledine and Paul Syverson, editors, *Proc. Privacy Enhancing Technologies workshop (PET 2002)*. Springer-Verlag, LNCS 2482, April 2002.
3. Oliver Berthold, Andreas Pfitzmann, and Ronny Standtke. The disadvantages of free MIX routes and how to overcome them. In H. Federrath, editor, *Proceedings of Designing Privacy Enhancing Technologies: Workshop on Design Issues in Anonymity and Unobservability*. Springer-Verlag, LNCS 2009, July 2000.
4. David Chaum. Untraceable electronic mail, return addresses, and digital pseudonyms. *Communications of the ACM*, 4(2), February 1982.
5. David Chaum. Blind signatures for untraceable payments. In D. Chaum, R.L. Rivest, and A.T. Sherman, editors, *Advances in Cryptology:Proceedings of Crypto 82*, pages 199–203. Plenum Press, 1983.
6. George Danezis. Mix-networks with restricted routes. In Roger Dingledine, editor, *Proceedings of Privacy Enhancing Technologies workshop (PET 2003)*. Springer-Verlag, LNCS 2760, March 2003.
7. George Danezis. Statistical disclosure attacks: Traffic confirmation in open environments. In Gritzalis, Vimercati, Samarati, and Katsikas, editors, *Proceedings of Security and Privacy in the Age of Uncertainty, (SEC2003)*, pages 421–426, Athens, May 2003. IFIP TC11, Kluwer.
8. George Danezis, Roger Dingledine, and Nick Mathewson. Mixminion: Design of a type III anonymous remailer protocol. In *2003 IEEE Symposium on Security and Privacy*, pages 2–15. IEEE CS, May 2003.
9. George Danezis and Len Sassaman. Heartbeat traffic to counter (n-1) attacks. In *Proceedings of the Workshop on Privacy in the Electronic Society (WPES 2003)*, Washington, DC, USA, October 2003.
10. Claudia Diaz, Stefaan Seys, Joris Claessens, and Bart Preneel. Towards measuring anonymity. In Roger Dingledine and Paul Syverson, editors, *Privacy Enhancing Technologies (PET 2002)*. Springer-Verlag, LNCS 2482, April 2002.
11. Roger Dingledine, Michael J. Freedman, David Hopwood, and David Molnar. A Reputation System to Increase MIX-net Reliability. In Ira S. Moskowitz, editor, *Information Hiding (IH 2001)*, pages 126–141. Springer-Verlag, LNCS 2137, 2001.
12. Roger Dingledine and Paul Syverson. Reliable MIX Cascade Networks through Reputation. In Matt Blaze, editor, *Financial Cryptography*. Springer-Verlag, LNCS 2357, 2002.
13. John Douceur. The Sybil Attack. In *Proceedings of the 1st International Peer To Peer Systems Workshop (IPTPS 2002)*, March 2002.
14. M. Kwiatkowska *et al.* PRISM web page. http://www.cs.bham.ac.uk/~dxp/prism/.

15. Elke Franz, Andreas Graubner, Anja Jerichow, and Andreas Pfitzmann. Comparison of Commitment Schemes Used in Mix-Mediated Anonymous Communication for Preventing Pool-Mode Attacks. In C. Boyd and E. Dawson, editors, *3rd Australasian Conference on Information Security and Privacy (ACISP'98)*, number 1438 in LNCS. Springer-Verlag, 1998.

16. David M. Goldschlag, Michael G. Reed, and Paul F. Syverson. Hiding routing information. In R. Anderson, editor, *Information Hiding: First International Workshop*, pages 137–150. Springer-Verlag, LNCS 1174, 1996.

17. Ceki Gülcü and Gene Tsudik. Mixing E-mail with Babel. In *Network and Distributed Security Symposium (NDSS 96)*, pages 2–16. IEEE, February 1996.

18. Markus Jakobsson. Flash Mixing. In *Principles of Distributed Computing - PODC '99*. ACM Press, 1999.

19. Markus Jakobsson, Ari Juels, and Ronald L. Rivest. Making mix nets robust for electronic voting by randomized partial checking. In *Proceedings of the 11th USENIX Security Symposium*, August 2002.

20. Dogan Kesdogan, Jan Egner, and Roland Büschkes. Stop-and-go MIXes: Providing probabilistic anonymity in an open system. In *Proceedings of Information Hiding Workshop (IH 1998)*. Springer-Verlag, LNCS 1525, 1998.

21. Ulf Möller, Lance Cottrell, Peter Palfrader, and Len Sassaman. Mixmaster Protocol — Version 2. Draft, July 2003. <http://www.abditum.com/mixmaster-spec.txt>.

22. Andreas Pfitzmann and Michael Waidner. Networks without user observability – design options. In *Proc. of EUROCRYPT 1985*. Springer-Verlag, LNCS 219, 1985.

23. Andrei Serjantov and George Danezis. Towards an information theoretic metric for anonymity. In Roger Dingledine and Paul Syverson, editors, *Privacy Enhacing Technologies (PET 2002)*. Springer-Verlag, LNCS 2482, April 2002.

24. Andrei Serjantov, Roger Dingledine, and Paul Syverson. From a trickle to a flood: Active attacks on several mix types. In F. Petitcolas, editor, *Proceedings of Information Hiding Workshop (IH 2002)*. Springer-Verlag, LNCS 2578, October 2002.

25. V. Shmatikov. Probabilistic model checking of an anonymity system. *Journal of Computer Security (selected papers of CSFW-15)*, 2004 (to appear).

A   Entropy Versus Number of Hops, for Each Topology

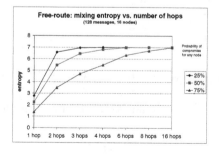

Fig. 7. Entropy vs number of hops, for cascade network (16 nodes)

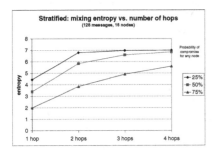 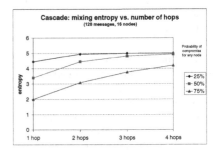

Fig. 8. Entropy vs number of hops, for stratified network (16 nodes)

Fig. 9. Entropy vs number of hops, for free-route network (16 nodes)

B Entropy Examples for Each Topology

B.1 Cascade

Consider a 2x2 cascade network as in Figure 1. Assume there are 128 messages in a batch, and that any node has $\frac{1}{4}$ chance of having been compromised. Let m be the targeted message, and suppose the adversary observed that the sender of m chose A as the first mix. Under the equal loading assumption, there are 63 other messages in addition to m that chose A as the first mix. Without loss of generality, we may assume that m occupies the first position in A's input buffer of length 64.

With probability $\frac{1}{4}$, mix A is hostile. In this case, m remains in the first position after passing through the mix. With probability $\frac{3}{4}$, mix A is honest. In this case, m appears in any of the 64 output positions of this mix with probability $\frac{1}{64}$ (note that m may not appear in the output buffer of mix B). The resulting probability distribution for m's position after passing through A is

$$
\underbrace{\frac{67}{256}}_{\frac{1}{4}\cdot 1+\frac{3}{4}\cdot\frac{1}{64}} \quad \underbrace{\frac{3}{256}}_{\frac{3}{4}\cdot\frac{1}{64}} \ldots \qquad \underbrace{0\ 0 \ldots 0}_{}
$$
$$
\text{position 1} \quad \text{positions 2..64} \quad \text{positions 65..128}
\tag{1}
$$

Next mix C is pre-determined by network topology, and the distribution it produces on its messages is the same as (1). Combining two distributions, we obtain that m appears in the cascade's output buffer with following probabilities:

$$
\underbrace{\frac{5056}{65536}}_{\frac{67}{256}\cdot\frac{67}{256}+\frac{3}{256}\cdot(63\cdot\frac{3}{256})} \quad \underbrace{\frac{960}{65536}}_{\frac{67}{256}\cdot\frac{3}{256}+\frac{3}{256}\cdot(\frac{67}{256}+62\cdot\frac{3}{256})} \quad \ldots \qquad \underbrace{0\ 0 \ldots 0}_{}
$$
$$
\text{position 1} \quad \text{positions 2..64} \quad \text{positions 65..128}
\tag{2}
$$

Entropy of this distribution is approximately 5.9082. Effective anonymity set provided by a 2x2 cascade with 25% density of hostile nodes and 128 messages per batch is 60 messages.

B.2   Stratified Array

The procedure for calculating mixing distribution for a stratified array is essentially the same as for a cascade, but there is an additional probabilistic choice. After the message passes through a mix, the next mix is selected randomly among all mixes in the next layer.

Consider a 2x2 stratified array as in fig. 2. Again, assume there are 128 messages in a batch, $\frac{1}{4}$ chance that a node is hostile, and that A was selected (in a manner visible to the adversary) as the first mix. The mixing performed by any single mix is exactly the same as in the cascade case, thus mixing distribution (1) after the first hop is the same in a stratified array as in a cascade.

After the first hop, however, mix C is selected only with probability $\frac{1}{2}$, while D may also be selected with probability $\frac{1}{2}$ (by contrast, in a cascade C is selected with probability 1). Distribution (2) has to be adjusted to take into account the fact that mix D, selected with probability $\frac{1}{2}$, has a $\frac{1}{4}$ chance of being hostile and thus leaving each received message in the same position.

$$\underbrace{\frac{4672}{65536}}_{\substack{\frac{1}{2}\cdot\frac{5056}{65536}+\frac{1}{2}\cdot\frac{1}{4}\cdot\frac{67}{256}\\ \text{position 1}}} \quad \underbrace{\frac{576}{65536}}_{\substack{\frac{1}{2}\cdot\frac{960}{65536}+\frac{1}{2}\cdot\frac{1}{4}\cdot\frac{3}{256}\\ \text{positions 2..64}}} \cdots \quad \underbrace{\frac{3}{512}}_{\substack{\frac{1}{2}\cdot\frac{3}{4}\cdot\frac{1}{64}\\ \text{positions 65..128}}} \cdots$$

Entropy of this distribution is approximately 6.8342. Effective anonymity set provided by a 2x2 stratified array with 25% density of hostile nodes and 128 messages per batch is 114 messages.

B.3   Free-route Network

Probability distribution is computed in exactly the same way for a free-route network as for a stratified array, except that the entire set of mixes is treated as a layer. Consider a 4x2 free-route network as in fig. 3. With 128 messages per batch, the buffer for each mix is 32 messages. If A is the first mix selected (and is hostile with probability $\frac{1}{4}$), the probability distribution after the message passes through A is

$$\underbrace{\frac{35}{128}}_{\substack{\frac{1}{4}\cdot1+\frac{3}{4}\cdot\frac{1}{32}\\ \text{position 1}}} \quad \underbrace{\frac{3}{128}}_{\substack{\frac{3}{4}\cdot\frac{1}{32}\\ \text{positions 2..32}}} \cdots \quad \underbrace{0\ 0\ \dots\ 0}_{\text{positions 33..128}}$$

The next mix is selected from among all four mixes with equal probability. A mix other than A is selected with probability $\frac{3}{4}$, and has $\frac{1}{4}$ chance of being hostile, producing the following probability distribution:

$$\underbrace{\frac{1216}{16384}}$$

$$\frac{1}{4} \cdot (\frac{35}{128} \cdot \frac{35}{128} +$$

$$\frac{3}{128} \cdot (31 \cdot \frac{3}{128})) +$$

$$\frac{3}{4} \cdot \frac{1}{4} \cdot \frac{35}{128}$$

position 1

$$\underbrace{\frac{192}{16384}} \quad \cdots$$

$$\frac{1}{4} \cdot (\frac{35}{128} \cdot \frac{3}{128} +$$

$$\frac{3}{128} \cdot (\frac{35}{128} + 30 \cdot \frac{3}{128})) +$$

$$\frac{3}{4} \cdot \frac{1}{4} \cdot \frac{3}{128}$$

positions 2..32

$$\underbrace{\frac{3}{512}} \quad \cdots$$

$$\frac{1}{4} \cdot \frac{3}{4} \cdot \frac{1}{32}$$

positions 33..128

Entropy of this distribution is approximately 6.7799 and effective anonymity set is 110 messages — slightly lower than in a stratified 2x2 array.

On Flow Correlation Attacks and Countermeasures in Mix Networks[*]

Ye Zhu*, Xinwen Fu, Bryan Graham*, Riccardo Bettati, and Wei Zhao

Department of Computer Science, Texas A&M University,
College Station TX 77843-3112, USA
{zhuye, bgraham}@tamu.edu,
{xinwenfu, bettati, zhao}@cs.tamu.edu

Abstract. In this paper, we address issues related to flow correlation attacks and the corresponding countermeasures in mix networks. Mixes have been used in many anonymous communication systems and are supposed to provide countermeasures that can defeat various traffic analysis attacks. In this paper, we focus on a particular class of traffic analysis attack, *flow correlation attacks*, by which an adversary attempts to analyze the network traffic and correlate the traffic of a flow over an input link at a mix with that over an output link of the same mix. Two classes of correlation methods are considered, namely *time-domain* methods and *frequency-domain* methods. Based on our threat model and known strategies in existing mix networks, we perform extensive experiments to analyze the performance of mixes. We find that a mix with any known batching strategy may fail against flow correlation attacks in the sense that for a given flow over an input link, the adversary can correctly determine which output link is used by the same flow. We also investigated methods that can effectively counter the flow correlation attack and other timing attacks. The empirical results provided in this paper give an indication to designers of Mix networks about appropriate configurations and alternative mechanisms to be used to counter flow correlation attacks.

1 Introduction

This paper studies flow correlation attacks and the corresponding countermeasures in mix networks. With the rapid growth and public acceptance of the Internet as a means of communication and information dissemination, concerns about privacy and security on the Internet have grown. Although it can potentially be used for malicious purposes, *Anonymity* is legitimate in many scenarios such as anonymous web browsing, E-Voting,

---

[*] This work was supported in part by the National Science Foundation under Contracts 0081761 and 0324988, by the Defense Advanced Research Projects Agency under Contract F30602-99-1-0531, and by Texas A&M University under its Telecommunication and Information Task Force Program. Any opinions, findings, and conclusions or recommendations in this material, either expressed or implied, are those of the authors and do not necessarily reflect the views of the sponsors listed above.

D. Martin and A. Serjantov (Eds.): PET 2004, LNCS 3424, pp. 207–225, 2005.

E-Banking, E-Commerce, and E-Auctions. In each of these scenarios, encryption alone cannot achieve the anonymity required by participants [1, 2].

Since Chaum [3] proposed the mix network, researchers have developed various anonymity systems for different applications. Although a significant amount of effort has been put forth in researching anonymous communications, there has not been much systematic study of the performance of mix networks in terms of anonymity degree provided and quality-of-services maintained. This paper focuses on the quantitative evaluation of mix performance. We are particularly interested in flow-based communication, which is widely used in voice over IP, web browsing, FTP, etc. These applications may have anonymity requirements, and the mixes are supposed to provide countermeasures that can defeat traffic analysis attacks.

We focus our analysis on a particular type of attack, which we call a *flow correlation attack*. In this type of attack, an adversary analyzes the network traffic with the intention of identifying which of several output ports a flow at an input port of a mix is taking. Obviously, flow correlation helps the adversary identify the path of a flow and consequently reveal other mission critical information related to the flow (e.g., sender and receiver). Our major contributions are summarized as follows:

1. We formally model the behavior of an adversary who launches flow correlation attacks. In order to successfully identify the output port of an incoming flow, the flow correlation attack must accurately measure the similarity of traffic flows into and out of a mix. Two classes of correlation methods are considered, namely *time-domain* methods and *frequency-domain* methods. In the time domain, *mutual information* is used to measure the traffic similarity. In the frequency domain, a matched filter based on the *Fourier spectrum* and the *Wavelet spectrum* is utilized.

2. We measure the effectiveness of a number of popular mix strategies in countering flow correlation attacks. Mixes with any tested batching strategy may fail under flow-correlation attacks in the sense that, for a given flow over an input link, the adversary can effectively detect which output link is used by the same flow. We use *Detection rate* as the measure of success for the attack, where Detection rate is defined as the probability that the adversary correctly correlates flows into and out of a mix. We will show that, given a sufficient amount of data, known mix strategies fail, that is, the attack achieves close to 100% detection rate. This remains true, even in batching strategies that sacrifice QoS concerns (such as a significant TCP goodput reduction) in favor of security.

3. While many mix strategies rely on other mechanisms in addition to batching alone, it is important to understand the vulnerability of batching. In our experiments, we illustrates the dependency between attack effectiveness for various batching strategies and the amount of data at hand for the attacks. These results should guide mix designers in the educated choice of strategy parameters, such as for striping or for path rerouting.

To counter flow correlation attacks, we investigate countermeasures based on theoretical analysis. We purposely synchronize the sending time of packets along a set of output links. This approach is more efficient than similar methods.

The remainder of this paper is organized as follows: Section 2 reviews the related work. Section 3 outlines our Mix network model, threat model, and a formal definition of the problem. Batching strategies used by existing mix networks are also discussed in this section. Section 4 introduces traffic analysis methodologies that may be deployed by an adversary. We consider both time-domain and frequency-domain traffic analysis methods. In Section 5 we evaluate the performance of mix networks in terms of detection rate and FTP goodput. Serious failure of mix networks in terms of providing flow anonymity is observed from the data we collect. In Section 6, we present an effective and efficient method that can provide a guaranteed detection rate with high FTP goodput. We conclude this paper and discuss the future work in Section 7.

2   Related Work

Chaum [3] pioneered the idea of anonymity in 1981. Since then, researchers have applied the idea to different applications such as message-based email and flow-based low-latency communications, and they have invented new defense techniques as more attacks have been proposed.

For anonymous email applications, Chaum [3] proposed to use relay servers, i.e. *mixes*, rerouting messages, which are encrypted by public keys of mixes. An encrypted message is analogous to an onion constructed by a sender, who sends the onion to the first mix. Using its private key, the first mix peels off the first layer, which is encrypted using the public key of the first mix. Inside the first layer is the second mix's address and the rest of the onion, which is encrypted with the second mix's public key. After getting the second mix's address, the first mix sends the peeled onion. This process proceeds in this recursive way. The core part of the onion is the receiver's address and the real message to be sent to the receiver by the last mix. Chaum also proposed return address and digital pseudonyms for users to communicate with each other anonymously.

Helsingius [4] implemented the first Internet anonymous *remailer*, which is a single application proxy that just replaces the original email's source address with the remailer's address. It has no reply function and is subject to all the attacks mentioned below. Eric Hughes and Hal Finney [5] built the *cypherpunk remailer*, a real distributed mix network with reply functions that uses PGP to encrypt and decrypt messages. The system is subject to a global passive attack and replay attack to its reply mechanism. Gülcü and Tsudik [6] developed a relatively full-fledged anonymous email system, *Babel*. Their reply technique does not need the sender to remember the secret seed to decrypt the reply message, but it is subject to replay attack. They studied the threat from the trickle attack, a powerful active attack. Another defect of Babel is that a mix itself can differentiate the forwarding and replying messages. Cottrell [7] developed *Mixmaster* which counters a global passive attack by using message padding and also counters trickle and flood attacks [6, 8] by using a pool batching strategy. Mixmaster does not have a reply function. Danezis, Dingledine and Mathewson [9] developed *Mixminion*. Although Mixminion still has many problems, its design considers a relatively complete set of attacks that researchers have found [8, 10, 11, 12, 13, 14]. The authors suggest a list of research topics for future study.

Low-latency anonymous communication can be further divided into systems using core mix networks and peer-to-peer networks. In a system using a core mix network, users connect to a pool of mixes, which provides anonymous communication, and users select a forwarding path through this core network to the receiver. *Onion routing* [15] and *Freedom* [16] belong to this category. In a system using a peer-to-peer network, every node in the network is a mix, but it can also be a sender and receiver. Obviously, a peer-to-peer mix network can be very large and may provide better anonymity in the case when many participants use the anonymity service and enough traffic is generated around the network. *Crowds* [17], *Tarzan* [18] and P^5 [19] belong to this category.

This paper is interested in the study of passive traffic analysis attacks against low-latency anonymous communication systems. Sun *et al.* [2] gave a quantitative analysis for identifying a web page even if encryption and anonymizing proxies are used. They took advantage of the fact that a number of HTTP features such as the number and size of objects can be used as signatures to identify web pages with some accuracy. Unless the anonymizer addresses this, these signatures are visible to the adversary. Serjantov and Sewell [20] analyzed the possibility of a lone flow along an input link of a mix. If the rate of this lone input flow is roughly equal to the rate of a flow out of the mix, this pair of input flow and outflow flow are correlated. They also briefly discussed some of the possible traffic features used to trace a flow. The attacks we will present later in this paper are very effective even when a large amount of noise exists. Other analyses focus on the anonymity degradation when some mixes are compromised, e.g. [17]. We understand that attacks used against message-based email mix networks can also threaten low-latency flow-based mix networks; however, we feel that traffic analysis attacks are also a serious problem for low-latency mix networks because of its QoS requirements. Our reasoning will be explained in detail in the following sections of this paper.

3   Models

3.1   Mix and Mix Network

A mix is a relay device for anonymous communication. Figure 1 shows the communication between users using one mix. A single mix can achieve a certain level of communication anonymity: The sender of a message attaches the receiver address to a packet and encrypts it using the mix's public key. Upon receiving a packet, a mix decodes the packet. Different from an ordinary router, a mix usually will not relay the received packet immediately. Rather, it collects several packets and then sends them out in a *batch*. The order of packets may be altered as well. Techniques such as batching and reordering are

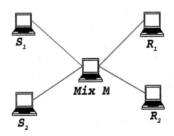

Fig. 1. A Single Mix

considered necessary techniques for mixes to prevent timing-based attacks. The main objective of this paper is to analyze the effectiveness of mixes against a special class of timing-based attacks.

A mix network consists of multiple mixes that are inter-connected by a network. A mix network may provide enhanced anonymity, as payload packets may go through multiple mixes. Even in such a mix network, it is important that each individual mix provides sufficient security and QoS so that the end-to-end performance can be guaranteed. Thus, our analysis on a single mix provides a foundation for analyzing the end-to-end performance of mix networks. We discuss in detail how to extend our work to larger and complicated mix networks in [21]. In fact, if we view a mix network (for example Onion routing [15]) as one *super mix*, the analytical techniques in this paper can be directly applied.

3.2   Batching Strategies for a Mix

Batching strategies are designed to prevent not only simple timing analysis attacks but also powerful trickle attacks, flood attacks, and many other forms of attacks ([9, 8]). Serjantov [8] summarizes seven batching strategies that have been proposed. We will evaluate each kind of these strategies. Our results show that these strategies may not work under certain timing analysis attacks. These seven batching strategies are listed in Table 1, in which batching strategies from S_1 to S_4 are denoted as *simple mix*, while batching strategies from S_5 to S_7 are denoted as *pool mix*.

Table 1. Batching Strategies

Glossary

n	queue size
m	threshold to control the packet sending
t	timer's period if a timer is used
f	the minimum number of packets left in the pool for pool Mixes
p	a fraction only used in Timed Dynamic-Pool Mix

Algorithms

Strategy Index	Name	Adjustable Parameters	Algorithm
S_0	Simple Proxy	*none*	no batching or reordering
S_1	Threshold Mix	$<m>$	if $n = m$, send n packets
S_2	Timed Mix	$<t>$	if timer times out, send n packets
S_3	Threshold Or Timed Mix	$<m, t>$	if timer times out, send n packets; elseif $n = m$ {send n packets; reset the timer}
S_4	Threshold and Timed Mix	$<m, t>$	if (timer times out) and $(n \geq m)$, send n packets
S_5	Threshold Pool Mix	$<m, f>$	if $n = m + f$, send m randomly chosen packets
S_6	Timed Pool Mix	$<t, f>$	if (timer times out) and $(n > f)$, send $n - f$ randomly chosen packets
S_7	Timed Dynamic-Pool Mix	$<m, t, f, p>$	if (timer times out) and $(n \geq m + f)$, send $\max(1, \lfloor p(n - f) \rfloor)$ randomly chosen packets

From Table 1, we can see that the sending of a batch of packets can be triggered by certain events, e.g., queue length reaching a pre-defined threshold, a timer having a time out, or some combination of these two.

Batching is typically accompanied by reordering. In this paper, the attacks focus on the traffic characteristics. As reordering does not change packet interarrival times much for mixes using batching, these attacks (and our analysis) are unaffected by reordering. Thus, our results are applicable to systems that use any kind of reordering methods. As such, in the rest of this paper, we will not discuss reordering techniques further.

Any of the batching strategies can be implemented in two ways:

Link-Based Batching: With this method, each output link has a separate queue. A newly arrived packet is put into a queue depending on its destination (and hence the link associated with the queue). Once a batch is ready from a particular queue (per the batching strategy), the packets are taken out of the queue and transmitted over the corresponding link.

Mix-Based Batching: In this way, the entire mix has only one queue. The selected batching strategy is applied to this queue. That is, once a batch is ready (per the batching strategy), the packets are taken out the queue and transmitted over links based on the packets' destination.

Each of these two methods has its own advantages and disadvantages. The control of link-based batching is distributed inside the mix and hence it may have good efficiency. On the other hand, mix-based batching uses only one queue and hence is easier to manage. We consider both methods in this paper.

3.3   Threat Model

In this paper, we assume that the adversary uses a classical timing analysis attack ([1, 22]), which we summarize as follows:

1. The adversary observes input and output links of a mix, collects the packet inter-arrival times, and analyzes them. This type of attack is passive, since traffic is not actively altered (by, say, dropping, inserting, and/or modifying packets during a communication session), and is therefore often difficult to detect. This type of attack can be easily staged on wired and wireless links [23] by a variety of agents, such as malicious ISPs or governments ([24, 25]).
2. To maximize the power of the adversary, we assume that she makes observations on all the links of the mix network.
3. The mix's infrastructure and strategies are known to the adversary. This is a typical assumption in the study of security systems. The above two assumptions create the worst case in terms of security analysis.
4. The adversary cannot correlate (based on packet timing, content, or size) a packet on a input link to another packet on the output link. Packet correlation based on packet timing is prevented by batching, and correlation based on content and packet size is prevented by encryption and packet padding, respectively.
5. To simplify the following discussion, we assume that dummy traffic is not used in the mix network. Some of the modern anonymous communication systems such as

Onion routing ([26]) do not use dummy traffic because of its heavy consumption of bandwidth and the general lack of understanding of to what extent exactly dummy packets contribute to anonymity.

6. Finally, we assume that the specific objective of the adversary is to identify the output link of a traffic flow that appears on an input link. Others have described similar attacks, but under simplified circumstances. Serjantov and Sewell [20], for example, assume that the flow under attack is alone on a link thus making its traffic characteristics immediately visible to the attacker. In this paper, we consider flows inside (potentially large) aggregates, thus making the attack generally applicable.

4   Traffic Flow Correlation Techniques

This section discusses the traffic flow correlation techniques that may be used by the adversary either to correlate senders and receivers directly or to greatly reduce the searching time for such a correlation in a mix network.

4.1   Overview

Recall that the adversary's objective is to correlate an incoming flow to an output link at a mix. We call this *flow correlation*. This kind of flow correlation attack is harmful in many scenarios. For example, in Figure 1, the adversary can discover the communication relationship between senders (S_1 and S_2) and receivers (R_1 and R_2) by matching senders' output flows and receivers' input flows. Using the flow correlation attack techniques, the adversary can find out a flow's sender and receiver if she catches a fragment of the flow in the mix network, thus breaking the anonymity despite the mix network. In a peer-to-peer mix network, the adversary can even reconstruct the path of this TCP connection by using flow correlation techniques. This subsection discusses the attack in more detail.

Figure 2 shows a flowchart of the typical procedure which the adversary may use to perform flow correlation. We now describe each step in detail.

(1) Data Collection. We assume that the adversary is able to collect information about all the packets on both input and output links. For each collected packet, the arrival time is recorded suing tools such as tcpdump [27] and Cisco's NetFlow [28]. We assume that all the packets are encrypted and padded to the same size, and hence only arrival time is of interest. The arrival times of packets at input link i form a time series

$$A_i = (a_{i,1}, \cdots, a_{i,n}) \tag{1}$$

where $a_{i,k}$ is the kth packet's arrival time at input link i, and n is the size of the sample collected during a given sampling interval. Similarly, the arrival times of packets at output link j form a time series

$$B_j = (b_{j,1}, \cdots, b_{j,m}) \tag{2}$$

where $b_{j,k}$ is the kth packet's arrival time at output link j, and m is the size of the sample collected during a given sampling interval. The packets come out from mixes in batches.

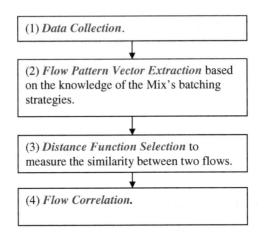

Fig. 2. Typical Flowchart for Flow Correlation

The length of sampling interval usually is much longer than the duration of a batch. Hence, a sampling interval typically contains many batches. We make the simplifying assumption that the traffic characteristic of the flow under consideration (the *input flow*) is known. This can be the case for example because the flow traffic characteristic is indeed observable at the input or at the input of the mix network.

(2) Flow Pattern Vector Extraction. With the above notation, the strategy of the adversary is to analyze the time series A_is and B_js in order to determine if there is any "similarity" between an input flow and an output flow of the mix. However, a direct analysis over these time series will not be effective. They need to be transformed into so called *pattern vectors* that can facilitate further analysis. We have found that effective transformation depends on batching strategies utilized by the mix. In Section 4.3, we will discuss specific definitions of transformations for different batching strategies. Currently, for the convenience of discussion, let us assume that A_i is transformed into pattern vector $X_i = (x_{i,1}, \cdots, x_{i,q})$. And time series B_j is transformed into $Y_j = (y_{j,1}, \cdots, y_{j,q})$. Note, here the two pattern vectors have the same length.

(3) Distance Function Selection. We define the distance function $d(X_i, Y_j)$, which measures the "distance" between an input flow at input link i and the traffic at output link j. The smaller the distance, the more likely the flow on an input link is correlated to the corresponding flow on the output link. Clearly, the definition of the distance function is the key in the correlation analysis. Section 4.2 will discuss two effective distance functions: one is based on mutual information and the other is based on the frequency-spectrum-based matched filter.

(4) Flow Correlation. Once the distance function has been defined between an input flow and an output link, we can easily carry out the correlation analysis by selecting the output link whose traffic has the minimum distance to input flow pattern vector X_i.

This approach can be easily extended to cases when multiple flows are aggregated over an input link [21]. The key idea is that by properly calculating the distance, we can find a correlation between one input flow and a set of output flows.

4.2   Flow Pattern Vector Extraction

In this subsection, we discuss how to choose pattern vectors X_is and Y_js. We will start with pattern vectors for the output link traffic first. Recall that batching strategies in Table 1 can be classified into two classes: threshold triggered batching (S_1, S_3, and S_5)[1] and timer triggered batching (S_2, S_4, S_6 and S_7). We will see that different classes should have different transformation methods.

For threshold triggered batching strategies, packets come out from the mix in batches. Hence, the inter-arrival time of packets in a batch is determined by the transmission latency, which is independent of the input flow. Thus, the useful information to the adversary is the number of packets in a batch and the time elapses between two batches. Normalizing this relationship, we define the elements in pattern vector Y_j as follows:

$$Y_{j,k} = \frac{\text{Number of packets in batch k in the sampling interval}}{\text{(Ending time of batch k) - (Ending time of batch k-1)}} \tag{3}$$

In the calculation, we may need to truncate the original time series $B_j = (b_{j,1}, b_{j,2}, \cdots, b_{j,n})$ so that only complete batches are used.

For timer triggered batching strategies, a batch of packets is sent whenever a timer fires. The length of the time interval between two consecutive timer events is a pre-defined constant. Thus, following a similar argument made for the threshold triggered batching strategies, we define the elements in pattern vector Y_j as follows:

$$Y_{j,k} = \frac{\text{Number of packets in the } k^{th} \text{time out interval}}{\text{(time of } k^{th} \text{ time-out) - (time of } (k-1)^{st} \text{ time-out)}} \tag{4}$$

$$= \frac{\text{Number of packets in the } k^{th} \text{ time out interval}}{\text{Pre-defined inter-time-out length}} \tag{5}$$

Again, in the calculation, we may need to truncate the original time series B_j so that only complete batches are used.

For the traffic *without batching* (i.e., the baseline strategy S_0 defined in Table 1), we use similar methods defined for timer triggered batching strategies as shown in (5).

The basic idea in the methods for extraction of pattern vectors is to partition a sampling interval into multiple sub-intervals and calculate the average traffic rate in each sub-interval as the values of the elements of traffic pattern vectors. The above two methods differ on how to partition the interval, depending on which batching strategy is used by the mix. We take a similar approach to extract pattern vectors X_is corresponding to Y_js. Again, the specific method of sub-interval partition depends on how the mix is batching the packets. Due to the space limitation, we will not further discuss the details of the methods developed. Readers are referred to [21] for details.

---

[1] S_3 could also be classified as timer-triggered. However, we treat it as threshold triggered because it may send out a batch when the number of packets received by the mix has reached the threshold.

4.3   Distance Functions

In this paper, we consider two kinds of distance functions: the first is based on a comparison of mutual information and the second on frequency analysis. The motivation and computation methods are given below.

Mutual Information
Mutual information is an information theoretical measure of the dependence of two random variables. In our scenario, we can view the pattern vectors that represent the input and output flows as samples of random variables. If we consider the pattern vectors X_i and Y_j to be each a sample of the random variables $\mathcal{X}_i$ and $\mathcal{Y}_j$, respectively, then $\{(X_{i,1}, Y_{j,1}), \cdots, (X_{i,q}, Y_{j,q})\}$ correspond to a sample of the joint random variable $(\mathcal{X}_i, \mathcal{Y}_j)$. With these definitions, the distance function $d(X_i, Y_j)$ between pattern vectors X_i and Y_j should be approximately inversely proportional to the mutual information $I(\mathcal{X}_i, \mathcal{Y}_j)$ between $\mathcal{X}_i$ and $\mathcal{Y}_j$,

$$d(X_i, Y_j) = \frac{1}{I(\mathcal{X}_i, \mathcal{Y}_i)} = -\frac{1}{\int\int p(x_i, y_j) \log \frac{p(x_i, y_j)}{p(x_i)p(y_j)}} \tag{6}$$

Here, we need to estimate marginal distributions ($p(x_i)$ and $p(y_j)$) and their joint distribution $p(x_i, y_j)$. In this paper, we use histogram-based estimation of mutual information $\hat{I}(\mathcal{X}_i, \mathcal{Y}_j)$ of continuous distributions [29], which is given as follows.

$$\hat{I}(\mathcal{X}_i, \mathcal{Y}_j) \approx \sum_{u,v} \frac{K_{uv}}{q} \log \frac{K_{uv}N}{K_{u.}K_{.v}} \tag{7}$$

where q is the sample size. The sample space is a two-dimensional plane divided into $U \times V$ equally-sized $\Delta X \times \Delta Y$ cells with coordinates (u, v). K_{uv} is the number of samples in the cell (u, v). ΔX and ΔY have to be carefully chosen for an optimal estimation.

Frequency Analysis
For timer-triggered batching strategies, we therefore use FFT or Wavelet on the sample X_i and Y_j to obtain the frequency spectrum X_i^F and Y_j^F. Then we apply matched filter method over X_i^F and Y_j^F. We take advantage of the fact that frequency components of the input flow traffic carry on to the aggregate flow at the output link. Matched filter is an optimal filter to detect a signal buried in noise. It is optimal in the sense that it can provide the maximum signal-to-noise ratio at its output for a given signal. In particular, by directly applying the theory of matched filters, we can define the distance function $d(X_i, Y_j)$ as the inverse matched filter detector $M(X_i^F, Y_j^F)$,

$$d(X_i, Y_j) = \frac{1}{M(X_i^F, Y_j^F)} = \frac{1}{\frac{<X_i^F, Y_j^F>}{||Y_j^F||}} \tag{8}$$

where $< X_i^F, Y_j^F >$ is the inner product of X_i^F and Y_j^F, and $||Y_j^F|| = \sqrt{< Y_j^F, Y_j^F >}$. Please refer to [30] for details about the calculation of FFT and Wavelet over a vector. Due to the space limit, please refer to [21] for detailed results of the Wavelet-based method, which has similar results to the FFT method reported in this paper.

5   Empirical Evaluation

In this section, we evaluate the effectiveness of a selection of batching strategies (listed in Table 1) for a mix under our flow correlation attacks. We will see the failure of a mix under our traffic flow correlation attacks and batching strategies' influence on TCP flow performance.

5.1   Experiment Network Setup

Figure 3 shows our experimental network setup. Our mix is implemented on Timesys/ Real Time Linux operating system for its timer accuracy [31]. The Mix control module that performs the batching and reordering functions is integrated into Linux's firewall system [32] using *Netfilter*; we use the corresponding firewall rules to specify what traffic should be protected. Two delay boxes D_1 and D_2 emulate the Internet propagation delay on different paths.

Our experiments reported here focus on TCP flows because of their dominance in the Internet. However, the results are generally applicable to other kinds of flows. The traffic flows in our experiments are configured as follows: An FTP client on node R_2 downloads a file from the FTP server on S_2. The traffic from S_1 to R_2 serves as the random noise traffic to the FTP client. The traffic from node S_1 to node R_1 is the cross traffic through mix M from the perspective of the FTP flow. We maintain the traffic rate on both output links of the mix at approximately 500 packets per second (*pps*). The objective of the adversary in this experiment is to identify the output link that carries the FTP flow.

5.2   Metrics

We use *detection rate* as a measure of the ability of the mix to protect anonymity. Detection rate here is defined as the ratio of the number of correct detections to the number of attempts. While the detection rate measures the *effectiveness* of the mix, we measure its *efficiency* in terms of quality of service (QoS) perceived by the applications. We use *FTP goodput* as an indication of FTP quality of service (*QoS*). FTP goodput is defined as the rate at which the FTP client R_2 receives data from the FTP server S_2. Low levels of FTP goodput indicate that the mix in the given configuration is poorly applicable for low-latency flow-based mix networks.

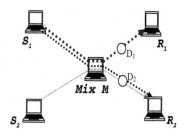

Fig. 3. Experiment Setup

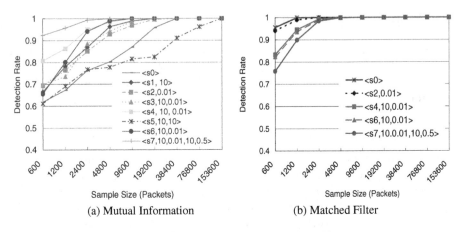

(a) Mutual Information   (b) Matched Filter

Fig. 4. Detection Rate for Link-based Batching

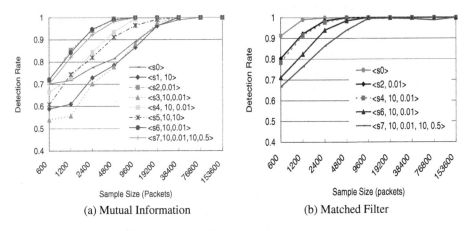

(a) Mutual Information   (b) Matched Filter

Fig. 5. Detection Rate for Mix-based Batching

5.3   Performance Evaluation

Effectiveness of Batching Strategies

Figure 4 shows the detection rate for systems using a link-based batching strategy. Figure 5 shows the detection rate for systems using a mix-based batching strategy as a function of the number of packets observed. A sample may include both FTP packets and cross traffic packets while FTP packets account for less than 20% of the number -sample size- of packets. Parameters in the legends of these figures are listed in the same order as in Table 1. Based on these results, we make the following observations:

1. For all the strategies, the detection rate monotonically increases with increasing amount of available data. The detection rate approaches 100% when the sample size is sufficiently large. This is consistent with intuition, as more data implies that there is more information about the input flow, which in turn improves the detection rate.

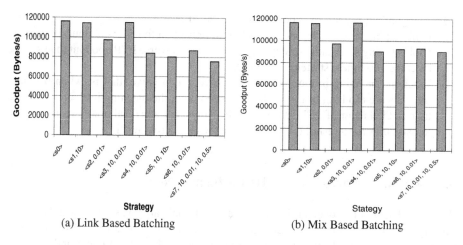

(a) Link Based Batching   (b) Mix Based Batching

Fig. 6. FTP Goodput

2. Different strategies display different resistances to flow correlation attacks. In general, pool mixes perform better than simple mixes based on matched filter detector.
3. Frequency-analysis-based distance functions typically outperforms mutual-information-based distance functions in terms of detection rate. For many batching strategies, the former performs significantly better. This is because there are phasing issues in frequency-analysis-based attacks. Therefore, lack of synchronization between data collected at input and output port has a minor effect on the effectiveness of the attack.
4. To compare mix-based batching strategy with link-based batching strategy, we find that no one dominates the other.

Overall, our data shows that the mix using any of batching strategies S_1, S_2, $\cdots$, S_7 fails under the flow correlation attacks. One of the reasons is that TCP flows often demonstrate interesting patterns such as periodicity of rate change and burstiness in particular when the TCP loop-control mechanism is triggered by excessive traffic perturbation in the mixes. Figure 4 and 5 show that flow correlation attacks can well explore this pattern difference between TCP flows.

Efficiency of Batching Strategies
As batching delays packets, one should expect that the overall performance (in terms of throughput) of TCP connections will be impacted by the mixes along their path. Figure 6 quantitatively shows the degradation of FTP goodput for a mix using different batching strategies.

In Figure 6, we compare FTP goodput between a strategy without any batching (S_0) and other batching strategies ($S_1, S_2, \cdots, S_7$). We still use the network setup in Figure 3. The traffic other than FTP is configured as follows: 400pps from S_1 to R_1 and 500pps from S_2 to R_2. Based on these experiments and the results illustrated in Figure 6, we make the following observations:

1. FTP goodput is decreased because of the use of batching.
2. Different batching strategies have different impact on the FTP goodput. In general, pool batching strategies (strategy S_5 to S_7) cause a worse FTP goodput than simple batching strategies (strategy S_1 to S_4).
3. When the batching in the mixes is excessively aggressive, that is, when batching intervals are too long or threshold values too high, the batching interferes with the time-out behavior of TCP and FTP, and in some cases, FTP aborts. This is the case in particular for threshold triggered mixes with no cross traffic.

6   A Countermeasure and Its Performance

From the discussion above, it is apparent that traditional batching strategies and reordering are not sufficient for mixes to effectively counter flow correlation attacks. Additional measures are needed. In this section, we introduce a relatively efficient and effective countermeasure and evaluate its performance in terms of FTP goodput.

6.1   Overview

A class of possible countermeasures can be developed based on the lessons learned in the previous sections. If a flow correlation attack relies on comparisons of pattern vectors of outgoing traffic, it will be ineffective when all packet vectors are identical. Thus, this type of flow correlation attacks can be effectively countered if a mix can make all the output flows look identical. As a result, assuming that we have the input flow vector X_i and l output flow vectors $Y_1, \cdots, Y_l$,

$$d(X_i, Y_1) = \cdots = d(X_i, Y_j) = \cdots = d(X_i, Y_l), \tag{9}$$

and the only analysis strategy for an adversary would be to randomly guess which output flow is correlated to an input flow. This results in a detection rate of $\frac{1}{l}$.

Because naturally the rates of traffic along all the output links of a mix are different, we have to appropriately insert dummy packets to make all the output flows behave in the same way. A challenge here is to insert a minimum number of dummy packets.

Such an output-control algorithm is illustrated in Figure 7. Mix M maintains two output queues, Q_1 for the link between Mix M and node R_1, and Q_2 for the link between

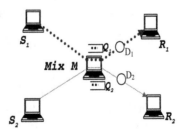

Fig. 7. Network Setup for the New Countermeasure

Data   : queues, in which packets are kept in deadline order by the mix
Result   : synchronized flows out of the mix
while *(1)* **do**
  if *(Q_1.Length > 0) and (Q_2.Length > 0)* **then**
      send the first packet from Q_1;
      send the first packet from Q_2
  else
      if *(Q_1.Length > 0)* **then**
          if *(Q_1.FirstPacket.Deadline > CurrentTime)* or *(Q_1.Length > Q_1.Threshold)*
          then
              send the first packet from Q_1;
              send a dummy packet for Q_2
          end
      else
          if *(Q_2.Length > 0)* **then**
              if *(Q_2.FirstPacket.Deadline > CurrentTime)* or *(Q_2.Length > Q_2.Threshold)* **then**
                  send a dummy packet for Q_1
                  send the first packet from Q_2;
              end
          end
      end
  end
end

Fig. 8. Algorithm for Output Traffic Control

Mix M and node R_2. At any time, if each queue has a packet, they are sent out in some pre-defined order, e.g., the packet in Q_1 first and the packet in Q_2 second. By doing so, one of the two queues will be always empty. Let us say, for the moment, that Q_2 is empty. A deadline is assigned to each packet waiting in Q_1. If a packet in Q_1 reaches its deadline, a dummy packet will be generated for Q_2. Then, the payload packet from Q_1 and the dummy packet from Q_2 are sent out in the predefined order. A dummy packet will also be generated for Q_2 if the queue length of Q_1 goes beyond a preset threshold. In this way, we can ensure a maximum delay on each packet, and we also guarantee that neither queue will overflow.

Figure 8 gives the new countermeasure algorithm on Mix M for the anonymity system in Figure 7. We can see that the output traffic of the Mix is now synchronized, and the adversary cannot observe any difference among the output flows.

This method can be easily extended and optimized for more complicated cases. The number of virtual output links of a mix can be very large since we assume a peer-to-peer mix network. Since we only maintain virtual queues, the overhead is limited. In the case of a large network with a small number of flows, there still needs to be a lower bound LB_Q of the number of virtual queues required for each mix to maintain anonymity. In other words, we do not necessarily need to synchronize every output link when traffic is slow, but we will synchronize a minimum number LB_Q of links. For example, if there is one virtual queue with a packet whose deadline is reached, we have to send out dummy packets to the other $LB_Q - 1$ virtual links.

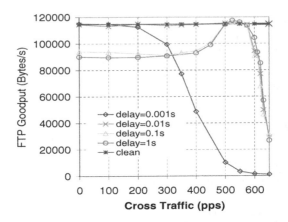

Fig. 9. FTP Goodput Using Output Traffic Control ("clean" means no output traffic control)

Output traffic control is not new and has been proposed for example in [33], where messages at the output ports are forwarded periodically[2]. The algorithm in Figure 8 is more efficient and probably more effective than the approach described in [33]. It is more efficient because packets are forwarded based on each queue's status: once each queue has payload packets, the first packet in each queue is sent out and packets suffer smaller delay at Mixes. It is likely more effective because periodic traffic patterns are very difficult to generate with sufficient accuracy. We showed in NetCamo [22, 34], for example, how high-accuracy traffic analysis can easily break periodic link padding schemes.

6.2   Performance Evaluation of Output Traffic Control

We are interested in how traffic flows traversing a mix affect each other. In particular, we evaluate the TCP performance. Again FTP is used as an example in the evaluation.

Figure 9 gives the FTP goodput measurement for our new scheme for the network setup in Figure 7. We set the threshold of each queue at *50* packets. The path from S_2 to R_2 has FTP traffic and UDP traffic of 400pps. Cross traffic in Figure 9 refers to the UDP traffic along the path S_1 to R_1. Both paths have a propagation delay of *0.3* second. We have the following observations from these experiments:

1. While not evident from Figure 9, the observed detection rate of the correlation attack is 50% in all the cases when the new countermeasure is used. This is expected, as the new method can guarantee a detection rate of $1/LB_Q$ where $LB_Q = 2$ in this case.
2. The goodput for the clean FTP is 114,628.83 bytes/s. When the delay parameter is set to 0.01s, the same goodput is achieved as long as the cross traffic is less than 525 pps. This is very significant. It indicates that, once the delay parameter is properly

---

[2] The paper is too vaguely written for us to figure out exactly what forwarding mechanism is used.

selected, our new method can achieve high throughput (as high as the case without mix) while guaranteeing a low detection rate.

3. For the cases of delay equal to 0.01s, 0.10s, and 1.00s, right after the cross traffic goes beyond 525 pps, all have their goodput drop rapidly. This is due to the fact that the cross traffic is so heavy that the FTP's TCP protocol detects congestion and adapts accordingly.

4. It is also interesting to note, that when the cross traffic is low and the value of delay parameter is large (say, the cross traffic is less than 500 pps and delay is equal to 0.10s or 1.00s), the goodput is low (about 93,000 bytes/s). This is consistent with intuition: if the cross traffic is low and delay is large, then the traffic of our FTP flow may have to wait longer than in other cases, resulting in a reduction of goodput.

5. Finally, in the case when the value of delay parameter is small, say, equal to 0.001s, the curve of goodput is monotonically decreasing. In this case, it is likely that a packet from the FTP flow will be transmitted due to the deadline expiration, rather than the arrival of a packet from the cross traffic. Thus, the cross traffic always contributes negatively to the goodput performance here by creating dummy packets.

7   Summary and Future Work

We have analyzed mix networks in terms of their effectiveness in providing anonymity and quality-of-service. Various methods used in mix networks were considered: seven different packet batching strategies and two implementation schemes, namely the link-based batching scheme and mix-based batching scheme. We found that mix networks that use traditional batching strategies, regardless of the implementation scheme, are vulnerable under flow correlation attacks. By using proper statistical analysis, an adversary can accurately determine the output link used by traffic that comes to an input flow of a mix. The detection rate can be as high as 100% as long as enough data is available. This is true even if heavy cross traffic exists. The data collected in this paper should give designers guidelines for the development and operation of mix networks.

The failure of traditional mix batching strategies directly leads us to the formation of a new packet control method for mixes in order to overcome their vulnerability to flow correlation attacks. Our new method can achieve a guaranteed low detection rate while maintaining high throughput for normal payload traffic. Our claim is validated by extensive performance data collected from experiments. The new method is flexible in controlling the overhead by adjusting the maximum packet delay.

Our study is the first that systematically models and analyzes flow correlation attacks and their countermeasures. The work presented in this paper is largely empirical. We are currently developing an analysis framework that allows quick, back-of-the-envelope calculations to assess the effectiveness of batching strategies in countering flow correlation attacks. It is an open question what statistical analysis methods an adversary may use. Performance bounds and estimates in terms of detection rate and throughput may be developed by following the approaches taken in [35] and [36], respectively.

References

1. Song, D.X., Wagner, D., Tian, X.: Timing analysis of keystrokes and timing attacks on ssh. In: Proceedings of 10th USENIX Security Symposium. (2001)
2. Sun, Q., Simon, D.R., Wang, Y., Russell, W., Padmanabhan, V.N., Qiu, L.: Statistical identification of encrypted web browsing traffic. In: Proceedings of IEEE Symposium on Security and Privacy. (2002)
3. Chaum, D.: Untraceable electronic mail, return addresses, and digital pseudonyms. Communications of the ACM **4** (1981)
4. Helsingius, J.:   Press release: Johan helsingius closes his internet remailer. http://www.penet.fi/press-english.html (1996)
5. Parekh, S.:   Prospects for remailers - where is anonymity heading on the internet. http://www.firstmonday.dk/issues/issue2/remailers/ (1996)
6. Gülcü, C., Tsudik, G.: Mixing E-mail with Babel. In: Proceedings of the Network and Distributed Security Symposium (NDSS), IEEE (1996) 2–16
7. Möller, U., Cottrell, L.: Mixmaster Protocol — Version 2. http://www.eskimo.com/~rowdenw/crypt/Mix/draft-moeller-mixmaster2-proto\%col-00.txt (2000)
8. Serjantov, A., Dingledine, R., Syverson, P.: From a trickle to a flood: active attacks on several mix types. In: Proceedings of Information Hiding Workshop. (2002)
9. Danezis, G., Dingledine, R., Mathewson, N.: Mixminion: Design of a Type III Anonymous Remailer Protocol. In: Proceedings of the 2003 IEEE Symposium on Security and Privacy. (2003)
10. Back, A., Möller, U., Stiglic, A.: Traffic analysis attacks and trade-offs in anonymity providing systems. In: Proceedings of Information Hiding Workshop. (2001)
11. Berthold, O., Langos, H.: Dummy traffic against long term intersection attacks. Proceedings of Privacy Enhancing Technologies workshop (PET 2002) (2002)
12. Berthold, O., Pfitzmann, A., Standtke, R.: The disadvantages of free MIX routes and how to overcome them. In: Proceedings of Designing Privacy Enhancing Technologies: Workshop on Design Issues in Anonymity and Unobservability. (2000)
13. Mitomo, M., Kurosawa, K.: Attack for Flash MIX. In: Proceedings of ASIACRYPT. (2000)
14. Raymond, J.: Traffic analysis: Protocols, attacks, design issues and open problems. In: Proceedings of Designing Privacy Enhancing Technologies: Workshop on Design Issues in Anonymity and Unobservability. (2001)
15. Syverson, P.F., Goldschlag, D.M., Reed, M.G.: Anonymous connections and onion routing. In: Proceedings of IEEE Symposium on Security and Privacy, Oakland, California (1997) 44–54
16. Boucher, P., Shostack, A., Goldberg, I.: Freedom systems 2.0 architecture (2000)
17. Reiter, M., Rubin, A.: Crowds: Anonymity for web transactions. ACM Transactions on Information and System Security **1** (1998)
18. Freedman, M.J., Morris, R.: Tarzan: A peer-to-peer anonymizing network layer. In: Proceedings of the 9th ACM Conference on Computer and Communications Security (CCS), Washington, DC (2002)
19. Sherwood, R., Bhattacharjee, B., Srinivasan, A.: p^5: A protocol for scalable anonymous communication. In: Proceedings of the 2002 IEEE Symposium on Security and Privacy. (2002)
20. Serjantov, A., Sewell, P.: Passive attack analysis for connection-based anonymity systems. In: Proceedings of European Symposium on Research in Computer Security (ESORICS). (2003)
21. Zhu, Y., Fu, X., Graham, B., Bettati, R., Zhao, W.: Correlation attacks in a mix network. Texas A&M University Computer Science Technical Report TR2003-8-9 (2003)

22. Fu, X., Graham, B., Xuan, D., Bettati, R., Zhao, W.: Analytical and empirical analysis of countermeasures to traffic analysis attacks. In: Proceedings of International Conference on Parallel Processing (ICPP). (2003)

23. Howard, J.D.: An analysis of security incidents on the internet 1989 - 1995. Technical report, Carnegie Mellon University Dissertation (1997)

24. F.B.I: Carnivore diagnostic tool. http://www.fbi.gov/hq/lab/carnivore/carnivore2.htm (2003)

25. Walton, G.: China's golden shield: Corporations and the development of surveillance technology in china. http://www.totse.com/en/privacy/privacy/pucc.html (2003)

26. Achives, O.R.D.: Link padding and the intersection attack. http://archives.seul.org/or/dev (2002)

27. tcpdump.org: tcpdump. http://www.tcpdump.org/ (2003)

28. cisco.inc.: Netflow services solutions guide. http://www.cisco.com/univercd/cc/td/doc/cisintwk/intsolns/netflsol/nfwhite.htm (2003)

29. Moddemeijer, R.: On estimation of entropy and mutual information of continuous distributions. Signal Processing **16** (1989) 233–246

30. MathWorks: Documentation for mathworks products (release 13). http://www.mathworks.com/access/helpdesk/help/helpdesk.shtml (2003)

31. TimeSys: Timesys linux docs. http://www.timesys.com/ (2003)

32. netfilter.org: Netfilter. http://netfilter.samba.org/ (2003)

33. Rennhard, M., Rafaeli, S., Mathy, L., Plattner, B., Hutchison, D.: Analysis of an anonymity network for web browsing. In: Proceedings of Workshops on Enabling Technologies: Infrastructure for Collaborative Enterprises (WET ICE). (2002)

34. Guan, Y., Fu, X., Xuan, D., Shenoy, P.U., Bettati, R., Zhao, W.: Netcamo: Camouflaging network traffic for qos-guaranteed critical allplications. IEEE Transactions on Systems, Man, and Cybernetics Part A: Systems and Humans, Special Issue on Information Assurance **31** (2001) 253–265

35. Fu, X., Graham, B., Bettati, R., Zhao, W.: On effectiveness of link padding for statistical traffic analysis attacks. In: Proceedings of the 23rd IEEE International Conference on Distributed Computing Systems (ICDCS 2003). (2003)

36. Padhye, J., Firoiu, V., Towsley, D., Krusoe, J.: Modeling TCP throughput: A simple model and its empirical validation. In: Proceedings of ACM SIGCOMM Special Interest Group on Data Communications (SIGCOMM). (1998)

Measuring Anonymity in a Non-adaptive, Real-Time System

Gergely Tóth and Zoltán Hornák

Budapest University of Technology and Economics,
Department of Measurement and Information Systems,
H-1111 Budapest, XI. Magyar tudósok krt. 2., Building I. B414
{tgm, hornak}@mit.bme.hu

Abstract. Anonymous message transmission should be a key feature in network architectures ensuring that delivered messages are impossible—or at least infeasible—to be traced back to their senders. For this purpose the formal model of the non-adaptive, real-time PROB-channel will be introduced. In this model attackers try to circumvent applied protection measures and to link senders to delivered messages. In order to formally measure the level of anonymity provided by the system, the probability will be given, with which observers can determine the senders of delivered messages (source-hiding property) or the recipients of sent messages (destination-hiding property). In order to reduce the certainty of an observer, possible counter-measures will be defined that will ensure specified upper limit for the probability with which an observer can mark someone as the sender or recipient of a message. Finally results of simulations will be shown to demonstrate the strength of the techniques.

1 Introduction

Anonymous message transmission techniques, such as MIX-net [1] or Onion Routing [2] aim to guarantee that no delivered message can be traced back to its sender. Research on such methods is currently under development but their theoretical analysis and description is not complete. Anonymous message transmission may be used for several real-life scenarios: in anonymous electronic election systems, in anonymous on-line shopping, in anonymous medical consulting and education or simply in electronic mailing.

Recent research in the field of anonymity focuses mainly on adaptive techniques [8,17]. Our approach on the contrary analyses a scenario, where the intermediate node providing anonymity is non-adaptive (i.e. message delay is independent of the actual message distribution). This way a truly real-time system can be constructed, where message-delay has a guaranteed maximum. Although there are connection-based systems among the active ones that aim to allow low-latency communication [2,13], they sacrifice aspects of the techniques described in this paper (e.g. mixing, dummy traffic) in order to become fast—on the other hand however they become vulnerable to some attacks as shown in [5].

D. Martin and A. Serjantov (Eds.): PET 2004, LNCS 3424, pp. 226–241, 2005.
© Springer-Verlag Berlin Heidelberg 2005

In this paper we focus largely on the probabilities with which an attacker can compromise the anonymity provided by our system. A similar approach is shown in Kesdogan et al. for the SG-MIX protocol [16]. Our approach is different in that they specify the user to determine the delay of a packet while traversing the channel, whereas in our model the channel is responsible for determining the delay.

In this paper we will consider only one relaying node (the PROB-channel) for providing anonymity. Reason for this is to analyze this simple scenario first as deeply as possible. Afterwards if the provided anonymity was evaluated, cascading our node similarly to de idea of MIX-nodes [1] will enable a more sophisticated construction. However this approach is out of scope for this paper.

We first introduce the formal model of the PROB-channel and explore what conclusions a passive observer can draw by only knowing public parameters and timing of events (sending & delivery time). Based on the model the source and destination hiding properties will be defined, which can act as a numerical measure for anonymity. The aim of these measures is the same as in [6,11]—to quantify the anonymity provided by the system. However instead of the entropy of the probability distribution we use the maximum of the probabilities for our quantitative analysis. Requirements necessary to limit the certainty of the adversary observer and to ensure given level of anonymity will also be introduced. Finally simulation results will be discussed that give a basic understanding about the operation of the channel.

2   Model of the PROB-Channel

The PROB-channel is responsible for providing anonymity in a scenario where senders send messages to recipients. First let us define the main characteristics of the channel informally:

- The channel is *real-time*, thus messages will be delivered before a message-invariant maximal delay. Other systems may work on a best effort basis (e.g. connection-based techniques: Onion Routing [2]) or do not consider time limits at all (e.g. MIX-nets [1]).
- The channel is *non-adaptive*, as its operation is not affected by properties and distribution of incoming messages, i.e. delay has static distribution. Other solutions prefer active operation, where the system is adaptive to the traffic at the expense of real-time guarantee (e.g. MIXMaster [15]).
- All input and output of the channel is *observable*, so an observer can detect all incoming and delivered messages.
- The channel is a *black-box*, since it is analyzed as a whole. The internal implementation is not specified and side-channel attacks are not considered. The observer cannot see what happens to the messages inside the channel and how they are encoded and delivered.
- The PROB-channel is required as there should be no direct connection between a sender and the receiver. As only one relaying node is inserted into the network topology, our system is a single *proxy* (just like anonymizer.com [14]). Other solutions, where no single relay can be trusted any more employ distributed systems with many relays forming a graph (e.g. Crowds [7]).

- We furthermore assume that messages passing through the channel are equally sized and properly encrypted, thus an observer can only draw conclusions from the timing of the messages, *content does not provide information*. This condition can easily be satisfied.

Our analysis started with the PROB-channel so that future evaluation of cascaded and active techniques can build on the conclusions drawn from this simple non-adaptive channel. We chose a real-time system, as our aim is to employ anonymity in interactive on-line services (e.g. web-browsing), where delay needs to be reduced below a certain limit. We use a black-box proxy model since we did not go into details about internal structure of the channel and left it as an open question how the transformation between sent and delivered messages will be realized. Finally an observable model was chosen since if one cannot be sure about what a potential observer might not perceive, then the worst should be assumed that he could perceive everything.

The model of the PROB-channel is the basis of our work considering anonymous message transmission techniques. Based on the results demonstrated in this paper future analysis will concentrate on active adversaries, which will probably require the usage of active channels. In the following in this chapter we will continue with the formal definition of the PROB-channel and introduce the adversary.

2.1 Description of the Environment

Let S denote the set of senders, R the set of recipients, and M the set of messages. Let $S(m_i)$ denote the sender of message m_i, $R(m_i)$ the recipient of message m_i, whereas $t_S(m_i)$ the time of sending of message m_i and $t_R(m_i)$ the time if delivery of message m_i. The system operates in continuous time, thus events cannot happen at the same time (no parallel entry into the channel). Time of transporting the message from the sender to the channel and from the channel to the recipient will not be considered. This simplification does not substantially affect the conclusions drawn.

2.2 Specification of the Channel

The channel delivers messages from senders to recipients. No messages are born inside the channel and messages won't be dropped by the channel. An incoming message from its sender will be delivered to its recipient after a delay with the following properties:

- the delay δ is a probability variable with a given $f(\delta)$ density function, $\delta = t_R - t_S$, where δ is message- and time-invariant;
- the channel will deliver all messages before a predefined, message- and time-invariant maximal delay δ_{max} (time-to-live) and after a predefined, message- and time-invariant minimal delay δ_{min}, thus $\forall_{m_i} [\delta_{min} < t_R(m_i) - t_S(m_i) < \delta_{max}]$.

Therefore channel C can be characterized by the parameters $f(\delta)$, δ_{min}, δ_{max}.

2.3   Message sending

In the following we assume that sender $s_a \in S$, $s_a = S(m_i)$ sends a message $m_i \in M$ to recipient $r_b \in R$, $r_b = R(m_i)$. Message m_i and the recipient's ID enter the channel in the encrypted form $\alpha_i := E_S(r_b, m_i)$ at time $t_S(m_i) = t_S(\alpha_i)$, whereas m_i will be delivered to the recipient in the form $\beta_i := E_R(m_i)$, encrypted with a different key, at time $t_R(m_i) = t_R(\beta_i)$ (see Fig. 1).

encrypted message: (common fixed size)   channel (static delay distribution)   encrypted by another key than α_i

original message from s_a original, delivered message to r_b

Fig. 1. Message sending through the PROB-channel

We assume furthermore that the adversary cannot break the applied encryption, thus he can decode nether α_i nor β_i. This could be achieved for example if at startup of the system each sender and recipient agreed a symmetric key with the channel (e.g. with the help of Diffie-Hellman protocol). Afterwards the sender s_a would use his key to encrypt the address of r_b together with the message m_i to form α_i. The channel would decrypt this packet, re-encrypt the message m_i with the recipient's key (thus create β_i) and forward it after the delay to the recipient, who could finally decrypt it with his key. Of course this simple scenario implies that the channel gains access to the contents of the plain message. However using security protocols (e.g. SSL, TLS) over the services offered by the PROB-channel would eliminate this problem.

2.4   The Observer

Let us now state what are the capabilities of a passive observer in this model. Such an observer can only eavesdrop encrypted messages, he cannot decrypt them (unless sent to him) nor can he modify, delete, replay or delay[1] messages. The aim of the observer is to match delivered messages (β_i) with their senders — or at least guess the link with good probability — and so get information about who communicates with whom.

We assume that the observer can eavesdrop all ends of the channel, this way he knows all encrypted messages sent and their time of sending, all delivered encrypted messages and their time of receipt. He also knows the parameters and the environment of the channel. Thus he is in possession of the following information:

- environment (S, R) and parameters $(f(\delta), \delta_{min}, \delta_{max})$ of the channel;
- $\varepsilon_S := \{\alpha_i := E_S[S(m_i), m_i]\}$, $\vartheta_S := \{t_S(\alpha_i)\}$ — sent messages and their time of sending;
- $\varepsilon_R := \{\beta_i := E_R[m_i]\}$, $\vartheta_R := \{t_R(\beta_i)\}$ — received messages and their time of receipt.

---

[1] Note that besides the traditional manipulation techniques an attacker can also delay messages in order to compromise anonymity.

This could be summarized as a passive adversary with knowledge of the system parameters.

Let Ψ denote the history of the system given by the following parameters: C, S, R, ε_S, ε_R, ϑ_S, ϑ_R. In the following we assume that the observer knows the full history Ψ of the system and he can perceive all the observable properties during the whole operation of the system. As we will see, the probability that a delivered message can be traced back to its sender, can even in this case be limited.

3   Confidence of the Observer

Let a specific history of the system be $\Psi^* := (C^*, S^*, R^*, \varepsilon_S^*, \varepsilon_R^*, \vartheta_S^*, \vartheta_R^*)$. In order to evaluate, which sender sent which message, for each delivered message β_k^* and for each sender s_l^* a probability $P_{\beta_k^*, s_l^*, \Psi^*}$ can be determined. If the observer knows the history Ψ^* of the system, he can conclude that β_k^* was sent by s_l^* with the probability $P_{\beta_k^*, s_l^*, \Psi^*}$:

$$P_{\beta_k^*, s_l^*, \Psi^*} = P[S(\beta_k^*) = s_l^* \mid \Psi = \Psi^*] \tag{1}$$

The observer naturally looks for the most probable source where $P_{\beta_k^*, \Psi^*} := \max_{s_l^*} P_{\beta_k^*, s_l^*, \Psi^*}$.

In order to trace back the messages to their senders the observer calculates the probabilities (1) and marks the most probable sender as the potential real sender of the message in question.

Equation (1) only formulates the aim of the observer, how the respective values could be calculated is not yet defined. In the following sections we are going to show two techniques (global and local back-tracing) that specify, how the adversary might calculate the numerical values from the history Ψ^* of the system.

The following sets need to be defined for simplifying upcoming equations. Let $\mu_{\beta_k^*, \Psi^*}$ denote the set of encrypted sent messages α_j^*, which might have left the channel as β_k^* (2) considering the properties of $f^*(\delta)$. Furthermore let $\eta_{\beta_k^*, s_l^*, \Psi^*}$ denote the set of α_j^* in $\mu_{\beta_k^*, \Psi^*}$, which were sent by s_l^* (3).

$$\mu_{\beta_k^*, \Psi^*} := \{\alpha_j^* \mid [t_R(\beta_k^*) - \delta_{max}^*] < t_S(\alpha_j^*) < [t_R(\beta_k^*) - \delta_{min}^*]\} \tag{2}$$

$$\eta_{\beta_k^*, s_l^*, \Psi^*} := \{\alpha_j^* \mid [\alpha_j^* \in \mu_{\beta_k^*, \Psi^*}] \wedge [S(\alpha_j^*) = s_l^*]\} \tag{3}$$

3.1   Global Back-Tracing

In order to compute the probabilities in (1) the obvious and optimal solution would be to perform global back-tracing, thus the observer would try all possibilities and choose the most probable one.

In order to do this, one has to generate all possible match combinations (the g_i-s) of sent and received messages (4). A match $g_i := \left\langle g_i^1, g_i^2, ..., g_i^{|M^*|} \right\rangle$ means that the delivered encrypted message β_k^* entered the channel as $g_i^k = \alpha_j^* \in \varepsilon_S^*$.

$$G_{\Psi^*} := \{ g_i := \left\langle g_i^1, g_i^2, ..., g_i^{|M^*|} \right\rangle \mid [g_i \in \underset{1 \le k \le |M^*|}{\times} \mu_{\beta_k^*, \Psi^*}] \wedge [\underset{1 \le j \le |M^*|}{\forall} \underset{\substack{(1 \le k \le |M^*|) \wedge \\ (j \ne k)}}{\forall} (g_i^j \ne g_i^k)] \} \tag{4}$$

After having all match combinations G_{Ψ^*}, based upon their probabilities the observer can calculate (1) as follows:

$$P_{\beta_k^*, s_i^*, \Psi^*} = \sum_{S(g_i^k) = s_i^*} P(g_i \mid \Psi = \Psi^*) \tag{5}$$

In order to get the values for (1), the probability of the matches (g_i-s)— which state that the delivered message (β_k^*) entered the channel from the respective sender s_i^* — need to be added up.

As it will be shown in section 6, uniformly distributed delay provides system optimum. In this case each g_i is equally probable, thus the probabilities can be calculated as follows:

$$P(g_i \mid \Psi = \Psi^*) = \frac{1}{|G_{\Psi^*}|} \tag{6}$$

Unfortunately global back-tracing is exponential by the number of sent messages and thus ineffective for practical use.

3.2   Local Back-Tracing

If the observer performs the delivered message → sender matching for each delivered message independently, then equation (7) gives the probability that s_i^* is the sender of β_k^* if history Ψ^* is known—a possible algorithm for (1).

$$P_{\beta_k^*, s_i^*, \Psi^*} = \frac{\sum_{\forall [\alpha_i^* \in \eta_{\beta_k^*, s_i^*, \Psi^*}]} f^*[t_R(\beta_k^*) - t_S(\alpha_i^*)]}{\sum_{\forall [\alpha_j^* \in \mu_{\beta_k^*, \Psi^*}]} f^*[t_R(\beta_k^*) - t_S(\alpha_j^*)]} \tag{7}$$

Equation (7) gives the probability as a quotient of the sums of the delay density function's values: in the numerator summation is done on the set of messages sent by the particular sender (i.e. any of his sent messages could have become this particular delivered message) and in the denominator summation is done on all sent messages in the respective time interval (i.e. this sum is constant for all possible senders for a particular delivered message).

Unfortunately local back-tracing has a great disadvantage. Originating from its local aspect even in a very simple scenario it can produce false results. Assume the following: two senders (s_0 and s_1) send messages to two recipients (r_0 and r_1) through the channel ($\delta_{min} = 1$ and $\delta_{max} = 4$ with uniform distribution). Messages are sent and delivered as follows:

Table 1. Message distribution example

Sent message	Sender	Time of sending	Delivered message	Recipient	Time of receipt
α_0	s_0	1.0	β_0	r_1	3.0
α_1	s_1	2.1	β_1	r_1	4.9
α_2	s_1	4.0	β_2	r_0	6.0
α_3	s_0	5.1	β_3	r_0	7.9

This example message distribution is shown on Fig. 2. It is obvious that β_0 can only originate from α_0, which implies that α_0 could not become β_1 and so on. However local back-tracing cannot handle this condition and considers α_0 for the calculations for β_1 and comes to an inadequate result: only β_0 and β_2 would be guessed correctly despite all messages in this scenario being tracable.

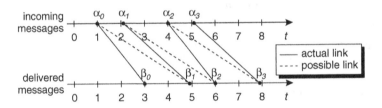

Fig. 2. Example message distribution

In this example the observer performing local back-tracing is only able to compromize the anonymity of the delivered messages β_0 and β_2. However for β_1 and β_2 both senders appear as potential subjects with an equal probability.

This example clearly illustrates the weakness of local back-tracing. It is to note that global back-tracing would have successfully linked incoming and delivered messages. However since only local back-tracing is feasible especially for larger sets of messages, in our work we will use locally back-tracing techniques for the drawn conclusions.

It has to be emphasized that a defense against a locally back-tracing observer is not guaranteed to work against an adversary performing global back-tracing. Our assumption is however that under special circumstances (see the MIN/MAX property with uniform message delay distribution in section 6) the history of the system can become resilient against both kinds of adversaries. On the other hand if the senders don't produce enough messages, in degenerate cases local back-tracing might not detect the real matching (e.g. if the sets $\mu_{\beta_k^*, \psi^*}$ are small).

4   Source- and Destination-Hiding Property

History $\Psi = (C, S, R, \varepsilon_S, \varepsilon_R, \vartheta_S, \vartheta_R)$ of a system is *source-hiding* with parameter Θ if the observer cannot assign a sender to any delivered message β_k with a probability greater than Θ:

$$\bigvee_{\beta_k \in \varepsilon_R} P_{\beta_k, \Psi} : \Theta \qquad (8)$$

Pfitzmann and Köhntopp [3] defined in their paper the term *sender anonymity*. Translated to the model of the PROB-channel this would mean that delivered messages are not linkable to a sender. Thus the source hiding property can be seen as a numerical measure for the sender anonymity. The aim of this measure is the same as in [6,11]—to quantify the quite elusive notion anonymity, however instead of the entropy of the probability distribution we use the maximal probability for our quantitative analysis. We have chosen this new measure for a simple reason: it is much more intuitive and does not disregard the important aspects of a practical measure.

Respectively also *recipient anonymity* was also defined. In our model this would mean that sent messages are not linkable to a recipient. For this purpose the destination-hiding property can be introduced.

Similarly to (1) the probability $P_{\alpha_j^*, r_i^*, \Psi^*}$ can be defined for each sent message α_j^* and for each recipient r_i^*. If the observer knows the history Ψ^* of the system, he can conclude that α_j^* was received by r_i^* with the probability $P_{\alpha_j^*, r_i^*, \Psi^*}$:

$$P_{\alpha_j^*, r_i^*, \Psi^*} = P[R(\alpha_j^*) = r_i^* \mid \Psi = \Psi^*] \qquad (9)$$

The observer naturally looks for the most probable destination where $P_{\alpha_j^*, \Psi^*} := \max_{r_i^*} P_{\alpha_j^*, r_i^*, \Psi^*}$.

Finally definition of the destination-hiding property is as follows: history $\Psi = (C, S, R, \varepsilon_S, \varepsilon_R, \vartheta_S, \vartheta_R)$ of a system is *destination-hiding* with parameter Ω if the observer cannot assign a recipient to any sent message α_j with a probability greater than Ω:

$$\bigvee_{\alpha_j \in \varepsilon_S} P_{\alpha_j, \Psi} : \Omega \qquad (10)$$

Naturally the observer can apply similar global and local back-tracing methods in order to compromise recipient anonymity as those defined in sections 3.1 and 3.2.

5   MIN/MAX Property

In order to be able to limit the possible value of equation (7) influencing the source-hiding property even in the worst case, restrictions have to be applied for the intervals between message sendings:

- First, summation in the numerator has to be performed on the smallest possible set. In order to achieve this, senders should not be allowed send more than one message in a given time interval.
- Second, summation in the denominator has to be performed on the greatest possible set. In order to achieve this, senders should be obliged to send at least one message in a given time interval. (If it is otherwise not achievable, senders should send *dummy* messages to randomly chosen recipients.)

The effect of dummy messages on anonymity has been analyzed by Berthold and Langos [9]. As it has been evaluated thoroughly, we do not handle requirements for contents, here only the frequency range for sending such messages is analyzed.

Considering the above limitations, history $\Psi = (C, S, R, \varepsilon_S, \varepsilon_R, \vartheta_S, \vartheta_R)$ of a system possesses the MIN/MAX property with parameters τ_{min}, τ_{max} ($\tau_{min} \leq \tau_{max}$), if it holds that no sender sends more than one message within a time interval τ_{min} (11) and all senders send at least one message in a time interval τ_{max} (12).

$$\forall_{s_l \in S} \ \forall_{\alpha_j | S(\alpha_j) = s_l} \ \xi_{s_l, \alpha_j} = \varnothing \tag{11}$$

$$\forall_{s_l \in S} \ \forall_{\alpha_j | S(\alpha_j) = s_l} \ -(\zeta_{s_l, \alpha_j} = \varnothing) \tag{12}$$

Where ξ_{s_l, α_j} is the set of sent encrypted messages, which were sent by sender s_l maximal τ_{min} after sending α_j (13) and ζ_{s_l, α_j} is the set of sent encrypted messages, which were sent by s_l maximal τ_{max} after sending α_j (14).

$$\xi_{s_l, \alpha_j} := \{ a_i \mid (S(a_i) = s_l) \wedge (t_S(a_i) > t_S(a_j)) \wedge ([t_S(a_i) - t_S(a_j)] < \tau_{min}) \} \tag{13}$$

$$\zeta_{s_l, \alpha_j} := \{ \alpha_i \mid (S(\alpha_i) = s_l) \wedge (t_S(\alpha_i) > t_S(\alpha_j)) \wedge ([t_S(\alpha_i) - t_S(\alpha_j)] < \tau_{max}) \} \tag{14}$$

If these conditions hold, for the probabilities (1) assigned to any delivered encrypted message and sender, a message-invariant upper limit $\hat{P}_\Psi$ can be given (15), and thus the source-hiding property can be guaranteed (assuming $\tau_{max} \leq [\delta_{max} - \delta_{min}]$):

$$P_{\beta_k, \Psi} \leq \Theta = \hat{P}_\Psi = \frac{\sum\limits_{i=1}^{\Delta_{min}} \max\limits_{(i-1)\tau_{min} \leq q < i \cdot \tau_{min}} f(q)}{|S| \cdot \sum\limits_{i=1}^{\Delta_{max}} \min\limits_{(i-1)\tau_{max} \leq q < i \cdot \tau_{max}} f(q)} \tag{15}$$

Where $\Delta_{max} = \left\lfloor \dfrac{\partial_{max} - \partial_{min}}{\tau_{max}} \right\rfloor$ and $\Delta_{min} = \left\lceil \dfrac{\partial_{max} - \partial_{min}}{\tau_{min}} \right\rceil$.

Unfortunately the same approach does not work for the destination-hiding property. The frequency of sending messages may be specified for the senders but the frequency of receipt cannot be specified for the recipients. Either the senders have to send messages uniformly distributed to all the recipients or the channel has to create dummy messages in order to ensure that each recipient receives the same amount of messages (with the same distribution). However coordinating the senders in a distributed environment seems to be difficult. On the other hand the option of dummy messages created by the channel moves us into the category of active channels, which is not the scope of this paper. Ultimately we have to realize that with the limitations of the PROB-channel the destination-hiding property cannot be realized efficiently.

6   Optimum — Uniformly Distributed Delay

Coming back to the source-hiding property, in the best case—while doing the local back-tracing—the observer can only pick randomly for a delivered message from those who sent a message in the relevant time frame ($\delta_{min} - \delta_{max}$).

Is the distribution $f(\delta)$ of the delay in a channel uniform (between δ_{min} and δ_{max} $f(\delta) = f_{max}$, otherwise zero), then with a history $\Psi = (C, S, R, \mathcal{E}_S, \mathcal{E}_R, \vartheta_S, \vartheta_R)$ for all delivered encrypted messages β_k we get:

$$P_{\beta_k,\Psi} = \frac{\max_{s_l}\left|\eta_{\beta_k,s_l,\Psi}\right|}{\left|\mu_{\beta_k,\Psi}\right|} \tag{16}$$

If Ψ has the MIN/MAX property with parameters τ_{min}, τ_{max} ($\tau_{max} \leq [\delta_{max} - \delta_{min}]$), then the upper limit in (15) can be brought into a simpler form:

$$P_{\beta_k,\Psi} \leq \Theta = \hat{P}_\Psi = \frac{\Delta_{min}}{|S| \cdot \Delta_{max}} \approx \frac{\tau_{max}}{|S| \cdot \tau_{min}} \tag{17}$$

If Ψ also fulfills the condition $\tau_{min} = \tau_{max}$ ($\tau_{max} \leq [\delta_{max} - \delta_{min}]$), meaning that each sender sends messages with a period exactly $\tau_{min} = \tau_{max}$, then the history of the system reaches the global optimum and the observer has to pick the sender for each delivered encrypted message randomly from all senders (from S):

$$P_{\beta_k,\Psi} \leq \Theta = \hat{P}_\Psi \approx \frac{1}{|S|} \tag{18}$$

Interpreting these we can formulate that with uniformly distributed delay the observer does not achieve anything by eavesdropping, he has to pick randomly from the senders who sent a message in the relevant time frame. If the senders satisfy the MIN/MAX conditions as well, then the level of anonymity can be controlled exactly.

7   Simulation Results

In this section simulation results will be introduced. Basically the following two aspects will be illustrated:

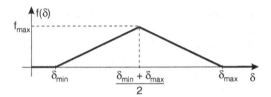

Fig. 3. Triangle distribution

- difference between *general* (see section 7.1) and *MIN/MAX* (see section 7.2) message sending and
- difference between *non-uniform* (triangle, see Fig. 3) and *uniform* distribution.

According to the categories above, four simulation scenarios can be defined. For each scenario, the following parameters were the same:

- there were 20 senders and 20 receivers;
- $\delta_{min} = 1$ and $\delta_{max} = 4$;
- simulation duration T = 2000: each sender was sending messages between time index 0 and T.

Each simulation scenario was repeated 20 times and the average of the results weighted with the total number of messages in the actual run are discussed in the following.

While the observer was performing local back-tracing three variables were maintained after the calculations for each message. Before each run these three variables were initialized to 0.

- *sure*—if the observer could successfully link the delivered message to its actual sender[2] then *sure* is increased by 1;
- *maybe*—if there were q senders with the same probability of sending the specified message then *maybe* is increased by q^{-1} and *failed* is increased by $1 - q^{-1}$;
- *failed*—if the observer could not link the delivered message to its actual sender (i.e. he linked the message to the wrong sender) then *failed* is increased by 1.

Note. In the following *Sure*, *Maybe* and *Failed* measure are the weighted averages of *sure*, *maybe* and *failed* divided by the average number of messages. On the diagrams below the quantity *Maybe* + *Sure* (the ratio with which the observer linked successfully messages to their real senders) is shown. As *Failed* = 1 – (*Maybe* + *Sure*), it is not shown on the diagrams.

---

[2] In order to check, whether the observer linked the right sender to a delivered message in the simulation there was an entity that knew the real sender of each message and this entity decided, whether the observer was successful or not.

7.1   General Message Sending

This section analyses the difference between uniform and another (in this case the triangle) distribution. For the scenarios *general* senders were used. Behavior of such senders is characterized by the parameter U:

- at initialization each general sender generates its own maximal delay U_{max}, which is a random number in the interval 0...U;
- then the sender repeatedly generates a random number in the interval 0...U_{max}, waits this amount of time and then sends a message to a randomly chosen receiver;
- message sending stops if a message sending happened after time T.

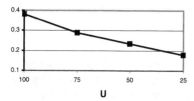

Fig. 4. General senders with triangle distribution

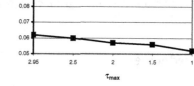

Fig. 5. General senders with uniform distribution

For numerical values, see section A.1 of the Appendix. It can clearly be seen on the diagrams above (Fig. 4 and 5) that uniform distribution reduces the chances of the observer significantly in contrast to another (in this case triangle) distribution.

7.2   MIN/MAX Message Sending

MIN/MAX sending was performed with parameter $\tau_{min} = 0.9$. Value of τ_{max} was chosen to be 1.0, 1.5, 2.0, 2.5 and 2.95. MIN/MAX senders were sending messages to randomly chosen recipients with random intervals between the message sending according to the appropriate τ_{min}, τ_{max} restrictions.

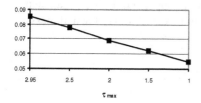

Fig. 6. MIN/MAX senders with triangle distribution

Fig. 7. MIN/MAX senders with uniform distribution

For numerical values, see section A.2 of the Appendix.

An increase in the number of messages could be observed, which implied basically the greater *Failed* ratio. Although uniform distribution (Fig. 7) is still better than the triangle one (Fig. 6), the absolute difference is not that substantial any more—the relative difference is still significant.

It can clearly be seen that the uniform distribution's $\hat{P}_\psi$ guarantees strong source-hiding property. Also note that the theoretical minimum of 0.05 for the certainty of the observer with 20 senders is almost achieved with uniform distribution with $\tau_{min} = 0.9$ and $\tau_{max} = 1.0$ (the actual value was 0.067, see section A.3 of the Appendix for more details).

It should also be mentioned that originating from the form of the triangle distribution equation (15) could not give usable upper limit for the certainty of the observer, thus source-hiding property in that case could not be guaranteed.

8   Conclusion

In this paper the formal model of the PROB-channel was introduced. Assuming a passive observer, we analyze what conclusions could be drawn for a non-adaptive, real-time relaying node based solely on observation of the timing of events and the parameters of the channel. With the help of a numerical measure of sender anonymity—the source hiding property—we show that the MIN/MAX approach combined with the optimal uniformly distributed delay, successfully prevents a locally back-tracing observer breaking the security of the PROB-channel. On the other hand global back-tracing (while having an exponential computational complexity) could achieve much better results against our system. Our assumption however is that under the circumstances pointed out in chapter 6 (e.g. MIN/MAX property and uniform distribution) the difference between global and local back-tracing is not substantial. Future analysis needs to prove this assumption.

Further research is also required to find out how our model has to be altered in order to guarantee recipient anonymity efficiently. It should be evaluated, how cascading such nodes can improve the resistance of the anonymity system against active attackers. Finally it should be investigated what an active attacker can accomplish against the model described here and how the PROB-channel should be extended to successfully protect against an active opponent. Probably an active channel is required that would dynamically react to the distribution of actual message arrivals.

Acknowledgements

The authors would like to thank George Danezis for his helpful comments and the anonymous referees for useful suggestions.

References

1. Chaum, D.: Untraceable Electronic Mail, Return Addresses, and Digital Pseudonyms. In *Communications of the ACM*, volume 24, number 2, pp. 84-88, 1981
2. Reed, M., Syverson, P., Goldschlag, D.: Anonymous Connections and Onion Routing. In *IEEE Journal on Selected Areas in Communication Special Issue on Copyright and Privacy Protection*, pp. 482-494, 1998
3. Pfitzman, A., Kohntopp, M.: Anonymity, Unobservability, and Pseudonymity – A Proposal for Terminology. In *Designing Privacy Enhancing Technologies*, Federrath, H. (editor), Springer-Verlag LNCS 2009, pp. 1–9, 2001
4. Back, A., Möller, U., Stiglic, A.: Traffic Analysis Attacks and Trade-Offs in Anonymity Providing Systems. In *Information Hiding: 4th International Workshop*, Moskowitz, I.S. (editor), Springer-Verlag LNCS 2137, pp. 245-257, 2001
5. Serjantov, A., Sewell, P.: Passive Attack Analysis for Connection-Based Anonymity Systems. In *ESORICS 2003*, Snekkens, E., Gollmann., D. (editors), Springer-Verlag LNCS 2808, pp. 116-131, 2003
6. Serjantov, A., Danezis, G.: Towards an Information Theoretic Metric for Anonymity, in *Privacy Enhancing Technologies (PET2002)*, Syverson, P., Dingledine, R. (editors), Springer-Verlag LNCS 2482, pp. 41-53, 2002
7. Reiter, M. K., Rubin, A. D.: Crowds: Anonymity for Web Transactions, *ACM Transactions on Information and System Security*, volume 1, number 1, pp. 66-92, 1998
8. Berthold, O., Federrath, H., Köhntopp, M.: Project "Anonymity and Unobservability in the Internet", *Conference on Freedom and Privacy 2000 (CFP 2000), Workshop on Freedom and Privacy by Design*, 2000
9. Berthold, O., Langos, H.: Dummy traffic against long term intersection attacks, in *Privacy Enhancing Technologies (PET2002)*, Syverson, P., Dingledine, R. (editors), Springer-Verlag LNCS 2482, pp. 110-128, 2002
10. Diaz, C., Seys, S., Claessens, J., Preneel, B.: Towards measuring anonymity, *in Privacy Enhancing Technologies (PET2002)*, Syverson, P., Dingledine, R. (editors), Springer-Verlag LNCS 2482, pp 54-68, 2002
11. Newman, R. E., Moskowitz, I. S., Syverson, P., Serjantov, A.: Metrics for Traffic Analysis Prevention. In *Privacy Enhancing Technologies (PET2003)*, Dingledine, R. (editor), Springer Verlag LNCS, 2003
12. Wright, M., Adler, M., Levine, B. N., Shields, C.: Defending Anonymous Communications Against Passive Logging Attacks. In *ISOC Symposium on Network and Distributed System Security*. 2002
13. Rennhard, M., Plattner, B.: Introducing Morphmix: Peer-to-Peer based Anonymous Internet Usage with Collusion Detection. In *Workshop on Privacy and Electronic Society (WPES)*, 2002
14. Anonymizer.com—Online Privacy Services, http://www.anonymizer.com
15. Möller, U., Cottrell, L., Palfrader, P., Sassaman, L.: Mixmaster Protocol — Version 2. Draft, 2002
16. Kesdogan, D., Egner, J., Büschkes, R.: Stop–and–Go MIXes: Providing Probabilistic Anonymity in an Open System. In *Information Hiding Workshop (IH1998)*, Springer Verlag, LNCS 1525, 1998
17. Boucher, P., Shostack, A., Goldberg, I.: Freedom Systems 2.0 Architecture. White paper, Zero Knowledge Systems Inc., 2000

Appendix A

In the Appendix numerical values of the simulations will be given.

A.1 Values for General Message Sending

In this section numerical values of the simulation of general senders (see section 9.1) will be given. General senders don't follow constraints to increase their anonymity, they send messages randomly. Table 2 shows the results with triangle distribution, whereas values for the uniform distribution can be found in Table 3.

Table 2. Results for general senders with triangle distribution

U	Sure	Maybe	Failed	Number of Messages
100	0.382	0	0.618	2811
75	0.288	0	0.712	4134
50	0.234	0	0.766	6560
25	0.179	0	0.821	12313

Table 3. Results for general senders with uniform distribution

U	Sure	Maybe	Failed	Number of Messages
100	0.141	0.156	0.703	2735
75	0.115	0.141	0.744	3622
50	0.096	0.103	0.801	5625
25	0.089	0.073	0.838	9000

It can clearly be seen that with triangle distribution the observer can always choose exactly one sender (*Maybe* is always 0). With uniform distribution the certainty of the observer is lower (overall *Failed* increases) and in several occasions he cannot choose between different senders (*Maybe* is not 0).

A.2 Values for MIN/MAX Message Sending

In this section numerical values of the simulation of MIN/MAX senders (see section 9.2) will be given. MIN/MAX senders enforce the MIN/MAX property for the distribution of sent messages, thus they greatly improve anonymity with the help of dummy messages. Table 4 shows the results with triangle distribution, whereas values for the uniform distribution can be found in Table 5.

Table 4. Results for MIN/MAX senders with triangle distribution

τ_{max}	Sure	Maybe	Failed	Number of Messages
1.0	0.055	0	0.945	42094
1.5	0.062	0	0.938	33320
2.0	0.069	0	0.931	27569
2.5	0.078	0	0.922	23525
2.95	0.085	0	0.915	20767

Table 5. Results for MIN/MAX senders with uniform distribution

τ_{max}	Sure	Maybe	Failed	Number of Messages
1.0	<0.001	0.052	0.948	42107
1.5	0.002	0.054	0.944	33317
2.0	0.002	0.055	0.943	27617
2.5	0.002	0.058	0.940	23473
2.95	0.002	0.060	0.938	20818

Comparing the results of MIN/MAX senders with general senders (see previous section), one can observe that the number of sent messages increased (dummy messages were introduced) and this resulted in a greater *Failed* ratio.

A.3 Upper Limit for the Confidence of the Observer

For MIN/MAX senders equation (15) gives a limit ($\hat{P}_\psi$) for the certainty of the observer. In the simulation actual values were the following (Table 6):

Table 6. $\hat{P}_\psi$ limits for MIN/MAX senders

τ_{max}	$\hat{P}_\psi = \Theta$ for triangle distribution	$\hat{P}_\psi = \Theta$ for uniform distribution	
	according to (15)	according to (15)	according to (17)
1.0	0.27	0.067	0.056
1.5	∞	0.1	0.083
2.0	∞	0.2	0.111
2.5	∞	0.2	0.139
2.95	∞	0.2	0.164

Panel Discussion — Mix Cascades Versus Peer-to-Peer: Is One Concept Superior?

Claudia Díaz[1,**], George Danezis[2,*], Christian Grothoff[3,*],
Andreas Pfitzmann[4,*], and Paul Syverson[5,*]

[1] Katholieke Universiteit Leuven, Belgium
Claudia.Diaz@esat.kuleuven.ac.be
[2] George Danezis, University of Cambridge, UK
George.Danezis@cl.cam.ac.uk
[3] Purdue University, USA
[4] Technische Universität Dresden, GER
pfitza@inf.tu-dresden.de
[5] Naval Research Lab, USA
syverson@itd.nrl.navy.mil

David Chaum's initial work on Mixes led to a vast number of proposals how to provide anonymous communication on the Internet. They all have in common, that a multiple of Mixes are used to establish a certain amount of anonymity. The most salient difference between those approaches is the way, how the Mixes are connected and organised.

Two idealised concepts set the range on a continuum of possible designs. On the one end, we have Mix cascades: dedicated servers joining traffic from a large set of users and uniformly redirecting it on a predefined route. The other end is defined by Peer-to-Peer (P2P) systems: widely distributed and equal client applications unpredictably routing their traffic over all possible routes. As these design options have implications on the achievable anonymity and performance, this panel discussion aims to elaborate the advantages and disadvantages of either concept.

As this major design decision has implications on several aspects, the panel is supposed to discuss the issue from multiple points of views: anonymity, deployment, availability, as well as performance.

The discussion is likely to focus rather on the appropriateness of attack models, than on details of analyses of certain implementations. This is intended, because we believe that the choice of attack models is an expression of the researcher's view of the world.

[**] Moderator.
[*] Panelists.

D. Martin and A. Serjantov (Eds.): PET 2004, LNCS 3424, p. 242, 2005.
© Springer-Verlag Berlin Heidelberg 2005

On the PET Workshop Panel "Mix Cascades Versus Peer-to-Peer: Is One Concept Superior?"

Rainer Böhme[1], George Danezis[2], Claudia Díaz[3],
Stefan Köpsell[1], and Andreas Pfitzmann[1]

[1] Technische Universität Dresden, Germany
{rainer.boehme, sk13, pfitza}@inf.tu-dresden.de
[2] University of Cambridge, United Kingdom
george.danezis@cl.cam.ac.uk
[3] Katholieke Universiteit Leuven, Belgium
claudia.diaz@esat.kuleuven.ac.be

Editors' note. Following the panel discussion on Mix Cascades versus P2P at PET 2004, we invited the original panel proposers to write a summary of the discussion for the proceedings. This is their contribution.

Abstract. After almost two decades of research on anonymous network communication the development has forked into two main directions, namely Mix cascades and peer-to-peer (P2P) networks. As these design options have implications on the achievable anonymity and performance, this paper aims to elaborate the advantages and disadvantages of either concept. After clarifying the scope of the discussion, we present arguments for Mix cascades and P2P designs on multiple areas of interest: the level of anonymity, the incentives to cooperate, aspects of availability, and performance issues. Pointed thesis and antithesis are given for both sides, before a final synthesis tries to articulate the status quo of the discussion.

1 Introduction

David Chaum's initial work [6] on Mixes led to a vast number of proposals on how to provide anonymous communication on the Internet. Some of these approaches have already been put into practice while others still rest as blueprints. They all have in common, that multiple Mixes are used to establish a certain amount of anonymity. The most salient difference between those approaches is the way, in which the Mixes are connected and organised. Two idealised concepts set the range on a continuum of possible designs. On the one end, we have Mix cascades: dedicated servers joining traffic from a large set of users and uniformly redirecting it on a predefined route. The other end is defined by peer-to-peer (P2P) systems: widely distributed and equal client applications unpredictably routing their traffic over all possible routes. The design of a Mix system has implications on the achievable anonymity and performance.

This article tries to cover a wide range of aspects, which are all related with this essential design decision. It is not so much focused on detailed analysis of certain specific implementations (e. g., [12, 13, 29]), but rather on the underlying explicit or implicit threat models. As the area of relevant aspects is broad and evidence still sparse, this paper is unlikely to deliver solid proofs. It should rather be regarded as an attempt to collect softer arguments—call it assumptions or beliefs—for both sides of the discussion. Arguments, which we consider as highly important, but which do not fit into the usually better grounded research papers because they are so hard to quantify [14, 26, 28]. Apart from documenting these points, we try to structure the discussion and eventually make it more salient to the community.

We assume that the reader is already familiar with the basic concepts of Mixes, so that our paper is structured straight off. In the next section, we propose a scheme to arrange the different approaches along two dimensions: *flexibility of routing* and *task sharing* (resources as well as trust and liability). In Section 3, we pick up the arguments for Mix cascades and evaluate the impact of the respective designs on four aspects: anonymity, incentives to cooperate, availability, and performance. We underline our claims with a number of pointed thesis. In Section 4 we contrast these points with arguments for peer-to-peer systems and assert a set of antitheses. Finally, a concluding synthesis is given in Section 5.

2   Classification of Approaches

To clarify the subject of the discussion, we propose to break down the properties of the different approaches on two dimensions. The first difference between Mix cascades and P2P networks is the freedom of choice of traffic routing. Typical Mix cascades offer no choice to their users while free choice of link partners—and hence full *flexibility of routing*—is a key feature of P2P concepts. The advantages and drawbacks of precisely this design issue have been addressed in the literature, for example in [5] and [8]. However, none of the pure concepts seems to dominate the other one in all aspects.

The second difference between Mix cascades and P2P networks concerns the organisation of the system. Mix cascades are typically provided by a small set of entities. Their Mixes are located at a small number of places, usually run on dedicated servers, and are administered by professionals. In contrast to this institutionalised approach, pure P2P networks avoid any exposed instances and organise themselves in a rather anarchical manner. All nodes act as equal peers and there is no allocation of duties. Hence, we name the second dimension *task sharing*. The division includes technical resources (e. g., load balancing) as well as intangible aspects such as trust and responsibility.

According to these two dimensions, we can arrange the different approaches for anonymity in networks in a two-by-two matrix as shown in Table 1 (p. 245).

The pure concept of Mix cascades is characterised by asymmetric task sharing and fixed routes. On the opposite, P2P networks consist of equal peers performing the same tasks and routing their traffic over a multiple of user-selected routes.

Table 1. Classification of different concepts for anonymous networks

Task sharing	Flexibility of routing	
	System defined	User's choice
Asymmetric	Mix cascade	Mix network
Symmetric	DC-net, Broadcast	P2P network

Table 2. Extended classification of approaches for network anonymity

Task sharing	System defined		User's choice	
	Fixed	Variable	Restricted	Free
Asymmetric	A_1	A_2	A_3	A_4
Symmetric	S_1	S_2	S_3	S_4

Mix networks are between these two extremes. They allow users to choose their respective routes, but still rely on dedicated Mix servers, which handle different tasks than the multiple of clients. Further topologies for anonymous network communication, such as DC-nets [7] and broadcast [20], exceed the scope of this discussion.

The proposed model helps to structure the topic of discussion, because certain advantages or disadvantages can be precisely linked with one of the dimensions. However, the routing dimension may need a further refinement, because argumentation on the pros and cons of the pure concepts tends to drift somewhere in the middle. For example, the literature responds to the critics of fully connected networks with restricted routes in sparse networks [8]. Also the recent *synchronous batching* approach tries to join the predictable timing feature from Mix cascades with decentralised topologies [17]. Thus it might be useful to subdivide the routing dimension into four sections, as shown in Table 2.

In the remainder of this paper we will discuss the impact of design decisions on each of the dimensions on the total quality of an anonymity service. The next section will show, why some scholars believe that the solutions A_1 and A_2 provide the highest anonymity, coupled with the best performance in case of A_1. In Section 4 we will elaborate why other researchers consider the solutions S_3 and S_4, or at least A_3 and A_4 as more desirable.

3   Arguments for Mix Cascades

The quality of anonymity services can be broadly divided into aspects of security and usability. However, as usability affects the size of the anonymity set, it also matters for the security of a system [2]. Hence, the ideal system can be described as follows: It provides anonymous access to, or sending of any information (*availability*), by hiding all information about the recipient's and/or sender's identity (*anonymity*) within a maximum large set of users (*incentives to cooperate*), with minimum degradation in usable bandwidth and response time (*performance*). To evaluate how Mix cascades and P2P networks perform in realising these goals, we analyse the impact of (1) *flexibility of routing* and (2) *task sharing* on the above-mentioned aspects.

3.1   Anonymity

The maximum anonymity that can be provided by Mix cascades means, that

– all other senders or recipients of the messages of a particular time interval, or
– all Mixes

have to cooperate to trace a message against the intention of its sender or recipient. A proof for this fact in a possibilistic as well as a probabilistic setting is given in [25][1].

The effects of flexible routing on anonymity are described in [5]. Assuming a globally listening and participating adversary, the authors conclude: "If only one Mix of a route is trustworthy, then the achievable anonymity is distinctly lower in a Mix network compared to a synchronously working Mix cascade" (p. 37).

Thesis 1. *P2P networks assume adversaries outside a closed group of people.*

So, it is evident that the requirements for an anonymity service heavily depend on the threat model considered. However, even if the threat model "all other senders or recipients ..., or all Mixes" is deemed too strong, there are good arguments for modifying the parameters rather than replacing the design. First, the anonymity level of a cascade can be downgraded by reducing the number of Mixes or the number of messages required per batch. Both measures have favourable side effects: They lead to an increase in performance and quality of service. Second, the upholding of a cascade design keeps the advantages of a clear structure of the system: In contrast to distributed approaches, cascades are easy to analyse and hence easy to prove.[2] This means that the system is more robust

---

[1] The idea of the proof is also outlined in this document: http://petworkshop.org/2004/talks/pfitza.pdf

[2] The degree of complexity of P2P systems apparently inspires researchers to write fancy papers. However, as a consequence of this complexity, some really important aspects are regularly either neglected (e. g., exit policies) or simplified with unrealistic assumptions (e. g., low number or small fraction, resp., of colluding nodes).

to remaining threats from information outside of the considered model. Third, when the threat model changes because stronger anonymity may be required in future, the switching costs are kept to moderate levels only if a cascade infrastructure is already set up: Changing parameters is far cheaper than switching to a new topology.

However, on the task sharing dimension, the low number of known Mix servers makes Mix cascades more vulnerable against adversaries that try to gain control over these servers [1]. Cascade proponents argue that symmetric task sharing in P2P networks is even more dangerous, because the peer nodes are run by end-users on out-of-the-box operating systems. This combination is less likely to withstand decent attacks compared to dedicated Mix servers administrated by security experts as in the asymmetric case. Equal peers in a symmetric architecture are also more likely to be down, hence forcing their users to change to another route. Frequent route switching increases the probability of using at least one time only collusive nodes.

Thesis 2. *P2P proponents err in assuming that the sheer number of nodes implies that only a minority colludes.*

This thesis has implications in terms of nodes, and in terms of links. The danger of a powerful attacker participating with a large set of nodes is quite well understood. Some measures have been proposed, such as reputation systems [15, 18], which make this attack more difficult at least. But a node does not necessarily need to be malicious because of its owner's bad intentions. It is also possible, that an attacker selectively throws out precisely those nodes, which impede his observation. Thus, the often-cited strength of distributed systems against *denial of service* (DoS) does at the same time attract active attackers, just because routes are dynamically switched and partial failures keep unnoticed. Here are obvious relations to aspects of availability, which are discussed in the next section.

3.2   Availability

Availability of anonymity services includes three steps: first, the possibility to reach an access-point, second, the correct operation of the Mixes and their communication, and third, the accessibility of requested information. The first step concerns possible blocking efforts of authoritarian states or organisations. Depending on the details of the filter method, a powerful blocker can always restrict access to anonymity services. However, it is obvious that publicly known or even central access points are more vulnerable than distributed networks.

Concerning the first step, symmetric systems dominate asymmetric ones if, and only if, their protocols do not unveil too much information about the network's topology (which else could be exploited to block packet forwarding—another rarely addressed aspect in the literature). Also the second step seems to be more robust with a symmetric structure because denial of service attacks would have to hit a large set of peers instead of some central servers. But Mix cascades can also be equipped with redundant backup servers. In addition, the professional administration makes Mix servers less vulnerable than user-run peers. The last step is probably the most difficult to discuss. If the peers used white-lists to manage their exit-policies (see below) the probability to get arbitrary information from the Internet would be quite low. However, institutionalised last Mixes of cascades are also likely to suppress access to certain content, depending on the respective jurisdiction.

Thesis 3. *Concerning availability, P2P seems to dominate the pure (no redundancy) cascade approach. Given redundant cascades, no concept is superior.*

3.3   Incentives to Cooperate

It is evident that a large user base is a prerequisite for strong anonymity. As a common implication, researchers discuss usability and performance aspects to evaluate the incentives to participate. These aspects depend on both flexibility of routing and task sharing.

Apart from that, also on the task sharing dimension, the responsibility of exit-nodes is a very important point, which is only marginally addressed in the literature [1]. For a risk averse user, being accountable for arbitrary crimes that are linkable with one's IP-address or computer is the major drawback of P2P structures. If the first case of, say, "music industry sues participant of P2P anonymity service" went public, the user-base is in danger to vanish. The juridical risk of participation is a major disincentive for users with honourable intentions.

Even if we assume that each user can restrict the access to a limited amount of obviously innocuous websites by administrating exit policies (usually black- or white-lists), the cost of managing these policies will exceed the resources for the majority of participants. As black-lists will never completely evade the risk, and demand a huge effort to keep them up to date, white-lists might be used. This will probably exclude most of the requested information from the network and thus render the system useless.

Thesis 4. *P2P systems are unlikely to receive support by an ample community.*

So, if the masses will be using Mixes at all, strong arguments suggest it will be Mix cascades. Talking about masses means considering the end users, individuals often described as spoiled and reluctant. Here, apart from what has been said before, performance will be an equally critical success factor.

3.4   Performance

P2P proponents often state that centralised routes set an upper limit to the service's performance and thus Mix cascades would perform worse. While the first statement is true, the second one needs further consideration. In fact, the batch size (or more general: the flushing strategy) sets the upper limit for the level of anonymity a service can provide. The frequency of packet arrivals determines the response latency of each Mix. Hence, up to a certain limit, packets pass Mixes the faster the more packets arrive. As Mix cascades usually are connected with higher bandwidth than distributed peers, the upper limit for a cascade is far beyond the limited bandwidth between P2P nodes. Because of this atypical relationship between volume and delay, Mix cascades dominate P2P systems in both, performance and batch size.

Thesis 5. *High load on cascades leads to reduced response latencies for a given batch size. P2P can never reach such capacity effects and therefore P2P always performs worse.*

Dummy traffic has been described as effective measure to prevent long-term intersection attacks [4]. The designers of many P2P systems suggest using dummy traffic—and hence using bandwidth—to reduce the risk of traffic analysis by an observing adversary. However, dummy traffic between two adjacent Mixes does not prevent attacks from insiders, i.e., Mixes, because they always can separate dummy packets from real data. To make dummy traffic indistinguishable from real data, it also has to be routed over multiple peers. This leads to further inefficiencies because dummy packets—now per definition indistinguishable—must be treated with the same quality of service as payload packets and thus cause additional load on already critical bottlenecks in the network topology.

Thesis 6. *Given an insider adversary, dummy traffic in flexible routing systems either is useless or jams connections. In both cases, performance suffers for little reward.*

Summing up all arguments on a more general level, we can put them into two points: First, the security of the cascade design can be proven with little assumptions. So we should not replace this design by a more obscure one, unless we have very good reasons. Second, many people tend to give up privacy if it is inconvenient. So if anonymity systems shall appeal a broader public then quality of service and low costs of maintenance are crucial. Mix cascades provide both very well.

4   Arguments for Mix Network Designs

Mix systems need to be trusted to hide the correspondence between input and output messages, something that cannot be proved or observed in any other way. There is a need to distribute Mix functionality in order to distribute this trust, necessary to provide anonymity, and in order to balance the load across the system. The Mix cascades provide some distribution of trust, but since all traffic is routed through all nodes in a Mix cascade no load balancing at all.

Antithesis 1. *Greater capacity, through load balancing, is a security property.*

General Mix networks allow for both distribution of trust and load balancing. Each new node that is added to the network provides extra capacity, and provided that there is sufficient traffic to prevent traffic analysis, increases the anonymity of all traffic. At the same time the latency of the anonymous communications remains relatively low, since path lengths do not need to grow nearly as fast as the size of the network [8]. This has to be contrasted with the Mix cascade approach, where new cascades need to be constructed to accommodate more traffic. These cascades do not mix traffic amongst them, and as a result provide less anonymity to their users. Therefore our thesis holds that a system that is able to mix together more traffic, is in the long run not simply more scalable. In the case of anonymity properties, that intrinsically rely on other people being present, it is also more secure.

Antithesis 2. *Robustness and availability are security properties.*

Mix cascades have intrinsic single points of failure. The failure of any node in the cascade will bring the operation of the whole cascade to a halt. Bypassing the failed node will require manual intervention, and key redistribution. This makes Mix cascades very fragile, in comparison with fully connected Mix networks, where failures in the network do not interrupt service: new routes that do not use the unavailable nodes are constructed, and used to route traffic.

The fragility of cascades makes them more susceptible to denial of service attacks. It is not necessary to subject the whole network to such an attack, since flooding a single node (such as the entry node to the cascade, that needs to be publicly visible) would be sufficient. The same applies for legal or compulsion attacks: it is sufficient to stop the operation of one node to disrupt all communications. Since by default there can be only fewer nodes participating in a cascade, due to the traffic load, such legal or compulsion attacks are easier to mount from a technical point of view.

Finally Mix cascades are vulnerable to even a small minority of insiders that would attempt to disrupt service by dropping packets, or flooding subsequent nodes. A rich literature exists on how to make cascade designs publicly verifiable, yet most of them rely on extremely expensive cryptographic primitives, and extremely complex protocols [24]. None of them has so far been implemented. On the other hand, two more practical suggestion to provide robustness, batch signing [6, 3] and random partial checking [22], can be equally well applied to Mix networks and Mix cascades.

Unreliable anonymous communication channels are likely to frustrate users and drive them away from using the system all together. This will reduce anonymity sets, and therefore lower the overall security of the channel. At the same time, denial of service itself can be used to assist other attacks, such as the $n-1$ attack [29].

Antithesis 3. *Trust means choice!*

The key to Mix mediated anonymous communications is that the user trusts that the Mixes will not reveal the relation between input and output messages. This choice cannot, and must not, be 'outsourced' to any other third party. Furthermore it is desirable to be able to easily set up a specific Mix node, for the use of particular communities that would trust it. Mix networks can easily accommodate such a trust model, and deployment model. On the other hand, the cost of running a cascade and its rigid structure makes it impossible for small communities to run trusted nodes, or to join and blend in the anonymity of larger groups.

The assumption that all but one Mix nodes are going to be corrupt, as the proponents of the cascade paradigm often do, is based on the false premise that there is a fixed set of nodes that everybody trusts and uses. On the other hand Mix networks allow for different users trusting different subsets of nodes. In extreme cases this would split the anonymity sets: two disjoint trusted groups will emerge, with different user bases. In most cases users will choose to trust overlapping sets of Mix nodes, in such a way that the anonymity sets are still confounded, and entangled. This provides maximal anonymity, and the ability of users or operators to make their own trust judgements.

Restricted routes networks, where the network graph is not complete, allows Mix server operators to make trust judgements, and only interconnect with a small set of others. This again increases the resilience of the network against Sybil attacks [19], or other ways a large number of corrupt nodes could infiltrate the network.

Antithesis 4. *Mix networks increase the* attack surface.

Mix networks allow traffic to come in and out of many nodes in the network. Therefore a Global Passive Adversary (GPA) or a Global Active Adversary (GAA) needs to make an effort proportionate to the number of nodes in the network to retain its capabilities. Furthermore using the peer-to-peer paradigm [21, 27] to do mixing increases even further the cost of the attacker, by multiplying the number and making nodes transient. Therefore it is likely that an attacker will never be able to attain the status of GPA or GAA.

This has to be contrasted with Mix cascade structures that offer very well defined entry and exit points. These can be observed at a fixed cost, and intersection attacks can be mounted against the participants [23, 9]. Combined with the intrinsically smaller anonymity sets, such an attack would be devastating. In other words by trying to protect against an assumed very powerful adversary, Mix cascades make the existence of such an adversary easily possible.

The single point of entry and exit also makes traffic analysis of anonymised streams easier. In the absence of a lot of cover traffic, which none of the fielded systems over the Internet have been able to provide, it is easier for an adversary to gain all the information necessary to perform traffic analysis [11]. Mix network based system, such as Onion Routing [16], face the same problems, but make it more difficult for an adversary to gain all the information necessary by using more nodes and links.

Antithesis 5. *Anonymity is hard, general purpose anonymous channels are even harder!*

Anonymising traffic between users requires the system to make all traffic 'look the same'. In the same way as Quality of Service algorithms operate, perfect anonymity systems require an intimate knowledge of the traffic characteristics they will carry. Anonymous remailers do so, by assuming that mail messages will be of a certain size, and can tolerate very high latencies. Peer-to-peer systems, that attempt to facilitate file sharing or covert communications try to use the application specific knowledge they have to construct more robust anonymous channel for their specific purpose. Mix networks are the natural structure of such channels since the established topologies, the trust judgements, and the pre-existing connections can be used to carry the anonymous channel and secure it.

On the other hand Mix cascades require a lot of cooperation to set up, that is specific to Mix cascade channel, and map with difficulty to any other pre-existing structure that nodes might have established amongst them. It is difficult to imagine how complete collaborative applications could be built to setup cascades.

Antithesis 6. *Mix networks offer the flexibility to handle unforeseen problems and opportunities.*

Mix cascades can be seen technically as a Mix network with an extremely restricted topology, namely a cascade. Systems that support Mix networks can therefore during their operation be turned into cascades [10], if it is proven necessary. On the other hand a cascade based system does not carry the information necessary (the routing information) to be easily converted into any other topology.

Mix networks can also be used to provide hybrid solutions relating to the topology. A solution such as a 'core cascade' with peer-to-peer nodes as the entrance points and the exit points, could for example be implemented. Mix network systems can also be modified more easily to environments, where cascades are not possible, such as anonymising ad-hoc wireless traffic, where messages have to travel across a set of wireless points restricted by the physical layout of the network.

5   Conclusions

In this paper we have discussed the issues that should be taken into account when choosing an anonymous communication system. We have classified existing systems according to the *flexibility of routing* and the *task sharing* dimensions.

The choice between symmetric and asymmetric systems and the appropriate flexibility of routing are dependent on the threat model considered; the requirements of the services that are implemented on top of the anonymous infrastructure, in terms of performance, anonymity and availability; and the incentives for the participants in the system.

In order to provide a good anonymity service, we need to attract a large number of users. Therefore the quality of service and the liability issues should be taken into account. In this respect, asymmetric systems seem to be more appropriate than symmetric systems because the users are not liable for other's actions, they require less resources and the available bandwidth is higher (better quality of service).

Regarding the resistance towards attacks, Mix networks require that the attacker is able to cover more surface of attack, given that the number of entry and exit points is larger. Moreover, Mix cascades are more vulnerable towards Mix failures, insider adversaries or denial of service attacks than Mix networks. Mix cascades require more trust from the user than Mix networks, given that the user cannot choose which nodes he wants to trust, nor he can add his own Mix to the cascade. Symmetric systems are more vulnerable to attacks than asymmetric systems because the security level of the nodes is lower. Contrary to the claims of many P2P designs, we state that the fact of having many nodes in the network does not imply that a strong attacker is not able to control a significant number of these nodes.

Symmetric systems typically offer a much larger number of entry and exit points than asymmetric systems. This is a feature that enhances the availability of the system, specially towards strong adversaries who want to prevent the users from accessing the anonymity service (these symmetric systems must conceal the topology of the network in order to prevent blocking the access to the service). Regarding the flexibility of routing dimension, Mix networks have better availability properties than cascades, because the number of entry and exit points is larger, and it is also more difficult for an adversary to provoke a denial of service attack that shuts down the anonymity service.

As final conclusion, we should say that more research and empirical data are needed in order to find concrete answers, as well as to develop policies or methodologies that can simplify the decision on the type of system we should implement according to the requirements of our application. We hope that this paper will help identifying the important issues that need to be taken into account by the designers of systems for anonymous network communication.

Acknowledgements

This paper summarises a panel discussion chaired by Claudia Díaz at the Privacy Enhancing Technologies Workshop 2004 in Toronto, Canada. It would not have been possible to collect this wide range of arguments without the input from the panelists, namely George Danezis, Christian Grothoff, Andreas Pfitzmann, and Paul Syverson, as well as many engaged contributions from the audience.

References

1. Acquisti, A., Dingledine, R., and Syverson, P.: On the Economics of Anonymity. In: Wright, R. N. (ed.): Financial Cryptography (FC 2003), LNCS 2742, Springer-Verlag, Berlin Heidelberg (2003) 84–102
2. Back, A., Möller, U., Stiglic, A.: Traffic Analysis Attacks and Trade-Offs in Anonymity Providing Systems. In: Moskowitz, I. S. (ed.): Information Hiding (IH 2001), LNCS 2137, Springer-Verlag, Berlin Heidelberg (2001) 245–257
3. Berthold, O., Federrath, H., Köpsell, S.: Web MIXes: A System for Anonymous and Unobservable Internet Access. In: Federrath, H. (ed.): Anonymity 2000, LNCS 2009, Springer-Verlag, Berlin Heidelberg (2001) 115–129

4. Berthold, O., Langos, H.: Dummy Traffic against Long Term Intersection Attacks. In: Dingledine, R., and Syverson, P. (eds.): Privacy Enhancing Technologies (PET 2002), LNCS 2482, Springer-Verlag, Berlin Heidelberg (2003) 110–128

5. Berthold, O., Pfitzmann, A., Standtke, R.: The Disadvantages of Free MIX Routes and How to Overcome Them. In: Federrath, H. (ed.): Anonymity 2000, LNCS 2009, Springer-Verlag, Berlin Heidelberg (2001) 30–45

6. Chaum, D.: Untraceable Electronic Mail, Return Addresses, and Digital Pseudonyms. Communications of the ACM **24** (1981) 84–88

7. Chaum, D.: Security without Identification: Transaction Systems to Make Big Brother Obsolete. Communications of the ACM **28** (1985) 1030–1044

8. Danezis, G.: Mix-Networks with Restricted Routes. In: Dingledine, R. (ed.): Privacy Enhancing Technologies (PET 2003), LNCS 2760, Springer-Verlag, Berlin Heidelberg (2003) 1–17

9. Danezis, G.: Statistical Disclosure Attacks: Traffic Confirmation in Open Environments. Proceedings of Security and Privacy in the Age of Uncertainty (SEC2003), Athens (2003, May) 421–426

10. Danezis, G., Dingledine, R., Mathewson, N.: Mixminion: Design of a Type III Anonymous Remailer Protocol. Proceedings of the IEEE Symposium on Security and Privacy (2003, May)

11. Danezis, G.: The Anonymity of Continuous Time Mixes. Paper presented at the Privacy Enhancing Technologies Workshop, Toronto, Canada (2004, May)

12. Díaz, C., Preneel, B.: Reasoning about the Anonymity Provided by Pool Mixes that Generate Dummy Traffic. Paper presented at the 6th International Workshop on Information Hiding, Toronto, Canada (2004, May)

13. Díaz, C., Sassaman, L., Dewitte, E.: Comparison between Two Practical Mix Designs. Paper to be presented at the 9th European Symposium on Research in Computer Security (ESORICS 2004, Sep 13–15), Sophia Antipolis, France

14. Díaz, C., Seys, S., Claessens, J., Preneel, B.: Towards Measuring Anonymity. In: Dingledine, R., and Syverson, P. (eds.): Privacy Enhancing Technologies (PET 2002), LNCS 2482, Springer-Verlag, Berlin Heidelberg (2003) 54–68

15. Dingledine, R., Freedman, M. J., Hopwood, D., Molnar, D.: A Reputation System to Increase MIX-net Reliability. In: Moskowitz, I. S. (ed.): Information Hiding. Fourth International Workshop, LNCS 2137, Springer-Verlag, Berlin Heidelberg (2001) 126–141

16. Dingledine, R., Mathewson, N., Syverson, P.: Tor: The Second-Generation Onion Router. Proceedings of the 13th USENIX Security Symposium (2004, August)

17. Dingledine, R., Shmatikov, V., Syverson, P.: Synchronous Batching: From Cascades to Free Routes. Paper presented at the Privacy Enhancing Technologies Workshop, Toronto, Canada (2004, May)

18. Dingledine, R., Syverson, P.: Reliable MIX Cascade Networks through Reputation. In: Blaze, M. (ed.): Financial Cryptography (FC 2002), LNCS 2357, Springer-Verlag, Berlin Heidelberg (2002)

19. Douceur, J.: The Sybil Attack, Proceedings of the 1st International Peer To Peer Systems Workshop (IPTPS 2002, March)

20. Farber, D. J., Larson, K. C.: Network Security Via Dynamic Process Renaming. Fourth Data Communications Symposium, Quebec City, Canada (1975, October) 8-13 – 8-18

21. Freedman, M. J., Morris, R., Tarzan: A Peer-to-Peer Anonymizing Network Layer. Proceedings of the 9th ACM Conference on Computer and Communications Security (CCS 2002), Washington, DC (2002, November)

22. Jakobsson, M., Juels, A., Rivest, R. L.: Making Mix Nets Robust for Electronic Voting by Randomized Partial Checking. Proceedings of the 11th USENIX Security Symposium (2002, August)
23. Kesdogan, D., Agrawal, D., Penz, S.: Limits of Anonymity in Open Environments. In: Petitcolas, F. A. P. (ed.): Information Hiding. Fifth International Workshop, LNCS 2578, Springer-Verlag, Berlin Heidelberg (2003)
24. Neff, C. A.: A Verifiable Secret Shuffle and its Application to E-Voting. Proceedings of the 8th ACM Conference on Computer and Communications Security (CCS 2001), ACM Press (2001, November) 116–125
25. Pfitzmann, A.: Diensteintegrierende Kommunikationsnetze mit teil-nehmerüberprüfbarem Datenschutz. Universität Karlsruhe, Fakultät für Informatik, Dissertation, Feb. 1989, IFB 234, Springer-Verlag, Heidelberg (1990)
26. Pfitzmann, A., Köhntopp, M.: Anonymity, Unobservability, and Pseudonymity — A Proposal for Terminology. In: Federrath, H. (ed.): Anonymity 2000, LNCS 2009, Springer-Verlag, Berlin Heidelberg (2001) 1–9
27. Rennhard, M., Plattner, B.: Practical Anonymity for the Masses with MorphMix. Proceedings of Financial Cryptography (FC '04), LNCS 3110, Springer-Verlag, Berlin Heidelberg (2004)
28. Serjantov, A., Danezis, G.: Towards an Information Theoretic Metric for Anonymity. In: Dingledine, R., and Syverson, P. (eds.): Privacy Enhancing Technologies (PET 2002), LNCS 2482, Springer-Verlag, Berlin Heidelberg (2003) 41–53
29. Serjantov, A., Dingledine, R., Syverson, P.: From a Trickle to a Flood: Active Attacks on Several Mix Types. In: Petitcolas, F. A. P. (ed.): Information Hiding. Fifth International Workshop, LNCS 2578, Springer-Verlag, Berlin Heidelberg (2003) 36–52

A Formal Privacy System and Its Application to Location Based Services

Carl A. Gunter[1], Michael J. May[1], and Stuart G. Stubblebine[2]

[1] University of Pennsylvania
[2] Stubblebine Research Labs

Abstract. There are a variety of well-known models for access control developed for purposes like formally modeling the access rights on files, databases, and web resources. However, the existing models provide an inadequate representation of a number of concepts that are important when modeling privacy rights in distributed systems. We present an analog of the access control matrix designed to model such concepts. Our formalism, which we call a *privacy system*, empashizes the management of data and actions that affect the privacy of subjects. We motivate privacy systems, describe them mathematically, and illustrate their value in an architecture based on *Personal Digital Rights Management (PDRM)*, which uses DRM concepts as a foundation for the specification and negotiation of privacy rights. This illustration is carried out throuh a case study of a privacy-respecting system for location based services. Our prototype, which we call *AdLoc*, manages advertising interupts on PDAs based on their location as determined by WiFi sightings in accordance with contracts written in the DRM language XrML.

1 Introduction

Privacy is a pivotal concern for data collected by and stored on computers. A variety of formal models have been proposed to characterize privacy based on cryptographic and information-theoretic critera, providing a rigorous definition of privacy. A closely related class of formal models formulate access control rules, which describe the rights of principals to perform actions and access data. These provide an abstract architectural perspective on privacy that can be supported by cryptographic techniques. Portions of what is needed are present in various formalisms. For instance, access control matrices provide an intuitive and fundamental model of the relationship between prinicipals, objects, and rights. Trust management systems provide a foundation for delegation, credentials, and decentralized operation. Role-based systems provide efficient ways to manage the relationship between principals and rights. However, the existing systems fall short on important issues like direct representation of the idea that data are *about* a specified principal whose privacy is at issue. They also fail to integrate the right range of basic concepts. The aim of this paper is to propose an analog of an

D. Martin and A. Serjantov (Eds.): PET 2004, LNCS 3424, pp. 256–282, 2005.

access control matrix primarily aimed at the representation and management of privacy rights. This entails the problems of representing, negotiating, delegating, and interpreting rights in a distributed context. We make three contributions: a formal system as a conceptual aid for analysis and design, an architectural approach to enable development based on common software platforms, and a case study to illustrate its characteristics and prove its scalability.

Our formal system, which we call a 'privacy system', describes an abstract concept of rights of principals to create and manipulate objects related to a principal which we call the 'subject' of the object. While existing models often include the concept of an owner of an object, the concept of privacy relating to an object is different in subtle respects such as the ways in which rights flow from the wishes and legal rights of the subject even when the subject no longer has access to the object (indeed the subject may never have had access to the object). A privacy system is similar to an access control matrix, but differs in several key respects. It is an abstract representation of a distributed system where enforcement concepts like a reference monitor (which inspired much of the early work on access control matrices) are unrealistic. It only indirectly deals with the rights of principals on objects, focusing instead on the rights of principals on other principals. The primary concept of interest is the ability of one principal to enter with another into an agreement that affects the privacy of a third. The system is formulated to enable the composition of simple kinds of rights into more complex ones and to facilitate standard representation with XML syntax. This enables easy implementation and clean interpretation of the syntax used to describe abstract rights.

Our architecture is based on the representation of privacy systems using *Personal Digital Rights Mangement (PDRM)* as a foundation for negotiations. Digital Rights Management (DRM) refers to the specification techniques and enforcement mechinisms being developed by vendors of intellectual property to protect intellectual property from piracy. PDRM uses the same mechanisms to enable individuals to license their private data. So, if DRM can be used to specify that a piece of music can only be rendered 10 times from a single processor, then PDRM can specify that a private telephone number can only be used once for a specific purpose. DRM requires an extensible foundation to deal with diverse kinds of intellectual property in various sectors (ebooks, digital music, movies, *etc.*). The industries in these sectors have focused significant effort on designing a suitable framework. This framework provides a tantalizing fit with privacy rights, which must also deal with a wide range of sectors (medical, financial, *etc.*). Our prototype approach is based on the use of the XrML digital rights language with negotiated privacy rights derived from specific sectors. For instance, we will show how P3P, a specification technique for privacy on the World Wide Web, can be incorporated in XrML contracts.

Our case study is our most detailed example of how to apply our theory and architecture. In the near future, a collection of devices and protocols will provide location information about the growing number of people who carry them. In particular, triangulation of cell phones, GPS satellite services (especially in vehicles), and information based on DHCP (especially for WiFi), will open a new range of interesting *Location-Based Services (LBS)*. They will also raise a wide range of privacy issues. Emerging architectures for these location-based services will ideally provide substantial individual control. This will entail a new level of user configuration for the location-reporting mobile embedded devices. Software that respects privacy requirements will be a crucial aspect of design for mobile embedded systems for consumers. We built a prototype privacy-respecting system for LBS based on WiFi sightings where the service is interupts on a PDA by advertisers. The idea that an advertiser could, say, pop up an advertisement on your PDA based on your location is, in the current spam-infested computing environment, almost a nightmare. However, consumers might want this for the right advertisers. This makes it an interesting case study in privacy enhancing technology. Essentially our system provides protocols for establishing a collection of rights that enables the target of the advertising to control access and protect her privacy to the degree she chooses, while the service providers will have digital licenses that show their rights to perform interupts on the user device for specified purposes and at permitted times, and that they retain the data only in accordance with rules agreed with the subject.

The paper has six sections. In Section 2 we summarize some of the literature related to formal models of privacy and access control and describe our approach within this context. In Section 3 we analyze the idea of using access control matrices as a model of privacy and discuss shortcomings for this purpose of a well-known example of an access control matrix system. In Section 4 we introduce a formal access control system that focuses on privacy. In Section 5 we carry out our case study for the use of PDRM to develop a privacy-protecting architecture for an LBS system for advertising on PDAs based on WiFi sightings. We then provide a brief conclusion.

2   Related Work

Early approaches for modelling protection systems include those by Graham and Denning [8], Lampson [10], and Harrison, Ruzzo, and Ullman [9]. A recent area of interest is trust management, which concerns checking authorization of unknown users [3] and there are attempts to connect these approaches [11]. DRM is a related area that focuses on managing access to disseminated digital content like music, movies, and text. The Open Digital Rights Language (ODRL) (odrl.net) and the eXtensible rights Markup Language (XrML) (www.xrml.org) typify work in this area. Usage CONtrol (UCON) [12] strives to unify the areas of access control, trust management and digital rights management.

This paper makes a similar attempt to unify these diverse areas, but we focus on the expression of privacy rights as the driving application and take what seems most needed from access control, trust management, and DRM. We aim to create a system that could, for instance, formalize standards for protecting the privacy of individually-identifiable health information [6]. Our formalisms describe mathematically the kind of transformations and access control decisions that must be made in managing such private patient information. Our architecture has elements in common with the Platform for Privacy Preferences [17], an effort to standardize privacy policies on the web. P3P is a browser-centric standard designed to put web site privacy policies in a machine readable format. A P3P Preference Exchange Langauge (APPEL) (`www.w3.org/TR/2002/WD-P3P-preferences-20020415`) enables users to prespecify their perferences so they can be matched against policies used by web sites. This language has received criticisms from many privacy activists [4,5,15] for being unenforceable and vague. Another related effort is the Enterprise Privacy Authorization Language (EPAL) (`www.zurich.ibm.com/security/enterprise-privacy/epal`) which provides an XML-based language for specifying privacy rules. Both P3P and EPAL can be used in connection with our formalism, architecture, and applications. We focused on the use of P3P in the study in this paper. Titkov *et. al.* [16] describe a similar system for privacy-respecting location aware services based on a broker agent architecture, persistent pseudonyms for each user, and P3P. We model the rules for private data transmission and manipulation more formally, introduce the notion of an explicit digital contracts between parties, and introduce the transmission of "fuzzy" location information rather than an all-or-nothing approach.

Our case study focuses on interrupt rights based on Location Based Services. The notion of selling interrupt rights for the purpose of controlling unwanted e-mail and telephone calls is studied in [7]. Fahlman's notion of controlling interrupt rights by forcing micropayments on unrecognized parties is interesting, but requires some significant revamping of the phone and email systems. In our design we hope to create a deployable system by relying in part on the effectiveness of audit and non-technical enforcement mechanims like the National Do Not Call Registry (`www.donotcall.gov`) or the legal protections associated with HIPPA.

There have been a number of legal studies related to interupt rights. Warren and Brandeis [18] famously formulate privacy in terms of the "right to be let alone". Their discussion of the right of a person to prevent unauthorized photographs from public circulation has many interesting parallels with modern discussions of location privacy. More recently, in the 108th Congress, HR71 [2], the "Wireless Privacy Protection Act of 2003," sought to require wireless providers to receive explicit approval from users before location information, transaction informatoion, and other kinds of data could be used. The bill also required that the wireless carriers "establish and maintain reasonable procedures to protect the confidentiality, security, and integrity of the information." With specific regard to wireless messaging, HR122 [1], the "Wireless Telephone Spam Protection Act," also from the 108th Congress, sought to place a ban on unsolicited commercial messages on text or graphic based wireless devices. It is unclear whether either of these bills will ever become law, but the inclination in government towards providing protections for location information and wireless messaging is clear.

The area of location privacy management has begun to develop, but still is lacking consensus, maturity, and theoretical and mathematical analysis.

The geographic location and privacy (geopriv) working group (`www.ietf.org/html.charters/geopriv-charter.html`) of the Internet Engineering Task Force (IETF) (`ietf.org`) has made some suggestions for how location information objects should be made and privacy policies formulated. The Geopriv system is based on XML and focuses on access rules and the creation of a trusted location server. Its goal is to allow people to let others track their location through location (data) objects that they publish while maintaining some user controls. Users define rules both on the location server and embedded in the location object that restrict how the data can be redistributed and retained and how accurate the information released to specific recipients is. Geopriv's goal is a set of languages and protocols that allow users to publish their location information on particular servers, have those servers securely distribute location information to authorized individuals, and maintain control over how others use the geolocation data.

The geopriv model is still evolving and most of its documents are works in progress. Its requirements document (already a standards track document in IETF) describes an architecture for running a location information management system. We borrow much of their architecture, but contribute a formal analysis of how information is distributed and collected, offer a richer model of rights and responsibilities, and suggest a manner to negotiate and compose different privacy policies. The access control/permissions model [13] being developed by geopriv is based on rule sets. We offer a contract-based system that is more powerful and flexible with respect to describing usage rights, object transformation policies, and controlling data retention.

Another location privacy system [14] provides a language for writing geolocation privacy preferences as well as an architecture that supports those rules. The focus is on designing a language that can be modelled mathematically and reasoned about formally, rather than one that is ready for immediate implementation. These assumptions result in a system that is less complex and more general than the Geopriv system described above. The language views location objects as having a lattice ordering determined by accuracy and traceability. This lattice structure is a convincing way of viewing the accuracy of location objects and identity, but stops there. We provide methods to express purpose, retention, usage, creation, and transfer rules. We borrow from this work the idea of object accuracy ordering when modelling the transformations that are done on objects before they are transferred between parties.

3   Background

The concept of an access control matrix is one of the oldest formalisms for describing access rights. The basic idea is to create a matrix indexed by principals $\mathcal{P}$ and objects $\mathcal{O}$. This is a function $R : \mathcal{P} \times \mathcal{O} \rightarrow \Sigma$ where Σ is a space of rights. For instance, we might have $\Sigma = \{r, rw, rwx\}$ for read-only, read/write, and read/write/execute rights. The matrix R provides an elegant abstraction: it describes the boundaries of a principal's ability to act on an object without the details about other constraints on this interaction. That is, it can indicate that principal p can execute object x without describing whether the actions of p will, in fact, execute x. This form of access control matrix is too simple for some purposes. In particular, it does not describe relationships between principals, such as whether one principal created another (if principals are like processes) or gave it access to the system (if principals represent users). It also does not by itself describe the events that cause its entries to change, such as the idea that a principal transfers a right on an object to another principal.

3.1   Graham/Denning Model

An early example of an extended access control matrix model that incorporates some of the key concepts related to events and constraints is the Graham/Denning model [8]. In this model, the access control matrix is a partial function $R : \mathcal{P} \times (\mathcal{P} + \mathcal{O}) \rightarrow \mathsf{pwr}(\Sigma)$ where pwr denotes the powerset operation. The space Σ is defined over a primitive set of access rights Σ_0 augmented with a few additional expressions. If $\sigma \in \Sigma_0$, then $\sigma*$ is a right to transfer σ as well as perform it. Distinguished rights include the idea that a principal is the owner of an object or that one principal has control over another. These rights govern a sequence of allowed events that describe the ability of principals to manipulate the rights on principals and objects. Events may be disallowed if the appropriate rights are not present. The following sequence of events illustrate the Graham/Denning model. We assume an initial principal p that creates other principals, which, in turn can create their own descendants.

1. p **creates** q; q **creates** r; q **creates** x. These events create two principals and an object. $R(p, q)$ and $R(q, r)$ are set to {control} and $R(q, x)$ is set to {owner}.
2. q **grants** $\sigma*$ **to** q **on** x. This creates a transferable right for q on x which is entered into $R(q, x)$. This is allowed because q owns x.
3. q **transfers** σ **to** r **on** x. This transfers the right σ to r for the object x setting the value of $R(r, x)$ to be σ. This is allowed because q has the right $\sigma*$ which allows it to transfer σ.
4. q **creates** s. Now $R(q, s)$ is {control}. Table 1 describes the state of the access control matrix R after this step.

Table 1. Sample Access Control Matrix

	p	q	r	s	x
p		control			
q			control	control	owner, $\sigma*$
r					σ
s					

5. r **transfers** σ **to** s **on** x. This is disallowed because the right of r is not transferable.
6. p **deletes** σ **of** r **on** x. This is disallowed because because p does not own x or control r.
7. p **deletes** r. This is disallowed because p does not control r.
8. p **deletes** q. This removes q from the access control matrix. It is allowed because p controls q.

A model of this kind improves on the basic access control matrix by adding relationships between principals and the effect that this has on the delegation of rights. It provides a useful basis for thinking about the management of access rights and the enforcement of these rights using an reference monitor. This provides a useful model of multi-user time-sharing systems.

3.2   LBS Scenarios

To analyze the suitability of an access control system like access control matrices as a model of privacy let us review it for use in an application space with rich privacy issues. For this paper we have chosen to focus on privacy associated with geo-location and LBS. Let us now turn to a collection of examples that illustrate the challenge. We identify three general classes of principals. First, there are the principals on which geo-location data is collected. Although these will typically be computers the data often gains its relevance because of its association with a human principal. Such prinicpals have interests in the privacy of the information that is collected. Let us refer to such principals as *subjects*. A second class of principals collects information about *sightings*, that is, they obtain information that a subject was at a location at a given time. Let us call these principals *holders* of geo-location data. A third collection of principals exploit location information to provide services. These principals can be called *providers*, but they may also play a role as *subscribers* to the data of the holders. They may provide a service to the subject, the holder, or some other party. Here is a collection of examples of these kinds of parties.

Subjects. Individuals concerned about privacy: Alice, Bob, Claire, Dan, *etc.* The devices that generate their location data: Alice's cell phone, Bob's GSM-equipped car, Claire's laptop making WiFi Internet connections, Dan's active badge, *etc.*

Holders. Principals willing and able to collect location information on entities with tracking capacity through sightings.

- *CellTrek* is a cellular provider that collects sightings using cellular triangulation based on the handsets of its subscribers.
- *Autorealm* is a telematics system for automobiles that tracks automobiles using GPS.
- *Canada On Line (COL)* is an ISP that tracks the locations of Internet connections made by its users based on information such as WiFi sightings.
- *Spartan Chemicals* is a complex of chemical plants where user movements are tracked in their facilities through the use of RFID tags.

Subscribers Providers of location based services based on collections of sighting information.

- *Friendsintown.com* correlates sightings using a kind of buddy system. These correlations are used to inform buddies if they are in the general vicinity of one another to facilitate a friendly get-together. For instance, Alice and Claire may be old college friends who travel frequently on business and like to get together for dinner if they are in the same city. Bob and Dan are computer science researchers working on similar problems and like to get together ahead of meetings if they are at the meeting site early.
- *Market Models* supplements geo-location information with demographic information from subscribers to produce statistical GIS information. For example, Market Models might have a profile of the incomes of individuals in Penn Station at noon. Market Models may have a model of how far from home a driver is when he passes a given restaurant on an interstate highway.
- *What's Here!* provides information to a PDA about the place where the PDA is currently located. What's Here provides a continuously updated map with a 'You Are Here' pointer on it. What's Here also uses context to determine likely interests of the holder. For instance, when a tracked subject enters the Penn Computer Science building, it provides a listing of the public seminars being held that day.
- *Travel Archive* keeps long-term records of travel for archival purposes such as long-term data mining or entertainment. For instance, SalesRUs uses travel archive to provide general information about its travel trends over time such as the average length and time of trips by its employees. Claire uses Travel Archive to keep long-term records of her travels so she can review family trips over the years (Did we visit Mother for Christmas in the year when Father died? Where was I when the Berlin Wall fell?).

3.3   Privacy in LBS

Let us now consider the privacy issues entailed in our complex of subjects, holders, and subscribers. It must first be noted that the distinctions are not at all rigid. For instance, a subject could hold location information about himself, holders may provide services themselves or subscribe to other holders, and subscribers like Travel Archive are clearly holders in their own right. However, a dominating feature of the scenarios is the fact that location information is typically data *about* a subject and this subject may well consider its use to affect her privacy. Arrangements to manage this privacy may take a variety of forms.

Several of basic LBS scenarios involve operations similar to the ones in the Graham/Denning model. For instance a principal may set a right on a location object so that another principal can read it. This looks like a typical operation on a time-share OS where an owner sets a permission on a file so another user can read it. However, it is an operation only indirectly involved in a typical scenarios for privacy management in these LBS systems. A more fundamental issue is the form and meaning of the contract between principals p and q that says q has the right to carry out sightings of p and report this data to a third principal r.

We classify the primary operations and relations of a privacy system as follows:

Transfer. What is the right of a principal p to transfer an object x to a principal q where x is about a subject r? This depends on rights of both p and q relative to r and features of x. For example, Autorealm may have the right to obtain very accurate information about the position and direction of Bob, but when this information is reported, with Bob's permission, to friendsintown.com, it should be reported with only metro-area accuracy. COL is only permitted to retain and transfer location information about Alice within a few minutes of its creation, but, once this information has been transfered to Travel Archive, it is retained as long as Alice continues her subscription with Travel Archive and can be transfered to Alice at any time during that subscription. Spartan Chemicals may be concerned about a security breach and transfers location information about Dan's active badge to the FBI, which does not offer Dan a subscription to see this data. Market Models is unable to obtain Dan's information from Spartan Chemicals, but Dan was happy to provide similar information through CellTrek in exchange for a reduction in his cellular bill. However, CellTrek cannot reveal his name in the location information it transfers to Market Models.

Action. What is the right of a principal p to carry out an action that affects the privacy of a principal q? This depends on the policy of p. For instance, friendsintown.com has a right to send email to Alice and Claire telling them someone on their buddy list is in town. Alice and Claire gave friendsintown.com this right. Spartan Chemicals has a right to question Bob about his reasons for being in a given location reported by his active badge. His employment contract gave this right to them.

Creation. Which principals p are allowed to create objects x whose subject is q? The right to create objects may be held by the subject only. For instance, Bob's telematic auto system may store location information in Bob's car, but Bob may choose to transfer this to Autorealm for various purposes. In other cases, the holder creates the object and it may not be directly available to the subject, as in the case of Spartan Chemicals. The right to create objects may exist for only a limited period of time. For instance, Claire might offer this to COL for a trial period of one month in order to explore the value of the service offered by What's Here!

Right Establishment. How are rights established for a principal p? For instance, Spartan Chemical may have an understanding with Dan that his location information may be passed to law enforcement officials as part of an ongoing investigation at the plant. The right of Spartan Chemicals to set a right for the FBI may derive from the rights they established with Dan. The right of Market Models to convey information derived from objects of Claire may derive from their rights as negotiated with COL, which, in turn, are related to the rights they established with Claire.

3.4   Limitations of Graham/Denning

Let us now consider some of the limitations of the Graham/Denning model with respect to the kinds of needs one infers from the requirements for privacy in LBS systems. Applying the model encounters the following limitations:

1. There is no explicit representation of the idea that an object is private data about a given subject.
2. There is only a limited analysis of the rights that exist between principals (as opposed to the rights between principals and objects).
3. There is no explicit representation of the way in which the objects are transfered (distributed) between the principals.
4. The concept of delegation is too limited.
5. There is no explicit representation for the idea that information transfers and actions are collaborations between principals.
6. There is no concept of the transfer of an object after a privacy-enforcing transformation.

Some of these can be addressed by an encoding, while others require an extension. Our system, which is described in the next section, deals with these limitations by focusing on a general view of abstract rights between subjects and the four operations and relations described above.

4   Privacy Systems

Assume we are given the following three spaces: *objects* $x, y, z \in \mathcal{O}$, *principals* $p, q, r \in \mathcal{P}$, and *actions* $a, b, c \in \mathcal{A}$. Let us model time as non-negative real numbers $t \in \Re$. Each object is assumed to have an associated *subject* $\mathsf{subj}(x) \in \mathcal{P}$, and an associated *creation time* $\mathsf{ct}(x) \in \Re$. We also assume that there is a distinguished *null object* $\perp_{\mathcal{O}} \in \mathcal{O}$ and a distinguished *null principal* $\perp_{\mathcal{P}} \in \mathcal{P}$ where $\mathsf{subj}(\perp_{\mathcal{O}}) = \perp_{\mathcal{P}}$ and $\mathsf{ct}(\perp_{\mathcal{O}}) = 0$.

Definition 1. *A privacy system is a tuple*

$$\langle \Sigma, T, U, V, W \rangle$$

where

- Σ *is a set of rights and* $\perp_{\Sigma} \in \Sigma$ *is a distinguished null right,*
- $T : \Sigma \times \Sigma \times \mathcal{O} \times \Re \to \mathcal{O}$ *is a publish/subscribe rights function,*
- $U \subseteq \Sigma \times \mathcal{A} \times \Re$ *is an action rights relation, and*
- $V \subseteq \Sigma \times \mathcal{O} \times \Re$ *is a creation rights relation.*
- $W \subseteq \Sigma \times \Sigma \times \Sigma \times \mathcal{P} \times \Re$ *is a right establishment relation.*   □

The intuitive explanation of the functions and relations in a privacy system $\langle \Sigma, T, U, V, W \rangle$ is as follows:

- $T(\sigma, \sigma', x, t)$ is a transformation of the object x that is determined by the policy σ of its publisher, the policy σ' of its subscriber, and the time t at which the subscriber receives the object. In some cases the value of the function will be a modified version of x that removes pre-specified types of sensitive information. If the policies of the publishing and subscribing parties accomodate full transfer, then the object x will be the value of this function, but in cases where the transfer is entirely disallowed, the value may be $\perp_{\mathcal{O}}$.
- $U(\sigma, a, t)$ indicates whether the right σ allows the action a at the time t. An action is usually based on a particular principal or object but the effect of an action is not described by the system.
- $V(\sigma, x, t)$ indicates whether σ allows the object x to be created at time t. The source of the object x is not described by the system. Typically it is obtained from an observation made by the creator.
- $W(\sigma_1, \sigma_2, \sigma_3, p, t)$ indicates whether a principal with the right σ_1 can, at time t, endow the right σ_2 to a principal with right σ_3 with respect to the objects of subject p. This will typically depend on the rights that the party endowing the rights has on the objects of p.

An informal example may be helpful before proceeding with further formalisms. Suppose Σ is a set of rights that indicate the right of a physician to collect and share the medical records of a patient. The relation W will indicate that a patient can endow upon a physician the right to collect and share data about the patient. The relation V will describe the right of a physician to create objects with the patient as their subject, by running tests for instance. The relation U will indicate that a physician may act in a certain way upon the medical information of a patient, by enacting a treatment, for instance. The effect of the treatment and whether the treatment is justified by the patient data are viewed as external to the privacy system.[1] The function T will indicate the right of the physician to share information with others. For instance, the physician may be able to share information about the patient with his partners without changing the object. The physician may be able to supply the object for research if it is transformed to protect the privacy of the patient. This may be done by changing the subject of the object to the null subject or by some more sophisticated technique.

The functions and relations in a privacy system are very general and cover quite a range of possibilities. For example, it is straight-forward to model the idea that a patient has a right that allows her to revoke the right of the doctor to create or distribute objects about her after a given time. To understand how we model actions of this kind, we need to introduce the concept of an event sequence.

---

[1] The physician may have a right to prescribe a drug, but choose not to do this because of its potential side effects. The basis for this decision is not modeled by the system. On the other hand, the system may model the idea that the physician does not have a right to impound the automobile of the patient, regardless of the results of his tests. Another party, such as a bank, may have rights to this action.

The concepts of publishing, subscribing, creating, establishing policies, and acting upon objects are modeled using a labeled transition relation over an assignment of objects and policies to principals. A *state* is a pair $S = \langle H, R \rangle$ consisting of a *holder state* $H : \mathcal{P} \to \mathsf{pwr}(\mathcal{O})$ and a rights matrix $R : \mathcal{P} \times \mathcal{P} \to \Sigma$. For each principal p, the set $H(p)$ represents the objects that p has obtained by direct observation or by subscription. The right $R(p, q)$ is the right of p with respect to the privacy of q. Four kinds of events are related to changes in this state.

1. A *set policy event* is a tuple of the form

$$p \textbf{ sets } \sigma \textbf{ on } q \textbf{ for } r \textbf{ at } t$$

   where p, q, r are principals, σ is a policy, and t is a time.
2. A *creation event* is a tuple of the form

$$p \textbf{ creates } x \textbf{ at } t$$

   where p is a principal, x is an object, and t is a time.
3. A *publish/subscribe* event is a tuple of the form

$$p \textbf{ gets } x \textbf{ from } q \textbf{ at } t$$

   where p is a principal called the *publisher*, x is an object, q is a principal called the *subscriber*, and t is a time.
4. An *action event* is a tuple of the form

$$p \textbf{ does } a \textbf{ on } q \textbf{ at } t$$

   where p is a principal, a is an action, q is a principal and t is a time.

We denote events and the space of events with the notation $e, f \in \mathcal{E}$. In each of the cases for an event e the value t in the tuple is called the *time of e*.

Definition 2. *Let R be a rights matrix over privacy system $\langle \Sigma, T, U, V, W \rangle$. Suppose e is an event and $S = \langle H, R \rangle$ and $S' = \langle R', H' \rangle$ are states. Then we write $S \xrightarrow{e} S'$ if one of the following four cases holds*

1. *$e = p$ setsσ on q for$r$ at$t$. The matrix R' is the same as R except $R'(q, r) = \sigma$. If $p \neq r$ then we must have*

$$W(R(p, r), \sigma, R(q, r), r, t).$$

   We say that p, q are the actors in the event and r is its subject.
2. *$e = p$ creates$x$ at$t$. The function H' is the same as H on principals other than p, but $H'(p) = H(p) \cup \{x\}$. In this case $\mathsf{ct}(x) = t$. It must be the case that*

$$V(R(p, q), x, t)$$

   where $q = \mathsf{subj}(x)$. We say that p is the actor in the event and q is its subject.

3. $e = p$ does a on q at t. We must have

$$U(R(p,q), a, t).$$

We say that p is the actor in the event and q is its subject.

4. $e = p$ gets$x$ from q at t. We must have $x \in H(p)$. The function H' is the same as H on principals other than q, but $H'(q) = H(q) \cup \{y\}$ where

$$y = T(R(p, \mathsf{subj}(x)), R(q, \mathsf{subj}(x)), x, t).$$

We say that p, q are the actors in the event and $\mathsf{subj}(x)$ is its subject.

A sequence of the form

$$S_0 \xrightarrow{e_1} S_1 \xrightarrow{e_2} \cdots \xrightarrow{e_n} S_n$$

is a valid event sequence if each of the indicated relations holds and, for each $i < n$, the time of e_i is strictly less than that of e_{i+1}. In general we will assume that such sequences begin with a value $\perp_{\mathsf{state}}$ representing a state in which $R(p,q) = \perp_{\Sigma}$ and $H(p) = \{\perp_{\mathcal{O}}\}$ for each p, q.   □

To save the need for writing subscripts, we generally drop the subscripts on $\perp_{\mathcal{O}}, \perp_{\mathcal{P}}$, and so on when this does not cause confusion.

The intuition behind actors and subjects is that the actors are the parties to a transaction that concerns private information about the subject of the transaction. The actors initiate events through joint agreement subject to the privacy rules they have with respect to the subject of the event.

Note the condition in the set policy event that allows the event p sets σ on q for p at t for any values of p, σ, q, t. This means that p is always able to negotiate rights on his data with other parties. This provides a somewhat liberal view of private information compared to current practice. By dropping this condition we generalize the system to accomodate the idea that parties must obtain rights to the objects of a subject by other means, as defined by W. This makes the examples below more difficult to describe (since they must describe this mechanism), so, for simplicity, we have restricted our attention to the basic case in which rights originate only from the subjects and can be changed by them at any time. The relation W determines all of the potential propogation of these rights and the operator T determines all ways in which data is transfered based on these rights. This raises issues with at least one of the examples in the previous section. For instance, a holder may not wish to change its right concerning transfering objects to their subject, as was the case with Dan and the FBI. However, if Dan and the FBI mutually agree, the data can be transfered to Dan regardless of any rights that may pertain to Spartan Chemicals.

In general we will be concerned about the question of whether a principal p can obtain (transformations of) objects with subject q *under the assumption* that p cannot create these objects directly but must obtain them by subscribing to a principal that is able to obtain them directly or by another subscription.

Similarly, we will want to ask whether a principal p can perform an action a with respect to subject q. This will be tantamount to asking whether this object can be obtained by p (possibly under the assumption that it cannot be created directly by p) and whether the action is allowed by the action rights of p at the time p wishes to perform the action.

Example 1. (Direct Permissions) Let $\mathcal{P}, \mathcal{A}, \mathcal{O}$ be any sets. The privacy system of *Direct Permissions (DP)* takes $\Sigma = \{\mathsf{dir}, \bot\}$. The value $\bot$ represents no permissions and the value dir represents direct permission. The operator and relations are defined as follows.

1. Define $T(\sigma, \mathsf{dir}, x, t) = x$. For all other arguments the value of T is $\bot$. That is, an object can be passed from one party to another only if the recipient has direct permission.
2. $U(\sigma, a, t)$ iff $\sigma = \mathsf{dir}$. That is, permission to perform action a is given to a principal only if it has direct permission from the subject of the action.
3. $V(\sigma, x, t)$ iff $\sigma = \mathsf{dir}$. That is, objects can only be created by principals with direct permission
4. $W = \emptyset$. That is, subjects must directly grant rights over their objects and actions. $\Box$

Proposition 1. *In a DP privacy system only principals with direct permission from p can create or obtain objects of p or perform an action a on p.* $\Box$

To illustrate direct permissions, let $\mathcal{P} = \{p_1, p_2, q_1, q_2\}$ consist of a pair of homes p_1, p_2 and offices q_1, q_2. Let $\mathcal{O}$ consist of a collection of telephone numbers, and let $\mathcal{A} = \{a\}$ represent the act of an office calling a home using the home telephone number object. Here is an example of an allowed sequence of events: (1) p_1 and p_2 set their own rights to dir; (2) p_1 and p_2 create telephone objects x_1 and x_2 respectively; (3) p_1 sets the right of q_1 to its objects and actions to dir; (4) p_1 and p_2 transfer their telephone objects to q_1 and q_2 respectively; (5) q_1 telephones p_1. In the second step p_1 and p_2 establish rights to create and call themselves using their telephone objects so $R(p_1, p_1) = R(p_2, p_2) = \mathsf{dir}$. In the fourth step q_1 comes to have $H(q_1) = \{x_1\}$, that is, the telephone object of p_1 is held by q_1. However, q_2 does not have permission to hold the telephone number of p_2 so the transfer of this number to q_2 only causes q_2 to obtain the null object $H(q_2) = \{\bot\}$. A nuance is worth noting: nothing in the privacy system says that q_1 needs the telephone object x_1 in order to call p_1. This is a domain-specific criterion.

Example 2. (Direct Time-Limited Permissions) Let $\mathcal{P}, \mathcal{A}, \mathcal{O}$ be any sets. The privacy system of *Direct Time-Limited Permissions (DTLP)* takes $\Sigma = \{\bot\} + (\{\mathsf{dir}\} \times \Re)$. The value $\bot$ represents no permissions and the value (dir, t) represents direct permission until time t. The operator and relations are defined as follows. We write $\mathsf{dir}(t)$ for (dir, t).

1. Define $T(\sigma, \mathsf{dir}(t'), x, t) = x$ provided $t' \geq t$. For all other arguments the value of T is $\bot$.
2. $U(\sigma, a, t)$ iff $\sigma = \mathsf{dir}(t')$ where $t' \geq t$.
3. $V(\sigma, x, t)$ iff $\sigma = \mathsf{dir}(t')$ where $t' \geq t$.
4. $W = \emptyset$. $\square$

Example 3. (Sharing With Partners) Let $\mathcal{P}, \mathcal{A}, \mathcal{O}$ be any sets and let $\mathsf{partner} \subseteq \mathcal{P} \times \mathcal{P}$ be a symmetric relation between principals. The privacy system of *Sharing With Partners (SWP)* takes

$$\Sigma = \{\bot\} + (\mathsf{dir} \times \mathcal{P}) + (\mathsf{indir} \times \mathsf{pwr}(\mathcal{P})).$$

It is defined in terms of the $\mathsf{partner}$ relation and a restricted set of actions $\mathcal{A}_{\mathsf{indir}} \subseteq \mathcal{A}$. The value (dir, p) represents direct permission to p from the subject and the value (indir, L) represents indirect permission from principals in L. The operator and relations for the privacy system are defined as follows. We write $\mathsf{dir}(p)$ and $\mathsf{indir}(L)$ rather than (dir, p) and (indir, L) repectively.

1. Define $T(\sigma, \mathsf{dir}(p), x, t) = x$ and, if $p \in L$, define $T(\mathsf{dir}(p), \mathsf{indir}(L), x, t) = x$. For all other arguments, the value of T is $\bot$. That is, an object can be passed from one party to another if the the recipient has a permission of 1 or has been given a permission by a partner.
2. $U(\mathsf{dir}(p), a, t)$ holds for any p, a, t and $U(\mathsf{indir}(L), a, t)$ holds if L is non-empty and $a \in \mathcal{A}_{\mathsf{indir}}$. That is, permission to perform action a is given if the permission is direct or a is a restricted action and the permission is indirect.
3. $V(\sigma, x, t)$ iff $\sigma = \mathsf{dir}(p)$ for some p. That is, objects can only be created when the permission is direct.
4. $W(\mathsf{dir}(p), \mathsf{indir}(\{q\}), \sigma, r, t)$ holds if $\mathsf{partner}(p, q)$. If $L' = L \cup \{p\}$ and $\mathsf{partner}(p, q)$, then

$$W(\mathsf{dir}(p), \mathsf{indir}(L'), \mathsf{indir}(L), q, t).$$

That is, parties with a direct permission can set an indirect permission for their partners. $\square$

To illustrate the SWP, consider financial institutions such as credit card companies that collect records on their customers and releases geneareal information and addresses to partner companies with the permission of customers. The customer has also given permission for such institutions to empower its partners with the ability to approach her by direct mail with product and service offerings. In an example series of events, a subject p provides a direct right $\mathsf{dir}(q)$ to an institution q who collects objects of p. Based on these objects, q decides to delegate a right concerning p to a partner r who receives objects x of p that lead it to send direct mail advertising to r. A *dis*-allowed sequence might begin with p giving a direct right to q and q attempting to provide an indirect right to one of its (non-partner) competitors. Another disallowed sequence would entail a principal with an indirect right attempting to confer this right on another principal.

Proposition 2. *In an SWP privacy system, only a principals with direct permission from a principal p can perform an action a that is not in $\mathcal{A}_{indir}$.*   □

5   LBS Case Study

The AdLoc location privacy and interruption rights management system mediates the rights of others to interrupt users with advertisements or coupons based on their location.

The system is comprised of a moblie client application, Geographical Location Service (GLS), Geographic Information service (GIS), and an advertising service application. We now describe the system and give an example.

5.1   PDA Application

The AdLoc test bed uses a Compaq iPaq running Microsoft PocketPC OS. All of the code for the program is written in Microsoft's Visual Studio .NET C# compiled for use on the Compact Framework. We used .NET for the prototype system because of its easy to use interface for XML Web Services. For the connection to the outside, a PCMCIA 802.11 wireless card is used. Due to battery limitations we chose to push location data only at certain intervals.

We chose 802.11 for location tracking since most wireless deivces are not yet GPS enabled. However, our architecture fully supports the devices devices obtaining their location from GPS.

5.2   GLS

The Geographic Location Service (GLS) is an XML Web Service that sits on the default gateway for the wireless network. It is coded in Microsoft .NET C# and its interface is XML. Its relative URL is "/GLS/", a location that could become a well known location for all GLS service instances. The requests that the web service accepts have no inbound arguments. Instead it responds to queries in a uniform manner. Its interface and behavior are described below.

- public string GetLoc() -
  GetLoc() returns the GLS's location in a human readable string. Our implemenation returns the city although one might return street address.
- public string GetGIS() -
  GetGIS() sends back IP addresses of Geographic Information Services (GIS) that can manage and distribute location information. Although most users will already have an existing relationship with one or more GIS, but the GLS provides one for those who don't.

5.3   GIS

The Geographic Information Service (GIS) is another Microsoft .NET C# Web Service entity which sits on an always available server. The code has two web service interfaces, one for clients/users and another for location service providers. It acts as the buffer between the two parties, enforcing rights and managing location data contract fulfillment. The GIS maintains lists of active location generating users as well as approved location service providers, so it acts as a central point of contact for many different classes of users.

Even though a particular GIS may have data from users in far flung locations, it may be useful to have certain GISes focus on particular geographic or logical areas. In that situation, a location service provider may discover a targeted audience by just focussing its attention on a particular GIS's user list. For example, a particular airport may maintain a GIS for all travellers waiting inside of it. In that case, an airline wishing to send flight information to waiting passengers might query the local GIS to discover which of its customers are nearby. In this particular case, it would be logical for the GLS on the airport's wireless network to provide the IP address of the airport's GIS as described above.

Since the GIS manages private information, all interactions with it require authentication and all private data is sent over encrypted channels. The facilities of .NET's Web Services tools are used to extensively in managing the X.509 certificates, encryption, and digital signatures required for the secure operation of the GIS. Specifically, all users sign their location object submissions and encrypt them using public key cryptography. Similarly, location service providers identify themselves with X.509 certificates and encrypt their communications with the server with public key cryptography.

Since the GIS manages private user data, it must be careful about who it allows to view its user list. Since GIS presence itself may indicate particular geographic proximity and may reveal information about user habits, only trusted service providers may interact with it. In order for a service provider to gain access to the server it must submit a digitally signed version of its privacy policy. The policy format is described below. If the submitted policy is in accordance with the minimum privacy standards for the GIS, the service provider is allowed access to the user list. This privacy policy is in addition to the digital contract checking that must be done before actions can be done by the service provider.

As part of its role as the buffer between users and service providers, the GIS acts as the facilitator of interrupts on the users. When a service provider has identified a user that it has an interrupt right on, it may send an interrupt message to the GIS to be delivered to the user device. When the user device connects to send new location objects to the GIS, it also accepts new approved strings to be displayed to the user. In our system, the PDA application contains a function to display a notification window on the PDA when new messages are received. When the user clicks on the window the new message(s) are displayed. The GIS is used as a buffer to reduce the potential problem of wireless spam. The PDA initiates all connections with the GIS and has an agreement with the GIS to manage communication rights. With just a single point of contact for all messages, users will have an easy time preventing unwanted messages from flooding them.

5.4   Policy Language

We use a policy language that is a blend of the digital rights language XrML and the World Wide Web Consortium's (W3C) Platform for Privacy Preferences (P3P)[17] notions. XrML is an expressive and easily extensible language for electronic contracts about digital media. P3P is a language with a comprehensive set of privacy rules, regulations, and enforcement options. Merging them together we achieve a language for contracts that can express rights and obligations about privacy requirements. The exact form of the digital contracts is described below.

The P3P language has constructs that express the privacy rights and obligations, similar to the requirements defined above in the formal semantics for our privacy system. The terms that we focus on in the development of our location data subscription system are as follows:

– Purpose - gives terms describing what kind of purposes the collected data can be used for. By declaring the purposes that the data may be used for, users maintain control over how their data is used by both the data collector and anyone who may acquire the data in the future.
– Retention - gives terms for relating how long the recipient may hold the data. The terms are not absolute terms, only relative terms: No-Retention, Stated-Purpose, Legal-Requirement, Business-Practices, Indefinitely
  With respect to the above defined formalisms, the Retention term in P3P models rules for data retention. Different parties in the system may have different rights of retention of the data, so data may pass from a party who has limited retention rights to one who has longer term rights. The particular limits of the retention rights for a particular party is defined by its contract with the user, not necessarily by the party from whom the data were obtained.
– Recipient - lists the parties who the location data can be shared with. The P3P specification has the following general categories to describe recipients: Ours, Delivery, Same, Other-Recipient, Unrelated, Public.
  With the exception of "Ours", all the categories include parties that have the right to autonomously use the data passed to them in unspecified ways. That looseness has been brought up in critiques of P3P, so when designing and implementing a real world privacy system more specific and well defined terms must be defined.

XrML is a digital rights language created to enforce copyrights and usage rights over proprietary digital media. It allows the creation of machine readable contracts that define specific rights to use and transfer media. We define some special use terms and elements for inclusion in the XrML contracts. Our structures identify contractual parties, digital objects, and rights that may be exercised over them. Contracts in the PDRM privacy system contain the following essential parts:

- Identity of the mobile device being tracked
- The user/subject of the location data
- The party receiving rights on the location data
- Validity period of the contract
- P3P privacy policy
- List of acceptable actions
- Digital signature of the user/subject

Since the contract is only signed by the user/subject, it can be viewed as a release by the user. Thus the contracts enforce the notion that users own location objects and maintain control over who can see them and how the data can be used. Interestingly, P3P was designed with the opposite notion - that companies own the data that they collect and make (non-binding and unenforceable) promises to users about how they plan on using them.

The location system we implemented focuses on interrupt rights [7] based on location information. In particular we describe in contract form the right for a service or company to send advertisements or coupons to a mobile user. We define only a limited set of actions for example purposes, but the language could be made as large as desired.

5.5   Advertising Example

We now describe how all the aforementioned pieces interact to provide a location based advertising/coupon service.

When Alice's PDA loads up the AdLoc software, it checks its adapter list to discover the default gateway. It then queries the gateway at the well known URL for a GLS service. The GLS service responds with its location. The PDA can also query for a listing of nearby or associated GISes.

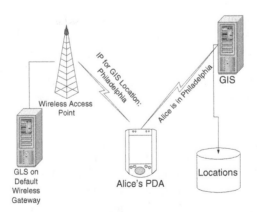

Fig. 1. Registering with the GIS

The PDA creates a location object it sends to the GIS. This action is equivalent to a create $(V(\sigma, x, t))$ action as described above. The GIS allows users to create objects about themselves, so the σ policy here is implicit.

The GIS retains each of Alice's location objects until a fresher one comes. The AdLoc software on her PDA sends out location objects every few minutes, each new object effectively erasing its predecessors. The GIS erases all location data older than 30 minutes. In summary, its σ can be written abstractly as:

```
<Retain>
    <TimeLimit>
        <M>30</M>
    </TimeLimit>
    <History-Level>1</History-Level>
</Retain>
```

A merchant M-Mart contacts the GIS to discover what PDA users are available. When it queries the GIS, it provides a public key certificate and digitally request. Included in the request is a privacy policy. The GIS checks M-Mart's policy against its default policy to decide to accept or reject the query. If it is accepted, M-Mart's certificate and signed privacy policy are stored in a local database for reference. The GIS sends back a full list of users available, but without their location data, only a pointer to how to contact them by email. At that point M-Mart's σ would look like this:

```
<Access-Level>
    <External-Contact-Info/>
</Access-Level>
```

The transfer of the objects with names and locations removed is a T transformation based on the above definitions.

M-Mart can then contact Alice and ask her for a signed digital contract allowing her to be contacted by PDA to receive coupons. M-Mart then presents that contract to the GIS and asks for more information about Alice's location. After receiving and verifying Alice's signed contract, M-Mart's σ for Alice would look like this:

```
<Access-Level>
    <Name/>
    <Location/>
    <External-Contact-Info/>
</Access-Level>
<Rights>
    <SendCoupon>
</Rights>
```

With the new σ, the GIS will send more specific information about Alice's objects whenever contacted next. Additionally, M-Mart can send digital coupons to Alice through the GIS or its AdLoc messaging proxy whenever Alice is available.

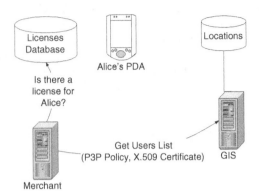

Fig. 2. Merchant gathering information from GIS

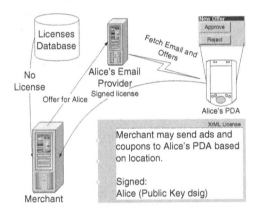

Fig. 3. Merchant acquiring license for contact

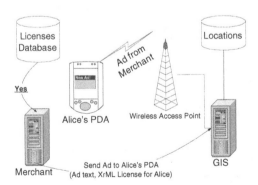

Fig. 4. Merchant sending an ad

6   Conclusions

We have described a formalism called a 'privacy system' that adapts access control matrices to the context of privacy. We have developed an architecture based on DRM that can carry out the negotiations to establish the rights in a privacy system. We have shown how 'Personal DRM' can be used to design a privacy-respecting system for LBS on WiFi sightings, and we have implemented this system for PDAs.

Acknowledgements

This work was supported by NSF grants CCR02-08996 and EIA00-88028, ONR grant N000014-02-1-0715, and ARO grant DAAD-19-01-1-0473 and a gift from Microsoft University Relations.

References

1. HR 122. Wireless telephone spam protection act.
2. HR 71. The wireless privacy protection act.
3. Matt Blaze, J. Feigenbaum, and J. Lacy. Decentralized trust management. In *Proceedings on IEEE Symposium on Security and Privacy*, 1996.
4. Electronic Privacy Information Center and Junkbusters. Pretty poor privacy: An assessment of P3P and internet privacy. 2000. www.epic.org/reports/prettypoorprivacy.html.
5. Roger Clarke. Platform for Privacy Preferences: A critique. 1998. www.anu.edu.au/people/Roger.Clarke/DV/P3PCrit.html.
6. US Dept of Health and Human Services. Standards for privacy of individually identiable health information. 2002. www.hhs.gov/ocr/hipaa/nalreg.html.
7. Scott E. Fahlman. Selling interrupt rights: a way to control unwanted e-mail and telephone calls. *IBM Systems Journal*, 41(4):759–766, 2002.
8. G. S. Graham and P. J. Denning. Protection: Principles and Practices. In *Proceedings of the AFIPS Spring Joint Computer Conference*, pages 417–429, 1972.
9. M.H. Harrison, W.L. Ruzzo, and J.D. Ullman. Protection in operating systems. *Communications of the ACM*, 19(8):461–471, 1976.
10. B. W. Lampson. Protection. In *5th Princeton Symposium on Information Science and Systems*, 1971. Reprinted in ACM Operating Systems Review 8(1):18-24, 1974.
11. Ninghui Li, John C. Mitchell, and William H. Winsborough. Design of a role-based trust management framework. In *Proc. IEEE Symposium on Security and Privacy, Oakland*, May 2002.
12. Jaehong Park and Ravi Sandhu. Towards usage control models: beyond traditional access control. In *Proceedings of the seventh ACM symposium on Access control models and technologies*, pages 57–64. ACM Press, 2002.
13. H. Schulzrinne, J. Morris, H. Tschofenig, J. Cuellar, and J. Polk. Policy rules for disclosure and modification of geographic information - draft-ietf-geopriv-policy-00.txt. Work in progress, 2003.

14. Einar Snekkenes. Concepts for personal location privacy policies. In *Proceedings of the 3rd ACM conference on Electronic Commerce*, pages 48–57. ACM Press, 2001.
15. Robert Thibadeau.   A critique of P3P: Privacy on the Web.   2000. `dollar.ecom.cmu.edu/p3pcritique/`.
16. Leonid Titkov, Stephan Poslad, and Juan Jim Tan. Enforcing privacy via brokering within nomadic environment. In *AT2AI-4*, 2004.
17. W3C. The Platform for Privacy Preferences 1.0 (P3P1.0). 2001. `www.w3c.org/P3P`.
18. Samuel D. Warren and Louis D. Brandeis. The right to privacy. IV(5), December 1890.

A   Example

This is an example license in which The Mobile Ad Company is given the right to send John Doe any ad it wishes to his cell phone (number 215-555-5050) so long as it keeps to the included privacy policy.

```xml
<?xml version="1.0" encoding="utf-8" ?>
<core:licenseGroup
     xmlns:core="http://www.xrml.org/schema/2001/11/xrml2core"
     xmlns:cx="http://www.xrml.org/schema/2001/11/xrml2cx"
     xmlns:dsig="http://www.w3.org/2000/09/xmldsig#"
     xmlns:sx="http://www.xrml.org/schema/2001/11/xrml2sx"
     xmlns:xsi="http://www.w3.org/2001/XMLSchema-instance"
     xmlns:priv="http://www.pdrm.org/XrMLPrivacy"
     xmlns:p3p="http://www.w3.org/2002/01/P3Pv1"
     xmlns:xs="http://www.w3.org/2001/XMLSchema"
     xsi:schemaLocation=
     "http://www.xrml.org/schema/2001/11/xrml2cx ../schemas/xrml2cx.xsd">

   <core:license
       licenseId="http://www.pdrm.org/examples/2003/SendAnyAd">
     <core:inventory>
        <!-- Device with ad -->
        <priv:mobile licensePartId="mobiledevice">
        <priv:locator>
          <priv:id>2155555050@MobileISP.com</priv:id>
        </priv:locator>
        </priv:mobile>
     </core:inventory>

     <core:grantGroup>
        <!--The company that is tracking us' specific key.-->
        <core:keyHolder>
          <core:info>
            <dsig:KeyValue>
                <dsig:RSAKeyValue>
                    <dsig:Modulus>...</dsig:Modulus>
                    <dsig:Exponent>...</dsig:Exponent>
                </dsig:RSAKeyValue>
```

```
        </dsig:KeyValue>
      </core:info>
  </core:keyHolder>
  <sx:x509SubjectName>CN=The Mobile Ad Company</sx:x509SubjectName>

  <!-- The person allowing the company to track him/her-->
  <core:issuer>
    <sx:commonName>John Doe</sx:commonName>
  </core:issuer>

  <!--The period for which the company may track the user. -->
  <core:validityInterval licensePartId="trackingPeriod">
    <core:notBefore>2004-05-20T19:28:00</notBefore>
    <core:notAfter>2004-07-29T19:28:00</notAfter>
  </core:validityInterval>

  <!--Grants Company the right to track the user through the
      permission period. -->
  <core:grant>
    <priv:PrivacyPolicy>
    <!-- Disclosure-->
    <p3p:ACCESS>
        <p3p:all/>
    </p3p:ACCESS>

    <!-- Disputes -->
    <p3p:DISPUTES-GROUP>
        <p3p:DISPUTES
            resolution-type="service"
            short-description="Customer service will
                              remedy your complaints.">
          <p3p:REMEDIES>
           <p3p:correct/>
          </p3p:REMEDIES>
        </p3p:DISPUTES>
    </p3p:DISPUTES-GROUP>

    <p3p:STATEMENT>
        <p3p:CONSEQUENCE>
        We collect your location information for development
        purposes and for tracking your individual movement habits.
        </p3p:CONSEQUENCE>
        <!-- Why we use it -->
        <p3p:PURPOSE>
          <p3p:develop/>
          <p3p:individual-analysis/>
          <p3p:individual-decision/>
          <p3p:current/>
        </p3p:PURPOSE>
```

```
              <!-- Who else can get this data -->
              <p3p:RECIPIENT>
                <p3p:ours/>
              </p3p:RECIPIENT>

              <!-- How long do we hold onto the data for -->
              <p3p:RETENTION>
                <p3p:legal-requirement/>
              </p3p:RETENTION>
            </p3p:STATEMENT>
          </priv:PrivacyPolicy>

          <!--The mobile device from the inventory-->
          <priv:mobile licensePartIdRef="mobiledevice"/>
          <!--The rights that we are giving-->
          <priv:sendanyad/>
        </core:grant>
     </core:grantGroup>
    </core:license>
</core:licenseGroup>
```

B   Example

This is an example license in which the Mobile Tracking Company is given the right
to retain John Doe's location data for the length of the contract. In particular, the
element `<core:grant>` grants the company the right to track the user through the
permission period. No rights are granted otherwise.

```
<?xml version="1.0" encoding="utf-8" ?>
<core:licenseGroup
     xmlns:core="http://www.xrml.org/schema/2001/11/xrml2core"
     xmlns:cx="http://www.xrml.org/schema/2001/11/xrml2cx"
     xmlns:dsig="http://www.w3.org/2000/09/xmldsig#"
     xmlns:sx="http://www.xrml.org/schema/2001/11/xrml2sx"
     xmlns:xsi="http://www.w3.org/2001/XMLSchema-instance"
     xmlns:priv="http://www.pdrm.org/XrMLPrivacy"
     xmlns:p3p="http://www.w3.org/2002/01/P3Pv1"
     xsi:schemaLocation=
     "http://www.xrml.org/schema/2001/11/xrml2cx ../schemas/xrml2cx.xsd">

     <core:license
         licenseId="http://www.pdrm.org/examples/2003/retentionTracking">
       <core:inventory>
          <!-- This is the location information we want to grant access
               to -->
          <priv:location licensePartId="locData"/>
       </core:inventory>

       <core:grantGroup>
```

```
<!--The company that is tracking us' specific key.-->
<core:keyHolder>
  <core:info>
    <dsig:KeyValue>
        <dsig:RSAKeyValue>
            <dsig:Modulus>...</dsig:Modulus>
            <dsig:Exponent>AQAQAA==</dsig:Exponent>
        </dsig:RSAKeyValue>
    </dsig:KeyValue>
  </core:info>
</core:keyHolder>
<sx:commonName>The Mobile Tracking Company</sx:commonName>

<!-- The person allowing the company to track him/her-->
<core:issuer>
  <sx:commonName>John Doe</sx:commonName>
</core:issuer>

<!--The period for which the company may track the user. -->
<core:validityInterval licensePartId="trackingPeriod">
  <core:notBefore>2004-05-20T19:28:00</notBefore>
  <core:notAfter>2004-07-29T19:28:00</notAfter>
</core:validityInterval>

<core:grant>
  <priv:PrivacyPolicy>
  <!-- Disclosure-->
  <p3p:ACCESS>
    <p3p:all/>
  </p3p:ACCESS>

  <!-- Disputes -->
  <p3p:DISPUTES-GROUP>
    <p3p:DISPUTES
     resolution-type="court"
     short-description="Take your case to the local court">
      <p3p:REMEDIES>
      <p3p:correct/>
      <p3p:law/>
      </p3p:REMEDIES>
    </p3p:DISPUTES>
  </p3p:DISPUTES-GROUP>

  <p3p:STATEMENT>
    <p3p:CONSEQUENCE>
    We collect your location information for
    development purposes and for tracking your
    individual movement habits.
    </p3p:CONSEQUENCE>
    <!-- Why we use it -->
```

```
                <p3p:PURPOSE>
                  <p3p:develop/>
                  <p3p:individual-analysis/>
                  <p3p:individual-decision/>
                  <p3p:current/>
                </p3p:PURPOSE>

                <!-- Who else can get this data -->
                <p3p:RECIPIENT>
                  <p3p:ours/>
                  <p3p:same/>
                  <p3p:unrelated/>
                </p3p:RECIPIENT>

                <!-- How long do we hold onto the data for -->
                <p3p:RETENTION>
                  <p3p:indefinitely/>
                  <p3p:legal-requirement/>
                </p3p:RETENTION>
              </p3p:STATEMENT>
            </priv:PrivacyPolicy>

            <priv:location licensePartIdRef="locData"/>

          </core:grant>
        </core:grantGroup>
        </core:license>
</core:licenseGroup>
```

Privacy-Preserving Trust Negotiations

E. Bertino[1], E. Ferrari[2], and A.C. Squicciarini[3]

[1] CERIAS and Computer Science Department Purdue University,
West Lafayette, IN, USA
bertino@cerias.purdue.edu
[2] Dipartimento di Scienze della Cultura, Politiche e Informazione,
Universitá degli Studi dell'Insubria, Como
elena.ferrari@uninsubria.it
[3] Dipartimento di Informatica e Comunicazione,
Universitá degli Studi di Milano, Milano
squiccia@dico.unimi.it

Abstract. Trust negotiation is a promising approach for establishing trust in open systems, where sensitive interactions may often occur between entities with no prior knowledge of each other. Although several proposals today exist of systems for the management of trust negotiations none of them addresses in a comprehensive way the problem of privacy preservation. Privacy is today one of the major concerns of users exchanging information through the Web and thus we believe that trust negotiation systems must effectively address privacy issues to be widely acceptable. For these reasons, in this paper we investigate privacy in the context of trust negotiations. More precisely, we propose a set of privacy preserving features to be included in any trust negotiation system, such as the support for the P3P standard, as well as different formats to encode credentials.

1   Introduction

The huge recent increase in web-based applications carried out on the Internet has been accompanied by an exponential amount of data exchanged and collected by the interacting entities. As the amount of exchanged information exponentially grows, privacy [1] has emerged as one of the most crucial and challenging issues. Current researchers are thus focusing on devising both systems for supporting on line resource sharing [2, 3] and on technologies for preserving user privacy in a standardized and automated manner [4].

Privacy is defined as "the right of individuals to determine when, how and to what extent information about them is communicated to others".[1] The most significant proposal for supporting privacy over Internet is the Platform for Privacy Preferences - P3P [5]. The designers of P3P have also developed a preference

---

[1] This definition is by Alan Westin, Professor of Public Law and Government, Columbia University.

D. Martin and A. Serjantov (Eds.): PET 2004, LNCS 3424, pp. 283–301, 2005.
© Springer-Verlag Berlin Heidelberg 2005

language, called APPEL [6], to allow users to express their privacy preferences, thus enabling automated matching of privacy preferences against P3P policies.

Privacy issues are particularly crucial when dealing with trust management. Today, among the various approaches that can be adopted for exchanging resources and services on the web, a promising model is represented by trust negotiations [3]. All existing trust negotiation systems are based on the disclosure of certain amount of sensitive information, usually conveyed by *digital credentials*, required to establish trust. However, although several efficient and powerful negotiation systems have been developed so far [7, 8, 9, 10, 11], none of them provides a comprehensive solution to protect privacy during the negotiation process. In particular, none of them supports P3P policies for expressing user privacy requirements and preferences in a standard way. Our belief is that trust negotiation has the potentiality for being widely used to establish trust during on-line negotiations, once it is complemented with privacy-preserving techniques. Starting from an analysis of the most relevant privacy pitfalls in trust negotiation, in this paper we revise all the key aspects of a trust negotiation, which are crucial in order to efficiently and effectively preserve privacy. Our philosophy is to exploit, whenever possible, existing standard privacy technologies, such as P3P and APPEL. The main innovative features we propose in this paper are the support for different credential formats, each of which provides a different degree of privacy protection, the notion of *context* associated with a policy, which allows one to both express privacy policies, and convey information which can be used to protect disclosure policies, and the integration of P3P policies at various steps of the negotiation. The work reported in this paper is built on top of a negotiation system named Trust-$\mathcal{X}$ previously proposed by us [12]. However, the extensions we propose in this paper are major extensions since our previous proposal, as the other existing negotiation systems, does not address privacy nor it does support any of the above mentioned features.

A work related to our is the work by Seamons et. al [9] which explores issues concerning support of sensitive policies, based on the use of of hierarchies in policy definitions. However, they do not address the issue of privacy policy support. The work by Winslett et. al, [10], provides a unified scheme to model resource protection, including policies. It currently represents one of the most significant proposals in the negotiation research area, and it is the approach that most influenced our work. However, the proposed approach does not deal with the issue of supporting privacy policies, neither it defines an ad hoc policy language. Finally, [13] provides an overview of some of the privacy problems that may arise during a negotiation. However, it does not provide a comprehensive solution to such problems, rather it mainly deals with protection of sensitive policies.

The remainder of this paper is organized as follows. Next section presents the main privacy pitfalls compromising trust negotiations, and outlines possible remedies. Section 3 overviews the Trust-$\mathcal{X}$ framework. Section 4 presents the Trust-$\mathcal{X}$ privacy language. Section 5 deals with a privacy based approach to trust negotiation. Section 6 presents Trust-$\mathcal{X}$ architecture, whereas Section 7 concludes the paper and outlines future research directions.

2   Privacy Pitfalls and Solutions in Trust Negotiations

One of the major concerns users have in adopting negotiation systems is that trust negotiation does not control or safeguard personal information once it has been disclosed. Nothing is usually specified about the use of the information disclosed during a negotiation. A possible solution to this problem is to integrate the negotiation system with the P3P platform [5]. The P3P platform can be used for stating how the personal information collected through credentials disclosure during on line transactions will be managed by the receiver. Another potential vulnerability of trust negotiation arises because of the common strategy of postponing actual credential disclosure. Indeed, during the policy evaluation phase, privacy can be compromised in several ways, since there are no guarantees about counterpart honesty until the end of the process. Policy disclosure can be used to determine the value of sensitive attributes without the credential ever being disclosed. Furthermore, during policy exchange it is not possible to determine whether a party is lying or not until the credentials are actually disclosed. Indeed, when a request for a sensitive credential is sent the counterpart typically replies by sending a counter request for the credentials necessary to disclose the credential originally requested. Thus, the receiver can infer that the counterpart can satisfy the request, obtaining clues about the possession of sensitive credentials, even if it never actually obtains the credential. As a result, a mendacious subject may practically gather the counterpart profile by falsely declaring possession of credentials. An ideal system should be able to prevent information leakage, without interfering with the negotiation process. A possible solution, proposed by Winsborough et al. in [11], is that of introducing the notion of attribute acknowledgment policies, in which a participant establishes for those attributes that she considers sensitive, whether or not she satisfies those attributes. However, the negotiation process results quite cumbersome and requires a user to specify an amount of policies, larger than her real necessity. An alternative solution is to disclose credentials as soon as a corresponding policy has been satisfied before the end of the policy evaluation phase. However, this strategy may result in unnecessary credential disclosures, as well as needless rounds of negotiation when failure is inevitable. A more promising approach is thus that of adopting a different perspective. Rather than introducing a policy for each sensitive attribute or jeopardizing private information by immediately disclosing credentials, policy expressiveness may be improved, by giving the user the possibility of specifying key information for driving the negotiation, while sending the policy. Finally, another issue related with credentials arises because of sensitive attributes.(e.g., age, credit rating). A credential may contain several sensitive attributes, and very often just a subset of them is required to satisfy a counterpart policy. However, when a credential is exchanged, the receiver anyway gathers all the information contained in the credential. Although some proposals exist [14, 15] for encoding digital credentials, no widely accepted standard exists for their representation which allows the possibility of a partial disclosure.

3   Trust-$\mathcal{X}$ Overview

This section briefly summarizes the main features of the Trust-$\mathcal{X}$ [12] system which is used as the reference system throughout the paper. Trust-$\mathcal{X}$ is a comprehensive framework for trust negotiation, providing both a language for encoding policies and certificates, and a system architecture. The language, named $\mathcal{X}$-TNL, is an XML based language and is specifically conceived for the specification of both certificates and policies. Trust-$\mathcal{X}$ certificates convey information about the parties and can be either credentials or declarations. Such certificates are collected into $\mathcal{X}$-Profiles, which are associated with each Trust-$\mathcal{X}$ entity.

Precisely, digital credentials are assertions describing one or more properties of a given subject, certified by trusted third parties. Declarations, by contrast, are self-credentials issued by their owner, collecting auxiliary information that do not need to be certified (such as for instance specific preferences) but may help in better customizing the negotiation. Since declarations are complementary information to be optionally exchanged, in what follows we focus only on credentials.

Protection needs for the release of a resource are expressed by *disclosure policies*. A resource can be either a service, a credential, or any kind of data that need to be protected. Disclosure policies regulate the disclosure of a resource by imposing conditions on the credentials the requesting party should possess. Disclosure policies for a resource can be gradually made known to the counterpart according to the degree of trust established, in order to ensure a better protection of the sensitive information exchanged. Trust-$\mathcal{X}$ also comprises an architecture for negotiation management, which is symmetric and peer-to-peer. A Trust-$\mathcal{X}$ negotiation consists of a set of phases to be sequentially executed. The idea is thus to disclose policies at first, in order to limit credential release, and then disclose only those credentials that are necessary for the success of negotiation. The key phase of a Trust-$\mathcal{X}$ negotiation is the policy evaluation phase, which consists of a bilateral and ordered policy exchange. The goal is to determine a sequence of credentials, called *trust sequence*, satisfying disclosure policies of both parties. More precisely, each time a disclosure policy is received the steps to be executed and the corresponding Trust-$\mathcal{X}$ modules involved are the followings:

- The party determines if the policy can be satisfied by any of the possessed credentials, querying the $\mathcal{X}$-Profile.
- The *compliance checker* checks in the policy base the protection needs associated with the credentials, if any.
- If a set of credentials and associated policies are actually found, the set of counter policies are extracted by the *policy base* and then sent to the counterpart.

Once a trust sequence has been determined, the credential exchange phase is executed. Each time a credential is received, the local compliance checker module checks local policy satisfaction and verifies at runtime the validity and ownership of the remote credentials. Functions required to carry out credential disclosure include verification of credential contents, checking for revocation, authentication of ownership. More details on the Trust-$\mathcal{X}$ system can be found in [12].

4   A Privacy Preserving Specification Language

In what follows we present the solutions we have devised to protect privacy during negotiations by proposing some extensions to the conventional languages for expressing policies and credentials. More precisely, we first propose an extension of the standard credential format to deal with privacy issues. Then, we introduce the notion of *context* associated with a policy, which can be used to attach privacy rules to a policy, as well as to protect policy disclosure and to speed up the negotiation process.

4.1   Private Credentials

During trust negotiations credentials play a key role, in that they represent the means to prove parties properties. Credentials must thus be unforgeable and verifiable. Typically, a digital credential contains a set of attributes specified using name/value pairs. The credential is signed using the issuer's private key and can be verified using the issuer's public key.

Our system supports two types of credential schemes. The first one is called *basic format* and represents the standard approach for credential encoding, that is, a digitally signed document containing a set of subject properties. The second proposal is called *privacy enhanced* format, and is based on a credential template supporting the disclosure of the credential in two different steps, keeping the sensitive content of the credential secret until the end of the negotiation. The proposed format also supports partial disclosure of credentials, to protect the privacy of sensitive attributes.

In the next sections we first illustrate the technique used to support partial attribute disclosure. Then, we present the privacy enhanced format, since this represents a novelty in the state of the art. We do not further elaborate on the basic format, since it has been already presented in [16].

Protected Attribute Credentials. An interesting approach to maximize privacy protection is to selectively disclose attributes within a credential, so that only the needed subset of properties is made available to the recipient of the credential. The best system currently available to allow partial disclosure of credentials relies on the use of the bit commitment technique [17], which enables users to commit a value without revealing it. By exploiting this technique within digital credentials it is possible to actually send credentials by revealing only the minimal set of attributes required during the negotiation. Although the idea of selectively disclosing credential attributes is not new [14, 18], this technique has never been thoroughly explored, especially in trust negotiations. The only work on this topic is from Jarvis [19]. This work focuses on selective disclosure of credentials during negotiations and provides a prototype implementation. Our focus, differently from [19], is to deeply analyze the impact of protected attribute

```
<HEADER>
<Student_Card credID='12ab', CredType= Student Card >
<Issuer HREF='http://www.ItalyCountry.com'
Title=KTHUniversity_Repository/>
<expiration_date> may 12th 2002     </expiration_date>
</HEADER>
<CONTENT>
      <name>
      <Fname> Olivia </Fname>
      XXXXXXXXXXXXXXXXXX
      </name>
      XXXXXXXXXXXXXXXXXXXXXXX
      <faculty> history </faculty>
      <badge_number> 328454</badge_number>
</CONTENT>
</Student_Card>
```

Fig. 1. Example of protected attributes in a privacy enhanced credential

credentials on trust negotiations, and devise new strategies to allow interoperability between users adopting various credential formats. Further, instead of using the bit-commitment technique we adopt a multi-bit hash commitment technique for attribute encoding, as the length of attributes will likely be longer than one bit. The general protocol followed to issue credentials with protected attributes is briefly summarized in what follows.

A credential requester first generates the set of attribute values for the credential. In order to create a credential with protected attributes the requester has first to create the corresponding private values to be used in place of the sensitive ones. Given a sensitive attribute a with value va the operations needed for its protection are: 1) generate a random string r; 2) compute p=va|r, that is, the concatenation of va with r; 3) compute v=hash(p), generated by invoking a hash-function one_way on p. These operations are performed for all the attributes of the credential that need to be selectively protected. Once the credential is ready, it is submitted to the credential authority, which verifies its content and the corresponding values, and finally signs it. During a negotiation, the credential can be sent by keeping secret the content of protected attributes. The disclosure of each private attribute is executed by sending the counterpart both va, the original value, and r, the random value, so that the receiver can compute va using the same hash function and verify the attribute validity. The remaining sensitive attributes of a credential that are not relevant for the negotiation can be left hidden, and never be disclosed to the counterpart.

Privacy Enhanced Credentials. The basic Trust-$\mathcal{X}$ credential is an XML document, digitally signed by the issuer, according to the standard defined by W3C for XML Signatures [20]. A credential is an instance of a *credential type*, which is a DTD (Document Type Definition) used as a template for credentials having a similar structure. Although the content of a credential is determined by the corresponding type, each credential, beyond the specific language used for its encoding, must always convey some general reference information about the corresponding credential type, the issuer, and its temporal validity. This set of information is crucial for proving that the credential, besides its specific content, is a signed and valid digital document issued by an entity reputed trusted.

The credential format we have devised, named *privacy enhanced credential template*, captures this reference information into a specific portion of the document, named *header*, which is kept separated from the private content of the credential, contained into a different portion of the document, referred to as the *content*. Further, credential content is structured by using the technique presented in the previous section, so that partial disclosure of attributes can also be achieved. This way of structuring credentials enables negotiating parties to adopt new strategies to gradually establish trust. Indeed, the header and content can be disclosed at different times during a negotiation. For instance, one possible strategy is to disclose the header to prove credential possession as the credential is involved into a negotiation, and keep the credential content secret until its disclosure at the end of the whole process. An alternative approach can be that of requiring attributes to be disclosed as soon as they are requested by a policy. Then, header disclosure can be immediately followed by disclosure of the required attributes and corresponding random values.

Although Trust-$\mathcal{X}$ provides an XML-based encoding of credentials, a privacy enhanced credential template is a language independent way of encoding credentials. Thus, in what follows we give a logic definition, abstracting from the specific Trust-$\mathcal{X}$ syntax. Formally, a credential type ct can be represented as a pair $< n_{ct}, p_{ct} >$, where n_{ct} is the name of the credential type, and p_{ct} is the set of corresponding attribute specifications. Each attribute specification contains the name and the domain. A privacy enhanced credential template can be modeled as follows.

Definition 1. *(Privacy enhanced credential template). Let $ct =< n_{ct}, p_{ct} >$ be a credential type, a privacy enhanced credential template for ct is a pair $< header\text{-}template, content\text{-}template >$ where:*

- header-template *is a set containing the following attribute specifications:*
  1) `credID`, *specifying the credential identifier;*
  2) `CredType`, *identifying the type of the credential;*
  3) `Expiration`, *specifying the credential expiring date;*
  4) `IssueRep`, *denoting the unique address of the issuer's server.*[2]
- content-template *is a list collecting attribute specifications p_{ct}.*   □

In the following definition and throughout the paper we denote with $sign(doc)$ and $hash(doc)$ the signature and the hash value computed over document doc. We are now ready to define a privacy enhanced credential.

Definition 2. *(Privacy enhanced credential). Let $p_{ct} =$<header-template, content-template> be a privacy enhanced credential template, and let k be the number of attributes collected in content-template. A privacy enhanced credential pc instance of p_{ct} is a tuple*
<header, content,sign(header|content)> *where:*

---

[2] Identified by a URI [21].

- *For each attribute specification p in* header-template, header *contains a pair (p-name, p-value), where p-name is the name of the attribute specified by p, and p-value is a value compatible with its domain;*
- *For each attribute specification p in* content-template, *content contains hash (p-name|p-value|random), where p-name is the name of the attribute specified by p, p-value is a value compatible with its domain, and random is a random string of bits;*
- *sign(header|content) is the signature computed over the header concatenated with the credential content.* □

Figure 1 shows an example of privacy enhanced credential, encoded using an XML compliant language.

A *credential proof* is a particular state of a privacy enhanced credential, where the header is plain and the content is hidden, that is, the attribute names, values and random numbers are not disclosed to the counterpart. The signature over the whole document in a credential proof can be verified. In what follows, when a credential proof for a credential *cred* has been disclosed, we say that *cred is proven*. Indeed, the credential receiver has an immediate proof of the credential, and a sufficient level of trust can be reached to advance the negotiation. During the policy evaluation phase, when a credential is requested, the credential proof can be safely released as the corresponding policy is satisfied, before having found a trust sequence. In this way the receiver party is ensured that the other party possesses the requesting credential, even if it cannot immediately access its content, unless explicitly required by parties adopted strategies. The protocol for proving a credential can be sketched as follows:

```
Requester::  Request cred
Cred_owner:: Send ⟨cred.header; hash(cred.p-name₁|cred.p-value₁|random1),
             ...hash(p-nameₖ|p-valueₖ|randomk)); sign((cred.header,
             hash(cred.p-name₁| cred.p-value₁|random1)), ...,
             hash(cred.p-nameₖ|cred.p-valueₖ|randomk)⟩
Requester::  Check cred.header
Requester::  Verifies sign(cred.header, hash(cred.p-name₁|cred.p-value₁|
             random1),..., hash(cred.p-nameₖ|cred.p-valueₖ|randomk))
```

The header of each credential is thus sent as plain text, whereas properties names and values are replaced with hash values. Hash values are generated for each attribute of the credential as introduced in Section 4.1. By using the issuer reference contained in the header, the credential receiver can verify credential ownership and validity. For example, during an on-line purchase, if a credit card is asked, one can directly verify by the bank whether the credential is still valid and whether the owner is actually the party who presented it, without knowing the credit card number until the success of the negotiation is not certain.

At the end of the policy evaluation phase, when a trust sequence has been found, all or a subset of random values are disclosed, allowing the receiver to verify credential properties and the actual attribute values. If the verification process fails, the receiver can eventually notify this to the issuer and abort the negotiation.

The protocol to reveal attribute content, say attribute $name_j$, is as follows:

Cred_owner:: Send $name_j, value_j, random_j$
Requester:: Compute $H = hash(value_j | random_j)$
Requester:: Verifies $hash(name_j | value_j | random_j)$ with H

Finally, it is worth to note that a credential proof is a powerful means to address those scenarios where a party is actually interested in verifying credential possession and not really in attribute credential values. As the header collects information proving credential possession header disclosure can immediately satisfies the policy without further exchanges. Typical scenarios are those requiring id cards proving membership to institutions like companies, libraries, gyms and so on.

4.2   Policy Language

Besides credentials, trust negotiation relies on disclosure policies, specifying trust requirements that must be satisfied in order to access the requested resource. Beyond the specific formalism adopted, disclosure policies are often modeled as expressions specifying two types of information: the target resource for which the policy is specified, and the credentials to be disclosed, eventually specifying conditions on them. Next definition formalizes this concept, according to the Trust-$\mathcal{X}$ syntax. The target resource is denoted as R, whereas the requested credentials are denoted by means of *terms*. A term specifies a credential name and eventual conditions against some of its attribute values.

Definition 3. (Rule) *[12] A rule is an expression of one of the following forms:*
1) $\mathbf{R} \leftarrow \mathcal{T}_1, \ldots, \mathcal{T}_n$, $n \geq 1$, *where* $\mathcal{T}_1, \ldots, \mathcal{T}_n$ *are terms and* $\mathbf{R}$ *is the name of the target resource.*
2) $\mathbf{R} \leftarrow \mathbf{DELIV}$. *This kind of policy is called* delivery policy.

A delivery policy states that no further information is requested for disclosing the requested resource. In what follows we assume each rule to be uniquely identified by an id.

Example 1. Alice is a student at KTH university wishing to obtain a loan for her university studies. NBG Bank offers special Student loans for promising students. Furthermore, NBG has an on-line service, called $HelpStudent$, to submit loan applications.

To complete the application $HelpStudent$ adopts a policy p_1 requiring a credit card to pay for the application fee. The corresponding rule is the following: $r = loan \leftarrow CreditCard$.

Although this specification captures all the basic information required to carry on a negotiation, it is not expressive enough to specify other crucial information that may be associated with a policy, such as, for instance, its usage, its prerequisites, or the privacy policies for the requested credentials. For this reason, in this paper we enhance the policy language by adding a set of information referred to as *policy context*. The goal is to integrate the basic rule defining a policy with a structured set of information to be used during trust negotiation process. Before formally defining a policy we thus need to introduce the notion of policy context.

Definition 4. (Policy context). *Let* $R \leftarrow T_1, T_2, ., T_n$ *or* $R \leftarrow DELIV$ *be a rule, and let* **rid** *be its identifier.*
A **context** *for* **rid** *is a pair:* $< \textbf{pol\_prec\_set}, \textbf{priv} >$ *where:*
- **pol_prec_set** $= \{p_1, \ldots, p_k\}$ *is a possibly empty set of policy identifiers,[3] named policy precondition set, where* $\forall\, p \in$ **pol_prec_set***, the corresponding rule is of the form* $R \leftarrow T'_1, T'_2, ., T'_k$*;*
- **priv** *is a privacy policy;*
All the components of a context are optional.   □

The context of a policy is thus a set of information to be associated with a given rule. More precisely, the *pol_prec_set* component is a set of policy identifiers such that at least one of the policy needs to be satisfied before the disclosure of the policy with which the precondition set is associated. The idea of policy preconditions is to protect sensitive policies by introducing an order in policy disclosure. In particular, policies belonging to a precondition set are related to the same resource required by the rule within which they are associated. This aspect has been extensively investigated by us in [12] and thus we do not further elaborate on it.

By contrast, the *priv* component is a new feature of a context and denotes a P3P privacy policy. The task of privacy policies is thus to complement disclosure policies, specifying whether the information conveyed by the credentials will be collected and/or used. Privacy policies may also specify the management of the portions of credential content (if any), not explicitly requested by the associated policy but anyway obtained as part of the credential. Indeed, upon receiving a credential, unless protected attributes are used, the recipient obtains the whole credential, and not only the attributes requested to satisfy the policy. We further reason on P3P policy encoding in Section 6. We are now ready to formally define a disclosure policy.

Definition 5. (Disclosure policy). *A disclosure policy is a pair*
$< \textbf{rid}, \textbf{context} >$ *where:* **rid** *is a rule identifier, and* **context** *is the optional context associated with the rule.*   □

Example 2. Suppose *HelpStudent* asks the applicant the ID Card after receiving the Credit Card, to check card ownership and collect applicant address information. Moreover, suppose that HelpStudent maintains a database of customers personal data. In particular, it collects applicant ID Card to proceed the loan application. The rule associated with the disclosure policy requiring ID Card will be (*loan* ← *idcard*), whereas a possible context is ($\{p_1\}, priv$), where p_1 is

---

[3] We assume that each policy is identified by a unique identifier.

```
<POLICY xmlns="http://www.w3.org/2000/P3PV1>
....
    <STATEMENT>
        <DATA-GROUP>
            <DATA ref="http://www.TrustX.repos.credtype#idCard.name">
            <DATA ref="http://www.TrustX.repos.credtype#idCard.lastname">
            <DATA ref="http://www.TrustX.repos.credtype#idCard.birthdate">
            <DATA ref="http://www.TrustX.repos.credtype#idCard.key">
                <CATEGORIES>
                <purchase/>
                </CATEGORIES>
            </DATA>
        </DATA-GROUP>
        <ACCESS> <contact_and_other> </ACCESS>
        <PURPOSE resolution-type="independent">
          <current/>
          <develop />
        </PURPOSE>
        <RECIPIENT> <ours/><same/></RECIPIENT>
        <RETENTION> <stated-purpose/> </RETENTION>
    </STATEMENT>
    <STATEMENT>
        <DATA-GROUP>
            <DATA ref="http://www.TrustX.repos.credtype#idCard.street">
            <DATA ref="http://www.TrustX.repos.credtype#idCard.stateprov">
            <DATA ref="http://www.TrustX.repos.credtype#idCard.postalCode">
            <DATA ref="http://www.TrustX.repos.credtype#idCard.country">
                <CATEGORIES><purchase/> </CATEGORIES>
            </DATA>
        </DATA-GROUP>
        <ACCESS> <contact_and_other> </ACCESS>
        <PURPOSE>
          <contact/>
          <individual-decision>
        </PURPOSE>
        <RECIPIENT> <ours/></RECIPIENT>
        <RETENTION> <business-practices/> </RETENTION>
    </STATEMENT>
</POLICY>
```

Fig. 2. Example of fine grained privacy policy

the id of the policy of Example 1, and *priv* is the privacy policy informing user about id card management. The associated P3P policy is shown in Figure 2.

We denote with the term *Policy Base* ($\mathcal{PB}$) the encoding of all the disclosure policies associated with a party. Next section shows how the privacy policy component of a policy context can be exploited to negotiate resources.

5   Privacy Preserving Trust Negotiations

In the following sections we show how the features presented so far, i.e., privacy enhanced credentials and contexts associated with a policy, can be used to carry on a privacy preserving trust negotiation.

5.1   Using Privacy Enhanced Credentials in Trust Negotiation

The following examples show how privacy enhanced credentials may be used to successfully complete a negotiation strongly protecting privacy, and simultaneously helping to deal with situations which would cause a negotiation failure adopting a traditional trust negotiation protocol.

Example 3. Suppose Alice is a patient of the *Health Clinic* and wants to buy the drugs she needs by an on-line pharmacy. Suppose that the pharmacy is allowed to sell this kind of drugs Alice needs either to doctors or by prescription of doctors working at the Health Clinic. Further, the pharmacy also needs to obtain Alice patient card issued by the clinic and a valid credit card, to complete the transaction. On Alice side, suppose that she is willing to disclose the requested credentials only if the pharmacy presents a credential proving pharmacy affiliation with the hospital since the patient id-card conveys sensitive information about Alice health. The corresponding rule will be: $Patient\_Card() \leftarrow Health\_Clin\_Aff()$. If the clinic is willing to disclose its affiliation only to clinic patients and/or doctors, then the adopted rule will be the following: $Health\_Clin\_Aff() \leftarrow Patient\_Card()$.

In a traditional negotiation, rules like the one in the above example will create a *negotiation deadlock*, thus causing negotiation failure, even if both parties possess the requested properties and associated credentials. Such deadlock may be avoided by using privacy enhanced credentials. During the policy evaluation phase parties may prove each other credential possession without actually revealing credential content until having received all the requested credential proofs. Selective disclosure of a credential can also be used to strengthen parties privacy protection. As a simple example, consider the scenario of a customer purchasing books from an on-line store. Suppose that the on-line store requires a credit and id card for both verifying credit card ownership and retrieving customer home address, in order to ship the book to the customer personal address. If the customer does not want to show his/her remaining information conveyed in the id-card (like the date and place of birth) he/she can send the id-card hiding all the sensitive information not strictly required by the on line store, without failing the process. Finally, note also that in such context the customer may choose whether to immediately send the requested attributes or wait until the policy evaluation has been completed and the requested credentials have been sent.

5.2   Privacy Policies in Trust-$\mathcal{X}$ Negotiations

A Trust-$\mathcal{X}$ negotiation is organized according to two main phases, the former devoted to policy exchange, and the latter to credentials disclosure. The key phase of the process is the policy evaluation phase where trust requirements are exchanged to determine possible sequences of credentials for successfully completing the negotiation. In addition, on top of the policy evaluation phase, Trust-$\mathcal{X}$ provides an *introductory phase*, to exchange preliminary information

```
<POLICY xmlns="http://www.w3.org/2000/P3PV1>

......
    <STATEMENT>
        <DATA-GROUP>
          <DATA ref="#dynamic.misc.data" >
              <CATEGORIES>
              <purchase/> <uniqueid/> <state/>
              </CATEGORIES>
          </DATA>
        </DATA-GROUP>
        <ACCESS> <contact_and_other> </ACCESS>
        <!-- Use (purpose)-->
        <PURPOSE resolution-type="independent">
        <current/>
        <develop />
        </PURPOSE>
        <RECIPIENT> <ours/><same/></RECIPIENT>
        <RETENTION> <stated-purpose/> </RETENTION>
    </STATEMENT>

    <STATEMENT>
        <DATA-GROUP>
            <DATA ref="#dynamic.misc.data" >
            <DATA ref="#user.home-info.online.postal" >
            <CATEGORIES><purchase/> </CATEGORIES>
        </DATA>
        </DATA-GROUP>
        <ACCESS> <contact_and_other> </ACCESS>
        <PURPOSE>
            <contact-required="opt-in"/>
            <individual-decision="opt-in"/>
        </PURPOSE>
        <RECIPIENT> <ours/></RECIPIENT>
            <RETENTION> <business-practices /> </RETENTION>
    </STATEMENT>
</POLICY>
```

Fig. 3. Example of coarse grained P3P policy

whose main goal is to reach an agreement on privacy requirements. Indeed, besides the specific way of approaching trust during negotiations, privacy concerns are a common feature of each Trust-$\mathcal{X}$ negotiation. The key component of the introductory phase is the *privacy agreement* sub-phase. The specific aim of the privacy agreement sub-phase is to reach a preliminary agreement on data collection and use before starting sensitive information exchange. The agreement, due to the mutual exchange of information characterizing a negotiation, is thus reached by communicating to the counterpart both privacy practices and preferences, using coarse grained P3P policies and privacy preferences rules. We assume user preferences are expressed using the APPEL [6] language, although other languages can be used as well (e.g., [22]). By specifying high level privacy policies, parties can communicate the types of data they will collect without having to enumerate every individual data. This type of policies can be implemented using P3P syntax by describing data using the `<dynamic><miscdata/><dynamic>` element and the categories to which the information to be exchanged belongs to. Once a prior agreement on data management is reached, parties can enter into the core of the process and start the policy evaluation phase. Note that under this approach the subsequent phases of a negotiation can be carried out without worrying about data collection and use. However, since parties are not aware of the actual counterpart requirements, resources requiring ad hoc privacy policies might be involved while evaluating parties policies. To cope with this possibility each policy context may contain in the optional *priv* field a P3P fine grained privacy policy. If desired by the parties, each policy can be sent accompanied by the related P3P policy, specifying how the information collected will be managed and for which purpose. Each time a P3P policy is received the receiver has to evaluate first the disclosure policy compliance and then check whether his/her privacy preferences comply with the P3P policy. Similar to privacy policies, privacy preference rules can also express either coarse grained preferences to be exchanged in the agreement phase, or more fined grained preferences associated with credentials reputed privacy sensitive, and be exchanged as the credentials are involved in the process.

Example 4. With reference to the loan scenario of Example 1, consider now two different privacy policies. The first P3P policy is an example of a coarse grained privacy policy to be exchanged during the privacy agreement phase. Suppose that, to accept student applications, HelpStudent needs to obtain certain information by the applicants, and store it for a week to check user compatibility with bank loan policies. However, HelpStudent also adopts a privacy policy stating that NBG offers personalized loan recommendations, for which it needs to collect customer personal information. The resulting P3P policy to be matched against the applicant privacy preferences is shown in Figure 3. The first STATEMENT says that customer personal information and miscellaneous purchase data (e.g., credit card number, type of loan required) will be used for completing the loan transaction. The second STATEMENT allows HelpStudent to use miscellaneous data for creating personalized recommendations and email them to the customer. The second privacy policy, reported in Figure 2, is an example of policy referring to a credential, (see Example 2). The policy states privacy practices related to credentials of type IdCard. Such policy is sent together with policies requiring user ID Card, and inform the user about the credential receiver intended use to collect user contact information to complete the electronic transaction.

6   Privacy-Enabled Trust-$\mathcal{X}$ Architecture

This section extends the Trust-$\mathcal{X}$ architecture [12] by privacy specific components. The privacy-enabled Trust-$\mathcal{X}$ system is composed by several components, sketched in Figure 4. As shown, the main components of the system are a *Policy Base*, storing disclosure policies, the *$\mathcal{X}$-Profile* associated with the party, a *Tree Manager*, managing the negotiation tree, and a *Compliance Checker*, testing policy satisfaction and generating request replies. The compliance checker also checks local policy satisfaction and verifies at runtime the validity and ownership of remote credentials. The goals of the system components are essentially to support policy and credential exchange and to test whether a policy is satisfied. In addition to those basic elements several modules for the

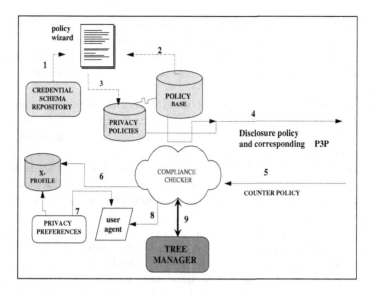

Fig. 4. Trust-$\mathcal{X}$ framework. Dashed lines denote off-line operations. Arrow labels denote the flow of the operations

management of privacy policies are also included. Current implementations of privacy systems [23] usually have two components deploying P3P. Web sites install privacy policies and reference files, at their sites, using tools like [24, 25]. Then, as users browse sites, their preferences are checked against site policies. This simple schema is not adequate in our context, in that we are dealing with both user and server sides. Indeed, each Trust-$\mathcal{X}$ entity acts during a negotiation as a server requesting personal data as well as a user disclosing personal information. The framework should thus support both sides during negotiations. In what follows we illustrate user and server modules separately. Then, we merge these two visions into a unique framework and show how they fit together. In presenting the modules we focus on P3P policies to be exchanged during the policy evaluation phase. We recall that (cfr. Section 5) P3P policies are also exchanged during the policy agreement phase. However, such policies are coarse grained since they refer to the whole negotiation and not to a specific credential. As such, they can be specified and evaluated using standard mechanisms adopted by web sites.

For a policy sender, the system should support the following actions:

1. mapping credential schema into data schema usable for privacy policy specification;
2. specifying privacy policies about these data using P3P;
3. providing agents supporting privacy policies among negotiations.

Creation of P3P policies can be executed off-line before negotiations start. The process is sketched on top of Figure 4 (dashed lines). As shown, the module in charge of encoding P3P is the Policy wizard. Given a disclosure policy dp, the module extracts the corresponding credential schema[4](see Figure 4, arrow 1) $C_1, .. C_n$ required by dp from the `credential schema repository`. This module is implemented as a credential chain tool, to retrieve credential schemes from public issuer repositories and by a local cache storing the most widely used schemes.

Once the required schemes are retrieved, credential content is considered, to identify data to be collected. Credentials content can be analyzed under two different perspectives. If the information to be collected is a set of properties and the credential actually represents only the envelope to transmit these data then the policy can be specified as a conventional P3P policy, that is, using built in data schemes and categories provided by the standard, without referring to the particular credential collecting the requested attributes. By contrast, if the key information is the credential itself, then the policy should refer not only to the attributes in the credential but also to the credential itself. For instance, if a web server wants to cache a whole credential to create a data base collecting customers data, it has to refer to the specific certificate, specifying its ID and issuer public key. In such cases it is mandatory to extend P3P data schema to encode the data structure underlying the credential. Privacy policies are encoded according to version 1.1. of P3P [26], that provides a new format for expressing P3P data schema in a simpler way than the previous one. The new format uses the XML Schema Definition (XSD) format which can be validated against an XML schema. Since Trust-$\mathcal{X}$ credentials are defined in terms of DTDs it is possible to encode the policy directly referring to the schema corresponding to a credential, by simply translating the DTD with XSLT [27] in XSD. An example of P3P policy referring to a credential schema is shown in Figure 2.

Once the corresponding data schema has been encoded the policy creation wizard can complete policy encoding, specifying data management (for which purpose the data will be collected, for how long, and so forth), defined according to the local privacy practice. The privacy policy is finally linked to the corresponding disclosure policy.

On the other side, the policy receiver must be equipped with tools for describing privacy preferences and matching policies against privacy preferences. Tools for describing privacy preferences can be implemented as ad-hoc policy editors, able to encode user preferences into a set of rules to be used to evaluate remote P3P policies. Policy matching, by contrast, can be executed by a user agent integrating the compliance checker module. The behavior of the user agent is modeled by function $Privacy\_matching()$, reported in Figure 5. The function is invoked each time a disclosure policy is received, even if it is not actually accompanied by a specific P3P policy. If a privacy policy is attached to the disclosure policy, a policy check is performed between the privacy policy and the preference rules of the receiving party, with respect to the credentials requested by the disclosure policy with which the privacy policy is associated. If no privacy policy is associated with the disclosure policy, then the preference rules are

---

[4] We use the term schema and type interchangeably, in this context.

Function Privacy_matching($priv$)
Input :
    $priv$: a privacy policy or an empty message;
Output :
    $Accept(priv)$ or $Refuse(priv)$
Precondition:
    $Priv\_nego$ is the remote P3P policy exchanged in the privacy agreement phase
    Gen_priv_pref are the local privacy preference rules exchanged in the privacy agreement
phase

begin
  if $priv \neq \emptyset$ *%matching privacy preferences*
    Let p_c be the policy associated with $priv$
    Let $Spec\_rules$ be the set of specific local preference rules not belonging to
Gen_priv_pref;
    if $\exists rule \in Spec\_rules$ for credentials requested in p_c **then**
      % Match is a function checking compliance between a privacy rule and a p3p policy
      if Match($rule, priv$)=TRUE **then**
      % there exists a specific rule for the requested credentials
        Return($Accept(priv)$)
      else Return($Refuse(priv)$)
    else
      if Match($priv\_pref, priv$)=TRUE **then**
        Return ($Accept(priv)$)
      else Return($Refuse(priv)$)
  else   % $p_c.priv = \emptyset$
    Let $Spec\_rules$ be the set of specific local preference rules
    in p_c credentials not belonging to Gen_priv_pref;
    if $\exists rule \in Spec\_rules$ for credentials requested in p_c **then**
      if Match($rule, Priv\_nego$)=TRUE **then**
      % there exists a specific rule for the requested credentials
        Return ($Accept(priv)$)
      else Return($Refuse(priv)$)
end

Fig. 5. Function Privacy_matching()

checked against the privacy policies exchanged during privacy agreement phase, denoted as *Priv_nego*, in Figure 5. Similarly, if no privacy policy is associated with the disclosure policy but a preference rule has been specified for the credentials requested by the policy, then the preference rule is checked against the coarse grained privacy policy exchanged during the privacy agreement phase. Modules characterizing the two sides are merged into a unique framework, and are complementary to each other. The first set of modules is used to integrate conventional disclosure policies sent to the counterpart with specific privacy policies. The latter, by contrast, acts as a further filter when remote policies asking for credentials conveying personal information are received.

As new features are added to Trust-$\mathcal{X}$, an increasing computational effort is required to carry out the process. For example, if a disclosure policy is sent together with a privacy policy, the compliance checker has actually to execute one or two additional operations (arrow 7) in order to check if the P3P policy fires. However, due to the simplicity underlying the P3P platform the time required to perform this kind of checking is minimal, and it does not really impact system performance. Moreover, it is expected that in most cases the overload caused by P3P policy exchange will be actually very limited and confined in the privacy agreement phase. Indeed, during the subsequent phase only additional privacy policies not covered by the previous ones may be exchanged, if required by the parties.

7   Conclusions

In this paper we have presented a system for trust negotiation specifically designed for preserving privacy during a negotiation. The system provides support for P3P policies, that can be exchanged at various steps of the negotiation, and for different credential formats, providing different degrees of privacy protection. In particular, the credential format we have provided achieves privacy protection by hiding the attribute names collected in a credential. However, the structure of a credential is sometimes required to be public during a negotiation, to ensure that the credential to be disclosed actually collects the required properties. We plan to further explore this issue in our future work.

We are currently developing a suite of strategies to carry on a negotiation, that exploit and extend the notion of context associated with a policy, to allow one to trade-off among efficiency, robustness, and privacy requirements. Additional future work includes an implementation of both the proposed system and the credential formats. Other extensions include the development of mechanisms and modules to semi-automatically design privacy policies to be associated with disclosure policies. Additionally, we plan to fully support P3P 1.1, once the new version will be standardized.

Acknowledgments. The authors thank Matthias Schunter for the many suggestions received on both the content and the presentation of the paper. The work reported in this paper has been partially supported by the EU under the TrustCoM project (Project n. IST-001945).

References

1. Westin, A.F.: Privacy and Freedom (1967) Atheneum, New York.
2. W. H. Winsborough, N.L.: Protecting sensitive attributes in automated trust negotiation. ACM Workshop on Privacy in the Electronic Society (2002)
3. M. Winslett, e.a.: Negotiating Trust on The Web. IEEE Internet Computing, Vol. 6, No 6 (2002) 30–37
4. R. Agraval, J. Kiernan, R.S., Yu, X.: Implementing P3P using database technology. 19th International Conference on Data Engineering (2003) Bangalore, India.
5. L. Cranor, M. Langheirich, M.M.: The Platform for Privacy Preferences 1.0 (p3p1.0) specification (2002) W3C Reccomandation, http://www.w3.org/P3P/brochure.html.
6. L. Cranor, M. Langheirich, M.M.: A P3P Preference Exchange Language 1.0 (appel1.0) (2002) W3C Working Draft.
7. P. Bonatti, P.S.: Regulating Access Services and Information Release on the Web. 7th ACM Conference on Computer and Communications Security, Athens, Greece (2000)

8. A. Herzberg, Mihaeli, e.a.: Access Control meets Public Key Infrastructure, or: Assigning Roles to Strangers. IEEE Symposium on Security and Privacy, Oakland, CA (2000)
9. K. E. Seamons, M.W., Yu, T.: Limiting the disclosure of Access Control Policies during Automated Trust Negotiation. Network and Distributed System Security Simposium, San Diego, CA (2001)
10. T. Yu, M.W.: A Unified Scheme for Resource protection in Automated Trust Negotiation. IEEE Symposium on Security and Privacy (2003) Oakland, CA.
11. Winsborough, W., Li, N.: Towards Practical Automated Trust Negotiation (2002)
12. E. Bertino, E. Ferrari, A.S.: Trust-X - a Peer to Peer Framework for Trust Establishment. To appear in IEEE TKDE, Transactions on Knowledge and Data Engineering (2004)
13. K. E. Seamons, M.W., Yu., T.: Protecting privacy during on line trust negotiation. 2nd Workshop on Privacy Enhancing Technologies (2002) San Francisco, CA.
14. Brands, S.: Rethinking Public Key Infrastructure and Digital Credentials. Mit Press (2000)
15. Herzberg, A., Mass, Y.: Relying Party Credentials Framework. RSA Conference (2001) San Francisco, CA.
16. E. Bertino, E. Ferrari, A.S.: X-TNL - an XML based language for trust negotiations. Fourth IEEE International Workshop on Policies for Distributed Systems and Networks, Como, Italy (2003)
17. Naor, M.: Bit commitment using pseudorandomness. Advances in Cryptology- 89 (1990) Lecture Notes in Computer Science, Vol. 435, New York.
18. P. Persiano, I.V.: User Privacy Issues Regarding Certificates and the TLS Protocol. Proceedings of the ACM Conference on Computer and Communication Security, Athens, Greece (2000)
19. Jarvis, R.: Selective disclosure of credential content during trust negotiation (2003) Master of Science Thesis, Brigham Young University, Provo, Utah.
20. World Wide Web Consortium: Extensible markup language (xml) 1.0 (1998) Available at: http://www.w3.org/TR/REC-xml .
21. World Wide Web Consortium: (Uniform resource identifiers, naming and addressing: Uris, urls, ...) Available at http://www.w3.org/addressing.
22. R. Agraval, J. Kiernan, R.S.Y.X.: An X-Path based preference language for P3P. Twelfth International World Wide Web Conference, Budapest, Hungary (2003)
23. World Wide Web Consortium: (References for p3p implementation) Available at: http://www.w3org/P3P/implementations.
24. IBM: (Ibm tivoli privacy wizard) Available at: www.tivoli.resource_center/maximize/privacy/wizard_code.html.
25. Center, J.J.R.: Jrc p3p resource centre (2002) Available athttp://p3p.jrc.it.
26. World Wide Web Consortium: P3p- the Platform for Privacy Preferences, version 1.1 (2003) Available at: http://www.w3.org/P3P/1.1/.
27. World Wide Web Consortium: Xsl transformations (xslt). version 1.0 w3c recommendation (1999) Available athttp://www.w3.org/TR/xslt.

Language-Based Enforcement of Privacy Policies

Katia Hayati and Martín Abadi

Department of Computer Science,
University of California, Santa Cruz

Abstract. We develop a language-based approach for modeling and verifying aspects of privacy policies. Our approach relies on information-flow control. Concretely, we use the programming language Jif, an extension of Java with information-flow types. We address basic leaks of private information and also consider other aspects of privacy policies supported by the Platform for Privacy Preferences (P3P) and related systems, namely the notion of purpose and the retention of data.

1 Introduction

Entities with a Web presence should not only define and publish their privacy policies but also ensure that they comply with those policies. A recent online survey [2] conducted by the Privacy Place [3] indicates that users may not mind when a website uses their personal information to tailor their browsing, but that they care about the possible misuse of this information and support punishments for misbehaving websites.

The problem of enforcing privacy policies has recently been attacked from several angles and in various domains (general enterprises [6], financial institutions [4], etc.). However, there have been no solutions at the level of programming languages. A language-level modeling of privacy policies should help programmers in avoiding inadvertent implementation mistakes. It should also facilitate the auditing of code by independent entities.

In a different context, there has been much work on restricting flows of information in programs (e.g., [9]), and on programming languages that support such restrictions (e.g., [13, 18, 19, 20, 21]). These restrictions can serve for guaranteeing integrity and secrecy properties. Although secrecy and privacy are related, it does not seem straightforward to reduce privacy policies (of the kinds considered in the privacy literature, and used in websites and elsewhere) to standard secrecy properties. Moreover, while privacy concerns are sometimes mentioned in some papers on those programming language, the papers do not show how to apply their techniques to enforcing privacy policies.

In this paper, we start to bridge the gap between those two lines of work. We explore how to use an information-flow system embodied in a programming language for guaranteeing that programs abide by their stated privacy policies. We address basic leaks of private information and also consider other facets of privacy policies.

D. Martin and A. Serjantov (Eds.): PET 2004, LNCS 3424, pp. 302–313, 2005.

In order to ground our work, we base our concepts of privacy on the Platform for Privacy Preferences (P3P) [23]. Although the P3P project is a young one, it has generated much interest and ongoing research (for example, about its implementation [1]). The goal of the P3P effort is twofold: to allow websites to specify their privacy policies concisely and precisely, and to enable users to specify their privacy preferences in order to check them automatically against the published policies of websites. A P3P file is an XML document that describes which information a website collects, what it intends to do with it, and how long it will be kept. A P3P file should also describe a way for a user to resolve a conflict with the website (for example, if the user believes information was mishandled). However, P3P is limited in scope. In particular, it is outside its scope to verify that websites really do abide by their stated policies in the implementation of their Web applications.

As a programming language, we use Jif [16, 17, 18]. It is an extension of Java that includes an enriched type system for specifying and checking information-flow security properties. It has not previously been used for providing privacy guarantees in a systematic way, but we believe that it is quite attractive for this purpose.

We show how we can use Jif for modeling and verifying aspects of privacy policies. Specifically, we consider three aspects of privacy: data cannot be (inadvertently) leaked; data is used at most for the purpose for which it was collected; and data is retained no longer than promised. These aspects constitute a core subset of the notions addressed by P3P. Of course, these notions are not specific to P3P privacy policies. They are also present, with variants, in other contexts, even beyond the Web.

The rest of this paper is organized as follows. Next, in Section 2, we present some further background material. In Section 3 we show how Jif can be used to give basic privacy guarantees. In Section 4 we explain how to represent purposes with principals. In Section 5 we treat retention guarantees. We conclude in Section 6.

2 Background

The problem of making it easier to control how private information is handled has been considered from many perspectives. Dreyer and Olivier [10] describe a system based on graph theory where entities are vertices in a graph and information flow between entities is represented by edges between vertices. In order to determine whether an inadmissible flow occurs, they use a graph reachability algorithm. Ashley, Powers, and Schunter [6] describe a system in which privacy information is attached to data. He and Antón [12] describe a system based on role engineering for modeling privacy policies. The authors also discuss P3P and lattices of purposes. Antón and her collaborators deplore the lack of a solution coming from the security sphere (see for example He's technical report [11] in addition to the previously cited paper). Privguard [15] is a system for protecting private data based on the purpose for which it was collected. It uses encryption to achieve security. The Enterprise Privacy Authorization Language (EPAL) in development at IBM [5] is an alternative to P3P. IBM has also developed the Declarative Policy Monitoring [8] and Reference Monitor technologies [14], designed to provide programming support for the enforcement of privacy policies written in EPAL or P3P. The enforcement appears to be done dynamically (for example in LDAP sniffers) and not at the language level. In addition to these projects, we are aware of some nascent efforts in this area (such as PAW [22]).

Type-based information-flow analysis for programming languages is a rich field, of which Jif is a prominent example. Work in the field is concerned with enforcing integrity and secrecy properties at the level of programs, relying on programming-language support. For example, Palsberg and Ørbæk [19] develop a λ-calculus with explicit trust operations, and equip it with a trust-type system; the SLam calculus [13] is a λ-calculus in which types express both integrity and secrecy properties.

While some of the foundational research in this area applies only to foundational calculi or "toy" programming languages, the techniques developed carry over to powerful, general-purpose programming languages. These include Jif (which, as mentioned in the introduction, is an extension of Java) and also Flow Caml (an extension of ML) [20, 21].

Jif provides mostly static information-flow checking via a type system based on the Decentralized Label Model [18]. The programmer must annotate variables, methods, and class declaration with a *label*. (Jif does not force the programmer to annotate every single variable: Jif infers labels not explicitly declared, and sets them to be as restrictive as possible.) A label specifies who owns data and who can read it. For example, the label {Alice:} means that Alice owns the data and only Alice can read it, and {Alice: Bob} means that Alice owns the data and Bob can read it too. The entities that own and read data are called *principals*. Principals are first-class objects (in the sense that they may be passed around). They are related to each other by the *acts-for* relation. If Alice acts-for Bob, then Alice can do everything Bob can do. The acts-for relation is reflexive and transitive. In addition, Jif supports a declassify operation, which enables the owner of a piece of data to give it a less restrictive label in certain circumstances.

3   Basic Control of Information Leaks

At a very basic level, Jif can be used to ensure that sensitive data is not leaked. For this purpose, we can represent categories of data (such as categories of sensitive data) with principals.

As an example, let us consider two principals, named SecretUserData and SharedUserData, and assume that SecretUserData acts-for SharedUserData. Then anything owned by SharedUserData is accessible by SecretUserData, but the converse is not true. Thus, while secret data may depend on shared data, leaks of secret data into shared data can be caught, as illustrated in the following code fragment:

```
// This code does not (and should not) compile.

int{SecretUserData: } credit_rating = 3;
// owned by SecretUserData and readable by no one else.

int{SharedUserData: } rebate;
// owned by SharedUserData, and can be accessed
// by SecretUserData.

if (credit_rating > 4) {
  rebate = 1;
  // ERROR: the (visible) value of rebate depends on the
  // (supposedly secret) value of credit_rating.
} else {
  rebate = 0;
}
```

This code fragment does not compile in Jif, because the value of `rebate` depends on the value of `credit_rating`. This dependency constitutes an inappropriate flow of information. If the value of a public variable depends on the value of a secret variable, then by observing the output of a program a non-authorized entity could infer information about the secret data.

As this example demonstrates, some of the most basic privacy properties can be supported by the Jif type system. In more elaborate examples, finer-grained data classifications can be used to indicate the intended recipients of a piece of data and other additional information. In any case, with Jif, the programmer has fewer worries that correctly labeled data will flow in unexpected or forbidden ways.

4   Purpose

In this section, we tackle the problem of modeling purposes in Jif. First, we review the definition of the notion of "purpose". Then we discuss how to represent purposes with Jif principals. Finally we briefly discuss the assurance problem: how can we make sure a program does what it promises to do?

4.1   What Is a Purpose?

Data is collected to fulfill a *purpose*. A purpose describes what the system intends to do with a piece of data. Examples include "tailoring the homepage of a website to the tastes of a particular client", "enabling a third-party shipping service to ship the goods to the client", "providing adequate medical care to a patient", and the like.

A purpose should be interpreted as an "upper bound", so the goal of a verifier is to make sure that the system does *at most* what it promised to do with the piece of data. To clarify this point, consider the example of an online bookseller that collects the user's mailing address for the purpose of shipping the purchased goods to the user. Then it is acceptable if the website actually does nothing with the address. For example, the user might have entered his address but then changed his mind about the particular purchase. On the other hand, the bookseller should not be allowed to do *more* than it promised. For example, it should not be allowed to sell the user's address to a telemarketing company.

Purposes can have a hierarchical structure. For example, the purpose of "traffic analysis" can be subsumed under the purpose of "website administration". Therefore, if a piece of data was collected with the purpose of helping with website administration, the system should be allowed to use it for the specific sub-purpose of "traffic analysis". The opposite, however, should not be true.

The P3P specification describes eleven specific purposes, and one catch-all "other" purpose which must be accompanied with a human-readable description. However, the notion of purpose can be more general than allowed in the P3P definition (which, for example, does not talk about sub-purposes). The model that we propose can adequately handle the P3P notion of purpose, and it is also powerful enough to describe a collection of purposes with sub-purpose relations, more broadly.

4.2   Modeling Purpose with Principals

The Model. We choose to represent a purpose with a principal in Jif. The programmer must create a principal for every purpose found in the policy. Data which is collected for a specific purpose is annotated as being owned by the corresponding principal. Methods which are needed for a specific purpose are annotated as bearing the authority of the corresponding principal.

This modeling achieves a number of goals. First of all, it ensures that correctly labeled data is going to be used only by the principals that have been explicitly granted authorization to use it. It also enables the programmer to make the program more explicit, as the purpose of methods is declared alongside them. In practice, the programmer does not need to annotate every single method, as Jif does some type inference. When type information is missing, type inference aims to find the most conservative label.

Consider the following code fragment. It shows a slightly more involved example than that of Section 3, and illustrates again how data cannot be misused. In this example WebAdmin and Marketing are two unrelated principals.

```
class LogProcessor {

    // the return type of total_hits is an int which
    // should be owned by WebAdmin and readable
    // by no one else.
    public int{WebAdmin: } total_hits() {
        ...
    }
    ...
```

```
}
...
int{Marketing: } hits = (new LogProcessor(...)).total_hits();
// ERROR: the label of hits is incompatible with
// the return label of total_hits().
}
```

An error is raised at compile time, preventing that data for `LogAmin` be made accessible to `Marketing`.

Sub-purposes. Sub-purposes are also easy to model via the acts-for relation. For example, if `LogAdmin` is a sub-purpose of `Admin`, then we can let the principal `LogAdmin` act-for `Admin`. So if a piece of data is collected for the (generic) purpose of `Admin`, it may in particular be used for the purpose of `LogAdmin`.

Suppose we have defined these two principals. We can then write the following code fragment:

```
InetAddress{Admin: } client_address = ...;
...
int{LogAdmin: } client_uid = client_address.hashCode();
```

The second assignment is legal even though `LogAdmin` uses a variable owned by `Admin`.

Multiple Purposes. Multiple purposes can be understood as another facet of sub-purposes. We can use the acts-for relation again to model data which is collected for several different purposes. The following construction is similar to the modeling of groups and roles in the Decentralized Label Model [18].

As an example, consider the purposes `LogAdmin`, `WebAdmin`, and `Admin` introduced above. Both `WebAdmin` and `LogAdmin` are sub-purposes of `Admin`, so we let both `LogAdmin` and `WebAdmin` act-for `Admin`. Suppose that the variable `client_address` is collected for both `LogAdmin` and `WebAdmin` purposes. Then we can label `client_address` with `Admin`, and it will be usable by both `LogAdmin` and `WebAdmin`.

Other examples may combine apparently unrelated purposes, such as the purpose `Marketing` defined above and the purpose `WebAdmin`. Suppose that we thought that a datum `unique_hits` should be used for both of these purposes. We can construct a new principal `Marketing_or_WebAdmin`, let `Marketing` and `WebAdmin` act-for the new principal, and use `Marketing_or_WebAdmin` in the annotation for `unique_hits`. In Jif this would not involve changing the already existing definition of `Marketing` or `WebAdmin`, because the superiors of a principal (those who act-for the principal) are declared alongside it.

While in principle one could construct an exponential number of compound purposes from a set of basic purposes, only those necessary for a particular program would have to be declared and used in that program. We expect these tasks to be of manageable complexity.

Conditional Purposes. Next, we discuss the situation (absent in P3P but present in other contexts [12]) where a piece of data `val` was collected for a purpose P but could be used for a purpose Q under certain well-defined circumstances. In Jif, `val` can have the label {P: }, but P can use the `declassify` operation when necessary.

The following code fragment illustrates this concept:

```
class Log authority(LogAdmin) {
// The class is annotated as bearing LogAdmin's authority.

  double{LogAdmin: } computeAvg(...) {
    ...
  }

  int{LogAdmin: } orderOfMagnitude(double{LogAdmin: } x) {
    ...
  }

  int{LogAdmin: Marketing} showAvg() throws SecurityException
    where authority(LogAdmin) {
    // The method is annotated as bearing LogAdmin's authority
    // so it is allowed to declassify data owned by LogAdmin.

    int{LogAdmin: } magn = orderOfMagnitude(computeAvg(...));

    if (certain_well_defined_circumstances) {
      return declassify(magn, {LogAdmin: Marketing});
      // returns magn with the new label
      // {LogAdmin: Marketing}.

    }
    else {
      throw new SecurityException();
    }
  }
}
```

The places in a program where the `declassify` operation appears constitute clear targets for detailed auditing. Thus, although the use of `declassify` may weaken the guarantees that can be established at the programming-language level, a Jif program with a few careful declassifications offers a better basis for enforcement than an arbitrary Java program.

Roles and Purposes. The principals that we use for representing purpose are regular principals in Jif. Myers and Liskov [18] have shown how to use principals and the acts-for relation to model *roles*. A principal may have several roles in an organization and wish to keep them separate. Roles are important in other contexts [12], and this modeling of purposes could be combined with the straightforward expression of roles to yield a richer system.

4.3 Assurance

It is important to realize that Jif, with our representation of purposes, will *not* guarantee that principals will perform only those actions that are necessary for the declared purposes. For example, we obtain no guarantee that a principal called WebAdmin will only administer a website, nor that a principal called Statistics will perform only statistical actions.

Nevertheless, information-flow checking does help. It can reduce the size of the code that needs to be examined in order to ensure that data is used only for the declared purposes.

In order to achieve higher assurance, one may combine the formal reasoning of the type system with a statement from the programmer (or some other responsible entity) certifying that the code does what it is supposed to do, and no more. This statement may in particular address any use of declassification operations. Ideally, it would be accompanied with a formal proof.

5   Retention

Another dimension of privacy is controlling how long user data may be retained. Although Jif does not have a built-in mechanism for expressing time or retention, in this section we show a treatment of retention that works within the existing Jif label system. We complete the section with another brief discussion of assurance.

5.1   Retention Periods

Our treatment addresses P3P's retention model, which defines five possible retention periods: no-retention, stated-purpose, legal-requirement, business-practices, and indefinitely. The label no-retention means that the data should be used only to complete the current action and should never be stored. Similarly, stated-purpose indicates that the data should be destroyed once the purpose for which is was collected is finished. This period could be longer than just the current transaction. For example, if a website collects a mailing address to share with an expediter, it might take a while to communicate the address to the expediter and complete the shipping. The retention legal-requirement indicates that the data will be retained for as long as is required by law. This period can vary, but for example the law sometimes requires banks to hold financial information for a year. The annotation business-practices is similar in intent, but here the considerations pertain to business rather than the law. The annotation indefinitely is the least restrictive: it indicates that the website may keep the data for any amount of time, but imposes no requirement.

It is of course possible that dealing with other models of retention would require changes and extensions to our approach.

5.2   Retention Labels

We can relate the idea of retention to information flow. A datum that may be retained only for a short time should not influence a datum that is retained for a very long time. For example, there should be no information flow from a variable with the label `no-retention` to a variable with the label `legal-requirement`.

Using this idea, we can represent retention periods within the existing Jif label system. We represent them as principals, much in the same way as purposes. Next we illustrate this encoding through an example; other encodings are possible.

In our example, `total_page_views` and `credit_rating` are variables intended for long-term retention, while `temp_cookie`, `credit_report_cookie`, and `viewed_credit_report` are variables intended for short-term use only (perhaps simply for displaying one webpage to the user). We omit the code that initializes the variables. For simplicity, we assume that these variables are all for the purpose of log administration, represented by the principal `LogAdmin`.

We introduce a principal for each retention period. In the example, we have two such principals, named `NoRetention` and `Indefinitely`, and we are concerned with preventing information flows from `NoRetention` to `Indefinitely`. Since flows in the opposite direction are admissible, we let `NoRetention` act-for `Indefinitely`.

Each of the variables has two owners: the purpose principal `LogAdmin` and a retention principal (one of `NoRetention` and `Indefinitely`). Labels with multiple owners, such as these ones, are supported in Jif. Intuitively, a component of a label with an owner A indicates A's policy. A label with multiple owners can be understood as the conjunction of the policies of all the owners.

```
int{LogAdmin: ; NoRetention: } temp_cookie;
boolean{LogAdmin: ; NoRetention: } viewed_credit_report;
int{LogAdmin: ; NoRetention: } credit_report_cookie;
int{LogAdmin: ; Indefinitely: } total_page_views;
int{LogAdmin: ; Indefinitely: } credit_rating;

// This assignment is OK (this ''if'' block typechecks).
if (viewed_credit_report) {
  credit_report_cookie = NO_SHOW_AD;
}
else {
  credit_report_cookie = SHOW_AD;
}

// This block typechecks too.
actsFor(NoRetention, Indefinitely) {
  // This ''if'' block executes only if it is the case that
  // NoRetention acts-for Indefinitely.
  // The reason we have to add a runtime check of this fact is
  // that acts-for relationships may change.
  if (credit_rating > 5) {
```

```
      temp_cookie = 1;
  }
  else {
    temp_cookie = 2;
  }
}


// ERROR: short-term information used in
// long-term variable.
if (viewed_credit_report) {
  total_page_views++;
}
```

Here, the value of `viewed_credit_report` is not allowed to influence the value of `total_page_views`, which may be kept indefinitely. Thus, the information-flow analysis addresses both purposes and retentions, simultaneously and independently.

5.3 Assurance

Much as for purposes, the Jif type system offers helpful support for retentions, but no actual "real-world" guarantees. For example, Jif does not have any independent information on the legal requirements associated with the label `legal-requirement`, and the Jif type system need not forbid storing data with the label `no-retention` on disk.

On the other hand, many such difficulties may be prevented if retention labels are correctly associated with system interfaces. In particular, the file-system interface could simply prevent the writing of data with the label `no-retention`. Thus, it may be possible to guarantee that data with the label `no-retention` is indeed ephemeral.

6 Conclusion

In this paper we present an approach for modeling and verifying some privacy properties in Jif, a programming language with an information-flow type system. We show how purposes and retention periods, in the sense of P3P, may be represented in Jif. We believe that this approach is rich enough to support additional privacy properties. In particular, we have developed some preliminary techniques for expressing the anonymous use of data.

So far we have focused on the checking of specific privacy properties on small pieces of code. We have not considered how our approach could apply to large software-engineering projects; we can only speculate on this question. Neither have we considered how those properties are assembled and expressed as a full policy. This policy may be written in P3P or a similar language, but it could also be represented by a Jif interface (analogous to a Java interface). In this case, the problem of checking compliance with the policy reduces to Jif typechecking.

For other policy languages, the problem of checking compliance may also be tractable provided those languages are given a precise semantics.

Acknowledgments

We thank Andrew Myers for encouragement, help with Jif, and comments on a draft of this paper, which in particular led to improvements in the treatment of retention periods. We also thank Stephen Chong for clarifying some tricky features of Jif, and Nathan Whitehead and the anonymous reviewers for many helpful comments.

This work was partly supported by the National Science Foundation under Grants CCR-0204162 and CCR-0208800.

References

[1] Rakesh Agrawal, Jerry Kiernan, Ramakrishnan Srikant, and Yirong Xu. Implementing P3P using database technology. In *Proceedings of the 19th International Conference on Data Engineering*, pages 595–606, March 2003.

[2] Annie I. Antón. The Privacy Place 2002 privacy values survey. http://william.stufflebeam.cc/privacySurvey/results/resultsPage.php, April 2003.

[3] Annie I. Antón. The Privacy Place. http://www.theprivacyplace.org, 2004.

[4] Annie I. Antón, Julie B. Earp, Davide Bolchini, Qingfeng He, Carlos Jensen, and William Stufflebeam. The lack of clarity in financial privacy policies and the need for standardization. Technical Report TR-2003-14, North Carolina State University, 2003.

[5] Paul Ashley, Satoshi Hada, Günter Karjoth, Calvin Powers, and Matthias Schunter. Enterprise Privacy Authorization Language (EPAL 1.1). http://www.zurich.ibm.com/security/enterprise-privacy/epal/Specification/, 2003.

[6] Paul Ashley, Calvin Powers, and Matthias Schunter. From privacy promises to privacy management: A new approach for enforcing privacy throughout an enterprise. In *Proceedings of the 2002 Workshop on New Security Paradigms*, pages 43–50, 2002.

[7] Michael Backes, Birgit Pfitzmann, and Matthias Schunter. A toolkit for managing enterprise privacy policies. In *8th European Symposium on Research in Computer Security (ESORICS 2003)*, number 2808 in LNCS, pages 162–180. Springer-Verlag, 2003.

[8] Kathy Bohrer, Satoshi Hada, Jeff Miller, Calvin Powers, and Hai fun Wu. Declarative Privacy Monitoring for Tivoli privacy manager. http://alphaworks.ibm.com/tech/dpm, October 2003.

[9] Dorothy E. Denning. *Cryptography and Data Security*. Addison-Wesley, Reading, Mass., 1982.

[10] Lucas C.J. Dreyer and Martin S. Olivier. An information-flow model for privacy (InfoPriv). In Sushil Jajodia, editor, *Database Security XII: Status and Prospects*, pages 77–90. Kluwer, 1999.

[11] Qingfeng He. Privacy enforcement with an extended role-based access model. Technical Report TR-2003-09, North Carolina State University, February 2003.

[12] Qingfeng He and Annie I. Antón. A framework for modeling privacy requirements in role engineering. In *Proceedings of the 9th International Workshop on
Requirements Engineering: Foundations for Software Quality*, pages 137–146. Es-
sener Informatik Beiträge, 2003.

[13] Nevin Heintze and John G. Riecke. The SLam calculus: Programming with secrecy
and integrity. In *Proceedings of the 25th ACM SIGPLAN-SIGACT Symposium
on Principles of programming languages*, pages 365–377, 1998.

[14] Richard Kevin Hill and Phil Fritz. Reference Monitor for Tivoli privacy manager.
http://alphaworks.ibm.com/tech/refmon, July 2003.

[15] F.A. Lategan and M.S. Olivier. Privguard: A model to protect private information
based on its usage. *South African Computer Journal*, 29:58–68, 2002.

[16] Andrew C. Myers. JFlow: Practical mostly-static information flow control. In
*Proceedings of the 26th ACM SIGPLAN-SIGACT Symposium on Principles of
Programming Languages*, pages 228–241, 1999.

[17] Andrew C. Myers. *Mostly-Static Decentralized Information Flow*. PhD thesis,
Massachussets Institute of Technology, 1999.

[18] Andrew C. Myers and Barbara Liskov. Protecting privacy using the Decentralized Label Model. *ACM Transactions on Software Engineering and Methodology*,
9(4):410–442, October 2000.

[19] Jens Palsberg and Peter Ørbæk. Trust in the λ-calculus. *Journal of Functional
Programming*, 7(6):557–591, November 1997.

[20] François Pottier and Vincent Simonet. Information flow inference for ML. *ACM
Transactions on Programming Languages and Systems*, 25(1):117–158, January
2003.

[21] Vincent Simonet. The Flow Caml System: documentation and user's manual.
Technical Report 0282, Institut National de Recherche en Informatique et en
Automatique (INRIA), July 2003.

[22] Jan C.A. van der Lubbe. PAW: Privacy in an Ambient World.
http://www.cs.kun.nl/paw, 2004.

[23] World Wide Web Consortium (W3C). The Platform for Privacy Preferences
Specification. http://www.w3.org/TR/P3P, April 2002.

Searching for Privacy: Design and Implementation of a P3P-Enabled Search Engine

Simon Byers[1], Lorrie Faith Cranor[2], Dave Kormann[1], and Patrick McDaniel[1]

[1] AT&T Research, Florham Park, NJ
{byers, davek, pdmcdan}@research.att.com
[2] Carnegie Mellon University, School of Computer Science,
Pittsburgh, PA
lorrie@cs.cmu.edu

Abstract. Although the number of online privacy policies is increasing, it remains difficult for Internet users to understand them, let alone to compare policies across sites or identify sites with the best privacy practices. The World Wide Web Consortium (W3C) developed the Platform for Privacy Preferences (P3P 1.0) specification to provide a standard computer-readable format for privacy policies. This standard enables web browsers and other user agents to interpret privacy policies on behalf of their users. This paper introduces our prototype P3P-enabled Privacy Bird Search engine. Users of this search service are given visual indicators of the privacy policies at sites included in query results. Our system acts as a front end to a general search engine by evaluating the P3P policies associated with search results against a user's privacy preference settings. To improve system performance we cache unexpired P3P policy information (including information about the absence of P3P policies) for thousands of the most popular sites as well as for sites that have been returned in previous search results. We discuss the system architecture and its implementation, and consider the work necessary to evolve our prototype into a fully functional and efficient service.

1 Introduction

As people increasingly use the Internet for shopping and other activities, the level of online privacy concern is rising [14]. Many web sites have attempted to address privacy concerns by posting privacy policies and participating in self-regulatory privacy programs. However, it remains difficult for Internet users to understand privacy policies [15], let alone to compare policies across sites or identify sites with the best privacy practices. The World Wide Web Consortium (W3C) developed the Platform for Privacy Preferences (P3P 1.0) Specification to provide a standard computer-readable format for privacy policies, thus enabling web browsers and other user agents to read privacy policies on behalf of their users [7]. However, the P3P user agents available to date have focused on blocking cookies and on providing information about the privacy policy associated with a web page that a user is requesting [8]. Even with these tools, it remains difficult for users to ferret out the web sites that have the best policies. We have developed a prototype P3P-enabled search engine called Privacy Bird Search that offers users the ability to perform Web searches that return privacy policy information along side search results.

D. Martin and A. Serjantov (Eds.): PET 2004, LNCS 3424, pp. 314–328, 2005.

1.1   P3P and APPEL

The P3P 1.0 Specification defines a standard XML format for a computer-readable privacy policy called a *P3P policy*. Although P3P policies contain some human-readable elements, they consist mostly of multiple-choice elements, which facilitate automated evaluation. A P3P policy includes elements that describe the kinds of a data a web site collects, the purposes for which data is used, potential data recipients, data retention policies, information on resolving privacy-related disputes, an indication as to whether a site allows individuals to gain access to their own data, and other information.

P3P became an official W3C Recommendation in April 2002 and has since been adopted by nearly a third of the most popular (top 100) web sites [4]. P3P user agent software is built into the Microsoft Internet Explorer 6 (IE6) and Netscape Navigator 7 web browsers. In addition, a P3P user agent called AT&T Privacy Bird can be downloaded for free and used as an add-on to the IE5 and IE6 web browsers. Other experimental P3P user agents are also available. In addition, a variety of tools have been developed to help web site operators generate P3P policies.

W3C also produced a specification for a language called A P3P Preference Exchange Language (APPEL) that can be used to encode user privacy preferences. APPEL is not an official W3C Recommendation; however, it has been implemented in Privacy Bird and other P3P user agents. APPEL is an XML-based language in which privacy preferences are encoded as rules that can be used to evaluate a P3P policy and control user agent behavior [6]. For example, an APPEL ruleset might specify that access to a web site should be blocked if the site collects data for telemarketing purposes without providing opportunities to opt-out.

1.2   Privacy Bird

AT&T Privacy Bird is implemented as an Internet Explorer browser helper object. The software adds a bird icon to the top right corner of the IE title bar. Users can configure Privacy Bird with their personal privacy preferences using a graphical user interface or by importing APPEL files. The preference interface allows users to select from pre-set high, medium, and low settings, or to configure their own custom setting. The user's preference settings are encoded as as APPEL rule set. At each web site a user visits, Privacy Bird checks for P3P policies. When Privacy Bird finds a policy, it uses an APPEL evaluation engine to compare the policy to the user's preferences. The Privacy Bird icon appears as a green "happy" bird at sites with policies that match a user's preferences. At sites with policies that do not match a user's preferences the icon appears as a red "angry" bird. The icon appears as a yellow "uncertain" bird at sites that have no P3P policy. A user can click on the bird to get a summary of the site's privacy policy, including the specific points where the site's policy differs from the user's preferences [9].

1.3   Related Work

A wide variety of web privacy tools are available that perform functions such as identifying web bugs, blocking cookies, reducing the amount of information transmitted by web browsers to web sites, and facilitating anonymous or pseudonymous browsing [8]. Several now-defunct dot coms offered privacy-related services including an electronic wallet linked to a privacy rating service (Enonymous) and a search engine dubbed "privacy friendly" because it did not have banner ads or cookies (Topclick). Neither of these services provided search results annotated with privacy information. Existing P3P user agents can make cookie blocking decisions based on P3P policies and display information about a site's privacy policies to users. However, none of these tools or services are designed to compare web site privacy policies or assist users in finding the sites with the best policies.

Tools and services are available to assist users in finding sites that match criteria unrelated to privacy. General web search engines find sites that match a user's text query. Google offers a SafeSearch feature in which sites with pornography or explicit sexual content are removed from search results. Shop bots and comparison shopping services find sites that sell a particular product, often offering the ability to compare these sites on the basis of price, reputation, delivery fees, and other criteria. However, currently none of these services offer comparisons based on privacy policies.

Studies have found that search engines are frequently used by most Internet users and that they serve as "gatekeepers" of Internet content [10]. Therefore, we believe that the search engine is the place where privacy policy information is likely to be of use most frequently.

After a user has conducted a web search and decided to visit a particular site, she has invested some time and effort and may be reluctant to turn away from that site even if she discovers that the site's privacy policy does not match her personal preferences. Without tools to assist her, she might have to visit several other sites before she finds one that has both the information or products she is looking for and a privacy policy that matches her preferences. In many cases such a site may not exist. As studies show that users typically do not visit more than two pages returned in a set of search results [13], it is unlikely that most users will undertake such a process to find a site that matches their privacy preferences.

A survey of Privacy Bird users showed strong interest in being able to do comparison shopping on the basis of privacy policies [9]. By adding Privacy Bird functionality to a search engine, we make it possible for users to determine which sites in their search results have policies that match their personal privacy preferences.

2   System Architecture

The Privacy Bird Search engine builds directly on the Google search engine service [2], and consists of four main architectural components: a policy acquisition module, a Google integration module, an APPEL evaluation engine, and a caching daemon. These components work in concert to acquire, maintain, and present a view of the P3P policies of sites returned by user search queries. This section gives an overview of the design and operation of this system.

The logical information flow and components of the Privacy Bird Search engine are illustrated in Figure 1. Users submit queries to the service through a search page provided by the Google integration model (step 1 in the figure). The integration model redirects the queries to Google, which returns results (2). The Google integration module checks the local cache for privacy policies associated with returned links. If available,

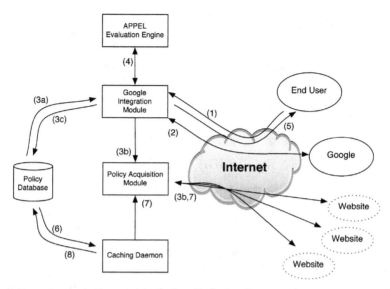

Fig. 1. Privacy Bird Search Engine Architecture - privacy evaluation results are generated by the evaluation of cached or real-time retrieved policies, and as directed by search results returned by the *Google* search engine

the policies are acquired directly from the policy database (3a). If not, the policy is acquired directly from the link's parent website using the policy acquisition module (3b) and placed in the database for future use (3c). The policies are evaluated using the APPEL evaluation engine, and results returned to the Google integration module (4). Finally, the search results are annotated with a red, yellow, or green bird (depending on the evaluation results) and returned to the original end user (5).

Working independently of user queries, the caching daemon maintains the freshness of the policy database. The daemon periodically queries the database for all expired policies (6), and uses the policy acquisition module to refresh them (7). Once re-acquired, they are pushed back into the policy database (8).

We use the automated P3P policy acquisition tool reported in [4] to obtain P3P policies, and refer interested readers to that publication for further details. The remainder of this section briefly describes the design of the other core components.

2.1   Google Integration

The Google integration module accepts user queries, submits them to the Google search engine, and returns annotated results to the user.

Depicted in figure 2, users enter search queries using a Google-style interface hosted on our server. The integration module submits queries to the Google search engine and retrieves encoded results. The integration module then checks each URL in the search

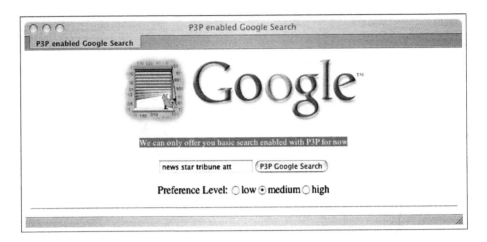

Fig. 2. Search Page

results to see whether it has a corresponding entry in the local P3P policy cache. If no
entry is found, it attempts to obtain a P3P policy directly from the web site. Next the
policies are evaluated and the results annotated and presented to the user in a Google-style
results page.

Illustrated in Figure 3, our current system simply places an appropriate Privacy Bird
icon next to each returned link. However, other presentation choices may be desirable. For
example, one may wish to reorder the links so that those with green birds are presented
first. In the extreme, one may eliminate all red or non-green birds entirely. We consider
the social and political implications of different result presentations inSection 5.

All of these tasks are performed by website scripting. The Google integration module simply joins the services of Google, the evaluation engine, and the caching daemon.
While intuitively simple, this requires some complex processing of the dissimilar arti-
facts used by each service. We consider the coordination of these services in depth in
Section 3.1

We have also added an advanced searching feature that causes the Google integration
module to return to the user any P3P policy information it has cached for a given site.
The prefix "p3p:" followed by a host and domain name signals a search for P3P policy
information.

As shown in Figure 4, a P3P policy search returns information about the location
of a site's P3P policy reference files, the content of any P3P headers, and the site's
cached P3P policies. In addition, the results page includes a hyperlink that submits the
site's policy directly to the W3C P3P Validator [1] to facilitate checking of policy syntax.
This advanced feature has been designed primarily for use by web site developers and
researchers.

---

[1] W3C maintains a free P3P validation service at http://www.w3.org/P3P/validator.
html. This service can be used to check the syntax of P3P policies and policy reference files,
and to verify that all P3P policies are properly located and referenced. This service is quite
useful for debugging P3P-related problems on web sites.

Fig. 3. Results Page

2.2   APPEL Evaluation Engine

A simpler P3P-enabled search service might establish a standard set of privacy preferences and evaluate all P3P policies against these preferences. However, this would eliminate one of the truly attractive features of P3P, choice. The APPEL evaluation engine gives us the ability to evaluate web site P3P policies against any APPEL-encoded privacy preference set without having to change any hard-coded rules.

For the purpose of demonstrating the feasibility of this concept in our prototype, we implemented an interface that includes three privacy settings, corresponding to three APPEL rulesets. In the future we plan to expand our interface to allow users to create or import rulesets. These rulesets could be maintained on the server[2] or placed in a cookie on the user's computer.

The three Privacy Bird Search settings are:

- *Low*: Trigger a red bird at sites that collect health or medical information and share it with other companies or use it for analysis, marketing, or to make decisions that may affect what content or ads the user sees. Also trigger a red bird at sites that engage in marketing but do not provide a way to opt-out.
- *Medium*: Same as low, plus trigger a red bird at sites that share personally identifiable information, financial information, or purchase information with other companies. Also trigger a red bird at sites that collect personally identified data but provide no access provisions.
- *High*: Same as medium, plus trigger a red bird at sites that share any personal information (including non-identified information) with other companies or use it to determine the user's habits, interests, or other characteristics. Also trigger a red bird at sites that may contact users for marketing or use financial or purchase information for analysis, marketing, or to make decisions that may affect what content or ads the user sees.

Currently, P3P policies are evaluated in response to each end user query. The red, yellow, or green bird result is used for annotation, but not stored beyond that request, i.e., there is no attempt to persistently store evaluation results. This misses an opportunity to optimize request processing costs, but as yet we have not seen evaluation as a limiting factor. We expect that this decision will effect the future scalability of the system, and will be revisited as needs dictate.

2.3   The Caching Daemon

The Privacy Bird caching daemon maintains the P3P policy database. Called `pb_daemon`, this daemon runs in the background and constantly scans the Internet for website P3P policies. Policies are refreshed as they become stale, and new site policies are discovered and subsequently monitored as directed by end-user queries. In this way, the service learns from users which policies it should be monitoring.

The P3P policy database is simply a collection of ASCII files containing the P3P policies of the monitored sites. A sub-directory is created for each site whose policies are being monitored. Each subdirectory contains all P3P policies, reference files, and a single informational file named *state*.

---

[2] The ruleset could be mapped to a unique identifier held in a user cookie. This would eliminate the need to communicate the potentially large policy, and allow policies to be used across browsers.

Fig. 4. P3P Policy Query Result Page

The *state* file contains a single line with the current state of the P3P-related files associated with the monitored site. The encoded data indicates whether the site is a "static" entry (see Section 3.3), the number of hits since its last refresh, the time of its next refresh, the time of its last reference, and a flag indicating that it should (or should not) be purged from the cache as soon as possible.

The P3P *EXPIRY* element dictates how long a downloaded policy should be considered valid. This tells the daemon exactly how long it can continue to use a downloaded policy, and when is should be discarded. As directed by the P3P specification, where EXPIRY is not set, a default expiration of 24 hours is assumed. As expected, the caching daemon holds a policy for this period if no EXPIRY is specified. Non-existence of policies are also cached in a similar way, save that no policies are stored in the directory. A site with no P3P policy is checked once every 24 hours to see if they have added one.

pb_daemon constantly scans the database for new entries, and purges old policy files and refreshes others dictated by EXPIRY information, if any. New sites are detected by periodically scanning the local database. The Google integration module stores acquired policies in the database. The policies are subsequently discovered at the next scan by the daemon. Because discovery occurs via the filesystem, the daemon need not directly communicate with the other components of the architecture. This vastly simplified the construction of the tool as it obviated the need for building specialized protocols for inter-process communication.

3   Implementation

We have implemented a prototype version of our Privacy Bird Search engine. The prototype has only basic user interface features and has not yet undergone performance testing. Eventually, we plan to evolve this prototype into a service that we can make available to the public via the Privacy Bird web site.

The following considers some of the low level implementation issues and challenges we faced during the construction of the Privacy Bird Search engine.

3.1   Google Integration Module

The Google integration module is built directly upon the Google search engine API [3]. Based on the SOAP [16] and WDSL [5] standards, this API provides a programmatic interface to the Google search engine. We found the Google API to be both well documented and easy to use. It allowed us to quickly integrate its service directly with our perl implementation of the integration module. In essence, this API reduced the job of implementing an Internet search to a quick and rather painless exercise.

The Google integration module is written entirely in perl. User cookies containing privacy preferences are decoded using simple perl subroutines and results recorded in process-local data structures. Call-outs to the APPEL evaluation engine allow us to access the evaluation tools, and results are again stored in the local data structure. The results of the Google query are extracted from the documented API structures, and used in the presentation functions.

Because of users' familiarity with it, the current implementation models the results after the Google results page. The Google integration module simply merges the search results with template files to generate the HTML source returned to the end users. This will allow us to quickly alter the feel of the results page as needs and user desires dictate. We plan to experiment further with different presentations as the prototype matures.

3.2   APPEL Evaluation Engine

While the evaluation of APPEL is intuitively simple, its implementation in software is complex and often difficult to debug [8]. The Privacy Bird APPEL evaluation engine first parses a P3P policy and an APPEL ruleset. Then it normalizes both policy and ruleset in several ways, including removing comments and white space characters and inserting default attribute values for attributes that have been omitted. Because P3P includes a somewhat complicated data model in which data elements may either be enumerated (for example, #business.contact-info.telecom.telephone.number) or identified by category (for example physical contact information), the APPEL engine must expand all data references so that rules about data categories can be applied to policies that include data elements and vice versa. The APPEL engine then applies each APPEL rule to the P3P policy in order to determine whether any of the rules fire. Evaluation of each rule involves an eight-part test that is applied recursively. The Privacy Bird APPEL engine collects description strings associated with each rule that fires and returns them to the calling application.

As the preceding discussion indicates, building an APPEL evaluation requires enormous domain knowledge and testing. Thus, rather than implementing a new APPEL evaluation engine, we have extracted the APPEL evaluation modules from the AT&T Privacy Bird software package [1]. However, this decision introduced an entirely different set of problems.

AT&T's Privacy Bird is a helper tool for Microsoft's Internet Explorer browser and requires a Windows operating system. We designed Privacy Bird Search entirely on the UNIX platform. Hence, we needed to port the code to a UNIX platform. The APPEL evaluation modules in Privacy Bird use Windows native libraries, which complicated the move to UNIX. For example, the Windows `String` API was used widely in the APPEL evaluation code. Similar to the `string` object in the ANSI Standard Template Library [12], the Windows `String` objects provide APIs for the safe and efficient manipulation of resizable buffers of alpha-numeric characters. Because this API was not available on UNIX, we had to build a custom string object and replace every `String` API call with an equivalent one. This required a fairly deep understanding of a large portion of code itself.

Because the original modules were integrated directly into the browser, we had to construct a new interface to the evaluation engine. For flexibility, we concluded that a command utility was the best way to access the evaluation engine. This lead to the following simple interface:

`appel_eval` *[user policy] [site policies]*

The *user policy* contains the APPEL privacy preferences. Based on user preferences or by default, the current Google integration module currently selects an APPEL policy encoding one the of three privacy preference profiles (e.g., high, medium, or low). The *site policies* are the collection of P3P related files retrieved directly from a site under consideration. The result of the APPEL evaluation is a Privacy Bird decision, which is printed to standard output in numeric form (e.g., 1, 2, or 3).

3.3   The Caching Daemon

The caching daemon is written entirely in perl. A number of APIs for the manipulation and use of the files created and maintained by the caching daemon (e.g., state files,

P3P policies) are directly implemented in the P3PSEARCH perl module.[3] The daemon itself is implemented in an executable pb_daemon perl script. As mentioned previously, pb_daemon does not communicate directly with the other components of Privacy Bird Search (e.g., via interprocess communication), but simply maintains the on-disk cache of P3P policies.

There are two classes of sites in the caching daemon. *Static* sites are those that are deemed important enough (e.g., appear frequently in searches) that fresh copies of the policies should always be maintained. Other non-static sites are those that the service acquires, but are free to be ejected from the cache should resource constraints mandate it. Static sites are identified in the caching daemon configuration as a single file of URLs, where each line contains the root of the site to which the policy applies. This file is read at startup and processed as described below.

The caching daemon is started using the following command line arguments:

pb_daemon [-r *refresh rate*] [-d *repository*]

Where the *refresh rate* is the rate at which the daemon rescans the P3P policy database, and the *repository* is the path to the the root of that database. The refresh rate defaults to 30 seconds, and the repository defaults to *./p3p_search_repository*)

The caching daemon operates as follows:

1. The daemon begins by initializing the list of static sites by reading the URLs included in the local (static_urls.dat) configuration file. Where a directory does not exist for a configured static site, one is created in the database. Where one exists, the local state file is read and its contents noted.
2. The daemon scans the database for directories not associated with statically defined sites. As before, the local state file is read and its contents noted.
3. The daemon queues the "stale" or missing policies for refresh (those entries which have not been refreshed in the last 24 hours, those with explicit and expired EXPIRY values, or those for which the daemon has no current information).
4. The policies are refreshed in the order in which they were queued. The policies and update state file are written to the appropriate directory once this process is completed. If the files cannot be retrieved, the stale files are removed and an empty state file written.
5. The main thread wakes every *refresh rate* seconds, rescans the database, and queues and refreshes the stale policies. This loop continues indefinitely.

The caching daemon does not refresh P3P policies directly. Rather, it forks a process for each site to be updated. This has the advantage that the daemon can easily parallelize updates. The current implementation forks a configurable number of update processes (by default, 5). Process termination is detected via the SIGCHLD signal, and the results obtained by rescanning the refreshed directory.

A key question for any such system is when to purge stale or unused site data. Some site policies may not be used frequently, or again. Hence, it is wasteful of resources to maintain the data. We are now considering several cache ejection strategies. The most

---

[3] The P3PSEARCH module also contains the APIs used by the Google integration module to acquire P3P policies from the end websites.

obvious strategies would be to cap the disk space usage and employ a commonly used cache ejection discipline when the usage is exceeded (e.g, least frequently used, least recently used).

A second, possibly more appropriate, approach would implement a neglection threshold: any policy which is not used for some period of time should be ejected. This would not only save disk space, but reduce the overhead of refreshing P3P policies and the associated state maintenance costs. An interesting question is whether to eject at all, as currently there are probably fewer than 5,000 P3P-enabled web sites on the Internet. Of course, as the use of P3P grows, this will be become a more important issue.

4   Performance

The current version of Privacy Bird Search is a prototype that has not yet undergone any performance optimizations other than the introduction of a caching daemon. It is implemented on a single 300 MHz UltraSPARC. The following discussion broadly considers the performance of the architecture and ways it can be improved. Ultimately, the performance must support scaling to a very large number of users.

While the current implementation is stable, the performance is less than optimal. The amount of time to return query results is impacted mostly by the time it takes to process a Google search request using the Google API, the time it takes to fetch P3P policies from web sites or from our cache, and the time it takes to evaluate P3P policies against user privacy preferences. It takes approximately 400 milliseconds to complete a search request using the Google search API (i.e., total first request to last response byte, with 30 search results returned). This response time will be affected by network conditions. The time it takes to fetch P3P policies from web sites varies considerably depending on web server performance and network congestion. Evaluating a single P3P policy is fairly quick, taking about 180 milliseconds to complete. However, if most of the 30 search results have P3P policies, this can add a delay of several seconds. Most of the cost of each evaluation is in launching the perl interpreter and disk I/O. The actual processing time by the APPEL evaluation engine is about 16 milliseconds.

We have not conducted a rigorous performance study. However, we have timed a number of search queries to get a feel for where the biggest performance costs are and where we might focus our optimization efforts. For example, searching for the term "lorrie cranor" can take a little over 25 seconds to return 30 results if no policies are previously cached. The same query takes about 6.4 seconds where policies are cached. The overwhelming amount of time spent in the uncached test is spent fetching P3P policies. In our current prototype policies are fetched serially—clearly, fetching P3P policies in parallel would improve performance considerably. Not only would this reduce total acquisition time, but it would allow us to evaluate policies while waiting for others to be returned. To further improve performance would require reducing policy evaluation time. Again parallel processing would improve performance considerably. In addition, if all the code were binary we could reduce the substantial overhead associated with launching the perl interpreter used to wrap the call to the binary evaluation tool. Minor performance gains could be achieved through optimization of the complicated APPEL evaluation code, including use of an XML parser optimized for this task.

Alternatively, caching evaluation results for each of our standard APPEL rule sets would improve performance, especially if caching was optimized to minimize disk I/O time. Each time the caching daemon retrieves a new policy the APPEL evaluation engine could be used to evaluate that policy for each of our standard APPEL rule sets (and perhaps also a set of popular user-defined APPEL files). The results of each evaluation could be stored as single bits.

When the policy cache is used, the performance of our prototype is reasonable for a prototype, but not for a production system. However, we believe the approaches outlined here will ultimately result in a stable and scalable system.

Note that because our implementation uses the Google API (as opposed to being integrated directly into a search engine) we had to build our own policy cache. A search engine may be able to implement privacy enhanced searching by integrating privacy tools with existing content discovery and management infrastructure. Moreover, we argue that the introduction of privacy features would represent a small incremental cost to an established search engine.

5   Discussion and Future Work

We have implemented a prototype P3P-enabled search engine that allows users to determine which of their search results are on web sites that have privacy policies matching their personal privacy preferences. We have demonstrated the feasibility of adding P3P functionality to a search engine. The next steps are to address performance and scaling issues, experiment with user interfaces, and investigate the types of P3P policies associated with web sites that are found using typical search queries.

Although our prototype system was developed with the intention of evolving into a fully functional and efficient service, we have not yet addressed all of the issues necessary to insure that the system will scale. As discussed in the previous sections, cache ejection, the policy of not caching evaluation results, and related issues may need to be revisited.

A number of user interface issues warrant further investigation. We would like to find an interface design that is easy to use and helps users find sites that are most likely to both match their queries and their privacy preferences. Our prototype Privacy Bird Search returns search results pages annotated with Privacy Bird icons. Users can then scroll through the search results to find those hits that have green bird icons. However, users tend not to look past the first screen or two of search results, and some search queries may not return green bird icons in the first two screens of results. Alternative interfaces might reorder search results so that green bird hits appear on top. However, this raises a number of questions. Should yellow and red birds also be taken into consideration when hits are reordered? If so, should sites with a policy that does not match a user's preferences be ranked higher or lower than sites with no policy at all? Should an attempt be made to order red bird hits according to the number of deviations from a user's preferences? For search results that return a large number of hits, should reordering be performed on only a subset of the hits (for example, the top 10 or top 100 hits)? Privacy Bird Search is designed as a front end to another search engine; however, a similar system built into a search engine could be positioned so that the privacy policy was taken into account in that search engine's ranking system. In that case a variety of options might be available to determine how much influence privacy policies have on ranking as compared with other factors. What kind of interface will best allow users to configure their preferences about privacy policies, ranking or search results, and other customizable features?

Ranking of search results on the basis of privacy policies raises usability issues as well as commercial and political issues. Because so many Internet users view the web primarily through the filter of a search engine, search engine ranking has enormous influence on what web sites users visit. This in turn influences the companies with which people do business and the ideas to which they are exposed [11]. If a popular search engine were to begin using privacy policies as a factor in search ranking it could influence web site operator decision-making about posting privacy policies and P3P policies. Depending on the approach to ranking, sites may have incentives to improve their policies. A search engine that offered only a standard privacy setting or that used a default preference set unless a user went to an advanced interface to configure preferences might influence sites to adapt their policies to match the standard or default setting. On the other hand, a search engine that ranked sites with no P3P policies higher than those with P3P policies that do not match a user's preferences might serve to discourage P3P adoption. Furthermore, because commercial sites are more likely to adopt P3P policies than non-commercial sites, reordering could reduce the chances that users would become aware of non-commercial sites.

In addition to annotating search results with privacy bird icons, we also plan to add a feature that will allow users to click on the bird icons to retrieve summary information about a web site's privacy policy, similar to the information provided by the Privacy Bird browser helper object [9]. This will include a summary of the site's policy, an explanation of why a site received a red bird, a link to any opt-out information provided by the site, and a link to the site's full human-readable privacy policy.

We previously developed software to gather data on P3P enabled web sites automatically. We have reported the results of our initial study of data collected using this software in [4]. However, no studies have yet attempted to use P3P to compare web site privacy policies systematically or determine the degree of variation of P3P policies across similar sites. Some factors that will determine the usefulness of a P3P-enabled search engine include the fraction of P3P-enabled sites among top hits to frequent search queries, and the fraction of those that tend to match users' privacy preferences. If few queries return hits that are both good matches to the query and have policies that match users' preferences, users are likely to find Privacy Bird Search more frustrating than useful. Future work in this area might include observations of Privacy Bird Search in use as well as simulations based on lists of most popular search queries.

Our work on Privacy Bird Search brings us a step closer to being able to provide privacy-related information to Web users at a time when it will be most useful. We were able to leverage our previous work developing the Privacy Bird browser helper object and automated tools for taking a census of P3P policies to develop this prototype. After further work on user interface, performance, and scalability issues we expect to be able to make Privacy Bird Search available to the public.

References

1. AT&T Privacy Bird, January 2004. `http://privacybird.com/`.
2. Google, January 2004. `http://http://www.google.com/`.
3. Google Web APIs Home, January 2004. `http://http://www.google.com/apis/`.
4. Simon Byers, Lorrie Faith Cranor, and David Kormann. Automated Analysis of P3P-Enabled Web Sites. In *In Proceedings of the Fifth International Conference on Electronic Commerce (ICEC2003)*, October 2003. Pittsburgh, PA.
5. Erik Christensen, Francisco Curbera, Greg Meredith, and Sanjiva Weerawarana. *Web Services Description Language (WSDL) 1.1*. W3C, 1.1 edition, March 2001. `http://www.w3c.org/TR/wsdl`.
6. Lorrie Cranor, Marc Langheinrich, and Massimo Marchiori. *A P3P Preference Exchange Language 1.0 (APPEL 1.0)*. W3C Working Draft, 15 April 2002. `http://www.w3.org/TR/P3P-preferences/`.
7. Lorrie Cranor, Marc Langheinrich, Massimo Marchiori, Martin Presler-Marshall, and Joseph Reagle. *The Platform for Privacy Preferences 1.0 (P3P1.0) Specification*. W3C Recommendation, 16 April 2002. `http://www.w3.org/TR/P3P/`.
8. Lorrie Faith Cranor. *Web Privacy with P3P*. O'Reilly and Associates, Sebastopol, 2002.
9. Lorrie Faith Cranor, Manjula Arjula, and Praveen Guduru. Use of a P3P User Agent by Early Adopters. In *Proceedings of the ACM Workshop on Privacy in the Electronic Society*, 21 November 2002. `http://doi.acm.org/10.1145/644527.644528`.
10. Eszter Hargittai. The Changing Online Landscape: From Free-for-All to Commercial Gatekeeping. In Peter Day and Doug Schuler, editors, *Community Practice in the Network Society: Local Actions/Global Interaction*. New York.
11. L. Introna and H. Nissenbaum. Shaping the Web: Why the Politics of Search Engines Matters. *The Information Society*, 16(3):1–17, 2000.
12. David R. Musser, Atul Saini, and Alexander Stepanov. *STL Tutorial and Reference Guide: C++ Programming With the Standard Template Library*. Addison-Wesley Professional Computing Series. Addison-Wesley, Reading, MA, 1996.
13. A. Spink, B.J. Jansen, D. Wolfram, and T. Saracevic. From E-Sex to ECommerce: Web Search Changes. *IEEE Computer*, 35(3):107–109, 2002.
14. Humphrey Taylor. Most people are "privacy pragmatists" who, while concerned about privacy, will sometimes trade it off for other benefits. *The Harris Poll*, (17), March 19 2003. `http://www.harrisinteractive.com/harris_poll/index.asp?PID=365`.
15. Joseph Turow. Americans and online privacy: The system is broken. Technical report, Annenberg Public Policy Center, June 2003. `http://www.asc.upenn.edu/usr/jturow/internet-privacy-report/36-page-turow-version-9.pdf`.
16. W3C. *Simple Object Access Protocol (SOAP) 1.1*, 2000. `http://www.w3c.org/TR/SOAP`.

Contextualized Communication of Privacy Practices and Personalization Benefits: Impacts on Users' Data Sharing and Purchase Behavior*

Alfred Kobsa[1] and Maximilian Teltzrow[2]

[1] School of Information and Computer Science
University of California, Irvine, CA 92697-3425, U.S.A
kobsa@uci.edu
http://www.ics.uci.edu/~kobsa
[2] Institute of Information Systems
Humboldt-Universität zu Berlin
Spandauer Str. 1, 10178 Berlin, Germany
teltzrow@wiwi.hu-berlin.de
http://www.wiwi.hu-berlin.de/iwi

Abstract. Consumer surveys demonstrated that privacy statements on the web are ineffective in alleviating users' privacy concerns. We propose a new user interface design approach in which the privacy practices of a website are explicated in a contextualized manner, and users' benefits in providing personal data clearly explained. To test the merits of this approach, we conducted a user experiment that compared two versions of a personalized web store: one with a traditional global disclosure and one that additionally provides contextualized explanations of privacy practices and personalization benefits. We found that subjects in the second condition were significantly more willing to share personal data with the website, rated its privacy practices and the perceived benefit resulting from data disclosure significantly higher, and also made considerably more purchases. We discuss the implications of these results and point out open research questions.

1 Introduction

Privacy plays a major role in the relationship between companies and Internet users. More than two third of the respondents in [1] indicated that knowing how their data will be used would be an important factor in their decision on whether or not to disclose personal data. It seems though that the communication of privacy practices on the Internet has so far not been very effective in alleviating consumer concerns: 64% of Internet users surveyed in [2] indicated having decided in the past not to use a website, or not to purchase something from a website, because they were not sure about how their personal information would be used.

* This research has been supported by the National Science Foundation (grant DST 0307504), Deutsche Forschungsgemeinschaft (DFG grant no. GRK 316/2), and by Humboldt Foundation (TransCoop program). We would like to thank Christoph Graupner, Louis Posern and Thomas Molter for their help in conducting the user experiment described herein.

D. Martin and A. Serjantov (Eds.): PET 2004, LNCS 3424, pp. 329–343, 2005.

Currently, the predominant way for websites to communicate how they handle users' data is to post comprehensive privacy statements (also known as "privacy policies" or "privacy disclosures"). 76% of users find privacy policies very important [3], and 55% stated that a privacy policy makes them more comfortable disclosing personal information [4, 5]. However, privacy statements today are usually written in a form that gives the impression that they are not really supposed to be read. And this is indeed not the case: whereas 73% of the respondents in [6] indicate having viewed web privacy statements in the past (and 26% of them claim to always read them), web site operators report that users hardly pay any attention to them.[1] [9] criticizes that people are turned off by long, legalistic privacy notices whose complexity makes them wonder what the organization is hiding. We clearly need better means for communicating corporate privacy practices than what is afforded by today's privacy statements on the web.

Communicating a company's privacy policy alone is not sufficient though. In situated interviews [10], users pointed out that "in order to trust an e-Commerce company, they must feel that the company is doing more than just protecting their data – it must also be providing them with functionality and service that they value." The way in which personal data is used for the provision of these services must be clearly explained. Current web privacy statements hardly address the connection between personal data and user benefits.

Thus, websites need more advanced methods for communicating to users both their privacy practices and the benefits that users can expect by providing personal data. In this paper, we will discuss and analyze such methods in the context of personalized websites [11]. Privacy protection is particularly important in such sites as they require more detailed user information than regular sites and therefore pose higher privacy risks [12].

We first survey existing approaches to communicate privacy practices to web site visitors that go beyond the posting of privacy statements, and indicate their merits and shortcomings. We then propose a new contextualized strategy to communicate privacy practices and personalization benefits. In Section 4, we describe a between-subjects experiment in which we compare this approach with a traditional form of disclosure. We focus on differences between users' willingness to share personal data, differences in their purchase behavior, and differences in their perception of a site's privacy practices as well as the benefits they received by sharing their data. The final section discusses the results and outlines open research questions.

2 Existing Approaches and Their Shortcomings

The currently predominant alternative approach to communicating privacy practices to website visitors is the Privacy Preferences Protocol (P3P). It provides website

---

[1] For example, [7] reports that on the day after the company Excite@home was featured in a *60 Minutes* segment about Internet privacy, only 100 out of 20 million unique visitors accessed that company's privacy pages. [8] indicates that less than 0.5% of all users read privacy policies.

managers with a standardized way to disclose how their site collects, uses, and shares personal information about users. However, the current P3P adoption rate stagnates at 30% for the top 100 websites, and only very slowly increases for the top 500 websites (currently at 22%) [13]. This relatively low adoption may be due to P3P's problematic legal implications [14], and the insufficient support to users in evaluating a site's P3P policy.

The latter problem is partly addressed by the AT&T Privacy Bird [15], which allows users to specify their own privacy preferences, compares them with a site's P3P-encoded privacy policy when users visit this site, and alerts them when this policy does not meet their standards. Upon request, the Privacy Bird also provides a summary of a site's privacy policy and a statement-by-statement comparison with the user's privacy preferences.

A few browsers also allow users to specify certain limited privacy preferences and to compare them with the P3P policies of visited websites. For example, *Internet Explorer 6* allows users to initially state a few privacy preferences and blocks cookies from sites that do not adhere to these preferences. The *Mozilla* browser goes one step further and allows users to enter privacy settings for cookies, images, popup windows, certificates and smart cards.

Finally, a simple non-technical approach is suggested by [9, 16]. The author correctly points out that the current lengthy and legalistic privacy statements "don't work". As an alternative, he suggests a "layered approach" which includes: one short concise notice with standardized vocabulary that is easy to follow and highlights the important information, and an additional long, "complete" policy that includes the details.

All these approaches suffer from the following major shortcomings though:

1. They require users to make privacy decisions upfront, without regard to specific circumstances in the context of a particular site or of individual pages at a site. This disregards the *situational nature* of privacy [17]. In fact, privacy preferences stated upfront and actual usage behavior often seem to differ significantly [18, 19].
2. The systems do not inform about the *benefits* of providing the requested data. For instance, respondents in [20] indicate to be willing to share personal data if the site offered personalized services.
3. They do not enhance users' *understanding* of basic privacy settings. For example, most users still do not know what a cookie is and what it can do.

Very recent work takes first steps to address some of these deficiencies. [21] aims at further enhancing the above-mentioned management of cookies and users' privacy in the *Mozilla* browser. Among other things, the authors study contextual issues such as how to enhance users' understanding of cookie settings, *at the time when cookie-related events occur* and in a form that is least distractive. [22] is concerned with the communication of privacy choices under the European Data Protection Directive [23]. From the privacy principles of this Directive, the authors derive four HCI guidelines for effective privacy interface design: (1) comprehension, (2) consciousness, (3) control, and (4) consent. Since single large click-through privacy policies or agreements do not meet the spirit of the Directive, the authors propose *"just-in-time* click-through agreements" on an *as-needed basis* instead of a large, complete list of service terms. These small agreements would facilitate a better understanding of decisions since they are made in-context.

3 A Design Pattern for Websites That Collect Personal Data

To adequately address privacy concerns of users of personalized websites, we propose user interface design patterns that communicate the privacy practices of a site both at a global and a local level. Similar to design patterns in object-oriented programming, interface design patterns constitute descriptions of best practices within a given design domain based on research and application experience [24]. They give designers guidelines for the efficient and effective design of user interfaces.

3.1 Global Communication of Privacy Practices and Personalization Benefits

Global communication of privacy practices currently takes place by posting privacy statements on a company's homepage or on all its web pages. Privacy statements on the web are legally binding in many jurisdictions. In the U.S., the Federal Trade Commission and several states have increasingly sued companies that did not adhere to their posted privacy policies, for unfair and deceptive business practices. Privacy policies are therefore carefully crafted by legal council. Rather than completely replacing them by something new whose legal impact is currently unclear at best, our approach keeps current privacy statements in the "background" for legal reference and protection. However, we argue to enhance this kind of disclosure by additional information that explains privacy practices and user benefits, and their relation to the requested personal data, in the given local context.

3.2 Local Communication of Privacy Practices and Personalization Benefits

As discussed in Section 1, tailored in-context explanation of privacy practices and personalization benefits can be expected to address users' privacy concerns much better than global contextless disclosures. Such an approach would break long privacy policies into smaller, more understandable pieces, refer more concretely to the current context, and thereby allow users to make situated decisions regarding the disclosure of their personal data considering the explicated privacy practices and the explicated personalization benefits.

It is unclear yet at what level of granularity the current context should be taken into account. Should privacy practices and personalization benefits be explained at the level of single entry fields (at the risk of being redundant), or summarized at the page level or even the level of several consecutive pages (e.g., a page sequence for entering shipping, billing and payment data)? Several considerations need to be taken into account:

Closure: Input sequences should be designed in such a way that their completion leads to (cognitive) closure [25]. The coarsest level at which closure should be achieved is the page level. This therefore should also be the coarsest level for the provision of information about privacy and personalization, even if this information is redundant across several pages.

Separation: Within a page, sub-contexts often exist that are supposed to be visually separated from each other (e.g. simply by white space). Ideally, the completion of each sub-context should lead to closure. Information about privacy and personalization should therefore be given at the level of such visually separated sub-contexts, even if this leads to redundancy across different contexts on a page.

Different sensitivity: [1] found that users indicated different degrees of willingness to give out personal data, depending on the type of data and whether the data was about them or their children. For instance, 76% of the respondents felt comfortable giving out their own email addresses, 54% their full names, but only 11% their phone numbers. Even when entry fields for such data fall into the same sub-context (which is likely in the case of this example), users' different comfort levels suggest to treat each data field separately and to provide separate explanations of privacy practices and personalization benefits that can address these different sensitivity levels.

Legal differences: From a legal perspective, not all data may be alike. For instance, the European Data Protection Directive distinguishes "sensitive data" (such as race, ethnic origin, religious beliefs and trade union membership) whose processing require the user's explicit consent. This calls for a separate explanation of privacy practices and personalization benefits of data that are different from a legal standpoint, possibly combined with a "just-in-time click-through agreement" as proposed by [22].

The safest strategy is seemingly to communicate privacy practices and personalization benefits at the level of each individual entry field for personal data. If a number of such fields form a visually separate sub-context on a page, compiled explanations may be given only if the explanations for each individual field are not very different (due to legal differences, different sensitivity levels, privacy practices or personalization benefits). A page is the highest possible level at which compiled contextual explanations may be given (again, only if the field-level explanations are relatively similar). Visually separate sub-contexts on a page should be preferred though, due to the closure that they require.

3.3 An Example Website with Global and Contextual Communication of Privacy Practices and Personalization Benefits

Fig. 1 shows the application of the proposed interface design pattern to a web bookstore that offers personalized services. The top three links in the left-hand frame lead to the global disclosures (to facilitate comprehension, we decided to split the usual contents of current privacy statements into three separate topics: privacy, personalization benefits, and security). The main frame contains input fields and checkboxes for entering personal data. Each of them is accompanied by an explanation of the site's privacy practices regarding the respective personal data (which focuses specifically on usage purposes), and the personalized services that these data afford.

As in the theoretical model of [26], a user achieves an understanding of the privacy implications of the displayed situation both intuitively (taking the overall purpose of the site and page into account) and through adequate contextual notice. The traditional link to a privacy policy can still be accessed if so desired.

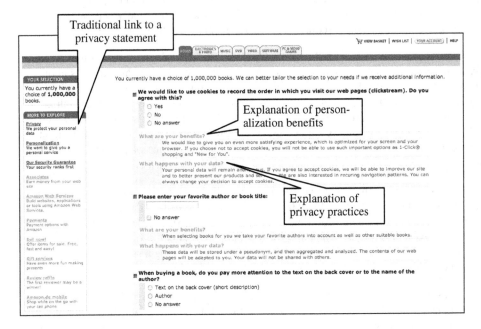

Fig. 1. Global and contextual communication of privacy practices and personalization benefits

4   Impacts on Users' Data Sharing and Purchase Behavior

We conducted a user experiment to empirically verify the merits of our proposed user interface design pattern in comparison with traditional approaches for the communication of privacy practices. In Section 4.1 we will motivate the specific research strategy that we pursued. Sections 4.2-4.5 describe the materials, subjects, design and procedures, and the results of our study. Section 5 discusses these results and points out interesting research questions that still remain open.

4.1   Background

Two kinds of methods can be applied to study users' reaction to different interface designs: inquiry-based and observational methods. In the first approach, users are being interviewed about their opinions with regard to the questions at hand. These interviews may be supported by representations of the proposed designs, ranging in fidelity from paper sketches to prototypes and real systems. In the second approach, users are being observed while carrying out tasks (either their customary ones or synthetic tasks). Both approaches complement each other: while inquiries may reveal aspects of users' rationale that cannot be inferred from mere observation, observations allow one to see actual user behavior which may differ from self-reported behavior.

This latter problem seems to prevail in the area of privacy. As mentioned above, [18, 19] found that users' stated privacy preferences deviate significantly from their actual behavior, and an enormous discrepancy can be observed between the number of people who claim to read privacy policies and the actual access statistics of these pages. Solely relying on interview-based techniques for analyzing privacy impacts on users, as is currently nearly exclusively the case, must therefore be viewed with caution. Our empirical studies therefore gravitated towards an observational approach, which we complemented by questionnaires. We designed an experiment to determine whether users exhibit different data sharing behavior depending on the type of explanation about privacy practices and personalization benefits that they receive (global alone versus global plus contextual). Our hypothesis was that users would be more willing to share personal data in the condition with contextual explanations, and that they would also view sites more favorably that use this type of disclosure.

4.2 Materials

We developed a fake book recommendation and sales website whose interface was designed to suggest an experimental future version of a popular online bookstore. Two variants of this system were created, one with contextual explanations of privacy practices and personalization benefits, and one without. Figure 1 shows an excerpt of the first variant, translated from German into English. The contextual explanations are given for each entry field (which is the safest of the strategies discussed in Section 3.2), under the headings "What are your benefits?" and "What happens with your data?" In the version without contextual explanations, these explanations are omitted.

In both conditions, the standard privacy policy of the web retailer is used. The three left-hand links labeled "Privacy", "Personalization" and "Our Security Guarantee" lead to the original company privacy statement (we split it into these three topics though and left out irrelevant text). In the condition with contextual explanations, the central policies that are relevant in the current situation are explained under "What happens with your data?" Such explanations state, for instance, that the respective piece of personal data will not be shared with third parties, or that some personal data will be stored under a pseudonym and then aggregated and analyzed. The explanation of the usage purpose is concise and kept in the spirit of P3P specifications [27].

A counter was visibly placed on each page that purported to represent the size of the currently available selection of books. Initially the counter is set to 1 million books. Data entries in web forms (both via checkboxes and radio buttons and through textual input) decrease the counter after each page by an amount that depends on the data entries made. The web forms ask a broad range of questions relating to users' interests. A few sensitive questions on users' political interests, religious interests and adherence, their literary sexual preferences, and their interest in certain medical subareas (including venereal diseases) are also present. All questions "make sense" in the context of filtering books in which users may be interested. For each question, users have the option of checking a "no answer" box or simply leaving the question unanswered. The personal information that is solicited in the web forms was chosen in such a way that it may be relevant for book recommendations and/or general customer and market analysis. Questions without any clear relation to the business goals of an online bookstore are not being asked. A total of 32 questions with 86 answer options are presented. Ten questions allow multiple answers, and seven questions have several answer fields with open text entries (each of which we counted as one answer option).

After nine pages of data entry (with a decreased book selection count after each page), users are encouraged to review their entries and then to retrieve books that purportedly match their interests. Fifty predetermined and invariant books are then displayed that were selected based on their low price and their presumable attractiveness for students (book topics include popular fiction, politics, tourism, and sex and health advisories). The prices of all books are visibly marked down by 70%, resulting in out-of-pocket expenses between €2 and €12 for a book purchase. For each book, users can retrieve a page with bibliographic data, editorial reviews, and ratings and reviews by readers.

Users are free to choose whether or not to buy one single book. Those who do are asked for their shipping and payment data (a choice of bank account withdrawal and credit card charge is offered). Those who do not buy may still register with their postal and email addresses, to receive personalized recommendations in the future as well as newsletters and other information.

4.3 Subjects

58 subjects participated in the experiment. They were students of Humboldt University in Berlin, Germany, mostly in the areas of Business Administration and Economics. The data of 6 subjects were eventually not used, due to a computer failure or familiarity with the student experimenters.

4.4 Experimental Design and Procedures

The experiment was announced electronically in the School of Economic Sciences of Humboldt University. Participants were promised a € 6 coupon for a nearby popular coffee shop as a compensation for their participation, and the option to purchase a book with a 70% discount. Prospective participants were asked to bring their IDs and credit or bank cards to the experiment.

When subjects showed up for the experiment, they were reminded to check whether they had these credentials with them, but no data was registered at this time. Paraphernalia that are easily associated with the web book retailer, such as book cartons and logos, were casually displayed.

In the instructions part of the experiment, subjects were informed that they would test an experimental new version of the online bookstore with an intelligent book recommendation engine inside. Users were told that the more and the better data they provided, the better would be the book selection. They were made aware that their data would be given to the book retailer after the experiment. It was explicitly pointed out though that they were not required to answer any question. Subjects were asked to work with the prototype to find books that suited their interests, and to optionally pick and purchase one of them at a 70% discount. They were instructed that payments could be made by credit card or by withdrawal from their bank accounts.

A between-subjects design was used for the subsequent experiment, with the system version as the independent variable: one variant featured non-contextual explanations of privacy practices and personalization benefits only, and the other additionally contextualized explanations (see Section 4.2 for details). Subjects were randomly assigned to one of the two conditions (we will abbreviate them by "no-ctxt-expl" and "ctxt-expl" in the following). They were separated by screens, to bar any communication between them. After searching for books and possibly buying one, subjects filled in two post-questionnaires, one online and one on paper. Finally, the data of those users who had bought a book or had registered with the system were compared with the credentials that subjects had brought with.

4.5 Results

Data Sharing Behavior. We analyzed the data of 26 participants in the conditions "no-ctxt-expl" and "ctxt-expl". We first dichotomized their responses by counting whether a question received at least one answer or was not answered at all. Whereas on average 84% of the questions were answered in condition "no-ctxt-expl", this rose to 91% in the second condition (see Table 1). A Chi-Square test on a contingency table with the total number of questions answered and not answered in each condition showed that the difference between conditions was statistically significant ($p<0.001$).

The two conditions also differed with respect to the number of answers given (see Table 2). The maximum number of answers that any subject could reasonably give was about 64, and we used this as the maximum number of possible answers. In condition "no-ctxt-expl", subjects gave 56% of all possible responses on average (counting all options for multiple answers), while they gave 67% of all possible answers in condition "no-ctxt-expl". A Chi-Square contingency test showed again that the difference between the two conditions is highly significant ($p<0.001$). The relative difference between the number of answers provided in the two conditions is even higher than in the dichotomized case (19.6% vs. 8.3% increase).

Table 1. Percentage of questions answered and results of Chi-Square test

	w/o contextual explanations	with contextual explanations	df	Chi-Square	p	N
% Questions answered	84%	91%	1	16.42	<0.001	1664

Table 2. Percentage of checked answer options and results of Chi-Square test

	w/o contextual explanations	with contextual explanations	df	Chi-Square	p	N
% Answers given	56%	67%	1	42.68	<0.001	3328

The results demonstrate that the contextual communication of privacy practices and personalization benefits has a significant positive effect on users' willingness to share personal data. The effect is even stronger when users can give multiple answers. We found no evidence for a significant difference of this effect between questions that we regarded as more sensitive, and less sensitive questions.

Purchases. Table 3 shows that the purchase rate in condition "ctxt-expl" is 33% higher than in condition "no-ctxt-expl" (note that all subjects saw the same set of 50 books in both conditions). A t-test for proportions indicates that this result approaches significance ($p<0.07$). We regard this as an important confirmation of the success of our proposed contextual explanation of privacy practices and personalization benefits. In terms of privacy, the decision to buy is a significant step since at this point users reveal personally identifiable information (name, shipment and payment data) and risk that previously pseudonymous information may be linked to their identities. A contextual explanation of privacy practices seemingly alleviates such concerns much better than a traditional global disclosure of privacy practices.

Access to the global company disclosures. We also monitored how often subjects clicked on the links "Privacy", "Personalization" and "Our Security Guarantee" in the left side panel (which lead to the respective original global company disclosures): merely one subject in each condition clicked on the "Privacy" link.

Table 3. Purchase ratio and result of t-test for frequencies

	w/o contextual explanations	with contextual explanations	df	Chi-Square	p	N
Purchase ratio	0.58	0.77	48	1.51	0.07	52

Rating of privacy practices and perceived benefit resulting from data disclosure. The paper questionnaire that was administered to each subject at the end of the study contains five Likert questions (whose possible answers range from "strongly agree" to "strongly disagree"), and one open question for optional comments. It examines how users perceive the level of privacy protection at the website as well as the expediency of their data disclosure in helping the company recommend better books.

The responses to the five attitudinal questions were encoded on a one to five scale. A one-tailed t test revealed that the agreement with the statement "Privacy has priority at <book retailer>" was significantly higher in condition "ctxt-expl" than in condition "no-ctxt-expl" ($p<0.01$). The same applies to subjects' perception of whether their data disclosure helped the bookstore in selecting interesting books for them ($p<0.05$). Note again that all subjects were offered the same set of books. The difference between the two conditions in the statement "<book retailer> uses my data in a responsible manner" approached significance ($p<.12$). More details about these results can be found in Table 4.

Table 4. Users' perception of privacy practice and benefit of data disclosure 1: strongly disagree, 2: disagree, 3: not sure, 4: agree, 5: strongly agree

| Item | N | no-ctxt-expl | | ctxt-expl | | Means$_{dif}$ | StdDev$_{dif}$ | t | df | p(t) 1-tailed |
		Means	StdDev	Means	StdDev					
Privacy has priority	41	3.35	0.88	3.94	0.87	0.60	0.28	2.16	39	0.01
Data helped site to select better books	56	2.85	0.97	3.40	1.10	0.51	0.28	1.85	54	.035
Data is used responsibly	47	3.62	0.85	3.91	0.83	0.29	0.25	1.17	45	0.12

5 Discussion of the Results and Open Research Questions

Our experiment was designed so as to ensure that subjects had as much "skin in the game" as possible, and thereby to increase its ecological relevance. The incentive of a highly discounted book and the extremely large selection set that visibly decreased with every answer given was chosen to incite users to provide ample and truthful data about their interests. The perceptible presence of the web book retailer, the claim that all data would be made available to them, and the fact that names, addresses and payment data were verified (which ensured that users could not use escape strategies such as sending books to P.O. boxes or someone they know) meant that users really had to trust the privacy policy that the website promised when deciding to disclose their identities.

The results demonstrate that the contextualized communication of privacy practices and personalization benefits has a significant positive effect on users' data sharing behavior, and on their perception of the website's privacy practices as well as the perceived benefit resulting from data disclosure. The additional finding that this form of explanation also leads to more purchases approached significance. The adoption by web retailers of interface design patterns that contain such explanations therefore seems clearly advisable.

While the experiment does not allow for substantiated conclusions regarding the underlying reasons that link the two conditions with the observed effects, the results are by all means consistent with recent models in the area of personalization research that include the notion of 'trust' in a company (e.g. [28]). One may speculate whether the significantly higher perceived usefulness of data disclosure in condition "ctxt-expl" can be explained by a positive transfer effect.

Other characteristics of our experiment are also in agreement with the literature. [29] found in their study of consumer privacy concerns that "in the absence of straightforward explanations on the purposes of data collection, people were able to produce their own versions of the organization's motivation that were unlikely to be favorable. Clear and *readily available* explanations might alleviate some of the unfavorable speculation" [emphasis ours]. [30] postulate that consumers will "continue to disclose personal information as long as they perceive that they receive benefits that exceed the current or future risks of disclosure. Implied here is an expectation that organizations not only need to offer benefits that consumers find attractive, but they also need to be open and honest about their information practices so that consumers [...] can make an informed choice about whether or not to disclose." The readily available explanations of *both* privacy practices and personalization benefits in our experiment meet the requirements spelled out in the above quotations, and the predicted effects could be indeed observed.

Having said this, we would however also like to point out that additional factors may also play a role in users' data disclosure behavior, which were kept constant in our experiment due to the specific choice of the web retailer, its privacy policy, and a specific instantiation of our proposed interface design pattern. We will discuss some of these factors in the following.

Reputation of a website. We chose a webstore that enjoys a relatively high reputation in Germany (we conducted surveys that confirmed this). It is well known that reputation increases users' willingness to share personal data with a website (see e.g. [31-33]). Our high response rates of 84% without and specifically 91% with contextual explanation suggest that we may have already experienced some ceiling effects (after all, some questions may have been completely irrelevant for the interests of some users so that they had no reason to answer them). This raises the possibility that websites with a lesser reputation will experience an even stronger effect of contextualized explanation of privacy practices and personalization benefits.

Stringency of a website's data handling practices. The privacy policy of the website that we mimicked is comparatively strict. Putting this policy upfront and explaining it in-context in a comprehensible manner is more likely to have a positive effect on customers than couching it in legalese and hiding it behind a link. Chances are that this may change if a site's privacy policy is not so customer-friendly.

Permanent visibility of contextual explanations. In our experiment, the contextual explanations were permanently visible. This uses up a considerable amount of screen real estate. Can the same effect be achieved in a less space-consuming manner, for instance with icons that symbolize the availability of such explanations? If so, how can the contextual explanations be presented so that users can easily access them and at the same time will not be distracted by them? Should this be done through regular page links, links to pop-up windows, or rollover windows that pop up when users brush over an icon?

References to the full privacy policy. As discussed in Section 3.1, privacy statements on the web currently constitute important and comprehensive legal documents. Contextual explanations will in most cases be incomplete since they need to be short and focused on the current situation, so as to ensure that users will read and understand them. For legal protection, it is advisable to include in every contextual explanation a proviso such as "This is only a summary explanation. See <link to

privacy statement> for a full disclosure." Will users then be concerned that a website is hiding the juicy part of its privacy disclosure in the "small print", and therefore show less willingness to disclose their personal data?

Additional user experiments will be necessary to obtain answers or at least a clearer picture with regard to these questions.

References

1. Ackerman, M. S., Cranor, L. F., and Reagle, J.: Privacy in E-commerce: Examining User Scenarios and Privacy Preferences. First ACM Conference on Electronic Commerce, Denver, CO (1999) 1-8, http://doi.acm.org/10.1145/336992.336995.
2. Culnan, M. J. and Milne, G. R.: The Culnan-Milne Survey on Consumers & Online Privacy Notices: Summary of Responses. Interagency Public Workshop:Get Noticed: Effective Financial Privacy Notices, Washington, D.C. (2001),
   http://www.ftc.gov/ bcp/workshops/glb/supporting/culnan-milne.pdf.
3. Department for Trade and Industry: Informing Consumers about E-Commerce. Conducted by MORI, London: DTI, London (2001),
   http://www.consumer.gov.uk/ ccp/topics1/pdf1/ecomfull.pdf.
4. GartnerG2: Privacy and Security: The Hidden Growth Strategy. (August 2001), http://www4.gartner.com/5_about/press_releases/2001/pr20010807d.html.
5. Roy Morgan Research: Privacy and the Community. Prepared for theOffice of the Federal Privacy Commissioner, Sydney (2001),
   http://www.privacy.gov.au/ publications/rcommunity.html.
6. A Survey of Consumer Privacy Attitudes and Behaviors. Harris Interactive, (2001), http://www.bbbonline.org/UnderstandingPrivacy/library/harrissummary.pdf
7. The Information Marketplace: Merging and Exchanging Consumer Data, March 13, 2001. Federal Trade Commission (2001),
   http://www.ftc.gov/bcp/workshops/ infomktplace/transcript.htm
8. Kohavi, R.: Mining E-Commerce Data: the Good, the Bad, and the Ugly. Seventh ACM SIGKDD International Conference on Knowledge Discovery and Data Mining, San Francisco, CA (2001) 8-13.
9. Abrams, M.: Making Notices Work For Real People. 25th International Conference of Data Protection & Privacy Commissioners, Sydney, Australia (2003), http://www.privacyconference2003.org/.
10. Brodie, C., Karat, C.-M., and Karat, J.: How Personalization of an E-Commerce Website Affects Consumer Trust. In: Designing Personalized User Experience for eCommerce, Karat, J., Ed. Dordrecht, Netherlands: Kluwer Academic Publishers (2004) 185-206.
11. Kobsa, A., Koenemann, J., and Pohl, W.: Personalized Hypermedia Presentation Techniques for Improving Customer Relationships. The Knowledge Engineering Review 16, (2001) 111-155. http://www.ics.uci.edu/~kobsa/papers/2001-KER-kobsa.pdf.
12. Teltzrow, M. and Kobsa, A.: Impacts of User Privacy Preferences on Personalized Systems: a Comparative Study. In: Designing Personalized User Experiences for eCommerce, Karat, C.-M., Blom, J., and Karat, J., Eds. Dordrecht, Netherlands: Kluwer Academic Publishers (2004) 315-332,
    http://www.ics.uci.edu/~kobsa/papers/2004-PersUXinECom-kobsa.pdf.
13. P3P Dashboard Report. (October 2003),
    http://www.ey.com/global/Content.nsf/US/ AABS_-_TSRS_-_Library.

14. Cranor, L. F. and Reidenberg, J. R.: Can User Agents Accurately Represent Privacy Notices? 30th Research Conference on Communication, Information and Internet Policy, Alexandria, VA (2002), http://intel.si.umich.edu/tprc/archive-search-abstract.cfm?PaperID=65.
15. AT&T Privacybird. (2002), http://www.privacybird.com/.
16. Abrams, M.: The Notices Project: Common Short Informing Notices. Interagency Public Workshop: Get Noticed: Effective Financial Privacy Notices, Washington, DC (2001), http://www.ftc.gov/bcp/workshops/glb/presentations/abrams.pdf.
17. Palen, L. and Dourish, P.: Unpacking "Privacy" for a Networked World. CHI-02, Fort Lauderdale, FL (2002) 129-136.
18. Spiekermann, S., Grossklags, J., and Berendt, B.: E-privacy in 2nd Generation E-Commerce: Privacy Preferences versus Actual Behavior. EC'01: Third ACM Conference on Electronic Commerce, Tampa, FL (2001) 38-47, http://doi.acm.org/ 10.1145/501158.501163.
19. Berendt, B., Günther, O., and Spiekermann, S.: Privacy in E-Commerce: Stated Preferences vs. Actual Behavior. Communications of the ACM (forthcoming).
20. Personalization & Privacy Survey. Personalization Consortium (2000), http://www.personalization.org/SurveyResults.pdf.
21. Friedman, B., Howe, D. C., and Felten, E.: Informed Consent in the Mozilla Browser: Implementing Value-Sensitive Design. 35th Hawaii International Conference on System Sciences, Hawaii (2002).
22. Patrick, A. S. and Kenny, S.: From Privacy Legislation to Interface Design: Implementing Information Privacy in Human-Computer Interfaces. In: Privacy Enhancing Technologies, LNCS 2760, Dingledine, R., Ed. Heidelberg, Germany: Springer Verlag (2003) 107-124.
23. EU: Directive 95/46/EC of the European Parliament and of the Council of 24 October 1995 on the Protection of Individuals with Regard to the Processing of Personal Data and on the Free Movement of such Data. Official Journal of the European Communities, (1995) 31ff, http://158.169.50.95:10080/legal/en/dataprot/directiv/ directiv.html.
24. van Duyne, D. K., Landay, J. A., and Hong, J. I.: The Design of Sites: Patterns, Principles, and Processes for Crafting a Customer-Centered Web Experience. Boston: Addison-Wesley (2002).
25. Shneiderman, B. and Plaisant, C.: Designing the User Interface, 4th ed: Pearson Addison Wesley (2004).
26. Lederer, S., Dey, A., and Mankoff, J.: A Conceptual Model and Metaphor of Everyday Privacy in Ubiquitous Computing. Intel Research, Technical Report IRB-TR-02-017, (2002) http://www.intel-research.net/Publications/Berkeley/120520020944_107.pdf.
27. The Platform for Privacy Preferences 1.0 (P3P1.0) Specification. W3C Recommendation 16 April 2002. (2002), http://www.w3.org/TR/P3P/.
28. Chellappa, R. K. and Sin, R.: Personalization versus Privacy: An Empirical Examination of the Online Consumer's Dilemma. Information Technology and Management, (forthcoming), http://asura.usc.edu/~ram/rcf-papers/per-priv-itm.pdf.
29. Hine, C. and Eve, J.: Privacy in the Marketplace. The Information Society 14, (1998) 253-262, http://taylorandfrancis.metapress.com/link.asp?id=033wvkeqd2weapjf.
30. Culnan, M. J. and Bies, R. J.: Consumer Privacy: Balancing Economic and Justice Considerations. Journal of Social Issues 59, (2003) 323-353.
31. CG&I-R: Privacy Policies Critical to Online Consumer Trust. Columbus Group and Ipsos-Reid, Canadian Inter@ctive Reid Report (2001).

32. Earp, J. B. and Baumer, D.: Innovative Web Use to Learn About Consumer Behavior and Online Privacy. Communications of the ACM Archive **46**, (2003) 81 - 83, http://doi.acm.org/10.1145/641205.641209.
33. Teo, H. H., Wan, W., and Li, L.: Volunteering Personal Information on the Internet: Effects of Reputation, Privacy Initiatives, and Reward on Online Consumer Behavior. Proc. 37th Hawaii International Conf. on System Sciences, Big Island, HI (2004) http://csdl.computer.org/comp/proceedings/hicss/2004/2056/07/205670181c.pdf.

Panel Discussion — Conforming Technology to Policy: The Problems of Electronic Health Records

Richard Owens[1,**], Ross Fraser[2,*], William O'Brien[3,*], and Mike Gurski[4,*]

[1] Executive Director, Centre For Innovation Law and Policy, University of Toronto
[2] Principal, Sextant Software Canada
[3] Associate Director, Corporate Security Bell Canada
[4] Information and Privacy Commission, Ontario

Privacy regulation often follows from the needs of particular sectors. This creates the risk of a patchwork of regulation for different sectors of activity, and of conflict and overlap amongst regulatory regimes. Where these risks are managed, however, citizens benefit from rules tailored to identified needs and sensitivities, and recipients of personal data benefit from more specific behavioral guides. The health care sector is perhaps the most active sector in attracting rules designed to enhance personal privacy. Several provinces in Canada have health care data specific legislation, and Ontario has a very sophisticated bill which is soon to become law. However, the creation and enforcement of such rules is fraught with difficulties and is highly systems dependent.

Also present is the overriding need for security. Unauthorised access and disclosure of health care records could compromise the credibility of the entire system. System security needs to prevent such access and disclosure for the duration of a patient's life, even alongside the rapid evolution of both security standards and data storage methods. It must occur within a system designed to facilitate instant access in emergencies, to accommodate socially beneficial secondary research uses of data, including data of identifiable individuals and populations, and it must occur in a potentially "leaky" environment of many, many points and hierarchies of access.

This panel will articulate its premises of reasonable privacy expectations in a health care setting, and then debate the role, choice and reasonable expectations of Privacy Enhancing Technologies in realising those expectations. The panel members have deep experience in these issues from a wide variety of perspectives, and will highlight the opportunities–and conundra–facing the privacy enhancing technologist in the health care sector and, by extension, other sectors of similar informational sensitivity.

[**] Moderator.
[*] Panelists.

D. Martin and A. Serjantov (Eds.): PET 2004, LNCS 3424, p. 344, 2005.
© Springer-Verlag Berlin Heidelberg 2005

Author Index

Lecture Notes in Computer Science

For information about Vols. 1–3422

please contact your bookseller or Springer